ALSO BY ERIC KLINENBERG

Heat Wave: A Social Autopsy of Disaster in Chicago

FIGHTING FOR AIR

FIGHTING FOR AIR

THE BATTLE TO CONTROL

AMERICA'S MEDIA

ERIC KLINENBERG

A HOLT PAPERBACK
Metropolitan Books/Henry Holt and Company
New York

Holt Paperbacks
Henry Holt and Company, LLC
Publishers since 1866
175 Fifth Avenue
New York, New York 10010
www.henryholt.com

A Holt Paperback® and ® are registered trademarks of
Henry Holt and Company, LLC.

Library of Congress Cataloging-in-Publication Data
Klinenberg, Eric.
Fighting for air : the battle to control America's media / Eric Klinenberg. —1st ed.
p. cm.
Includes index.
ISBN-13: 978-0-8050-8729-1

1. Broadcasting policy—United States.   2. Mass media policy—United States.
I. Title.
HE8689.8 .K625 2007
302.230973—dc22   2006049627

Henry Holt books are available for special promotions and
premiums. For details contact: Director, Special Markets.

Originally published in hardcover in 2007 by Metropolitan Books

First Holt Paperbacks Edition 2008

Designed by Kelly S. Too

Printed in the United States of America

For Caitlin

CONTENTS

FIGHTING FOR AIR

THE EMPTY STUDIO

At approximately 1:39 a.m. on January 18, 2002, a 112-car Canadian Pacific Railway train carrying hazardous chemicals derailed just outside Minot, North Dakota, the fourth largest city in the state. According to the operating crew, the train had been traveling at forty miles an hour, and the accident happened when they attempted to slow down after hitting a rough spot on the tracks. Thirty-one cars jumped off the rails, and several burst open, spilling about 240,000 gallons of anhydrous ammonia, a toxic compound commonly used as a fertilizer, into a woodsy neighborhood called Tierrecita Vallejo, "Lovely Land of the Valley."

Minot, a quiet town with a population of nearly thirty-seven thousand nestled into a low-lying valley below the Canadian border, developed with the expansion of the rail lines and is now known for its air force base and annual state fair. In winter, arctic air grips the region, freezing winds howl through the streets, and residents hunker down. On the morning of the accident the winds were unusually gentle, and instead of dispersing, the anhydrous ammonia quickly formed a vapor plume that covered the crash site, spread to the adjacent residential area, and floated ominously toward town. Once they realized what was happening, the train crew unhitched their two locomotives and hurried into Minot. The conductor used his personal cell phone to call Ward County 911.[1]

OPERATOR: 9-1-1, what's the emergency?
CALLER: Uh, uh, this Minot Dispatch?

OPERATOR: Yes, it is.
CALLER: We've got an emerg, just had a derailment. We've got an explosion. Oh, it's around Tierrecita, Tierrecita Val, Vallejo, uh, CP Rail, we just had a derailment and we've got an explosive. Over.

OPERATOR: Okay. Uh, do you know what kind of chemicals are on board, sir?
CALLER: Uh, we've got hazardous material and I can smell stuff now.

Although the Ward County 911 dispatchers do not see much action in the dead of winter, they had an emergency management plan in place. After taking the conductor's call, the operator paged the Minot Rural Fire Department, and within two minutes the chief and assistant chief responded. They sent six units from the rural fire hall to the accident site, requested mutual aid from the Minot City Fire Department and the Burlington Fire Department, and notified the Air Force Base Hazardous Materials Team. Ward County also sent officers from its Sheriff's Department to the scene.

Local officials had to issue a public warning with information about the spill as well as instructions on how civilians could stay safe. Emergency personnel were familiar with anhydrous because local farmers use it regularly, and their advice was simple: Stay indoors, away from the spill. Cover your mouth with a wet washcloth if you have trouble breathing. Turn off your home furnace. Do not try to drive through the cloud. Anhydrous takes oxygen out of the air and is capable of shutting down car engines. In large enough doses, anhydrous shuts down the human respiratory system, too. Even limited exposure burns the eyes, the skin, and the lungs. The emergency crews feared that some civilians who smelled or saw the toxic cloud would leave their homes in hope of outrunning it, only to put themselves in harm's way.

Four minutes after the train crew first reported the crash, dispatchers received a call from two panicked parents whose child had run out into the toxic air.

MALE: We're out at, um Tierrecita Vallejo, 625 37th Street Southwest . . . We don't know what's going on. Something sparks and flew. It reeks in our background. We're gonna try, get out of the house.

OPERATOR: Okay, um. What

FEMALE: What is happening here?

MALE: *(talking to female: What, What is it?)* It's bad. We're gonna try to go to the neighbors. What is it? . . . It smells really bad. I don't know if, uh, a train blew up or . . .

OPERATOR: Yeah, there is, there is a train derailment there.

MALE: Okay . . . Where is Kelsey at?

FEMALE: She ran.

MALE: God damn.

OPERATOR: Everybody in the room?

MALE: No, we don't. My daugh, she sent my daughter out.

OPERATOR: Outside?

FEMALE: Oh, shit.

MALE: Yell at her.

MALE: Becky?

FEMALE: Kelsey. Come back, Kelsey, come back. Kelsey, can you come back.

MALE: God damn it, Becky. What in the hell are you doing in the middle of the night.

OPERATOR: Do, do you have everybody there now?

MALE: No, we don't. My daughter isn't there. I don't have anything on. They're all dressed and she sent her out but it smells really bad outside.

OPERATOR: Okay, yeah, just.

MALE: Is she here?

FEMALE: No, honey, she's gone.

OPERATOR: Ma'am?

FEMALE: My daughter ran out the front door.

OPERATOR: She ran out? How old is your daughter?

FEMALE: She's twelve . . . Is she gonna die out there?

MALE: I don't know.

FEMALE: You guys have to hurry please . . .

Two minutes later the office fielded another urgent call.

OPERATOR: 9-1-1, what is your emergency?

FEMALE: Hi. There's some emergency at our house at Tierrecita
Vallejo. I don't know what it is but there was a huge, huge crash.
There's smoke everywhere outside.

OPERATOR: Right. We're aware of it. We have fire units en route,
okay? You need to stay

FEMALE: What is going on?

OPERATOR: You need to stay calm until we can figure out what, what's
going on, what to do. Okay. Stay calm. If there's gonna be any
evacuations, we will announce it. Okay. But you need to stay in
your house.

FEMALE: We can't hear if you announce anything.

Within minutes of the accident, calls to 911 were coming in by the
dozen. Those who lived near the accident or were driving close by heard
the explosions and saw fires burning. Some who were farther away
smelled chemicals in the air and worried that there had been a bomb at
the local military base. The toxic cloud grew to some five miles long,
two and one-half miles wide, and 350 feet high, penetrating into the
homes of approximately fifteen thousand people, waking up some and
causing widespread fear and confusion among those who stumbled
around their homes trying to assess what was happening.[2] Minot residents complained that their eyes, lungs, and nasal passages were burning,
and told dispatchers that they didn't know how to protect themselves.
"What should we do?" one resident asked his wife as she spoke with the
operator. She repeated the question. "What should we do?"

INSTEAD OF CALLING 911 TO FIND OUT WHAT HAD HAPPENED AND WHAT
they should do, most people in Minot turned on their televisions and
radios, which had proven to be reliable sources of emergency public
health and safety information since the Cold War, when President Harry
Truman charged broadcasters with responsibility for the service. Not
only were broadcast companies then uniquely positioned to conduct
crisis communications on a massive scale; they also had a special duty

to do so: the government required that they meet public-interest obligations in exchange for a license to use the nation's airwaves and for
regulatory enforcement that prevented other operators from sending
signals over their designated frequencies. In 1951, Truman established
the CONELRAD (Control of Electromagnetic Radiation) system, a federal program which when activated (by emergency tones sent through
a predetermined chain of stations) required all of the nation's television
channels and FM radio outlets to immediately broadcast warnings
before shutting down their signals, preventing foreign enemies from
taking over the spectrum during a military attack. As part of the program, selected AM stations would move to one of two designated frequencies, 640 kHz or 1240 kHz (each of which was tagged with a
triangle-in-circle "CD Mark" on radio dials built between 1953 and
1963), from which they could securely issue safety announcements. "At
the first indication of enemy bombers approaching the United States,"
explained a civil defense publication from the 1950s, "the CONELRAD
stations, 640 and 1240, are your surest and fastest means of getting
emergency information and instructions. Mark those numbers on your
radio set, now!"

After the Cuban Missile Crisis, disaster planners recommended
improving the technology so that local officials could activate the system
during a range of public safety threats, and in 1963 they introduced
the Emergency Broadcast System (EBS) for warnings during natural
disasters, civil emergencies, or military attacks. U.S. law required radio
and television broadcasters to conduct weekly tests of their EBS systems,
and most Americans who watched television or listened to the radio
between 1963 and 1997 remember hearing the bracing, two-tone signal, along with a flat yet reassuring voice announcing, "This is a test of
the Emergency Broadcast System. This is only a test."

In 1997 the federal government updated EBS with a new technology, the Emergency Alert System (EAS). According to the Federal Communications Commission (FCC), EAS improves crisis communications
because its "digital system architecture allows broadcast stations,
cable systems, participating satellite companies, and other services to
send and receive emergency information quickly and automatically
even if those facilities are unattended."[3] The president, state and local
governments, and the National Weather Service can also use EAS to
override local broadcasts, an innovation designed to protect the public

by expanding the number of authorities who can trigger an alert when disaster strikes.

After the derailment, dispatchers in Minot knew to direct callers to the airwaves—specifically, to KCJB AM910, the designated emergency broadcaster—for directions on how to stay safe. Radio service is especially useful during a crisis, operators explained, because battery-powered devices work even when the power is out.

OPERATOR: 9-1-1, emergency.
CALLER: Um, I called awhile ago about a power outage and ammonia smell . . .

OPERATOR: Well, you just need to stay in your house with the doors and windows closed until we direct you differently . . .
CALLER: Okay. Well, how will we find out?

OPERATOR: Uh, we will get that out, out on cable TV or KCJB radio.
CALLER: Cause our, uh, electricity's out . . . So we can't get TV.

OPERATOR: Okay. What about a radio?
CALLER: Well, we have a little, uh, a little transistor one.

OPERATOR: Okay. That would be the thing to use then.
CALLER: But what, what channel?

OPERATOR: KCJB.
CALLER: What?

OPERATOR: 910.
CALLER: 910 . . . Okay. Well, we'll try that. Thanks.

But the caller quickly discovered that KCJB, and every other radio station in town, were not reporting any news or information about the anhydrous spill. Instead, all six of Minot's name-brand stations—Z94, 97 Kicks, Mix 99.9, The Fox Classic Rock, 91 Country, and Cars Oldies Radio—continued playing a standard menu of canned music, served up by smooth-talking DJs trading in light banter and off-color jokes while the giant toxic cloud floated into town.

Although the broadcasts originated in Minot, every one of the town's non-religious commercial stations was owned and operated by the San Antonio–based conglomerate Clear Channel Communications, which acquired the outlets in 2000 and replaced locally produced news, music, and talk programs with prepackaged content engineered in remote studios and transmitted to North Dakota through digital voice-tracking systems.[4] Clear Channel consolidated operations for its Minot stations into two central offices, neither of which had a live staff member interrupt the regularly scheduled automated shows to issue an alert immediately after the spill.

POSTAL WORKER KENNY MOE WAS DRIVING HOME FROM A LATE SHIFT ON the morning of the accident.[5] "I saw a haze in front of me and I thought there was a fire," he reported. But since there was no special warning on the radio, he presumed that there was nothing especially dangerous ahead. Moe continued on the highway, traveling directly into the blinding cloud. "It hit my eyes like two ice picks. It was like somebody dumped acid in my eyes. I thought I could drive out of it." But he couldn't see past his own car. "I rolled down my window and wham, that stuff hit me. My face muscles were just twitching and stuff was running out of my nose. When you're sucking that stuff in, it's pure chemical." Moe managed to turn onto another road, and he sped away from the fumes. "I got home and fell to the ground." He called 911, but the line was busy, so he dialed an emergency assistance number and urged the operator to send more staff to the accident. Then, fighting off nausea and burning sensations in his mouth, lungs, throat, and hands, he and his wife, Jen, got back in the car to rescue her mother from the valley. "My wife, by the time we got there, could hardly breathe . . . You go into a cloud of smoke for 20 minutes and your whole life is different."

John Grabinger, a thirty-eight-year-old who ran a hardware store, lived a few blocks from the crash site with his wife, MaLea, and neither knew how to respond to the infusion of poison in the air. The couple ran to the window after hearing the explosions and saw an overturned tanker car lying a stone's throw from their home. They decided to flee in their pickup truck, but John, at the steering wheel, was blinded by the vapor. He crashed into a neighbor's garage, and he and his wife crawled out into the cloud. MaLea suffered lung inhalation injuries, temporary respiratory failure and serious lip and feet burns from direct contact with the anhydrous, but she made it into the home of her neighbor Linda Juntunen. Her husband did not. Juntunen called 911. "There's a man down in his driveway," she reported. "His wife came into our home and she's very, very sick." John's body lay still on the ground. He had inhaled a lethal dose of the fumes.

Minot residents who stayed inside their homes were growing anxious because they were blocked from getting information about what was happening around them and were unable to learn how to stay safe. At roughly 3:00 a.m., a frustrated caller told 911 that local broadcasters had failed to issue an alert.

> OPERATOR: 9-1-1, what is your emergency?
> CALLER: Well, I'm wondering about this anhydrous, uh?
>
> OPERATOR: Sir, you're to stay in your home. Treat it like smoke. Turn your furnace off. Put towels underneath the doors. Go in your bathroom. Turn the shower on and cover your face with wet towels . . . And stay there until further instructions by law enforcement.
> CALLER: Okay, cause the PA system doesn't work, it's
>
> OPERATOR: I understand that. It's, also, we've been putting it on over the cable TV and the radio.
> CALLER: Which radio station?
>
> OPERATOR: All the radio stations, sir.
> CALLER: I've been, had it on. I haven't heard it once.

An hour later, Dick Levitt, a staff member at Minot's noncommercial radio station, Christian broadcaster KHRT, called 911 to ask why the emergency broadcaster was not covering the disaster.

> OPERATOR: Minot Police Department, Lt. Lockrem. Can I help you?
> CALLER: Ah, yes. Ah, this is Dick Levitt out at KHRT radio. And, um, I, ah, know we've got a problem in the city, but I have not been able to get any information whatsoever to be able to put out over the airway. And, I'm calling to find out what do I do? Where do I get it?

According to Minot officials, the city's dispatchers were so busy fielding calls that no one checked to see if the local radio stations were alerting listeners to the spill. Operators continued instructing residents like Levitt to tune in to one of its designated emergency broadcasters, the radio station KCJB-AM and the television station KMOT. "We're telling people to tune in to the radio, and they're just getting music," said Lieutenant Fred Debowey, who grew up in Minot. "It was awful."

KMOT-TV, an NBC affiliate with a production facility in Minot, was off the air at the time of the chemical spill, with no early morning crew. Yet dispatchers were able to reach the news director at home, and he hurried to the station. Officers also tracked down the news director for KXMC-TV, a CBS affiliate and the only other television channel with a transmitting station in Minot, and asked him to warn viewers about the accident. Both stations began issuing alerts soon thereafter, yet many Minot residents had lost power and could not turn on their sets.

Finding a real person at the radio stations proved to be more difficult. The Minot dispatchers tried using the EAS system, which should have allowed officials to automatically override the radio broadcast and issue their warnings directly, without the collaboration of radio staff. But Chief Dan Draovitch and Lieutenant Debowey of the Minot Police later said that the system failed, due to breakdowns at both the emergency office and at KCJB. "The EAS programming would dump every time we got a power surge," Debowey told me. "So it didn't operate." Minot officials also tried using the outdated EBS technology, which they kept operational because, Debowey explained, "[they] could still use it locally to get through to the stations when [they] needed some help." Minot officials say that the EBS had passed a test the previous week. This time, however, it too failed.[6]

With neither emergency communications system functioning, the dispatchers attempted the tried-and-true old-fashioned approach: picking up a telephone and calling KCJB directly. Local authorities knew that KCJB was running with automated technology, yet they hoped that someone would be working the late shift. No one at Clear Channel's stations picked up the telephone when they called the office. "We rang it and we rang it and we rang it and he never answered," Debowey said.

What was happening at KCJB, or at Clear Channel's central Minot offices? Steve Davis, the company's senior vice president of engineering, insists that a Clear Channel employee was working in Minot that morning, and that its own radio staff was "attempting to learn what was happening."[7] Don May, who has worked at KCJB for forty years, told me that he was home in the hills when the train derailed. A police lieutenant tracked May down by phone after failing to contact anyone at the station, and the radio veteran quickly made his way toward the studio. "I live above the valley, but to get to the station I had to go through it. It took me about twenty-five minutes to get through the spill; it would normally take three or four minutes, but I couldn't see. I had to drive through the anhydrous myself. When I got there all of our telephone lines and all of the lines at the police department were jammed. The fellow who was there that night had no idea what was transpiring. He couldn't call out because every time he picked up the phone there was someone on the line." May said that he got on the air about two hours after the accident and made an announcement about it, but that there was no way for him to update his information.

Neither of these accounts adequately answer the only question that matters for the people of Minot: if there was someone in Clear Channel's radio office at the time of the spill, and the enormous volume of incoming calls from residents concerned about the emergency clearly indicated that a crisis was unfolding, why didn't that person go on the air and issue an alert?

SOME TIME PASSED BEFORE THE SCALE OF THE DAMAGE COULD BE assessed. The Minot Rural Fire Department estimated that the toxic cloud had covered the homes of about 40 percent of the city population, or roughly fifteen thousand people. In Tierrecita Vallejo, toxic gas saturated the area after the accident, and after three hours Minot officials decided that it was no longer safe for the community's residents to stay in place. Firefighters drove buses into the neighborhood and evacuated residents to a triage area. The evacuees were not allowed to return to their homes until March, more than six weeks after the accident.

John Grabinger was the only fatality from the toxic spill. The Moes and Kelsey, the twelve-year-old girl who fled her home after the derailment, sustained injuries from exposure, as did seventeen emergency responders and two members of the train crew. In all, approximately 330 people were treated for immediate health problems while more than 1,000 people needed medical care for recurring illnesses in the next month. The long-term consequences of their exposure remain unknown, but Minot residents continue to suffer a variety of afflictions. It's impossible to know how many would have escaped harm if the local media had sounded a warning, telling residents what was happening and how they could stay safe.

The people of Minot remain haunted by the fact that many of the core institutions on which they relied for basic services failed during the crisis. Their emergency communications system crashed when local officials could not properly operate their equipment. And their radio system broke down—not only because a new technology malfunctioned, and not because the broadcasters were biased—but because the company that had established control over all of Minot's non-religious commercial stations had pulled valuable human resources out of the community, leaving no one available or alert enough to issue a warning when the public needed them most.

I FIRST HEARD ABOUT THE COMMUNICATIONS BREAKDOWN IN MINOT A few months after it happened. At the time I was living in Chicago, where I had just finished writing a book about a treacherous heat wave in 1995 that killed 739 people in a single week. Although Chicago is a major U.S. city with a local media known for aggressive news coverage, key features of the disaster—why certain neighborhoods were especially vulnerable, why the city refused to call in additional ambulances and paramedics, and how the mayor and city council avoided holding hearings to learn more about what happened—were never explained. Stories on the catastrophe disappeared soon after the weather changed, and eight years later, when a three-week heat wave killed approximately thirty thousand people across Europe, public officials in France, Germany, Italy, and Spain insisted that they were unprepared because nothing like it had happened before and no one had previously reported on the dangers of extreme heat.

Chicago and Minot are hardly the only American cities to experience recent disasters; nor are they the only places where tears in the social fabric—for which the local media serve a crucial, binding role—made the damage caused by chemicals or the climate more severe. Dramatic communications failures in both places were not anomalies but social dramas that highlighted problems with the increasingly consolidated systems of news and cultural production that shape our media and, in turn, our public and political life, everyday.

What has happened to our nation's rich and diverse supply of local media outlets? Like most Americans, I found it difficult to keep track of the countless media mergers reported by the business press during the 1990s, let alone to assess the meaning of those multicolored consolidation charts displaying which large conglomerate had dumped or acquired which other conglomerate, split into separate divisions, or changed its name. But by any measure the speed and scale of concentrated media ownership during the past ten years is remarkable—as is the extent to which the White House, Congress, and the Federal Communications Commission have gutted legislation that historically had protected the public's interest in open, competitive, and locally engaged media, and replaced it with new laws designed to promote private gain.

The map of the media landscape may be confusing from above, but at ground level the dramatic consequences of concentration are all too recognizable in the local office buildings where communications workers in all media are anxious about losing their hard-won jobs when the next wave of downsizing hits or when a distant company takes over their own. I saw some of these fears firsthand when I conducted ethnographic research in Chicago newsrooms during the late 1990s and early 2000s, revisiting the institutions that failed during the heat wave to examine whether the acute problems brought to light because of the catastrophe—the lack of local reporters covering street-level conditions, and the commercial pressures that helped to bury a deeper investigation into what went wrong—also affected their coverage of the city in ordinary times.

I was not the only one startled by the level of upheaval in the local newsrooms; nearly every journalist I met worried about how the changes stemming from consolidation and convergence in their industry would affect both their craft and their career. After listening to their concerns I decided to expand my fieldwork, traveling across the nation's cultural landscape to survey what communications scholars call the *media ecosystem*—the dynamic and interconnected set of local and national newspaper, television, radio, and Internet producers and products—on which we depend for news, information, and entertainment, and in which the average American spends half of her waking moments—about eight hours per day.[8]

In the radio industry, I learned about hundreds of DJs, news reporters, and talk show hosts who lost their programs after conglomerates such as Clear Channel bought their stations and installed digital voice-tracking systems to replace local talent. In the television industry, I discovered stations that scheduled local news programs throughout the day but refused to increase the staff levels, choosing instead to recycle the same stories and use scripted packages, including promotional video news releases from businesses and government agencies, to fake local reports. In the newspaper industry, I observed big-city newsrooms where rows of empty desks and unused chairs marked the number of journalists and local beats that management had eliminated. In the alternative weekly market, I read the same cultural coverage, syndicated columns, and phone sex advertisements in papers on both coasts and many cities in between. I even downloaded the same stories from Web sites produced by local media outlets that differed only in their customized graphics, designed to match each particular publication's style.

Yet I did not encounter signs of cultural and journalistic desertion in every part of the landscape. In some of the same places where the effects of consolidation and cost cutting were most devastating, dramatic regeneration, in the form of citizens determined to restore health and vitality to their local media ecosystem, was under way, with blogs, community Internet sites, wireless access services, grassroots journalism publications, even old-fashioned, low-power radio stations becoming abundant. Projects such as these cannot fully compensate for the loss of professional reporters, producers, and editors who have the financial resources and special training that help support ambitious original journalism, particularly investigative reporting, enterprising coverage of powerful private or public institutions, and hard-hitting daily news coverage. But by 2005, citizens cum local media producers had nonetheless made an imprint on the communities they served, occasionally altering the way commercial media operated, too.

I also observed the emergence of a new, or at least newly invigorated, group of activists—millions of citizens and hundreds of civic groups, representing all political persuasions and regional locations, who are so concerned about how consolidation changed their media that they are demanding better and more responsible service from both the private companies that dominate the news and culture markets and the government officials who have squandered their public-interest obligations.

There have been dramatic transformations in the U.S. media ecosystem during the past decade, but the process of shaping a new media
landscape for the digital age is by no means complete. In the next few
years, the future health of the nation's media ecosystem will be determined by interactions among and between all of these players: Big
Media conglomerates, upstart chains, locally owned and operated outlets, government regulators, elected officials, citizen journalists, public-
interest organizations, and grassroots activists fighting for reform.
Until recently, the most important contests between these groups took
place behind closed doors, in the corporate backrooms and federal
agencies where ordinary people have little access or influence. But
today that is changing, and for one simple reason: Americans know
how much is at stake.

FIGHTING FOR AIR TELLS TWO OVERARCHING STORIES THAT WOULD BE
common knowledge were it not for the crisis in communications that
they address: first, how Big Media companies parlayed bold political
entrepreneurialism and the federal government's blind faith in the
power of markets and technology to win historic concessions from
Congress and the Federal Communications Commission, which they
used to dominate local markets from coast to coast. The pattern is now
familiar: just as Starbucks knocked out independent coffee shops and
Wal-Mart killed the corner store, media conglomerates have devastated locally produced newspapers, television stations, and radio programs throughout the country. But with media the stakes are higher,
because both cultural diversity and democracy in America require a
rich and varied supply of news and information in the public sphere,
where communities, large and small, debate policy options, determine
where to invest public resources, and decide how to protect the vulnerable or defend themselves.

We already know the hazards of replacing home-cooked meals
made from farm-raised meats, fruits, and vegetables with a steady diet
of Big Macs, supersize fries, and extracrispy wings from the fast-food
chains that saturate America's highways and byways. The second big
story in *Fighting for Air* is an account of how citizens and civic groups
discovered that the twenty-four-hour, all-you-can-eat buffet of stale

news is crushing creative and independent voices, destroying the rich American tradition of local reporting, and clogging the informational arteries that make democracy work. Concerned citizens may disagree over whether the media are biased (and, if they are, whether they tilt left or right); whether coverage of the war in Iraq is sanitized to promote its popularity or dramatized to undermine the campaign; or whether Jon Stewart and Stephen Colbert offer more penetrating analysis than Tucker Carlson and Bill O'Reilly. But they share one widespread conviction: that the distinctively local voices, personalities, and sources of news and entertainment that used to animate radio, television, newspapers, and alternative weeklies have been crushed by an onslaught of cookie-cutter content. Media conglomerates, they believe, are estranging Americans everywhere from the sights, sounds, and cultural styles that once made their hometowns feel special, like home.

Media activists have a model. Some forty years ago a network of community organizers built a vast environmental movement—and permanently changed the political landscape—when they recognized that the pollution in their backyards came from a governmental and corporate culture that let the almighty dollar overshadow the public health. "We have subjected enormous numbers of people to contact with these poisons, without their consent and often without their knowledge," wrote Rachel Carson. "When the public protests, confronted with some obvious evidence of damaging results . . . it is fed little tranquilizing pills of half truths . . . The public must decide whether it wishes to continue on the present road, and it can do so only when in full possession of the facts."[9]

Today groups such as Free Press, the Youth Media Council, and the Prometheus Radio Project are following in the environmentalists' footsteps. They use local cases and draw on the rhetoric of public health to reveal the costs citizens pay when their government capitulates to corporate interests, abandoning its commitment to the nation's well-being. They demand accountability from the chains and conglomerates that have seized control of the airwaves and from the political officials who have entrusted the public interest to technology and the market. They call for original, locally focused content that shows respect for the places they live and serves the needs of citizens and communities. They believe that their cause is the most pivotal issue currently facing the American people, because the quality of media affects whether and how the electorate can make informed decisions about every other political matter—from welfare to warfare, housing to health care, criminal justice to campaign finance, and plans for homeland security, no matter whether they are made to address risks for towns such as Minot or large metropolises such as Washington, D.C., and New York City.

They are fighting for air.

1

IN THE PUBLIC INTEREST

Disasters have long shaped U.S. media policies, because crises throw into stark relief the status quo that, absent dramatic benchmarks, is otherwise so hard to apprehend. In April 1912—exactly ninety years before the chemical spill in North Dakota—another radio alert system failed, and the death toll of that more famous disaster led directly to the nation's first broadcast media policy. When the luxury ocean liner the *Titanic* hit an iceberg en route from England to New York City, radio operators aboard the ship used its wireless radio system to broadcast a distress signal. The message, which included information about the craft's nautical position, immediately reached two boats that were a half-day's distance by sea, as well as the *Carpathia,* whose one radio operator heard the distress call "by a lucky fluke," leading him to direct the captain to travel the fifty-eight miles separating them from the doomed ship. "When it arrived at the scene three and a half hours after hearing the distress call," reported the radio historian Susan Douglas, "it could only rescue those who had managed to get into the lifeboats." More than fifteen hundred others drowned with the ship. There were at least two boats traveling closer to the *Titanic* that evening. The *California* could have reached the *Titanic* in about an hour, but its wireless operator slept through the distress calls. *Lena* was some ninety minutes away, yet the freight steamer did not have a wireless on board.[1]

Wireless communications among those following the disaster ashore also failed. Friends and relatives of passengers who used radios to get news about the *Titanic* and make inquiries about who survived were stymied in their efforts due to the extraordinary traffic on the system, the speed of which had another downside: vast circulation of misinformation, which generated widespread complaints about "ceaseless interference, cruel rumors, and misleading messages that filled the air from unknown sources during the disaster." Douglas explained that "out of this early congestion of inquiries emerged the message reporting that the *Titanic* was moving safely towards Halifax. When the American and British press learned that this news was completely false and that the *Titanic* had, in fact, sunk, its editors were appalled. The amateurs were accused of manufacturing the deception and were universally condemned."[2]

Problems with wireless communication during the *Titanic* disaster generated new congressional proposals for radio policies to protect public health and safety on the seas, including ensuring that ships maintained a wireless system that was manned at all times, an auxiliary power source in case the engine malfunctioned, and a formal procedure for reporting emergencies. But the most significant policy initiatives involved federal regulation of the airwaves on which the wireless operated, an unprecedented move in the United States that made the government responsible "to insure to the people of the United States an uninterrupted wireless service twenty-four hours a day for every day of the year," because the private sector had proved incapable of policing itself.[3] Political officials demanded that amateur operators, who were stigmatized as "wireless meddlers" and became scapegoats for the communications breakdown, be forced off prime spots on the broadcast spectrum, constrained from using powerful signals, and converted from active, talking participants to passive listeners. The most influential newspapers and magazines would eventually join the Progressive Era chorus for government control, too; at the same time, upstart entrepreneurs advocated measures that would rein in the space for amateurs while opening up the airwaves for new commercial projects.

A mere four months after the *Titanic* disaster, the broad coalition of media companies and civic reformers got its wish. On August 13 Congress passed the Radio Act of 1912, which, as Douglas explained, "required that all operators be licensed, that stations adhere to certain wave allocations, that distress calls take priority over all other calls, and that the secretary of commerce and labor be empowered to issue licenses and make other regulations necessary to sort out the wireless chaos." For the first time, the government would control property rights and manage the airwaves, allocating certain wavelengths (or portions of the spectrum) to the military, the private sector, and to individual amateurs depending on their needs, investments, and potential contributions to the "people's interests."

The 1912 legislation paved the way for the Radio Act of 1927 and the Communications Act of 1934, which created the Federal Communications Commission (FCC), an independent regulatory agency made up of seven commissioners who are appointed by the president and confirmed by the Senate. (The number of commissioners was reduced to five in 1983.) The FCC's responsibilities extended far beyond managing communications during disasters. Congress charged the new agency with setting media policies of all kinds, and particularly with generating rules to ensure that local media markets would be competitive and diverse. The commission, whose rulings are often narrowly decided because the president can only give his party a one-seat majority, played a key role in establishing the notion that promoting the public interest should be the guiding principle of media policy. During the twentieth century, however, media policies that advanced the interests of corporate broadcasters often trumped proposals that would have better served citizens. The FCC's political will to live up to its stated ideals has varied depending on the values of its commissioners and the goals of the political party in charge.[4]

The FCC did establish some important precedents for the nation's approach to media regulation. Under the FCC's oversight, the government would formally treat the airwaves as natural resources that, like the air itself or national parks, belong to the people. Over time, the FCC defined the core goal of federal media policies as the promotion of "diversity," "localism," and "competition" in American towns and cities, and it set strict ownership limits to maintain a robust flow of ideas into the public sphere. Although the commission allocated great control of the spectrum to national networks and commercial broadcasters, corporations could only secure official licenses as "trustees" of the airwaves by promising to meet certain "public-interest" standards and to provide "public-service" programs, including news and other shows with no commercial sponsors.[5] During the last seventy years, the FCC has regularly reexamined whether its policies help advance its core objectives, even as it has maintained many of its original principles, and its mission to promote strong local coverage, diverse content, and open competition remains sacrosanct.

SCHOLARS OF AMERICAN POLITICAL CULTURE, FROM ALEXIS DE Tocqueville and John Dewey to Richard Hofstadter and Cass Sunstein, have emphasized the crucial role that local media play in creating as well as informing communities and citizens. Before the advent of radio, that task largely fell to newspapers. As Tocqueville famously said, "Without newspapers there would be hardly any common action at all." Robert Park, a newsman who became the founding figure of American urban sociology, claimed that in cities the local press replaces gossip as the social institution that binds residents to one another. Joseph Medill, the editor and co-owner of the *Chicago Tribune* and onetime mayor of Chicago, wanted his paper to provide another public service, helping migrants and immigrants acculturate to the city and nation that would become their new home. Hofstadter described Medill's project eloquently: "[The newspapers] found themselves undertaking the . . . ambitious task of creating a mental world for the uprooted farmers and villagers who were coming to live in the city. The rural migrants found themselves in a new urban world, strange, anonymous, impersonal, cruel, often corrupt and vicious, but also full of variety and fascination . . . The newspaper became not only the interpreter of this environment but a means of surmounting in some measure its vast human distances." Even established city dwellers benefited from the metropolitan press, wrote the historian Gunther Barth. Because it "reduced anxiety and solitude" among those "yearning for contacts with each other and their world."[6]

There was no shortage of sensationalism and partisan politics in nineteenth-century newspapers. The "penny papers" of the 1830s targeted working-class readers with human-interest stories about ordinary people, criminals, and local politicians, while the "yellow papers" of the 1890s were notorious for their inflammatory coverage of controversial topics. But the distinctive feature of American city papers has always been their use of local news reporters to hit the streets and gather primary facts about urban life. Urban newspapers developed a beat system for producing regular coverage of key institutions, such as city hall and the urban political machine, the local economy and labor market, sports franchises, factories, the stock market, the neighborhoods, and entertainment venues. They also cultivated relationships with local advertisers, whose contributions not only helped to make publishing profitable but also gave each city's printed pages a decidedly local look and feel. Local subjects became progressively more prevalent in city papers during the nineteenth century. As new publications targeting the fast-growing urban population made newspaper markets more competitive, publishers lured readers by increasing both the number of stories concerning local events and the proportion of original articles written by local reporters rather than clipped from national sources.[7]

The great diversity and intensely local focus of modern American newspapers helped them earn the reputation as watchdogs over the powerful political and corporate interests that shaped American cities. Just as, according to the late urban scholar and activist Jane Jacobs, ordinary civilians safeguard neighborhoods by acting as "eyes on the streets," modern American urban news organizations promised to protect entire metropolitan communities by serving as "eyes on the city," attuned to the dangerous consequences of corrupt officials, greedy developers, failed public projects, or mismanaged disasters.[8]

Not all newspapers lived up to this mission, and most American cities have had their share of media organizations that used their printing presses or broadcast licenses to promote their own interests, even at the expense of the people they served. Yet local news companies that proved their commitment to the public interest through serious journalism and civic contributions established a public trust with the communities they served. Historically, this ethic of responsibility to the collective good evolved organically, out of deeply rooted local ties. Walter Lippmann, whom some consider the dean of American journalism, attributed the durability of America's free press to these abiding local attachments: "There is," Lippmann argued, "a fundamental reason why the American press is strong enough to remain free. That reason is that the American newspapers, large and small, and without exception, belong to a town, a city, at most to a region."[9]

Lippmann and other proponents of local news were hardly parochial; they understood that, no matter how globally connected the world is, most people live locally; that local institutions—schools, hospitals, police departments, tax boards, and the like—exert tremendous influence on our lives; that local media producers are uniquely capable of reporting on and opining about the issues that directly impinge upon us and our communities, and of explaining how and why regional, national, and international events hit home.

In addition, the local media can also exert tremendous power. According to Phyllis Kaniss, the University of Pennsylvania communications scholar who authored the most recent comprehensive academic study of city newspapers and television stations, messages from local media "are as capable of killing a multimillion dollar development project as helping it sail through a lengthy public approval process, as potent in winning a politician votes as in ousting an entire agency's management from their appointed positions. Local news plays a crucial role in the policy decisions of local officials to implement new initiatives or to eliminate and modify existing programs . . . Local news can affect private decisions as well. It can send people packing to move out of homes in the city or suburbs and determine whether they send their children to public or private schools or let them play in the nearby park."[10]

In 2001 the *Seattle Times,* where local management was embroiled in a bitter struggle to preserve its autonomy, reported that patients had died prematurely in clinical trials run by the Fred Hutchinson Cancer Research Center, and that doctors and administrators had financial interests in the drugs under review. In lawsuits, the families of five of the patients alleged that they had never been told about the institution's stake in the experiments; nor had they been adequately informed about the risks of participating. Although one family won its initial suit, all parties are still appealing. Until the *Times* investigation, neither Seattle residents nor other potential patients in the region could have known that some of the center's experiments were dangerous. In 2005 the *Sacramento Bee* (which is owned by the McClatchy Company, one of the few newspaper chains to maintain its large investments in local reporting staffs), published a three-part series on the Pineros, migrant foreign workers who were injured or killed on U.S. Forest Service projects. In its nine-month investigation, the *Bee* discovered that the Forest Service had not merely failed to adequately train the ten thousand Pineros or provide proper safety equipment, but repeatedly "abused" the laborers by forcing them "to live in squalor" and ridiculing them on the job. The series not only won honors and awards but also led the government to promise immediate reforms.[11]

Local news stories are consequential even when they don't address matters of life and death. The *East Hampton Star,* a family-owned weekly since 1885, has been a steady voice for historic and environmental preservation in a region where real estate development, especially for ultrawealthy New Yorkers shopping for second homes, has long threatened to transform the landscape. In a 2003 issue, the paper featured one story on "regenerative designs" such as underground parking garages and multifamily apartment complexes (rather than single family homes) that could reverse growth and "retain East Hampton's most environmentally sensitive marshes and woodlands, while returning to a pristine state some land already built upon"; and another explaining a confusing public plan to protect local wildlands and groundwater sources. The *Star,* which is one of the few newspapers in the United States to publish every letter to the editor it receives (at considerable cost to the owners), keeps residents informed and engaged, helping to create a collective, if contested, sense of place. In this way, the *Star* makes self-governance and social participation available to its readers, revealing how the business of business becomes the people's business when it affects public life.

When they stake a claim in the communities where they operate, the media contribute to the vitality of local democratic politics by shedding light on important issues that private citizens do not have the time, inclination, or expertise to uncover or understand on their own. In the process, local media can provide a forum from which dissenting voices reach the public, and also help to mediate disputes between self-interested groups. Local news organizations like the *Star* have been especially important players in debates about urban and suburban growth; although in many American towns and cities the local media have aggressively advocated development to serve their own interests, in others the local media have helped hold back projects that threatened to overrun the area.

In a classic article on urban growth machines written in 1976, the sociologist Harvey Molotch argued that "the newspaper tends to achieve a statesman-like attitude in the community and is deferred to as something other than a special interest by the special interests. Competing interests often regard the publisher or editor as a general community leader, as an ombudsman and arbiter of internal bickering and, at times, as an enlightened third party who can restrain the short-term profiteers in the interest of more stable, long-term, and properly planned growth. The paper becomes the reformist influence, the 'voice of the community,' restraining the competing subunits, especially the small-scale, arriviste 'fast-buck artists' among them."[12]

The impact of local news does not end at home. Today we can look back on the history of local journalism and recognize its role in identifying emerging social problems, political projects, and cultural trends that—once documented and publicly reported—grow from city stories into national or international issues. Whether it was the *Memphis Commercial Appeal*, the *Columbus (Georgia) Enquirer-Sun*, or the *New York World* documenting the rise of the Ku Klux Klan in the late 1910s and 1920s, reporters like Ted Poston and Carl Rowan covering the growing civil rights movement at the grass roots, Randy Shilts and the *San Francisco Chronicle* documenting the rise of the HIV/AIDS epidemic in San Francisco, or the *Boston Globe* staff uncovering sexual abuse by Catholic priests, locally engaged reporters and news organizations have served the public interest and helped effect social change.

No matter if the object of investigation is development and sprawl, corrupt city governments, organized violence, racial discrimination, self-interested medical researchers, or public health crises, penetrating local journalism contributes to the collective welfare of communities and residents—even those who don't pay attention to the coverage. The reason, as the legal scholar C. Edwin Baker argued before a U.S. Senate hearing on media ownership in 2004, is that the presence of large, diverse, aggressive, and independent local journalistic staffs, and the constant threat of critical attention that they impose, provide a strong disincentive for powerful institutions and individuals to engage in harmful, unethical, or illegal conduct. Without "eyes on the city," Baker explained, political officials and corporations feel emboldened to promote their own interests, even at the public's expense.[13]

ONE SET OF "EYES ON THE CITY," THOUGH, IS NOT SUFFICIENT TO GUARantee critical attention. The effectiveness of media depends on the vitality and diversity of available news sources. From Thomas Jefferson and

James Madison onward political theorists have argued that the local media are most effective, and the public sphere is most dynamic, when it includes competing perspectives. Of course, an open market for news and information means some unsavory organizations are always part of the mix, and the history of local journalism is full of ugly episodes. Many small, independently owned news companies have produced parochial, discriminatory, and incendiary content, and even the most stalwart advocates of locally controlled journalism have warned about the damage done by bigoted or profiteering publishers.

As Upton Sinclair put it in 1919 in his self-published study of American journalism, *The Brass Check:* "The average country or small-town editor is an entirely ignorant man; the world of culture is a sealed book to him. If you go to the small town in Pennsylvania or Arkansas or Colorado . . . you find [the editor] getting a regular monthly income from the copper-interests, whatever happens to be dominant in that locality. You find him heavily subsidized at election-time by the two political machines of these great interests."[14] Sinclair's concerns about local publishers hardly softened his contempt for the day's newspaper moguls. Yet they did convince him that there are no simple solutions to the problems generated by America's for-profit media.

We can only imagine what Sinclair would have written about the *Newark Weekly News,* a locally owned and operated paper published by Howard Scott and launched in 2005 with a $100,000 no-bid contract from the city council and then-mayor Sharpe James, who wanted an organ for promoting "good news" about the beleaguered city. Among the paper's regular features are glowing accounts of city council members, full-page ads promoting city programs, and reports based on leads from local officials. "Do we have critical reporters on staff? No. Do we have investigative reporters? No," Scott told the *New Jersey Star-Ledger.* "Our niche is the good stuff."[15] The city of Newark is hardly the only government to offer citizens propaganda disguised as legitimate news, but it is certainly the most unabashed.

Just as there are some corrupt local publishers, so too is there an ever-dwindling set of national chains that have maintained their commitment to local journalism that promotes the public interest. Today most Americans recognize that there are differences between Wal-Mart, which faces lawsuits from a class of potentially more than one million current and former employees who charge it with sex discrimination, off-the-clock labor, and contracting with sweatshops, and Costco, which is widely praised for its good pay (its average hourly wage was seventeen dollars in 2005) and benefits; or between McDonald's and In-N-Out Burger, the chain praised by Eric Schlosser in *Fast Food Nation* for its fresh ingredients, friendly customer service, and low prices.[16] Media chains always had a similar variety of managerial styles. But in recent years intense pressure from financial analysts and large shareholders who demand profit margins several times the 5 or 6 percent now typical of Fortune 500 firms has made it practically impossible for publicly traded companies to sustain their investments in the sizable local staffs required to watch over a city. Those that do have either a two-tiered stock system that allows family owners to maintain managerial control (as is true for the New York Times Company and the Washington Post Company), or a special strategy that concentrates on growth markets with special opportunities and leaves out any other places (as is the case for the McClatchy Company).[17]

FOR NO MATTER WHO CONTROLS THEM, CONSOLIDATED MEDIA companies—be they made up of newspapers, television and radio stations, or a combination of them all—compromise the quality of democratic politics and cultural life when they grow out of touch with the communities in which they operate. In the last decade, though, Congress and the FCC have relaxed ownership restrictions in all media. The government did not so much "deregulate" the market, because broadcasters depend on tight state supervision to protect their exclusive domains in the airwaves. Instead, the federal government "re-regulated" the industry so that Big Media companies could expand and consolidate ownership across outlets, even though such arrangements threatened the localism, diversity, and competition that are supposed to drive U.S. media policy, and resulted in massive downsizing of the local reporters, editors, and DJs who produce original content for cities and towns.

These re-regulatory projects affected every major and minor media market, but their impact was particularly severe in the radio industry. Prior to 1996, the FCC exercised caps on the number of radio stations that a media company could own at the national level. It set the limit at seven AM and seven FM stations in 1953, and, in 1984, under pressure from broadcasters who insisted that loosening radio regulations would increase their efficiency and profitability, the commission modified the caps to allow for twelve and twelve. In 1992 the limits were expanded to eighteen and eighteen, and then to twenty and twenty in 1994.

With the Telecommunications Act of 1996, Congress and the FCC eliminated the national station ownership limit altogether and raised local limits from four to as high as eight stations, allowing Big Media groups to merge operations on an unprecedented scale. Following the 1996 rule change, ambitious radio companies such as Cumulus Media, Viacom/ Infinity, and Citadel Broadcasting Corporation joined Clear Channel in the race to take over hundreds of stations and establish dominance in particular markets. Despite the eight stations local limit in the largest cities, the FCC's idiosyncratic counting method still made it possible for single corporations to own nine or more stations in some thirty-four specific metropolitan areas around the country. By the early years of the twenty-first century there were markets in Kansas, Wyoming, Florida, Oregon, and Ohio where one company, Clear Channel or Cumulus, owned more than half the local stations; and others in New York, Texas, Maine, Iowa, and Georgia where two companies owned more than 60 percent between them.

As the Citadel Broadcasting Corporation openly acknowledges, small and midsize markets are the best to take over because they are "less competitive, have fewer signals, derive a significant portion of their revenue from local advertisers and offer substantial opportunities for further consolidation."[18] Not that Big Media companies avoid big cities. Clear Channel owns fifteen stations that reach Washington, D.C., fourteen in Pittsburgh, thirteen in Detroit, twelve in Cleveland and Newark, and eleven in Los Angeles, Boston, and Cincinnati.[19]

Whether buying into large markets or small, Big Media spent billions of dollars to acquire stations immediately after the Telecommunications Act became law. There were more than 10,400 commercial radio stations in the United States when the Telecom Act went into effect in 1996. During the two-year industry-wide shopping spree that followed the relaxed regulations, media companies bought and sold more than 4,400 of them, over 40 percent of the field, reducing the number of individual owners by 700 (or about 14 percent). Less than twelve months after the new rules became law, Neil Hickey, a contributing editor at the *Columbia Journalism Review*, reported that in the radio industry alone, "Westinghouse/CBS purchased Infinity Broadcasting for $4.9 billion, creating a radio colossus of 77 stations and achieving dominant power in the nation's top ten radio markets, with multiple stations in each," while "Chancellor Broadcasting Co. bought twelve radio stations from Colfax Communications for $365 million, giving it 53 stations in 15 markets."[20] *USA Today,* whose parent company, Gannett, had led the consolidation movement in the newspaper industry, warned about the "unprecedented wave of consolidation" that took radio "from a kitchen-table culture of mom-and-pop business to one at home in the boardrooms of the nation's largest companies."

Small, independently owned and operated radio stations were hit especially hard by the wave of acquisitions, as were minority station owners, whose numbers dropped 8 percent (from 350 to 322)—the largest decrease since the FCC began tracking them in 1990—when they were forced to compete against or sell out to Big Media groups. By 2005, the FCC reported that only 3.6 percent of all broadcast radio and television stations were minority-owned, while a mere 3.4 percent were owned by women. "I don't think anybody anticipated that the pace would be so fast and so dramatic," said FCC chairman William Kennard, defending himself against critics who charged him with allowing the industry to dictate the terms of its own regulation. "The fundamental economic structure of the radio industry is changing from one of independently owned operators to something akin to a chain store."[21]

In Texas, to take one example, radio consolidators were rounding up as many stations as they could handle. Lowry Mays, then the president and CEO of Clear Channel Communications, purchased his first local station, KEEZ-FM (now KAJA-FM) in San Antonio, in 1972. During the early 1990s he expanded his national holdings to the legal limit of forty, and in the months following the 1996 act he turned his relatively unknown company into one of the nation's largest radio operators, acquiring outright or obtaining interest in sixty-six new stations to top one hundred overall. Mays was downright cautious compared to his old Austin associates, R. Steve Hicks, the radio entrepreneur and cofounder of SFX Broadcasting, and his billionaire brother, Thomas Hicks. Backed by what analysts estimated as a $700 million equity commitment from Hicks, Muse, Tate & Furst, the investment firm where Tom was cofounder, chair, and CEO, Steve created a new company,

Capstar Broadcasting Corporation, to take advantage of the deregulated marketplace. Capstar purchased 350 radio stations, including all the SFX stations that the Department of Justice allowed it to take, between 1996 and 1998.[22] As Lisa Dollinger, Capstar's former vice president of corporate communications and now the chief communications officer at Clear Channel, told me, "The Hickses saw what had happened in the 1996 Telecom Act, and they went out and bought as many small and midsized stations as they could. Capstar became the largest radio group in the country overnight."[23]

Standardization of broadcast content made such rapid consolidation possible. Randy Michaels, the former CEO of Clear Channel's radio division, compared its programming format with the menus at national burger franchises, telling the *Wall Street Journal* that "a McDonald's manager may get his arms around the local community, but there are certain elements of the product that are constant. You may in some parts of the country get pizza and in some parts of the country get chicken, but the Big Mac is the Big Mac. How we apply those principles to radio we're still figuring out."[24]

National media chains have in fact shown little interest in letting customers have it their way. Rather than offering homemade broadcasts done specially for the people and places they serve, companies like Clear Channel produce standardized national and regional shows that have the artificial flavor of local broadcasts. Announcers prerecord voice bits and music selections into four-hour segments that take them less than twenty minutes to produce, and pretend familiarity with places they've never been and local traditions they've never experienced. On one Clear Channel show, for example, the San Diego–based personality "Cabana Boy Geoff" Alan raved about a "wild and crazy party" in a local club where, he said, "I personally saw a number of you hook up with people you had never hooked up with before." He then conducted an interview with the pop star duo Evan and Jaron Lowenstein, during which Evan announced that a town was "actually far more beautiful than I expected it to be": "It's actually really nice, so happy to be here." "We've got some good people here," Alan agreed, then asked listeners to call the station with questions for the musicians. Yet the show had been taped weeks earlier, in Southern California. The DJ had not attended the party, nor ever visited the town, and the Lowensteins could not answer the calls. Listeners were hearing a doctored script, produced in a studio far away, and—until they began turning off their radios in favor of satellite service, the Internet, and MP3 players—no one at Clear Channel cared what the audience had to say.[25]

ALTHOUGH CITIZENS MAY BE DISSATISFIED, BIG MEDIA COMPANIES across the board have taken Clear Channel's business strategy as a model for how they can profitably expand. In today's media market, established conglomerates such as Viacom, Disney, News Corporation, and General Electric, as well as emerging giants such as Gannett Company and the Tribune Company, are centralizing operations and cutting costs while customizing content just enough to offer local variation—chicken in some places, pizza in others, and everywhere the Big Mac.

Take Sinclair Broadcast Group, the upstart television chain known for airing partisan nightly news coverage and scheduling "news specials" such as *Stolen Honor,* in which Vietnam veterans spewed unfounded accusations at Democratic presidential candidate John Kerry just weeks before the 2004 presidential election. In the media industry, Sinclair is best known for pioneering NewsCentral, an innovative if short-lived system for producing local television news coverage for affiliates in its fleet of just under sixty stations with a central cast working in a suburban Baltimore studio. Or Village Voice Media, the alternative weekly publisher that recently merged with New Times, the Phoenix-based chain whose irreverent managers developed a standard format for blending local investigative features with cookie-cutter cultural coverage and copious sex ads in cities throughout the country. After the merger, which left the Southwestern executives in charge of the Village Voice brand, the company owned seventeen alternative weeklies in major markets such as New York, Los Angeles, Miami, Houston, Seattle, Denver, and San Francisco, giving it control of about 25 percent of the Association of Alternative Newsweeklies market.

In the Midwest, the Tribune Company has grown from its roots in Chicago to become the nation's leader in "convergence" news production, in which staff from newspapers, broadcast television and radio stations, cable channels, magazines, Web sites, and entertainment subsidiaries work "across platforms," creating "content" (not simply journalism) that is customized for different markets and media. Tribune's bold growth strategy captured the attention of media conglomerates around the globe, while raising concerns from industry watchdogs and consumer groups. For the Tribune model of "cross-ownership" of broadcast and print outlets in the same market is possible only if a corporation can get around standard federal media policies that prohibit such arrangements unless—as is the case for Tribune's properties in Chicago, New York, and Los Angeles—a company is given a special waiver or grandfathered in by law.

Media policies do little to prevent ambitious companies such as Tribune, Sinclair, Viacom, and News Corporation from acquiring properties beyond the standard limits. During the past two decades it has become common practice for Big Media companies to challenge the federal government's ownership restrictions by conditionally buying outlets in places where they are over the limit, and then requesting waivers, pressing legal cases, or mounting political campaigns so that the law comes into compliance with them.

Major media companies spend lavishly on marketing and lobbying projects that put spotlights on their leading roles as creative cultural entrepreneurs whose mission is to inform, entertain, and serve the public. What they leave unsaid, however, is their other identity as political entrepreneurs and powerful interest groups, whose fundamental purpose is not to promote the interests of citizens but, like all publicly traded companies, to generate high revenues and increase stock values for their shareholders. There is, of course, a strong American tradition of doing well in the media business by doing good journalism and entertainment. But in recent decades most media chains have used a different strategy, increasing profits by cutting their costs, eliminating reporters, DJs, and producers in cities where they control enough of the market that consumers have few other places to turn for local news and culture.

The rise of national media conglomerates and the fall of locally owned and operated newspapers, television channels, and radio stations have helped to facilitate the industry's divestment from the places where they operate. In 1945, for example, roughly 80 percent of American newspapers were privately owned, often by families that were willing to sacrifice potential profits to maintain their journalistic principles and preserve their readers' trust. Today, however, more than 80 percent of American newspapers are owned and operated by publicly traded corporations, many of which are merely subsidiaries of larger conglomerates whose executives are unwilling to compromise income for the good of cities they rarely visit or towns they've never seen.

Not that the FCC is unaware of the industry's influence. In addition to the revolving door through which regulators routinely exit to take high-paying jobs in the companies they once regulated, Big Media companies get influence the old-fashioned way: they pay for it. According to a report on the legislative process behind media re-regulation published by the CPI in 2003, "FCC officials have been showered with nearly $2.8 million in travel and entertainment over the past eight years, most of it from the telecommunications and broadcast industries the agency regulates . . . The $2.8 million paid for FCC commissioners and agency staffers to attend hundreds of conventions, conferences and other events in locations all over the world, including Paris, Hong Kong and Rio de Janeiro." The National Association of Broadcasters was the leading industry sponsor, doling out $191,472 to FCC officials traveling to its events. The FCC chairman, who was most responsible for setting the commission's agenda, "chalked up the most industry sponsored travel and entertainment among active commissioners during the period covered by the study—44 trips costing $84,921."[26]

Lobbying by the media industry is especially intense when Congress and the FCC are actively debating regulatory changes. In the early 1990s, for example, the networks and aspiring radio giants helped to lead a high-powered, low-profile campaign on the Capitol, urging political officials to roll back the ownership caps that restrained consolidation among radio and television companies. The effort intensified after the Republican Party took control of Congress in the 1994 elections, and in the next two years the media industry's lobbying expenses skyrocketed while political contributions from the communications and electronics sector soared from $30,727,095 to $60,914,552. By comparison, 1996 contributions were $51,593,530 from agribusiness, $46,578,676 from energy and natural resources, $13,089,979 from defense.[27] In the view of CPI founder Charles Lewis, such conduct from major media interests leaves little question that "the FCC is in the grips of the industry," captured by the very companies it is supposed to regulate.

The money was well spent: the expensive lobbying campaign of the mid-1990s, for example, culminated in the 1996 Telecom Act. Arguing that the economic downturn of the early 1990s had imperiled the media business, with stations and channels across the country suffering operating losses, aspiring consolidators claimed that more mergers would allow them to reduce costs and increase profits. Whether and how concentration would protect competition, diversity, and localism was left unsaid.

Andrew Jay Schwartzman, president and CEO of the Media Access Project, a nonprofit law firm that works on media policy in Washington, D.C., acknowledged that Big Media's lobbying narrative had some truth to it, up to a point. Many broadcasters did indeed lose advertising revenue during the recession of the early 1990s. "The media business is always cyclical that way," he told me. But the real source of their trouble at the time was that some companies "bulked up quickly and took on a lot of debt after the FCC raised ownership caps in the 1980s and again in 1992. They paid high prices for radio properties, expecting them to keep generating the same levels of income. And when the market slowed they were exposed." The broadcast industry had been pushing for relaxed ownership laws since the 1980s, and in the mid-1990s it simply used the brief economic downturn as an excuse to call for gutting the caps. "Many of the stations that were in the red during the early 1990s were there because of their debt, and others were family-owned stations that put people in their families on the payroll in no-show jobs so they could take money out. The industry was doing just fine. The 'crisis' they talked about to get a policy change was a fake crisis."

The tremendous political clout of the media and telecommunications industries derives not only from their big budgets for lobbying and well-connected trade associations, but from the belief of elected officials (who spend much of their time raising money to buy advertising from broadcast companies) that the industry's influence determines the fate of policy proposals, political campaigns, and, in turn, their own careers. Indiscreet members of Congress say that FCC officials, senators, and representatives are "reluctant regulators," because they fear being singled out and targeted with a backlash of negative coverage from the Big Media companies they are supposed to check.[28] Officials sometimes benefit from their relations with Big Media in more concrete ways, too.

The Hicks brothers of Capstar Broadcasting Corporation are illustrative of such mutually profitable relationships. No mere bystanders to the 1996 act, the Hickses, according to their own press materials, played a key role in persuading Congress to raise the local ownership caps and abandon the national limits outright. Hicks, Muse, Tate & Furst was already the the nation's largest active investor in the broadcast industry, and it stood to profit handsomely from aggressive deregulation. Steve, who purchased his first radio station at age twenty-nine and took over stations in several southern states soon thereafter, was the Hicks family leader on media policy. Capstar's Web site boasts that Steve devised the Local Marketing Agreement (LMA), the legal loophole that allows one media company to effectively lease and operate stations it does not technically own, thereby evading ownership limits in a local market.

For the Hicks brothers, as for other media executives, political entrepreneurialism is the fundamental source of financial success. As a regent of the University of Texas under Governor George W. Bush, Tom Hicks lobbied to create and then chair the UT Investment Management Company (UTIMCO), which would manage the system's multi-billion-dollar budget. Soon after taking it over, Tom was at the center of a statewide scandal when journalists discovered that UTIMCO awarded $450 million in contracts to companies whose executives were close friends of Hicks, major donors to the Bush family, or business partners with Hicks's companies. In 1998 Hicks made a direct contribution to the governor's wealth by leading a group that purchased the Texas Rangers for $250 million in what the *Texas Observer* called a "sweetheart deal." The future president had spent $605,000 on his 1.8 percent share of the team, and he personally earned between $10 million and $14 million on the sale.

IF LOBBYING HAS BEEN ONE SECRET TO BIG MEDIA'S POLITICAL SUCCESS, storytelling, which news and entertainment companies are uniquely equipped to do effectively, has been another. In the past decade major media companies have told two, mutually exclusive stories, depending on whether the audience is made up of political officials and regulators or citizens and shareholders. Each story has a different moral and a different implication, so it's not surprising that media executives don't tell them both at once.

Before Congress and the FCC, Big Media managers always insist that the industry is in crisis—as in the early 1990s—besieged by competition from the Internet, satellite services, bloggers, citizen journalists, and personal listening devices. As their hard-luck story goes, only the elimination or drastic reduction of ownership limits can save major media conglomerates and, by extension, the public goods they offer. Testifying in a U.S. Senate hearing on media consolidation in July 2001, Mel Karmazin, the former president and chief operating officer of Viacom, used such a story to challenge the very premise of the debate. "Thank you for this opportunity to testify before you today on the topic of media consolidation and broadcast ownership," he opened. But "instead of 'media consolidation,' I prefer to call it media competition, because that's what consumers are enjoying today." After complaining about dwindling audiences and revenues for Viacom's then-subsidiaries such as CBS and Infinity (one of the nation's leading radio companies), Karmazin reported that "it is bewildering and astounding that there is a debate raging anew here in Washington over the limits on national broadcast television station ownership."[29]

What Karmazin left out is the happier story that Viacom's own Web site provided to potential investors at the time. "Viacom is a leading global media company, with preeminent positions in broadcast and cable television, radio, outdoor advertising, and online. With programming that appeals to audiences in every demographic category across virtually all media, the company is a leader in the creation, promotion, and distribution of entertainment, news, sports, music, and comedy. Viacom's well-known brands include CBS, MTV, Nickelodeon, Nick at Nite, VH1, BET, Paramount Pictures, Infinity Broadcasting, Viacom Outdoor, UPN, TV Land, Comedy Central, CMT: Country Music Television, King World, Spike TV, Showtime, and Simon & Schuster."

Karmazin was in good company at the hearing. Jack Fuller, then-president of Tribune Publishing, the newspaper subsidiary of the Tribune Company, offered in his testimony a variation on Viacom's theme. "In an environment where people's choices for obtaining information have radically multiplied, there is no risk of one voice dominating the marketplace of ideas," Fuller assured the committee. "Today in clamorous cities such as Los Angeles, Chicago, and New York, it is frankly a challenge for any voice—no matter how booming—to get itself heard . . . Let firms own newspapers and broadcast television stations and people who get all their news from broadcasting today will hear new voices."[30]

Tribune Company president, chairman, and CEO Dennis FitzSimons shared a different version of market conditions with the corporation's shareholders just a few years later. "Here's a quick look at how this [cross-ownership strategy] has worked for us in Chicago, where we offer consumers varied media choices like the Chicago *Tribune, RedEye,* and WGN television and radio. We also own *Chicago* magazine, *Hoy/ Chicago,* CLTV, our 24-hour cable news channel, and Tribune Direct, our direct mail operation. And we have a strong Internet presence with our newspaper sites Chicagosports.com and Metromix.com, our very successful entertainment site. Together, the weekly reach of these properties is 6.4 million people *or more than 90% of the market.*"[31]

Americans and their elected officials may not know which of Big Media's own stories they should believe, but they are beginning to realize that entrusting media conglomerates with even more control of the public airwaves is a losing proposition.

THE TIMING OF AMERICA'S LOCAL MEDIA DEVASTATION COULD NOT BE worse. We live in an era of extraordinary upheaval and conflict. The United States is now engaged in a war that has no foreseeable endpoint, a war made possible because the government misled the majority of its citizens into believing that Iraq had given substantial support to Al Qaeda in planning 9/11, and a substantial minority into thinking that inspectors had discovered weapons of mass destruction in Iraq or that world public opinion supported the war.[32] Strange outbursts of extreme weather are punishing the planet, with catastrophic storms hitting cities everywhere, and policy makers are searching for ways to handle emerging natural and manmade catastrophes. Millions of good jobs, and some entire industries, are disappearing as multinational firms relocate facilities to countries with low prevailing wages. Public programs, such as health care, education, and possibly social security, are being transferred into the hands of private sector companies with no proven performance records. As metropolitan regions are sprawling outward, city centers are gasping for new life. Scientists warn of a coming energy crisis and insist that our modern habits are unsustainable. Record numbers of citizens are incarcerated. And we can only speculate about unreported issues and trends—especially at the local level—that are shaping the ways we live and die. Our need for media that serves the public interest by helping citizens and communities make informed decisions has never been greater.

2

REMOTE CONTROL

John Brandt always wanted to work in radio. "I didn't know anything about the business, really. But I loved the music, the DJs, the banter. The excitement of it all. I listened all the time, and I couldn't imagine a better thing to do with my life." In 1964 he moved to Ogallala, Nebraska, a western cattletown and farmer's settlement that boomed after becoming a stop on the Union Pacific Railroad, but today, after decades of agricultural decline, has a population a tad under five thousand people. "I worked in the grocery store, and then at the Holiday Inn," Brandt told me on a crisp winter morning in 2006, with a deep, soothing voice that was made for the medium. "Then I got hired at the town's only radio station, KOGA."

It was a small AM station, with a 500-watt signal and a license to broadcast full power during daytime hours and low power, at 150 watts, after dark. In December, when the sun sets early, KOGA was off the air by 4:15 p.m. (AM radio signals travel farther after nightfall, and small stations were often restricted to reduce interference with other stations.)[1] KOGA could reach eighty thousand people. "We had to *broad*cast," Brandt recalled fondly. "Which means we tried to have something for everyone who could pick up our signal. And we packed the programs with local and regional content. We don't have a lot of drama around here, no 'if it bleeds it leads' material. But we covered the county fairs. We announced town meetings. We did radio obituaries—which is a real service, because the towns around here have either weekly or biweekly papers, and a lot of times we were the only ones to report that there would be a funeral for someone who died between the editions. We did high school sports, a tremendous number of games, for something like seventeen schools. And we had *Midwest Opinions*, our daily forty minutes of around-the-coffee-table talk. Thirty-seven years later, I'm still here."

The general manager who first hired Brandt shared his passion for radio. Ray Lockhart came to KOGA in 1967 with plans to build the sleepy station into a local powerhouse. "Before he came the owners were doing absolutely nothing," Brandt remembered. "There were three of them—two men from Ogallala, one from Oshkosh—and they gave him a ten percent stake in the company. Ray knew that simple good business practices could make us a lot more money. You can do real well by just being professional." Lockhart created discount pricing schemes for advertising packages and standardized the station's billing system. But his entrepreneurialism extended beyond the financial side of the business. "Ray was an amazing innovator. He had an intuitive sense about what we could do with local radio," said Brandt. "We did market reports all through the day. We did local talk. And all the music formats—Top Forty, big country, even a polka every hour, because the people who did music programming liked it. At the time I was on the air from six to nine in the morning. I did the morning music—Creedence Clearwater Revival, Willie Nelson. We'd have to wait for Ray to leave town to play songs like 'Jumpin' Jack Flash.' At the time, Ray and I would do *Midwest Opinions* together a little after eight. Then I'd go out and sell ads for the rest of the day."

The reforms were a hit. KOGA gained more listeners. Advertisers bought airtime in bulk and paid on time. Profits increased, and so did Lockhart's ambitions. "In 1972 he got us a nighttime license. And then around 1973 we got an FM station."[2] By 1974 Lockhart's changes at KOGA had proven so successful that he decided to buy out his partners, and he took over controlling interest in the company. Around that time another group started a competing FM station in Ogallala, yet it couldn't win over KOGA's listeners, and ultimately Lockhart bought it for himself. Although Ogallala, like many other small U.S. towns, did not have much local market competition, it did have a hometown owner committed to providing a diverse set of offerings.

. . .

THE LATE 1960S AND EARLY 1970S WERE A REVOLUTIONARY PERIOD FOR
music radio, with stereo sound on the emergent FM dial attracting
young listeners because AM programmers, relying heavily on the standard playlists that proliferated as leading stations used Top 40 formats
to compete with television in the 1950s, had dulled the edges of the
nation's leading outlets. FM broadcasting technology, which differs from
AM broadcasting because it modulates the frequency, not the ampli-
tude, of radio waves, was invented by RCA's radio whiz kid, Edwin
Howard Armstrong, between 1928 and 1933, when it was patented.
FM signals did not travel as far as then-dominant AM stations, but they
transmitted a higher fidelity broadcast because they could separate and
layer sounds for stereophonic effect. Armstong was certain that FM
would transform the radio business, yet David Sarnoff, RCA's general
manager and future president, decided to build the company around
television rather than radio innovations, and neither RCA nor any other
major media company invested significant resources in FM stations
until the 1960s.[3]

The federal government played a crucial role in launching FM music
radio and, in turn, advancing its goals of increasing the diversity and
competition of local broadcast media. In the 1960s regulators grew concerned that AM stations owners were using their FM outlets to simul-
cast AM programs (and thereby double the chance that listeners would
find their broadcasts while scanning the dial) rather than play different
content, and in 1964 the FCC ruled that, beginning in January 1967,
companies that operated AM and FM stations in cities with more than
one hundred thousand people could not simultaneously replicate more
than half of their programming. The new rule forced radio stations to
choose between investing in new content or going off the air.

KFRE-FM in San Francisco was one of the many stations where
managers, convinced that FM radio would never be commercially viable,
looked for someone to take over the studio.[4] The timing was fortu-
itous. Tom "Big Daddy" Donahue had recently left his DJ job at another
Top 40–format AM station where he was not allowed to play new
bands, such as the Doors, the Grateful Dead, and Jefferson Airplane,
that were breaking out in San Francisco. Donahue was incredulous
about the situation, in which he was a leading DJ participating in an

inspiring moment of musical innovation and cultural change—one whose symbolic center was his own city—and he was unable to broadcast the sounds on local radio.

When Donahue heard that some AM stations were killing their FM affiliates because of the FCC rule change, he began dreaming about a way to resurrect them by taking advantage of the programming freedom and high-fidelity stereo sound they offered. He convinced the owners of KFRE to let him run the station. Using the call letters KMPX, Big Daddy created what the Los Angeles DJ Jim Ladd termed "the very first FM rock station on planet earth."[5] DJs such as Donahue became spokesmen for a new generation of youthful idealists. The first "freeform" FM stations did not only break rock music; they also placed "a strong emphasis on community issues affecting the young," wrote the radio historian Susan Douglas, "and the news and public service announcements emphasized the station's organic relationship to its locale."

The main source of FM's allure was that station managers encouraged DJs to explore new music, playing songs they selected personally rather than songs selected for them. In the 1950s and early 1960s, Douglas explained, marketing experts persuaded managers at popular AM music stations to rely on *Billboard* rankings and records of jukebox plays, rather than on the idiosyncratic tastes of on-air talent, who were susceptible to both bribes from record producers and cultural appeals to promote "race music," such as blues and R&B. AM DJs began complaining that they had been straitjacketed by management, and many fled to the FM dial. "In 1965," said Richard Neer, a former DJ at what was once New York City's premier rock station, WNEW-FM, "there were a lot of stations playing forty records, and . . . there weren't any visionaries in the business of radio. Everyone was wearing suits and very uptight and very programmed." With FM, however, "the disc jockeys had total freedom to play whatever records they chose. They could say what they wanted, whenever they wanted." According to Ladd, putting together a music program used to be "like painting a picture aurally. It wasn't one song after another, unrelated . . . Back then, you were telling stories . . . If you picked a Bob Dylan record and followed it with a particular Stones record, there was a reason for that on many different levels. It wasn't just that the Dylan record was hot and the Stones record was a new release."[6]

The freedom to determine what songs to play was one thing, but the greatest glory and joy for DJs came from discovering new bands, and in cities with vibrant cultural scenes disc jockeys kept their ears to the ground so they could hear fresh acts. Since the late 1960s urban disc jockeys have played important roles in breaking music with a decidedly local flavor: folk and psychedelic rock in San Francisco; rhythm and blues in Detroit; funk in Philadelphia; new wave and hip-hop in New York City; house in Chicago; grunge in Seattle.[7] Early FM DJs aimed to delight listeners, of course, but not simply with market-tested songs that were guaranteed to please. "We created taste," said Nat Asch, the original programming director at WNEW-FM. "Whatever we had at that time, we presented it and said try this. If you don't like it, we're going to go into the toilet, but that's none of your concern, try it. We surrounded that music with people who could extend what we presumed was interesting about what we presented . . . We led rather than reflected."[8]

Disc jockeys at WLIR, Long Island's famous rock station, shared this mission. The station's official history proudly claims that "LIR was already adding cuts from Blondie, Talking Heads, and The Ramones to the latest Rolling Stones or Neil Young album cuts in the 1970s," paving the way for these new artists on the air. Like the DJs at WNEW, programmers at WLIR featured live recordings of up-and-coming bands at venues such as CBGB and Max's Kansas City, sometimes getting them on the radio before they had a record. Rodney Bingenheimer used the same techniques at KROQ in Los Angeles. Bingenheimer, who helped to break dozens of major acts, from the Go-Go's to Van Halen and the Sex Pistols, told the *Los Angeles Weekly* that "what was fun was when bands used to come up to KROQ, like Bad Religion would show up and give me a tape, and by the time they get in their car and drive off, it's already on the radio . . . I used to play Oasis before they were signed—on cassette demos!" In Boston, bands such as Aerosmith (from nearby New Hampshire) and the J. Geils Band credit Maxanne Sartori of WBCN for playing their music until it broke into the national market. Sartori, whom *Rolling Stone* praised for "consistently boost[ing] local bands," made her biggest catch at the Newberry Street Music Fair, where a young rocker named Ric Ocasek impressed her so much that she began playing demos from his group, Cap'N Swing. Soon after, she introduced Ocasek and his bandmates to the former Modern Lovers and DMZ drummer David Robinson, and together they formed the Cars.[9]

DJs at small-town stations such as KOGA in Ogallala had their own aspirations. Although they were unlikely to launch new bands into fame, they played the essential role of introducing their audience to new music styles, social trends, and ideas, acting as cultural brokers between the local community and the national or international scene. Radio personalities in New York and Los Angeles may have had well-known voices, but only a rare few enjoyed the public recognition routinely afforded to their counterparts in small towns and cities, where constant appearances made their faces famous.

Paradoxically, the popularity of FM radio compromised the future of live broadcasting at small stations. While managers at stations the size of KOGA understood the importance of employing good talent, they also had a strong incentive to keep costs down and profit margins up in their modest markets—even the low salaries paid to DJs cut into the bottom line. As the FM dial gained popularity, small-station owners began to rely on automated programming technology, which could pump out a steady stream of music without a DJ in the studio. Douglas estimated that by the mid-1970s up to one-seventh of FM stations used "assembly line" systems to "stay on the air for hours with virtually no human intervention."[10] This early automation relied on audiotaping technology; in the absence of chains that could distribute content to stations in multiple markets, individual radio stations preprogrammed their broadcasts mainly by recording in their own studios. "We started using the tape automation around the time we got the FM station," Brandt recalled. "We used an old Harris System, big reels of tape that would play music, with another machine that would play commercials." Lockhart, KOGA's owner, used similar devices in his other stations, where tape technology provided material for late-night broadcasts through the 1980s and early 1990s. The system worked fine—unless it didn't, in which case the stations had to scramble to find someone who could do the show live, or else go off the air.

The technological breakthrough that would put an end to such system failures—and, ironically, also to innovative programming—was developed in the world of small radio. Kevin Lockhart, who was born just five years before his father began working at KOGA, grew up in the radio business, working as a DJ, manager, and salesman at the family stations before serving four years in the U.S. Army, where he learned some basic technical skills even though, he told me, "[he] didn't have any real training as an engineer." In late 1989 Kevin had just returned to Ogallala, where his father, who by then had also acquired two stations in Colorado, was frustrated because the automated tape system at one of his outlets was failing. "Replacing the old tape recorders would cost about three or four thousand dollars per machine," Brandt explained. "And Ray asked why we couldn't just record programs in the computer." Kevin didn't have a good answer, except for the fact that they didn't have software for the job, which meant that if they wanted a computer automation system they would have to develop it on their own. "They were working in the basement of our office," Brandt recalled. "My desk was down there, so I was around for it all. Kevin had some friends who helped. And they were trying to record a CD into a computer, to play it out, and then match the wave form. I remember the day they came running to my office in the basement screaming that they had done it. 'We've got CD quality,' they said. It was quite a moment."

After the first breakthrough, Kevin camped out in the basement and continued developing the software. "I just played around on the computer and tried to come up with things," he modestly explained. Not only did the new system solve the problems at Ray Lockhart's own stations, which never numbered more than ten. "By 1991 we found something that worked well enough to put on the market." They created a new company, Prophet Systems Innovations, and Brandt, by then a veteran sales manager, began demonstrating the computer automation system at national trade shows. "We were a small-market radio station and we developed it for small markets, that's how we were thinking," Brandt said. "But we had a guy who wanted to make it applicable for big-market stations, too. He helped to develop it, adding features like laugh tracks and audience applause. He made it user-friendly, and adaptable, because he knew that's what the large stations would need if their hosts were going to tape whole shows."

By the mid-1990s Prophet's small staff had built a central file server that facilitated high-speed transmission of radio content, and a wide-area network system—for "WANcasting"—that allowed managers of multistation radio companies (which were then limited to forty stations nationally) to see and control what was playing on all their outlets at once. With Prophet's sophisticated voice-tracking system, radio stations could store music or talk shows on exportable and manipulable digital files, rather than on CDs or records, and DJs could craft their programs by adding commentary, news, traffic, and commercials into the electronic mix. Computer monitors would graphically display exactly how much time each song left for opening and closing voice-overs, so programmers could avoid talking through the lyrics and ensure high-quality production values. The technology was extraordinary. Brandt remembered: "I would show people the technology, and executives from CBS and all the major stations were stunned. They couldn't believe that we could do all this with a computer. The first group to actually buy a system from us was the Christian radio station in Las Vegas. It cut their [programming] expenses to almost nothing."

But politics, not religion, would turn the Prophet computer system into gold. A number of federal policies worked to speed American media corporations—television and print, as well as radio—into the digital age. After taking office in 1993, President Bill Clinton and Vice President Al Gore made a high-profile push for new laws that would relax regulatory constraints on large telecommunications companies and encourage private-sector investment in a new "Information Superhighway." The private sector responded by energetically pursuing high-tech production and distribution systems. While the Democrats, hoping to secure the financial support of major telecommunications corporations, focused on infrastructure projects for "telephony," big broadcasting companies organized an expensive lobbying campaign to promote their own interests. The resulting Telecommunications Act of 1996 proved to be decisive for Prophet's future. "We were developing this before the 1996 Telecom Act," Kevin told me, chuckling a little at his luck. "We had an internal fight about it, because the programmers thought we wouldn't get enough business to make it work, but my father and I had been following the debate around radio ownership, and we insisted that we go forward." The Lockharts immediately understood that the new federal rules would forever change their family business. But it took longer to recognize that media conglomerates, which were prepared to begin their feeding frenzy at the moment President Bill Clinton signed the Telecom Act into law, would take advantage of Prophet's automated programming system to transform the entire radio industry, substituting machine-made shows by "cyber jocks" who could program a four-hour segment in less than thirty minutes for the live talent and local programming that the Lockharts themselves had always valued. "It surprised us how quickly the supergroups emerged," said Kevin. "Then we realized—oh my goodness, this is going to be something else."

STEVE HICKS OF CAPSTAR HAD RECOGNIZED THE POTENTIAL COST SAV-ings from a computerized radio programming system even before he started his megabusiness. But as he began acquiring hundreds of new stations, each with its own payrolls to fill, he took an urgent interest in technology that would dramatically reduce the company's labor needs. In January 1997 Capstar invited a half-dozen leading automation companies to Austin for a "dog and pony show," giving each a week to demonstrate its products. Prophet was by no means the only company working on digital automation. Yet "we were," Kevin Lockhart recalled, "about six months ahead of everyone else. We were the only one that could connect the system right there, from Austin to Nebraska."

Capstar was at first only cautiously optimistic about Prophet. After all, Prophet had fewer than ten employees working in an unknown midwestern town of about five thousand people. The company would have to prove that it could handle a big job; to do so, Kevin agreed to connect the first eleven stations in the system at cost before scaling up. He went to Austin and managed the job brilliantly, and after the first successful implementation Capstar asked him to expand the automated system into its entire station group.

Capstar's business model was based on replacing original local shows and the people who made them with programs recorded in its Austin facility. To do this, though, engineers would have to wire each station into the matrix, and that required traveling to the small-market towns that Lisa Dollinger called "the sticks." In the following months Dollinger, then Capstar's PR director, worked closely with Prophet as it fully automated Capstar's fleet of local stations, and she has fond memories of the time. Together, Lockhart, Dollinger, and a team of engineers traveled the nation in an RV, installing the new systems in an effort they described as "Nerds on Tour."

Back in Austin, Capstar programmers perfected the art of mass customized digital programming, in which ersatz local commentary would be inserted into long segments of automated content. Voice tracking allowed Capstar to create the impression that the old ways of DJing remained in place, even though the on-air talent at many stations was replaced by personalities who worked outside the state where their shows aired, and the primary responsibility of the new DJs had shifted to performing the role of local radio host. With Prophet's technology, a broadcaster committed to efficient production could have one employee record more shows in an eight-hour workday than was previously possible in a full week. It could also operate with no one in the studio, no matter what the time of day. As Prophet's promotional Web site advertises, its VoiceTRAC software is "able to record a perfect 4 hour shift in under 30 minutes! You don't have to be a superhero to sound like one . . . Record your voice tracks up to 2 weeks in advance. Read song notes and access music beds/audio via the button bar while you record. *Sound live and local.*"[11]

"Capstar pioneered voice tracking," Dollinger told me. "We hired DJs who were very good and specialized for different formats. We had thirty-five or forty DJs and these gorgeous studios, and they would voice-track for all our different markets. They would introduce songs or read the weather forecast or make a service announcement, just short messages. We also had out-of-market talent doing them for some areas. The local station would communicate with them, so the talent out-of-market knew which issues and themes to push for which place." Capstar had indeed engineered a radical system: it helped take FM radio back to the heyday of Top 40 AM radio in the 1950s, this time updated with a fake local twist.

According to Dollinger, the net results of the conversion to digital automation included improved technical engineering and more professional operations at small-market stations. It would have been practically impossible for large radio companies to produce this blend of customized and standardized content with the old tape-recording technology, she told me.

Prophet allowed small-market audiences to get "top talent" and encouraged them to believe that the DJs knew all about their town. Steve Hicks was so pleased with the outcome at Capstar, and so eager to establish control over the technology that made it all possible, that he bought Prophet Systems and all of Lockhart's stations for his own company.

. . .

LOCKHART'S FORMER STATIONS WERE ALREADY ACCUSTOMED TO DIGITAL automation, but workers at most other radio stations Capstar took over were less enthusiastic about voice tracking, since for them the rise of more automated production translated into the downsizing of local production staff, a loss of local control, and overall job insecurity. Tricia Nellessen, who worked as a DJ on KKIX, a country station in Fayetteville, Arkansas, described the impact of the computerization process after GulfStar Communications, a subsidiary of Capstar, bought KKIX and its sister station, KKZQ, along with two other stations in the market, KEZA and KJEM. According to a scholarly article she published with Robert Brady, before GulfStar took over, KKIX and KKZQ employed live DJs in all their broadcasts and employed program directors who selected music based on their knowledge of the local market. After the transition, GulfStar reduced the number of local staff and implemented a new production model. "Although management did not explicitly suggest that the staff should be deceptive about the station's reliance on voicetracking," Nellessen and Brady wrote, "steps were taken to give the appearance that the shows were live."[12]

One of Nellessen's former colleagues reported in the same article: "I know that if I'm caught in the store by a listener who asks how she could have just heard me on the air, I'll tell her I'm voicetracked. But, honestly, we all try to keep up the illusion that it is live unless we're backed into a corner and have to tell." The staff worked hard to achieve this illusion. Employees were told to keep the phones on hold when airing a voice-tracked program, so that callers would hear a busy signal and believe, falsely, that the host was speaking with other audience members. "There were numerous moments where DJs were left wondering what to say when a listener called in and asked to talk to (or even meet) an air talent who was actually based out of another city. Most programming staff members usually came up with an excuse like 'He just stepped into a meeting' or 'Oh, she's out of the control room and I'm not sure where she is, may I take a message?'"

In Nellessen's and Brady's view, GulfStar was using voice tracking not only to deceive Fayetteville listeners but to outright abandon them and evade its stations' public-interest obligations. Although KKIX station managers often wrote to the automation studio to advise the cyber jocks about local issues, their messages could hardly substitute for the knowledge and experience of radio hosts who worked and lived in the area. The result was that "stations begin to sound less localized and more homogenized. Air staff used to describe local events; public service announcements were made for local organizations; and the staff was on site to broadcast the latest news and weather conditions. In 2000, the staff . . . mentions local conditions, but cannot provide specifics because the staff is not really at that location." Worse, listeners complained, were the on-air personalities piped in from Austin, who often mispronounced the names of towns, neighborhoods, and prominent people in the area. If local radio once helped to create communities and build common identities, now it was estranging them by destroying the sounds that made listeners feel at home.

Capstar was not the only big radio company to use voice tracking, and as other big radio companies developed systems similar to Prophet's, reports of lost local programming, automated news services, and the sale of radio airtime for program-length infomercials were beginning to concern the industry's leading figures. In 1998 the former NBC News president Lawrence Grossman complained that "the new radio entrepreneurs have slashed station budgets and eliminated what they view as costly nonessential operating expenses such as news staffs and even wire services." Moreover, he warned that "except at public radio and a few all-news stations, radio reporters have become a vanishing breed . . . The current trend is to 'outsource' radio headline news without letting the audience know—not just cutting back on station news coverage but eliminating all reporters."[13]

While commercial stations across the country downsized their newsrooms and integrated voice-tracked programs into evening and, alarmingly, daytime hours that had rarely been automated, citizens longing for better journalism flocked to National Public Radio. Between 1996 and 2006 NPR's audience of "unique listeners" (who tune in at least once a week) doubled, from 12.5 million to 25 million.[14] The public broadcaster is best known for its national programs, but as radio consolidators (as the companies that acquired large station groups are commonly called) eliminated local content on the commercial dial a number of NPR affiliates discovered that they could increase their audience by increasing their supply of live, locally oriented shows.

At Chicago's WBEZ-FM, the general manager, Torey Malatia, added original programming and cut back on NPR's syndicated shows because he believes his station "really [has] a function and responsibility . . . to be a resource for the people who live here, and that comes first." That idea, he told me as we sat in his office on Navy Pier, where the dramatic skyline unfolded before us, has "died in mainstream radio. So we have to create content that draws its distinctiveness from this place, from the stories around us, and the character of the community we serve. Our programming has to resonate with a unique and identifiable voice, because unless it does, we don't give people a reason to feel we're doing something that's irreplaceable in their lives."

Steve Edwards, a precocious talent who hosts WBEZ's popular city affairs program *Eight Forty-Eight*, developed a large following among Chicago radio listeners by adhering to the programming principles Malatia established. Speaking with me on a schoolyard bench in my old neighborhood, Edwards identified the feeling that citizens everywhere experience when they hear the flimsy or fake local content produced by Big Media: "They don't respect where I live." "Radio is an intensely personal medium," he explained. "You take radio with you in your car, your bathroom, your shower sometimes. You have your headphones. There's a flavor of radio that is intimate and personal and, by extension, local. And there's a tradition of local radio in this country. So when you're in Chicago, it sounds like you're in Chicago, and people talk like they're from Chicago. They talk about Chicago things, and through that the radio station actually creates a community around it. It's locally based. It used to be that if you went to Kansas City or Georgia or New York, you'd hear different things. And if you heard the same thing, it would be spoken with different accents and hopefully different opinions and views in each town. What strikes me as a listener is that I wake up with that same person everyday, and he or she starts my day with news and culture or traffic and a funny joke. And I *know* him; I *know* her. When that voice is piped in via satellite, when the same songs are played eighteen times a day, when the anchor doesn't know how to pronounce certain towns in my state—that's offensive to me. They don't appreciate, don't respect me. They don't respect my family, my community."

. . .

VOICE-TRACKED PROGRAMMING CAN DO MORE THAN ALIENATE LISTEN-
ers; it can endanger them. Years before the toxic spill in Minot, Tricia
Nelleson and the radio workers she interviewed in Arkansas warned
that automated stations might fail to provide emergency warnings
before, during, and after a local crisis. Nelleson was confident that the
Emergency Alert System would function during a major disaster. Yet
she was also skeptical that the radio stations would have adequate
staff to handle smaller problems, and she doubted that they would be
able to provide the level of local news, service, and information that
citizens need after the emergency broadcast ends and the community is
left to assess what happened and recover. Employing real people to
work in the studio might cost big radio companies more than using
cyber jocks, but the public benefits—in good times and bad—would be
priceless.

Consider what happened in South Dakota's Grizzly Gulch forest
during the summer of 2002, just five months after the disaster in
Minot. For more than a decade a DJ who calls himself Jack Daniels has
hosted the weekday morning program on X-Rock, a heavy-metal and
hard-rock station in Spearfish, South Dakota, that broadcasts to the
Deadwood, Sturgis, and Rapid City markets in the western part of the
state. Along with his partners, Tom Collins and Jim Kallas (who recently
replaced Collins), Daniels serves up a playlist—AC/DC, Metallica,
Ozzy, Disturbed, Saliva—that's in tune with the mythically lawless
subculture of the old mining region. Like many morning drive-time programs, the show features animated and occasionally lewd commentary,
along with a Web site full of bikinied models and off-color jokes. As
Daniels put it, "We're not on the level of Howard Stern, but we take
some huge chances."

X-Rock is owned and operated by Duhamel Broadcasting Enterprise, a family-run business that enjoys a loyal base of support, in part
because it has been in South Dakota for over fifty years. When Jack,
Tom, or Jim offends someone, they are likely to hear about it. They've
all lived and worked in the area for decades, their kids went through
its public schools, and they bump into listeners in grocery stores, restaurants, and community meetings. So does their boss, Bill Duhamel,
who began his career as a late-night DJ on KOTA, which his mother,

Helen, purchased in 1953 to prevent an out-of-state company from taking over what was then Rapid City's only radio station. Today the Duhamel family owns and operates four radio stations in the Black Hills, a television station in Rapid City, and three satellite stations serving the sparsely populated region spanning from western South Dakota to eastern Wyoming and the Nebraska Panhandle.

In May and June of 2002 Jack Daniels and Jim Kallas were busy with their usual programming and promotional work, hosting parties at local bars and making celebrity appearances at car dealerships and weekend festivals. Although South Dakota has a small population, summer is a crowded season. Nearly 2 million travelers cross the jagged mountains, rock tunnels, and tall stone spires on Needles Highway to see American bison, elk, and bighorn sheep in the Black Hills National Forest and Custer State Park, or to gaze up at Mount Rushmore and the Crazy Horse Memorial nearby. Some half million others ride to Sturgis for the world's largest motorcycle rally, roaring along the quiet mountain roads on Harley-Davidsons and painting the towns a leathery black. For X-Rock, where programmers describe their core audience as "eighteen- to thirty-four-year-old men in T-shirts," early summer is prime time.

Normally the summer weather in the Black Hills is pleasantly arid, with gusty winds that circulate the sweet smells of ponderosa pine, quaking aspen, and spruce trees across the big, open sky; the 2002 season, however, began inauspiciously. In May and June a series of severely hot and dry days caused drought conditions in three-fourths of the state, leaving spring wheat, summer crops, pastures, and hay to deteriorate under the unrelenting sun. More ominously, the scorching climate parched the soil and vegetation, turning the typically verdant landscape into a tinderbox forest. West of South Dakota, similar conditions had already proven disastrous, fueling twenty major fires in nine states, including devastating infernos in Arizona and Colorado. By June 26 the flames had consumed 2.5 million acres of land, and meteorologists warned that the fire season was only beginning.

Around 2:00 p.m. on Saturday, June 29, a gust blew trees into a power transmission line in South Dakota's Grizzly Gulch, and sparks from the contact ignited a conflagration. Within minutes, strong winds of up to forty miles per hour picked up the flames and carried them to adjacent trees, which lit up like kindling. Officials immediately called in local firefighters and emergency personnel, yet they were outmatched. The fire spread quickly through the wildlands, with gusts propelling the blaze several hundred yards in seconds. The flames advanced toward Deadwood, which was jammed with thousands of weekend tourists who listened as the sounds from the roaring fire and falling trees echoed through town.[15]

Karla Wiederhold was at home in Lead when the fire started in 2002. "My friend was out having a cigarette, and he screamed, 'Hey, look, there's a plume out there.' But I didn't think it was a fire. We're in a mining town, and there's smoke sometimes. Then the smoke turned black." She turned on her radio. "I heard that Deadwood was on fire, and I panicked. My mother is there, and I couldn't reach her by phone. I wanted to go and get her, but the police department told us to stay home."

Deadwood was already in danger. The fire spread to one thousand acres as gusts pushed it over the highways, into the hilly neighborhoods, and close to downtown. Then governor William Janklow ordered an evacuation, and soon a long line of cars formed on Highway 85, descending to safer terrain. Local officials and the American Red Cross opened an emergency shelter on the Black Hills State University campus in Spearfish, and after it filled up, the National Guard set up another nearby. People searching for relatives posted messages at the makeshift communications center. "I am looking for Esther Roth, Lanny Roth. Please have family call Perry." The local cellular tower and some phone lines were down, and residents struggled to get basic information about the conditions of their homes or the fate of their families and friends. With lines of communication dried up, anxiety spread through the region as quickly as the flames.

Jack Daniels does not usually work on Saturdays, but on June 29 he was doing a special live broadcast from a car dealership in Spearfish. He saw the forest fire himself, as he was driving near Deadwood after he finished the broadcast. X-Rock immediately began relaying vital information. I turned on the radio, Daniels recalled:

> And Jim Kallas, my program director, is on the air, directing everybody to the emergency area where the Red Cross was. Remember, this is six days from the Fourth of July; they estimate the crowd at fifteen to twenty thousand people inside tiny Deadwood. All the hotels are

totally filled, you know, and they're knocking on doors saying, "Leave your luggage, get in your car, and get out of here."

I drove toward the radio station because I knew we had to go on the air. I walked in, and Jim said, "Hey, you go on." It was perfect timing, because all these people had just been displaced, they didn't know where to go, no idea whatsoever, and I swear to you within five minutes, all our phones lines lit up. Next thing you know, I'm on line one: "Hey, my name is Gladys Johnson, I'm from Indianapolis, and we've just been evacuated from a hotel in Deadwood. I'm looking for my daughter." And so it just became this gigantic, Mayberry thing, just telling stories over the radio and connecting people with other people.

Before long Tom Collins arrived at the studio, and—as all the other local stations continued with their regular programming, breaking in with occasional news updates—Daniels, Collins, and Kallas spent the next ten hours hosting an impromptu broadcast fully dedicated to the emerging disaster. Local reporters, firefighters, and residents who stayed home despite the evacuation order called in to help track the blaze, and evacuees clustered around radios in shelters, cars, and hotels to learn about the state of the homes, businesses, neighbors, and friends they left behind. According to Kallas, "We called the whole staff in, about ten people—our sales staff, our announcers, our part-timers, whoever was around. The sales staff was answering phones and taking down information."

Carol Reif, whom I visited at the Adams Museum and House in Deadwood, recalled that "people were really frantic. They would call the station because their mother was in central city, and pretty soon neighbors would call and say don't worry about your mother, we'll take care of her. Jack and Tom were the main communication center. They were like the counselors, helping us calm down." Daniels remembered hearing from the first callers that day. "They didn't know where to turn. They would have just sat there in the dark with nothing. You listen to the other radio stations, they were acting like nothing happened."

One evacuee remembered how her family was spread out around the area, and said that it was difficult to stay in contact. "We were in hotel rooms, we had no communication with anyone, but we had the radio. The TV wasn't giving you play-by-play. It gave you news, not very good news. They didn't tell us anything we needed to know. The way we kept in touch was Jack Daniels and Tom Collins. It was absolutely amazing. I don't think they even ate."

Daniels and Collins rested early on Sunday morning, and another crew, including Kallas and the afternoon man, Kevin Morgan, took over the live broadcast for a few hours while they slept. The duo was back on the air by 8:00 a.m. Sunday, at which point the uncontained fire spanned over 4,500 acres. Plumes of black smoke hovered menacingly above the Black Hills, while horrifyingly spectacular orange, yellow, and pink light colored the morning sky. More than 250 emergency workers were on the scene, along with forty-four fire engines and seven heavy air tankers dropping slurry from the sky. The winds calmed, but the fire moved on, feasting on the dry terrain and the buildings in their path, building energy before the next gust pushed them onward. The Grizzly Gulch fire became the top priority of the federal fire service, and hundreds more workers—including 123 inmates from the state corrections system and the most elite Hotshot crews in the federal response service—rushed to the area. By midday local officials decided to evacuate Lead, too, leaving some fifteen thousand displaced people in the hills. Stores posted signs saying "Pray for Rain."

X-Rock continued its live broadcast, taking in hundreds of calls per day, and Duhamel management decided to run around-the-clock disaster coverage even though, Daniels said, its competitors continued to air regular programs, music, or syndicated talk shows. Daniels recalled: "We were on, like, anywhere between fourteen and seventeen hours a day. People were listening to get updates on the fire, and we weren't going anywhere. We weren't going to kick back into Metallica or Pantera. People knew that we were live and we were staying live."

Bill Duhamel endorsed the decision. As he said, "At least in our company, we've done this [kind of special coverage] probably about a dozen times through the years with fires and things. It's the expected thing to do. It just comes as the tradition of the company; it's a function of our philosophy and the manager's involvement. If you're local, you probably have it."

The broadcast quickly became a civic project, capturing not only the attention of people near the fire but also the interest of listeners beyond South Dakota. After learning about the X-Rock coverage, an

Internet service began streaming the feed online. Soon distant listeners, many of whom had friends and family in the Black Hills, e-mailed the station to thank the staff.

The local fire story was national news, and, as Daniels explained, the small X-Rock staff was generating information from unusual sources.

> There were some hill boys, you know, who have always lived out there and know that area inside and out. They made up their minds, they weren't going to go anywhere, just weren't going to go. So they start calling me, and they were actually doing a play-by-play of the fire over the radio. They were looking from a bird's-eye view of the fire as it was rolling out of Deadwood and Lead. We were teasingly calling them Wolf Blitzer.
>
> We also had firefighters coming off the lines, calling X-Rock and telling us what they were seeing. There was interaction between the firefighters and the people that evacuated and couldn't find their kids and animals. Someone would call and say, "Tell Rose Emanuel I just picked up her Siberian husky and he's in my truck." Then Rose would call five minutes later, and she'd be *weeping* over the radio.
>
> Eventually it got to the point where the emergency officials let our people go in. They got two of our guys, Paul James and Kevin Morgan, and took them into these places, put them in the fire suits and the hats, and actually took them to the fire lines. The local authorities realized very quickly that this radio station was voicing this whole deal, so not only did they let our people remain in there, they protected them.

The firefighters had other urgent concerns, since lingering high temperatures and low humidity levels made controlling the fire all the more difficult. By Monday, July 1, they had contained 10 percent of the conflagration, but the flames now spread over 6,200 acres, and 684 emergency personnel battled back. On Tuesday the fire remained steady, and local officials allowed residents to return to Deadwood for the first time in three days. The crews continued their battle for five more days, completely containing the blaze on Sunday, July 7. Although nearly 11,000 acres of land had burned during the weeklong conflagration, the emergency workers had protected all but seven homes and eleven buildings in the area, and not a single person had perished.

Citizens and officials praised firefighters for their extraordinary work, but they also gave special thanks to the X-Rock team for its public service during the crisis. Bill Duhamel received calls of appreciation from Governor Janklow and Senators Tom Daschle and Tim Johnson. The shock jocks got special citations from the mayors in the nearby towns. "It was funny," Daniels said. "You do all these things for years on the radio: introduce some records, tell stupid jokes, show up on the car lot, go to the bars on Friday nights and do wet T-shirt contests. And then all of a sudden you're placed in a position where something goes seriously wrong and you're challenged. For that one time, you realize the importance of local broadcasters and what they are actually *supposed to do.*"

3

CLEAR CHANNEL COMES TO TOWN

Robert Short Jr. grew up in a segregated Syracuse, New York, neighborhood during the late 1960s and 1970s, where as a young black male he developed "a strong moral commitment to the African American community" and "a love for rhythm and blues music" that, he told me, would ultimately drive him to "do something crazy": start a radio station. Short went to Ohio for college, then returned home in 1980 to work as an accountant. "I was doing well," he recalled, with a somber, matter-of-fact tone. "I made enough to buy a house, which I owned outright. I had a family. And I built up a pretty big record collection, too." As a teenager, Short had enjoyed listening to Syracuse radio, but after living out of state he realized that something was missing from his hometown's offerings. "The city had no heartbeat, no rhythm. Music radio was all country and western, rock, Top 40; there was nothing like an urban format. The only black music was the crossover artists: Michael Jackson, the Commodores, Gladys Knight, Marvin Gaye. And even then we'd only hear the big commercial hits, the ones everyone knew and had heard a thousand times. Not Marvin Gaye live in the London Palladium singing 'Let's Get it On.' Nothing special, no songs from the vault. And you know, without a heartbeat, you've got no life."

In 1980 about one-fifth of the city's 170,000 residents were African American, yet there had never been a black-owned radio station in Syracuse, and, according to Short, "blacks here never had a real voice."

"At first I just complained about it," he recalled. "Then it dawned on me: instead of waiting for someone else to do something, why don't I do it myself?" Short began shopping for an FM station, but he quickly learned that the cost of entry was prohibitively high. During his search, however, some contacts informed him that the FCC, which had long been pressured by civil rights groups to increase minority representation on the airwaves, was concerned that Syracuse had no stations serving its sizable black population. In fact, the commission planned to license a new station designed for African American listeners, and in 1988 it formally opened the application process.

"There was a thirty-day window to apply, and I decided to do it. I knew it would be expensive, but not *how* expensive. And I knew it would be long, but not *how* long. I would say that I spent $175,000 to $200,000 of my own money just to get through the process. It lasted *six years*. The legal fees alone were over $100,000; then there were engineering studies, research, consulting, FCC filing fees. I mortgaged my house. I got cash advances and maxed out my credit cards. I borrowed money from my parents and my siblings. I risked everything. The big companies [competing for the license] dragged out the process to weed out the small players. And if you drop out, you lose everything you put in."

Short Broadcasting won rights to the license in 1993, but by then he had run out of resources and had to find new investors. It took about a year to raise the capital and build the station, and in May 1995 WRDS 102.1-FM went on the air. R&B music was the soul of WRDS, and during its initial months the station relied on satellite services and syndicated African American personalities, such as Tom Joyner and Doug Banks, who were airing for the first time on Syracuse radio. "Some people complained about the syndicated programs," Short acknowledged, "and I tried not to use them too much. But we had to get off the ground." Once the station was established, Short indeed made community programming, civic affairs, and locally oriented talk shows key parts of the mix. "My vision," Short explained, "was to have an urban station that would unify the black community. The mainstream news would really only cover the black community of Syracuse when there was a problem. They focused on shootings, on drug busts, on crime. We covered town meetings. We addressed issues in the schools. Discrimination. We brought people who were affected by all this into the studio to discuss issues that got no attention. If there were controversies in the Syracuse black community, we'd try to air them, too. The school district didn't like me, because I was always giving editorials about the state of our inner-city schools. But we had kids who weren't passing the fourth-grade reading test. I'm a product of the Syracuse public schools, and my own kids were in them at the time. This stuff really mattered to me. It was personal."

Unlike most large commercial radio stations, Short treated the public-service responsibilities required of local broadcasters as opportunities for community building, not as burdensome obligations. "I started a station-sponsored Unity Day, when we'd have a big BBQ at the beach, play volleyball, bring in music. We invited all the local organizations to come together. The health clinics did immunizations, tested for blood pressure and diabetes. We had corporate partners give bike helmets to kids. We had all the service agencies, the fire and police departments. It was great." Short's own public-service passion involved working with kids. "I must have spoken at every high school in the city. I talked about staying in school, being a black business owner, having role models. We sponsored Little League teams for neighborhoods that couldn't afford them, bought them uniforms and gear. And we did special programs, like field trips to the radio station and to the Knicks exhibition game in Syracuse. It was their only chance to see professional basketball players live, and they'll never forget it."

WRDS attracted listeners immediately. "Within a year everyone knew of our station," Short reported. "Initially we were around number ten in the market, with about four percent of the audience. But we usually had the highest time-spent-listening of all the stations, and we were often number one or two with eighteen- to thirty-four-year-olds. Eventually we got as high as the top six or seven stations in the Syracuse market. This was about a twenty-million-dollar market, and so if we could pull in five percent of it that was a million dollars, enough to make things work." The local advertising market was difficult to crack, partly, Short explained, because some businesses proved uninterested in target marketing to African American listeners. "That's just something the black media has to face." Yet gradually the station's sales representatives made inroads, and Short was cautiously optimistic that the advertisers would follow the audience.

Then the Telecommunications Act of 1996 went into effect. "The playing field changed right beneath our feet," Short said. "I was competing against some big companies before, but it was relatively fair battle because they couldn't monopolize the whole advertising pie. Clear Channel moved in and took over seven stations, and a lot of small broadcasters sold their licenses. Clear Channel's operating costs were unbelievably low, because they moved their stations together, turned them into jukeboxes with voice-tracking technology and syndicated programs—which they also owned!—and they had one general manager oversee the whole group. Clear Channel had the top sales reps; they even own Katz Media Group, which represents more stations than anyone else, and they offered special advertising packages to big customers who bought into their group. They also owned the billboards, which you need for radio promotions. They owned the theaters, so it was hard to promote your own concerts. And they owned SFX Entertainment, which books the talent, which means they basically owned the artists. They would squeeze you out, and the little guys just couldn't compete. The system was just too difficult, all the way around."

WRDS was more than a business for Short. Both his dreams of running a radio station and his commitment to enriching the cultural life of Syracuse's African American community made him reluctant to sell out even when the advertisers pulled back their purchases. When fees spiked for the Arbitron ratings service, to which Short subscribed so that his sales representatives could deliver the same market data to advertisers that Clear Channel offered, he was forced to pare down the staff. But Short's partners were less willing to endure regular beatings from the ruthless giant that dominated the Syracuse market, and they persuaded him to sell WRDS to another competitor, Radio Corporation (later renamed Galaxy Communications) in 2000, after only five years on the air. Radio Corporation converted WRDS-FM into WZUN-FM, switched from the urban format to light rock, and when that failed experimented with two other styles of programming. Clear Channel took advantage of changes in WZUN's format to convert one of its own stations to the urban contemporary style. It played similar music to WRDS, Short said, but the conglomerate's approach to station management was completely different. "They don't line up special programs to get the kids into basketball games. They don't have anyone going into the schools. They do zero community work. They don't give our community a voice. They don't want us to have a voice. They just want us so they can sell ads."

In January 2003, Short appeared before the U.S. Senate Committee on Commerce, Science, and Transportation at a hearing on media ownership, where he testified: "WRDS is a victim of the 1996 Telecommunications Act . . . It was not my desire to sell WRDS when we did. We sold because . . . Clear Channel was able to exercise market power with advertisers in a manner with which we were unable to compete."[1] Short, who had served on the board of directors for the National Association of Black Owned Broadcasters, regretted that "because of the Telecom Act, there are only a few remaining African American broadcasters." Today he continues to work occasionally in media, recently coproducing a documentary about Dorothy Gilliam and Ernest Withers, two black journalists who covered the civil rights movement. But Short's entrepreneurial energy is now focused on a small business that sells gift baskets in a local mall, and whose public-service contributions to Syracuse are relatively modest.

IN OCTOBER 1999, ONE YEAR BEFORE CLEAR CHANNEL'S STATIONS squeezed Short Broadcasting out of Syracuse, then president and CEO Lowry Mays announced that his fast-growing conglomerate would spend $23.5 billion to merge with, and effectively absorb, AMFM, whose vice chairman and CEO of the new media division was his old friend Steve Hicks. "The Mays team," *Business Week* reported, put together the deal "in little more than five days. 'Once we had the ability to move, we moved like lightning,'" said Lowry's son and future successor, Mark Mays.[2] AMFM was hardly Clear Channel's first major purchase of another radio consolidator. In 1998 Clear Channel paid approximately $6.5 billion to acquire Jacor Communications, the Covington, Kentucky, company that spent more than $1 billion purchasing stations and programs after the 1996 Telecom Act passed, building up to 206 stations in twenty states by July 1998. When Clear Channel acquired its rival, it hired Randy Michaels, the flamboyant former shock jock who was Jacor's CEO, as president of its radio division.[3]

Clear Channel was just one of about a dozen ambitious corporations that were selling equity and borrowing heavily to take over stations throughout the country in hopes of establishing dominance in the radio market after passage of the Telecom Act. AMFM had itself formed just two months before, when Capstar and Chancellor Media

Corporation combined to form the nation's largest radio station group, with 463 outlets. Viacom, which took over CBS and its Infinity Broadcasting radio divison in 1999, was in the midst of building an empire of approximately 180 stations, the majority concentrated in major cities with large audiences and lucrative advertising markets. At the same time Cumulus Media, an Atlanta-based company that focuses on small- and midsize cities, was assembling a fleet of more than 250 stations. By 2002 there were twenty-one companies that owned more than 40 stations (the cap before 1996), with the ten largest—Clear Channel, Viacom/Infinity, Cumulus, ABC/Disney, Cox Communications, Citadel Broadcasting Corporation, Entercom Communications, Emmis Communications, Radio One, and Univision Hispanic Broadcasting Corporation—controlling 67 percent of the industry's revenues. According to the Future of Music Coalition (FMC), a Washington, D.C., nonprofit that does research on how media policies affect the interests of recording artists and listeners, the result is an oligopoly: "Virtually every geographic market is dominated by four firms controlling 70 percent of market share or greater," and "in smaller markets, consolidation is more extreme."[4]

None of the radio giants can compete with Clear Channel, which by the end of its feeding frenzy controlled nearly 1,240 stations, several times more than its main competitors. Clear Channel also owned the nation's leading programs, because in the deal with Jacor it obtained Premiere Radio Networks, a syndicator whose list of some seventy talk, entertainment, news, and sports shows includes those by Rush Limbaugh, Dr. Laura Schlessinger, and Glenn Beck, and the *American Top 40* program. Premiere shows aired on roughly seven thousand stations, which meant that the great majority of U.S. radio outlets would have to rely on the industry giant for key programming.[5] In addition, Clear Channel acquired Prophet Systems Innovations (as well as Ray Lockhart's three stations in Ogallala), whose automated programming technology would make the integration of these disparate properties that much smoother.

By 2002 Clear Channel employed 60,000 people in 63 countries and generated $8.4 billion in revenues. According to its corporate fact sheet, Clear Channel's various holdings reach roughly 154 million people, or 75 percent of the U.S. population over the age of eighteen. Its U.S. radio stations enjoy a weekly audience of 110 million listeners, and its

26,000 annual concerts, family events, and sports competitions attract more than 66 million people. Clear Channel also owns and operates 41 television stations, 240 foreign radio stations, and more than 144,000 advertising displays, "including billboards, street furniture, transit panels and airport and mall signage," as well as 655,000 displays "in more than 60 countries throughout Europe, Asia, Australia and Africa."[6] It even owns a leading industry trade publication, *Inside Radio*. The previous publisher, Jerry Del Colliano, had been critical of Clear Channel's managerial practices.[7] Although Clear Channel is best known for its radio operations, it's easy to see why Mays told *Fortune* magazine: "If anyone said we were in the radio business, it wouldn't be someone from our company . . . We're not in the business of providing news and information. We're not in the business of providing well-researched music. We're simply in the business of selling our customers' products."[8]

Yet that was a business that Lowry Mays had not yet mastered, particularly when it came to local radio, and listeners, especially young ones, were turning away in droves. In September 2002 Duncan's American Radio, one of the industry's leading market research services, warned that radio listenership had sunk to a twenty-seven-year low, and three years later Abritron reported that Americans were tuning in to radio three hours less per week than they had in 1993.[9] There's no question that the recent emergence of satellite radio, Internet radio, MP3s, and personal listening devices has threatened the future of traditional broadcast radio stations. But before any of these external threats posed real problems, Clear Channel had become the industry's own worst enemy, flooding the airwaves with standardized formats, automated programs, rip-and-read journalism, endless commercials, and a uniform diet of politically partisan, parochial talk shows that dulled local radio and pushed large segments of the audience off the dial.

LOSING LISTENERS IS ALWAYS BAD FOR RADIO COMPANIES, BUT FOR Clear Channel the downward spiral of audience ratings was especially bad news. The problem was not simply that the company had acquired about nine hundred more stations than its largest competitor, but also that it was still paying for them. To finance its media properties, all of which came with considerable operating expenses, Clear Channel had accumulated about $9 billion of debt by 2003, as well as a BBB- credit rating and a "negative" stock outlook from Standard and Poor's.[10] Like other media conglomerates that had borrowed heavily to expand their holdings during the booming market of the 1990s, in the early 2000s Clear Channel faced intense pressure from investment bankers to increase its profit margins. The radio division was able to eventually raise advertising rates once it pushed out smaller competitors and established a dominant presence in local radio markets. According to Jon Mandel, the co-CEO of the multibillion-dollar media marketing company Media-Com, Clear Channel leveraged its stronghold on radio advertising in cities where it had multiple stations to force "large cost increases over what supply and demand would have caused in a free market." The result, he testified to the U.S. Senate Committee on Commerce, Science, and Transportation, is a "consolidation tax" that is paid first by businesses and then passed on to consumers. "In Atlanta, costs are 155 percent higher than free market, which is a consolidation tax of $144.5 million per year. New York radio is overcharged by 30 percent. $156 million per year . . . The people and businesses of Austin are overcharged by 95 percent . . . And in Tulsa, Atomic Burrito has to sell a lot more beans or lay a worker off to cover the $4,200 per year, 12 percent consolidation tax on their radio advertising."[11]

Revenues from the "consolidation tax" were hardly enough to satisfy the analysts on Wall Street. So Mays accelerated a trend that the Hicks brothers had started in Austin, consolidating its local stations into one or two central locations, downsizing staff, and using its own properties, such as Prophet (the digital automation system) and Premiere Radio Networks (the syndicator), to substitute voice-tracked or national programs for live, local broadcasts. At Capstar, the Hickses justified their extensive use of voice tracking by arguing that the "hub and spoke" digital programming system helped them bring top talent to small and midsize markets that otherwise could not afford it. Clear Channel made similar claims, only it was now using voice tracking to replace live talent in the nation's largest cities, including Chicago, where, according to a report by the Cornell University Labor Studies Center, "six radio stations are run from one building," and Washington-Baltimore, where "eight stations are operated from one building and are programmed by just one employee."[12]

It's impossible to know exactly how many radio jobs Clear Channel eliminated or how much it saved in labor costs. The American Federation

of Television and Radio Artists (AFTRA), the national labor union representing journalists, broadcasters, and artists, estimated that the company eliminated between 1,500 and 4,500 positions between 2000 and
2004, and Todd Spencer, the former managing editor of the radio trade
publication *Gavin,* reported that industry pressure from consolidation
resulted in a net loss of 10,000 radio-related jobs between 2000 and
2002. In *Salon* Eric Boehlert claimed that cyber jocking saved Clear
Channel "tens of millions in salary." In addition to the layoffs, AFTRA's
national director of legislative affairs, Tom Carpenter, told me, Clear
Channel reduced labor costs by paying cyber jocks a fraction of the
standard DJ salary. "In Chicago during 2001, they were paying people
at the KISS station as little as three thousand dollars, and usually six to
eight thousand dollars a year to do a voice-tracking shift for a show
that would have cost them at least forty thousand dollars [a year] to do
live." Moreover, Carpenter explained, Clear Channel treated its employees and its union so badly that labor organizers dubbed it "the Wal-Mart
of the radio industry." The Cornell study, for example, cited union leaders who complained that Clear Channel had introduced "business and
employment practices that effectively dilute [collective bargaining]
agreements and undermine pay standards."[13]

Sweeping labor cuts dramatically, if also inevitably, changed the
company's programming. With digital editing, Clear Channel took fake
local broadcasting to new levels, running phone contests in which listeners didn't know that they were competing with a national audience
or employing DJs who fabricated experiences in places they had never
been. Clear Channel's radio hosts were hardly bashful about the process.
In 2002 the *Wall Street Journal* reported that "Cabana Boy Geoff"
Alan had been staging local shows for Boise, Idaho; Medford, Oregon;
and Santa Barbara, California from Clear Channel's San Diego studio;
and *Salon* revealed that "a DJ named Randi West has aired simultaneously on Clear Channel stations in Cincinatti; Louisville, Ky.; Des
Moines, Iowa; Toledo, Ohio; Charleston, S.C.; and Rochester, N.Y."[14]
Months later, the Clear Channel personality Jon Ballard told Knight
Ridder about the challenges of recording his commentary and banter
with local reporters (who talked back to the recordings) in Detroit
from his base studio, WWDC in Rockville, Maryland. "It was a little
wild at first because I had never even been to Detroit until April. I had
to rely on the Internet to know what the hot spots in town were so I

could talk about them on the air."[15] As word about voice tracking spread through media circles, critics—especially those inside the industry—dubbed the radio empire "Cheap Channel" and warned that its short-term profit seeking would ultimately devalue the medium. Clear Channel, they insisted, was chipping away at its own pot of gold.

LISTENERS COULD HEAR THE DIFFERENCE THAT AUTOMATED PROGRAM-ming makes during regular conditions. In disasters, however, the conse-quences of Clear Channel's dependence on voice tracking and syndication were devastating. On August 14, 2003, roughly 50 million people across the Northeast, Midwest, and Ontario, Canada, experienced a prolonged blackout after a series of mishaps that began in Ohio. Com-ing just two years after 9/11, the breakdown provoked widespread anxiety: Had the United States been attacked? Was something even more dangerous about to happen? At the local level, however, the loss of electricity generated more immediate problems, shutting down street lights, elevators, subway systems, air conditioners, fans, refrigerators, television sets, computers, and electrically charged telephones. Cities faced elevated public health risks, particularly for the elderly and infirm, as well as the threat of public looting and violence. Residents rushed to their radios, as they always do during crises involving power outages, because most other communications technologies were useless.

David Rubin, the dean of Syracuse University's S. I. Newhouse School of Public Communications, was on campus when the electricity went out, and he immediately went to his car and turned on WSYR 570-AM to learn what was happening. As the local news leader and a leading local station since 1922, WSYR had won considerable praise for its on-the-ground coverage of a major storm during Labor Day weekend in 1998, and it retained loyal listeners even after Clear Channel acquired it, along with six other Syracuse stations, in 1999. Lowry Mays singled out his pride in the Syracuse operations during the Senate testimony he delivered while sitting next to Robert Short Jr., from WRDS. "In Syra-cuse," he gloated, "Clear Channel saves appoximately $200,000 a year by operating its stations as a unit instead of as stand-alone properties."[16]

Driving home from campus, the dean realized that instead of reporting on conditions in Syracuse, the city's leading news station was providing information about the subways in New York City. "What got me really upset is that WSYR kept using the feed from CNN to get news about New York City and other parts of the Northeast. The local coverage was weak and sporadic. WSYR didn't have reporters in place, so it was vamping to cope with it. I only heard one local reporter on the air, and she was on the air only once." Rubin was so upset by the absence of local coverage from Clear Channel that he wrote an editorial about the problem for the *Syracuse Post-Standard*. "When the power goes out, as it did on Aug. 14, local radio is the public's information lifeline," Rubin explained, adding that, in exchange for their licenses to use the airwaves, radio companies pledge that they will become part of the nation's security system when disaster strikes. In 1998, WSYR had responded aggressively to an unusually powerful storm. Rubin praised the station for providing "information, reassurance and a sense of community," and called its coverage "heroic."

During the blackout, Rubin presumed that WSYR would provide a similar level of disaster reporting, calling in additional personnel, assigning journalists to beats in key city agencies, and bumping paid advertisements off the air. He expected WSYR to offer some national reporting, too, but like most other listeners he tuned in primarily for local news and reliable information about what was happening in Syracuse and how he should respond. "I heard almost none of this (except the ads, which kept on coming as usual)," the dean complained. "News Director Bill Carey was in the anchor seat and seemed to be all alone, without a local reporting staff to turn to. He was a general without any troops in the field. After brief local segments, he switched to a CNN feed that had a national, not local, focus."[17]

Clear Channel responded immediately to Rubin's op-ed, with an explosive letter written by Bill Carey, then its Syracuse news director. "As a listener," Carey wrote, Rubin is entitled to complain about WSYR's disaster coverage. But Carey argued that the dean "was decidedly not . . . an expert in journalism" qualified to comment on his station's reporting. According to the Clear Channel executive, Rubin's job was "primarily an administrative position and a fund-raising post," and not one that required teaching about the media. Moreover, Carey alleged that Rubin was "a search committee's third choice for the job," that he had not "worked in the trenches of broadcast or print journalism," and that the only publicly available writing by the dean "involves reviews of chamber music." His closing lines packed a stronger punch: "I have always made it a policy to immediately return the calls of 'respected' members of the Newhouse faculty. That, Mr. Rubin, is why you have not heard from me."[18]

Rubin, in fact, had been a magazine writer for thirty years, authored a major textbook on the media, edited a journalism review, worked on the PBS program *The Inside Story,* and—as the university was quick to point out—been its top choice for the deanship. But Clear Channel's managerial blunder was even more significant than those editorial mistakes. Even after its failure to issue warnings during the toxic crisis in Minot, the conglomerate's response to serious criticism of its disaster coverage was to impugn the critic rather than to improve its news reporting. Flabbergasted, Rubin wrote another article for the *Post-Standard,* sharpening his argument about the extent to which Clear Channel had decimated the news department, then confronted the company to back up the "community service" rhetoric that it came by so cheaply. "I challenge Mr. Carey to compare the number of journalists employed at the station fifteen years ago with the number employed now. I challenge him to compare news budgets. I challenge him to compare the amount of local material on the air, as opposed to the cheap, syndicated talk-show filler that the station airs constantly."[19] Carey did not respond.

LITTLE WONDER THE PROBLEM REPEATED ITSELF ELSEWHERE JUST A FEW weeks later, during the heart of hurricane season. In September 2003 Hurricane Isabel came ashore in Henrico County, Virginia, where about 260,000 people live on the outskirts of Richmond. Newsradio WRVA 1140-AM in Richmond is the official emergency broadcaster for Henrico County, where it had operated its high-power signal since 1925. It was purchased by Clear Channel in 1992. Robert Orndorff, a local radio enthusiast who ran the Richmond Radio Web site, reported that between 2000 and 2001, just after the AMFM merger, Clear Channel downsized the staff, eliminating the local morning show and several on-air personalities and replacing them with syndicated content. Tamra McKinney, the county's director of public relations and media services, tried to work out a plan for postdisaster public-service broadcasting with Clear Channel, but no one at the company office was available to help. "With a hurricane you know it's coming. We called all the radio stations in town and requested a back-up emergency number, but Clear Channel never responded. They just didn't call us back. Clear Channel owns seven stations, and if you can't get through to one, you can't get through to seven."

According to Patricia O'Bannon, an elected official on the local Board of Supervisors, and then-chair of the Virginia Association of Counties' Telecommunications and Utilities Steering Committee, the hurricane hit early in the evening, and WRVA broadcast the official emergency alert as it is required to by law. The problem with its disaster coverage became apparent after the hurricane ended and thousands of local residents needed basic information about how to protect themselves. Clear Channel, having dramatically reduced the local reporting and in-studio staff at its fleet of Richmond stations, had neither the personnel at its stations or in the field to cover the crisis, nor the public-service commitment to suspend its regular programming for the good of its listeners.

O'Bannon said that the hurricane took out the area's water system, the back-up system for its water-pumping system, the electricity, and telephone service in most of the county. Communications lines were down, and even driving through the streets to issue warnings with a bullhorn was difficult, because so many trees were down in the roads. "We needed to put an announcement on the radio not to drink the water," she explained. "Because if you allow the water to settle into the pipes, it can pick up corrosions and grow new bacteria." The treated water had indeed settled in the pipes for two days, and residents needed to know that they had to flush out the contaminated water after the pumps were restored. O'Bannon told me: "About one hundred thousand people didn't have phone service, and we needed to get that information out right then. We tried to reach out to Clear Channel, but they were playing Rush Limbaugh, a guy out of Pennsylvania, some guy out of Atlanta. It wasn't local. Tamra kept calling Clear Channel, and she was told that she had to call a remote location. When she did that, she got a message that said the offices were closed. But she needed the information on the radio right then. She called and called, but got nothing."

McKinney got through to Clear Channel the next morning, when the water had been flowing for a few hours. According to O'Bannon, "They told her that she was too late to get on the news for that morning. She then asked if she could purchase ad time [to use for public-service announcements], and she was told no, that it was all booked up and that even if they could, they would have to broadcast it all over the region. [The ads] they were going to put on Rush Limbaugh [were] going to be all over the region, and they would have a few minutes of local news. They didn't keep up with the reporting after the storm had passed, even though we were left with nothing and in crisis."

After the hurricane, McKinney returned to Clear Channel to arrange a better system for future emergencies. "We tried to work out a contract where we would purchase time on each of the stations during crises. We were talking money, and we offered to put down a retainer. We wanted a guarantee that we would have a minute or two, every hour on the hour, to get information out. But they weren't interested in that. They said no. That's because they would then have to have someone there [in the studios], and they don't."

O'Bannon acknowledged that Clear Channel met its legal obligation to broadcast an emergency alert, but she questioned whether the company also met the loose public-interest standards that the FCC seldom enforces. The problem, she insisted, was that Clear Channel refused to do anything beyond what was required by law. "Our radio stations reneged on their responsibilities" to Virginians, proving Clear Channel cared about the money in local markets but not about the people who lived in them. "We still haven't come up with a new policy to deal with this kind of problem. We need to be ready right now, in case something happens. And we can't rely on Clear Channel."

BY THE TIME OF THE HURRICANE, HOWEVER, AMERICAN RADIO LISTENERS did know that they could rely on Clear Channel to deliver familiar products wherever they operated. The company had built up big-brand radio formats to an unprecedented scale, establishing KISS-FM stations in forty-seven markets, MIX-FM stations in two dozen others, and a variety of MAJIC oldies, country, and classic-rock outlets that always sound the same. Even the commercials, which approached twenty minutes per hour on some Clear Channel broadcasts, compared to approximately ten to twelve before consolidation, took on similar tones.

Clear Channel, like most other media conglomerates, did not like to tell listeners that it owned so many stations, but as concerns about its homogenous programming spread throughout the country, citizen groups, media critics, and other Big Media companies began complaining that the radio giant was destroying diversity, competition, and local coverage in the airwaves. "Fingers are pointed at the alleged misdeeds of Clear Channel," testified Lewis Dickey Jr., the chairman, president, and CEO of Cumulus Broadcasting, which operates more than three hundred stations and has to scramble to avoid being tarnished by Clear Channel's reputation, "and assumptions are incorrectly made that every radio company engages in the same practices."[20] When Randy Michaels, chief of the radio division, announced that Clear Channel was working to apply the business principles of McDonald's to the radio industry, he helped create a public relations crisis for everyone in the industry.

Jenny Toomey, the executive director of the Future of Music Coalition (FMC), led one of the earliest and most effective campaigns to protest the way Clear Channel and other leading consolidators were polluting the cultural environment. Toomey, a disarmingly cerebral musician, entrepreneur, and firebrand activist in her early thirties, joined with colleagues Kristin Thomson and Peter DiCola to produce a technically sophisticated research report, *Radio Deregulation: Has It Served Citizens and Musicians?* which she presented while sitting beside Lowry Mays at the Senate hearing on media ownership in January 2003.[21] "Bear Stearns, the investment bank, had published a study showing that the format variety had gone up after consolidation," Toomey told me. "The National Association of Broadcasters and all the big radio companies cited it whenever they could as proof that the deregulation was good for programming diversity. But when we looked closely at what they meant by *format variety*, we realized that they were actually using the term to cover up how much their programs overlapped."

Testifying before the Senate, Toomey made a strong distinction between *format variety*, which refers to the number of program formats available in a typical market, and genuine *format diversity*. Citing recent playlist data and charts, the FMC documented substantial overlaps among the new formats, which meant supposedly distinct formats were actually playing the same songs. "For example," Toomey explained, "Urban and CHR/Rhythmic overlap at a 76 percent level. 38 of their top 50 songs are the same. Then there's the rock cluster. Rock, Alternative, and Album-Oriented Rock overlap considerably, between 36 percent and 58 percent depending on which pair among those three you consider . . . Adding a CHR/Rhythmic station to a market that already has an Urban station adds format variety. But it doesn't add any programming diversity."[22] The UCLA sociologist Gabriel Rossman had demonstrated this in his scholarly research. Using playlist data for a national sample of FM music stations, Rossman had compared independent stations and stations owned by chains of different sizes. His main finding: "The larger the station's owner, the less diverse its play, both internally and relative to its peers."[23] Armed with such fine-tuned analysis, Toomey charged that "the radio industry has measured itself—and encouraged policy makers to measure it—with an inadequate statistic." While promoting its commitment to "new music" and "more variety," Clear Channel was actually delivering more of the same.

JUST HOW CLEAR CHANNEL AND OTHER LARGE RADIO CONSOLIDATORS selected the music to play for their listeners was also generating suspicions. In 1960 Congress passed prohibitions against *payola*—derived from *pay* and *Victrola* (the brand name for a line of phonographs)—because major record companies had been paying radio stations to play their songs, at once gaining publicity, marginalizing independent and small producers, and creating unfair conditions for market competition. Although racial discrimination, anxiety over the growing popularity of rhythm and blues music among whites, and threats to the market position of leading recording companies motivated the crackdown on payola, the legislation did help to limit open corruption in radio programming.[24] By 2001 reports of widespread "legal payola"—in which "independent promoters" representing record labels were bribing DJs and programmers with cash and gifts to get their clients on the air, and with no admission of the practice by radio stations—began to attract attention from Congress and the FCC.

According to Eric Boehlert, who authored a series of articles describing the $150-million annual business in legal payola that developed after deregulation, "Most listeners don't know it, but virtually every song they hear on FM commercial radio has been paid for—indirectly—by five major record labels." Independent promoters, or indies, have moved into the market to fill the legal gap that forced a separation between radio stations and record companies. "Indies pay for the right to exclusively represent radio stations. The up-front fee is roughly between $100,000 and $400,000, depending on the size of the market. Once that deal is signed, the indie sends out weekly invoices to record companies for every song added to that station's playlist . . . Roughly $800 per song in middle-sized markets and $1,000 and more in larger markets, up to about $5,000 per song." To get around the indies, Clear Channel offered record companies the chance to have their bands play before its programmers—for $35,000 a shot. Boehlert reported that the company was also negotiating an exclusive contract with one of the largest indie promoters, Cincinnati-based Tri State Promotions and Marketing, to form an alliance of independent promoters on which every label would become dependent when it tried to produce a hit.[25] Paying for airtime would by no means be sufficient for making a hit record, since many heavily promoted albums fail miserably. But in a consolidated radio landscape, it was increasingly necessary.

Under pressure from critics and regulators, in 2003 Clear Channel announced that it would stop using independent promoters. Yet in 2005, when Attorney General Eliot Spitzer of New York State began releasing results from his investigation into the practice, it was clear that traditional payola—with record labels making direct, illegal payments to stations—had become rampant. Spitzer's investigation established that major labels were paying powerhouse radio companies such as Clear Channel and Infinity to get airtime for top artists who, an outsider might believe, would not need the extra push. Among his many findings: in 2002 Sony BMG gave a San Diego station director a thirty-two-inch plasma TV to put Jennifer Lopez's album *This Is Me . . . Then* on the radio; and in 2003 a Sony employee wrote a Clear Channel programmer to ask, "What do I have to do to get Audioslave on WKSS this week?!!? Whatever you can dream up I can make it happen."[26] Sony BMG reached a $10-million settlement to end the investigation in the summer of 2005, but weeks later the FCC—prodded by the Democratic commissioner Jonathan Adelstein, an amateur musician who made payola one of his main priorities—announced that it would open its own payola inquiry. "The FCC staff is working with voluminous evidence right now," Adelstein said, because the case is "potentially the most widespread and flagrant violation of FCC rules in the history of American broadcasting."[27]

Of course, most musicians and record labels cannot afford to pay for the chance to get on the air. Both legal and illegal payola penalize aspiring and independent artists, especially those whose creative music does not fit neatly into a standard pop format. Payola also penalizes top artists, because labels take a share out of their proceeds to pay the promoters. In 1999 Don Henley and Sheryl Crow cofounded the Recording Artists' Coalition to help musicians regain collective bargaining power in a field where consolidation had weakened their position. Speaking before Congress, Henley complained that "a recording artist has a much better chance of getting radio airplay if the promotional budget for a record is large, than if the record is good. And then adding insult to injury, the promotional fees paid to the independent promoters are recouped either in whole or in part against the artist's royalties . . . This unprecedented control over the music industry by the conglomerates is hurting the music business and the culture. It is preventing talented, new artists from emerging and is generally casting a pall over [the] industry."[28]

Other critics and musicians went farther, arguing that consolidation inflicted "cultural damage" on everyone because it blocked an important process through which new music percolates up from the local to the national scene. Clear Channel is hardly the only source of the bottleneck. Viacom owns CBS Radio (formerly Infinity Broadcasting), as well as MTV, VH-1, and BET, the three leading outlets for music videos and music promotion on television. At the Museum of Television and Radio forum, "The Rise of Rock FM," the DJ Jim Ladd expressed his contempt for radio consolidators and the consultants on whom they rely for programming: "If you listen to any radio station in Los Angeles, California, you are listening to a pre-programmed list. People with great talent . . . have been reduced to loading machines in an assembly line. It's the most sickening thing in the world. I can't listen to the radio station I work for . . . After 25 years, after working at KMET, after being number one in my time slot . . . when I go back to work on Monday I will have a confrontation with someone who has never worked in that market telling me I don't know what I'm doing and if I would only follow the format things would be great at the station . . . Now, I don't want to at all give the impression that I don't like consultants. But if we could all get together as a mob after this, arm ourselves with automatic weapons and go find these bastards . . . Tomorrow, radio would be different."[29]

Michael Guido, a music industry attorney, whose clients include Velvet Revolver, said on the PBS television series *Frontline* that consolidation and standard formatting had deeply eroded the influence of local DJs. "In the early days of the music business, the record business, you could find a DJ in Cleveland, like Alan Freed, or in Buffalo, who would fall in love with a record, start playing it, people would react to it, and you could start a record off that way. It's much more difficult to do now with two or three conglomerates controlling all the radio formats."[30]

Simon Renshaw, the manager for the Dixie Chicks and a board member of the Recording Artists' Coalition, testified before Congress that "the possibility of an act 'breaking out' on a singular station or singular market has been severely diminished because of consolidation . . . In addition to the problems that consolidation and centralized playlists have brought to individual artists, one should not overlook the cultural damage [that] is inflicted by these practices. One has to wonder whether any of the great musical trends in contemporary music could have happened in today's radio environment. Would the Motown or Stax sounds ever have been heard, would the Beach Boys have exploded out of Southern California, would the grunge sounds from Seattle ever have ignited a new generation of music lovers? Many of the most important musical styles have been ones that developed and matured locally and were brought to the forefront by local radio stations, championing their local music." According to Jon Rintels, the executive director of the Center for Creative Voices in Media, "If Clear Channel had controlled radio during the Fifties the way they control it today, we'd still be listening to Frank Sinatra."[31]

CLEAR CHANNEL ALSO TAKES A HEAVY-HANDED, TOP-DOWN APPROACH to its political programming. According to prominent musicians and talk show hosts, the company's partisan projects (both on and off the air) had a chilling effect on free speech during the early days of the War on Terror, and many musicians worried that they would be punished— banned from playlists at major music stations, condemned by syndicated personalities, or canceled from concert schedules—if they did what artists have always done: speak their minds, especially if they oppose the war or the sitting president.

There was no mistaking the allegiances of Clear Channel's executives and board members, since the Mays and Hicks families had been backing President Bush since he entered Texas politics, and they remained major contributors to conservative causes. According to the Center for Public Integrity, 63 percent of Clear Channel's political donations went to Republicans, including $667,550 to the Republican National Party Committee and $116,870 to Bush, making it one of the most partisan givers among media conglomerates, which typically hedge their political bets to maintain good standing with both parties.[32] There was also little question that hard-core right-wing commentators such as Rush Limbaugh, Dr. Laura Schlessinger, and Michael Savage anchored Clear Channel's AM offerings and helped establish its public image as a partisan corporation. So after 9/11, when a list of about 150 songs deemed inappropriate to broadcast—including John Lennon's "Imagine," Neil Diamond's "America," and anything by Rage Against the Machine—went out to Clear Channel's stations, critics cried censorship. When I spoke with Lisa Dollinger, who parlayed her service doing PR for the Hicks brothers at Capstar into an executive job as chief communications officer at Clear Channel, she insisted that a regional programmer, not Clear Channel's central office, circulated the list as a suggestion, and that there was never a corporate ban.

The charges that Clear Channel engaged in political censorship after 9/11 and during the 2004 elections transcend what's on the company's playlists. On October 1, 2001, Clear Channel fired the veteran Bay Area radio personality and community affairs director David "Davey D." Cook, soon after he broadcast one long and widely discussed interview with Barbara Lee, the lone U.S. congressional representative to vote against authorizing war in Afghanistan, and another with the politically progressive musician Boots Riley, on his KMEL-FM public affairs show *Street Knowledge*.[33] Cook, who also hosted a KMEL music show called the *Local Flava Hour* and wrote the Beats 'n' Breaks column for the *San Francisco Bay Guardian*, had worked his way up through the KMEL hierarchy to become a leading figure in the local music scene and a nationally recognized authority on hip-hop culture. His strong ties to local artists and commitment to getting their work on the air helped KMEL, which launched the careers of Bay Area musicians such as Tupac Shakur and MC Hammer, earn the nickname "the people's station." Clear Channel claimed that his termination was part of a routine station cutback. But his dedicated listeners found that hard to believe, given his popularity and long history with the station, not to mention the absence of another community affairs director at KMEL. According to the local music writer Jeff Chang, "Cook's firing seemed to symbolize the end of an era in which community input, local music, and progressive politics had a place at KMEL, and it triggered thousands of e-mails, faxes, and . . . rowdy picket lines at the station."[34]

Cook was so outraged by the apparent politics of his firing that he began looking into Clear Channel's conduct in other cities where it had bought out minority-owned stations and targeted young African American audiences with an urban format. When we met in Berkeley, he denounced Clear Channel for abdicating its public-service responsibilities to black communities that had been better served under previous management, scaling back its civic projects and firing community affairs personnel, reducing airtime for local artists and flooding the airwaves with negative messages. Speaking before an FCC hearing, Cook complained that "in San Francisco, after 9/11 Clear Channel put up a dozen posters on all their billboards that had public affairs advertisements about giving to the Clear Channel Fund, being patriotic. Did you notice that they didn't tell you about one voter registration campaign, they didn't interview one candidate on any of the stations, didn't do any sort of election coverage or encouragement to a community where you have 70 percent of the people not voting?" Cook is one of the few radio personalities willing to openly criticize the industry's dominant employer, and he has been off commercial radio ever since.

The list of Clear Channel radio personalities who claim that the company punished them for airing political views grew during the build-up to war in Iraq, and again during the 2004 presidential campaign. Both Roxanne Walker, who won the South Carolina Broadcaster Association's 2002 Radio Personality of the Year award, and the generally conservative Charles Goyette, named best local talk show host by the *Phoenix New Times* in 2003, said that Clear Channel penalized them (Walker was fired; Goyette was moved out of his prime airtime)

for their antiwar positions. Walker, who sued Clear Channel for illegally terminating her employment at WMYI-FM in Greenville due to
her political opinions, (the case was settled in April 2005) told the
Greenville News that, after being pressured to tone down opposition
to the war in Iraq during conversations with her conservative cohosts,
"[she] was forced out because [she] would not comply with their
orders to be silent." In the *American Conservative*, Goyette wrote that
his program director told him, "With you, I feel like I'm managing the
Dixie Chicks," and that the company wanted to fire him but found it
difficult because of his "well-drafted contract."[35] During the same
period, Clear Channel's syndicated radio personality Glenn Beck—
who famously called Michael Berg, the father of Nicholas Berg,
the American businessman who in May 2004 was kidnapped and
beheaded in Iraq, "despicable" and a "scumbag" after he criticized
President Bush and the war—received tremendous corporate support
to organize eighteen "Rally for America" events in cities throughout
the country.[36]

By far the most vocal, and most famous, radio personality to charge
Clear Channel with political censorship is Howard Stern. Clear Channel dropped Stern from its stations after the FCC fined it $495,000 for
airing programs on which he violated indecency regulations. But Stern,
who was retained by Infinity's stations, insisted that Clear Channel
axed him for political rather than economic reasons. On his program
Stern said, "There's a lot of people saying that the second that I started
saying, 'I think we gotta get Bush out of the presidency,' that's when
Clear Channel banged my ass outta here. Then I find out that Clear
Channel is such a big contributor to President Bush, and in bed with
the whole Bush administration, I'm going, 'Maybe that's why I was
thrown off: because I don't like the way the country is leaning too much
to the religious right.' And then, bam! Let's get rid of Stern. I used to
think, 'Oh, I can't believe that.' But that's it! That's what's going on
here! I know it! I know it!"[37]

Though Clear Channel's exact motivations for taking Stern off the
air are impossible to discern, its aggressive moves to keep antiwar content off its radio and outdoor billboards have been readily apparent,
especially after members of Congress complained that they too had
been censored by the media giant. In April 2003 U.S. congressional representative Jan Schakowsky, the ranking Democrat on the House Com-

merce Consumer Protection Subcommittee, announced on the floor that Clear Channel had refused to accept paid advertisements that were critical of the war from herself and fellow Illinois representative Danny Davis.[38] And in July 2004 the public-interest group Project Billboard sued Clear Channel for refusing to put up its political ad, an image of a bomb with the text "Democracy Is Best Taught by Example, Not by War," on a Times Square billboard during the Republican National Convention. Clear Channel, which had used its billboards throughout the country to post patriotic messages supportive of the president and the war, announced that it had rejected the ad because it was "distasteful" and "politically charged." Yet it also refused to put up an alternative Project Billboard poster, with the same text alongside a dove.[39] Ultimately the two sides settled, and Project Billboard displayed its ad at a different site.

Six months after the controversy, Clear Channel announced that it would partner with another media giant with a zeal for partisan political activism: Fox News. Under terms of the five-year deal, the News Corporation would provide an hourly five-minute newscast at the top of the hour and a one-minute segment at the bottom of the hour to more than one hundred of Clear Channel's talk stations, including outlets in major metropolitan markets. "Working this closely with a premier national news provider for the majority of our news/talk stations makes overwhelming sense," said John Hogan, then CEO of Clear Channel's radio division.[40] For once, not a single media critic disagreed with the company's promotional spin.

TODAY, DISTRUST OF CLEAR CHANNEL RUNS DEEP, AND UNDER ITS LEADership the broadcast radio industry has dug itself into a hole from which it may never emerge. Ask radio enthusiasts what makes the medium special, and they're likely to respond similarly: Done well, radio is personal, intimate, edgy, and local. It helps build communities and supports subcultures, with each station contributing distinctive sounds to the chorus on the dial. It entertains, delivering new music and fresh ideas. It provides essential news and information. It is a lifeline when disaster strikes. Ask most anyone—listeners, musicians, DJs—whether commercial radio is doing any of these things in the age of Clear Channel, and, again, the answer is an emphatic, often angry, no.

"Radio Sucks" has become a catch phrase of our time, getting nearly 12 million Google hits as of April 2006.

Eventually Clear Channel got the message, and as the FCC prepared to rule on another round of proposals for further media deregulation, the conglomerate began a high-profile campaign to appease its critics—especially inside the Beltway, where even congressional leaders and FCC staff who had supported the Telecomunications Act of 1996 were embarrassed by what had happened to radio. In early 2003 Lowry Mays transferred the controversial radio chief Randy Michaels (who soon left the company) and replaced him with John Hogan. Hogan quickly brought on Lisa Dollinger (formerly of Capstar) to spearhead the division's new PR campaign, and within two years she was promoted to chief communications officer for the entire conglomerate. Lowry Mays retired in October 2004, after suffering from a cerebral blood clot. His older son Mark became CEO and president, positions he held until February 2006, when his brother Randall, who was already the company's chief financial officer, took over as president while Mark remained CEO.

Clear Channel's new leaders were determined to listen to their critics and understand their language and core concerns, lest they drive even more listeners off the dial. The radio division scaled back its use of voice tracking, added new local music programming, and built up an online New Music Network that invites registered musicians to upload songs on its Web site. Although its political contributions and radio programming continue to weigh heavily in favor of the Republicans, Clear Channel responded to complaints about its partisan agenda by launching an hourlong weekly talk show with Jesse Jackson (albeit typically on an early morning weekend hour when listeners are scarce), and converting several of its stations to the liberal Air America political-talk format. In July 2004 the company announced that it would reduce the number of commercial minutes per hour after too many dissatisfied advertisers complained that their spots were lost amid the "clutter" of long commercial breaks. "We heard you," its PR campaign said. "Less is more."[41] Tom Carpenter, of AFTRA, reports that the company had even become a more fair negotiator. "We now have a pretty productive relationship with Clear Channel," he told me in the summer of 2005. "They say that they've learned a lesson that voice tracking is not necessarily the best way to run their stations."

Under Dollinger's leadership, the communications office began issu-ing regular press releases to promote the company's local coverage, news reporting, and community involvement. It also added a "Local Spirit" Web site, featuring an interactive map along with text reporting that "community service is the core of our culture" and that "Clear Channel people embody the local spirit of giving that is transforming, bringing people together, and working to give hope and assistance to those in need."

CLEAR CHANNEL RESERVED ITS LARGEST PR CAMPAIGN FOR HURRICANE Katrina, in August and September of 2005, when it set out to self-consciously demonstrate the depth of its public-interest commitments. The conglomerate owns seven stations in New Orleans and six in Baton Rouge, and its state-of-the-art facilities, including a central studio space in Baton Rouge and many of its broadcast towers, survived the storm. So, too, did the facilities at Entercom, a big television and radio company whose six radio stations in New Orleans, including the con-servative talk station WWL-AM, are part of its fleet of roughly one hundred national outlets. WWL, which also runs a broadcast tele-vision channel, is one of the few local radio stations to employ a sizable reporting staff, and it was the only New Orleans station that broadcast through the hurricane, when residents, lacking electricity or phone service, depended on the medium. But after its downtown office began flooding, WWL had to evacuate its staff to an emergency studio, where its operations would be limited. Ken Beck, an Entercom national news and talk programming director, called Gabe Hobbs, who has a similar position at Clear Channel, to ask if they could help each other during the crisis. According to the *Wall Street Journal,* Beck offered to share WWL's programming with Clear Channel, which "didn't have the same news resources as Entercom." Hobbs had another idea: the rival groups could merge temporarily, moving their staffs to Clear Channel's Baton Rouge complex. Beck "jumped at the opportunity," and soon the competitors were working together as the United Radio Broadcasters of New Orleans.[42]

It was an ingenious arrangement. Clear Channel was resource rich: the powerful conglomerate secured helicopters to transport staff mem-bers to Baton Rouge and trucks to deliver fuel for the backup power generators. Clear Channel called in its expert engineering teams to repair damaged broadcast systems, and it maintained excellent working conditions in its high-tech studios. All Clear Channel lacked were radio reporters, the living, breathing, locally connected broadcasters who could do what both national and New Orleans newspaper and television journalists were doing with such enthusiasm: hitting the streets to cover the catastrophe and provide scared and stranded residents with vital information about the state of their city. Fortunately for the people of New Orleans, that's what Entercom, with one-twelfth the number of national outlets, could offer, and as a result they got the kind of news coverage that citizens in places where Clear Channel is the only major operator do not.

Clear Channel's communications office immediately publicized the successful collaboration, and within days leading national newspapers, television stations, and trade publications ran glowing stories about United Radio Broadcasters. Dick Lewis, Clear Channel's regional vice president, told the *Los Angeles Times* that as a teenager he decided to go into radio after his family drove into a tornado, and "it was the radio that gave us our sense of calmness, our touch with the outside world." At Clear Channel, he explained, "We provide entertainment to fill up the time . . . All we're doing is filling up the time, to be here until something of significant magnitude happens."[43] (His comment, at least, helps explain Clear Channel's belief about the value of regular radio programming, and it shows why the company had no problem replacing original local broadcasts with voice-tracked programs and syndicated content that "fill up the time.")

The *Times* reported this self-serving rhetoric without a hint of skepticism, leaving out any mention of the controversies surrounding Clear Channel's failures during previous catastrophes. At its San Antonio headquarters, the conglomerate saturated its online "Local Spirit Press Room" with dozens of press releases touting the fund-raising initiatives sponsored by its stations: "Clear Channel Radio-Duluth Collects Life-Saving Supplies for Gulf Coast Region." "Clear Channel Radio's Mullins in the Morning Inspires Listeners to Help Devastated Hurricane Region." "Clear Channel Radio Encourages Nurses to Volunteer in Stricken Gulf Coast Region." "Clear Channel Radio Listeners Donate Almost 10 Tons of Cash."[44] The stream of self-congratulatory public statements continued through September, October, and November. Clear Channel had worked hard to hide the problems with its broadcasts during other disasters, so its remarkable efforts to get and take credit for its contributions during Katrina raised eyebrows among critics who suspected ulterior motives. But the radio giant was desperate for good publicity and for respect from federal regulators: it was about to launch another political campaign to expand its local radio holdings.

IN OCTOBER, JUST ONE MONTH AFTER KATRINA, THEN PRESIDENT AND CEO Mark Mays called for Congress to further increase local radio station limits (which remained capped at six in midsize markets and eight in large markets) to ten in midsize markets and twelve in metropolitan areas with more than forty-five stations. "Specifically free radio needs Congress to relax outdated restrictions on our operations," Mays declared. "Free radio is not asking for much more room." The bold public call for lifting radio ownership caps represented a tactical shift for Clear Channel, which in previous years had advanced its regulatory activism backstage. Between 2002 and 2003 the company's lobbying expenditures soared from $68,675 to $1,860,000, and in 2004 it invested $1,720,000.[45]

Financial analysts understood why the company was spending so aggressively. In late 2005 Bloomberg News Service warned that Clear Channel may fall into the junk bond market, while Moody's, Fitch Ratings, and Standard & Poor's warned that Clear Channel stock could lose its investment grade rating because of the conglomerate's debt, then $6.6 billion, and its difficulty raising advertising revenues in the medium it had done so much to damage.[46] Yet citizens and officials charged with serving the public interest saw little reason to throw Clear Channel a lifeline. "We already have too much concentration in ownership," said North Dakota senator Byron Dorgan, who has been a leading voice for media reform since he learned how Clear Channel mismanaged the Minot disaster in his state. "How much bigger does one need to get?"[47]

Even for Clear Channel, the answer is mixed. While lobbying to eliminate ownership limits, during 2005 Clear Channel joined media conglomerates such as Viacom and Time Warner in deciding that its experiment in corporate synergy had failed. Market analysts considered its outdoor advertising a growth business because digital technologies allowed billboard owners to sell rotating ad space to multiple clients and increase traffic on expensive sites. But both the radio division, despite annual profit margins of around 40 percent, and the entertainment division, with margins of 6 percent, were experiencing declining annual profits that dragged down the company's overall market value. In response, during 2005 Clear Channel announced plans to break its radio/television, entertainment, and outdoor advertising units into three separate publicly traded companies. Clear Channel would continue to control the broadcast and advertising companies, but it pledged to spin off 100 percent of Clear Channel Entertainment and create a new board of directors for the corporation.[48]

Clear Channel had hardly given up on broadcast radio. In fact, its executives expressed confidence that the autonomous radio corporation will become even more profitable once the advertising market rebounds and the broadcast signal converts from analog to digital—a change that will allow each station on the FM dial to multicast (or transmit at least two separate streams of programming)—effectively multiplying its available commercial time. "Right now," said Carpenter, of the labor union AFTRA, "they're planning to take their broadcast signal and split it into multiple streams with digital. They'll staff live broadcasters on the primary channels and use a lot of cyber jocking on the others." But the conversion to digital broadcasting also gives the FCC a chance to support innovation in radio, just as it did some forty years ago by forcing AM stations to offer new content, rather than simulcasts, on their FM outlets. If, for example, the FCC required broadcasters to air original, locally produced programs rather than voice-tracked and syndicated shows on the new digital frequencies, the policy could, once again, bring bounce back into the airwaves and usher in a radio renaissance.

CLEAR CHANNEL IS BIG ENOUGH TO HEDGE ITS BETS ON ITS BROADCAST holdings, however, and in recent years it has quietly become a major investor in the new media that threaten the future of traditional radio. In 1999 Clear Channel made a $75-million investment in XM Satellite Radio, one of the two leading providers, and it is already a leader in Internet radio as well.[49] Although Clear Channel's most ardent critics once hoped that the conglomerate would be crippled by threats from new technologies, it has staked out so much property in the emerging media market that John Hogan said, "The Internet and iPod are not challenges—they are business options for us."[50]

Clear Channel investors may be well served by the company's new media strategies, but there is little evidence that listeners who care about what is happening in their own communities will be. Local content is conspicuously absent from satellite radio.[51] On a recent cross-country driving excursion, the writer Walter Kirn enjoyed national programs from CNN, FOX, NPR, and an "Old Skool Rap" station while he drove, without warning, directly into a tornado with winds up to 180 miles per hour. "The new technology connects you to the world—but not the one outside your window," Kirn reported. Satellite radio "often makes me feel as though America were a high-tech hologram and I were a futuristic ghost . . . Having passed through the canyonlands of Utah while listening to Caribbean pop and having crossed the Black Hills of South Dakota immersed in a disco channel called the Strobe, I feel after a year of nonstop driving (50,000 miles in all) that I haven't, in fact, gone anywhere except deeper and deeper inside my radio."[52] After a decade of consolidation, Americans in all parts of the country know exactly what that sounds like.

4

NEWS FROM NOWHERE

On December 1, 2004, a cheerful and charismatic meteorologist named Vytas Reid delivered bad news about the weather to television viewers in Buffalo, New York, who at least were expecting it. "We did get to see our snow last night," Reid reported, lifting his eyebrows and sighing audibly so that the camera would capture the familiar resignation of a man who had been through countless northeastern blizzards and expected to see many more. The extreme climate only made the colorful topographic maps and WeatherRider FlyThru animation segments generated by AccuWeather's Galileo Weather System all the more captivating. The veteran newsman invited his audience to join him at the radar screen. "We'll take a look at what's coming our way." On the same day, at the same time, Reid also reported the weather for a television station in Flint, Michigan, where conditions were also bleak. "We got to see *fifty*-mile-per-hour gusts south of us," Reid exclaimed, amazed at the area's bad luck. The winds were calmer in Baltimore, Maryland, and Raleigh, North Carolina, however, where Reid was also the local meteorologist. He dutifully told viewers about the climate "we got to see" earlier in the day but warned that, alas, a cold snap was on its way.

Neither Reid nor any of the seven other meteorologists who worked in his newsroom that winter actually experienced the weather conditions that they reported to cities across the country from inside the Sinclair Broadcast Group's glass-encased, modern headquarters in a Hunt Valley, Maryland, office park. Instead, they prepared for their segments by downloading climate data from the AccuWeather system, scripting banter to share with anchors, and studying geography and regional pronunciation from their library of atlases, as well as what the staff meteorologist James Wieland called "notebooks with little quirky things about each market we're in." Then they walked into one of Sinclair's five one-person meteorology studios to stage a live, local forecast before robotically controlled cameras that they operated with a joystick. When they finished digitally recording a segment, the meteorologists sent it to the stations through a Telestream program called ClipMail. The technology was breathtakingly sophisticated. "If we had a bunch of twelve-year-old boys in here, we could run the whole station," said Sinclair vice president and on-air personality Mark Hyman, my host and guide for the unforgettable day I spent inside the eerily lifeless, space-age news facility. "The price of a robotically controlled camera is basically the same as the price of a manned camera. But you're not paying labor costs, health care, or payroll tax." Wieland reminded us of another benefit. "A robot doesn't call in sick."

Wieland, a handsome man whose receding hairline and large forehead belied his age (early thirties), didn't have much downtime either. "I'm doing three times the amount of forecasting here as I was before, in Myrtle Beach, South Carolina," he told me. "I do at least three cities daily, sometimes more if we're short-staffed." Whether reporting to Cincinnati, Rochester, Pittsburgh, or Las Vegas, Wieland looked and played the part of a local meteorologist. "Last year we sent our weather team to their specific markets to do community service," he explained. "And a lot of people were surprised that we're not even there." "Viewers don't care if James is in a studio in Oklahoma City, or College Park, or here," added Hyman, who monitored all of my conversations in the building and jumped in whenever his staff strayed from the message management wanted them to convey. "There isn't anyone in the U.S. who collects their own weather data, and so what we're doing here is not so different."

Hyman was being disingenuous. Journalists throughout the television industry considered Sinclair's NewsCentral system revolutionary, and business managers viewed its ambitious directors, whose legal team had pushed the FCC's local ownership limits to the breaking point, as fearsome renegades. In the mid-1990s Sinclair was a tiny and unknown speck on the media landscape. But by 2004 Sinclair had

become infamous: not only did the family-run corporation own and operate more U.S. stations than any other company—sixty-two channels in
forty markets, reaching at least 24 percent of American viewers[1]—it
also pioneered the high-tech, top-down production system through which
a staff of on-air personalities including Reid and Wieland recorded
national and local "must carry" content (weather, sports, news, editorials, and specials) that was transmitted to each "online" station in its fleet.
With NewsCentral, Hyman and his similarly opinionated boss, President and CEO David Smith, could dictate programming decisions that
other broadcasters, including the networks, routinely delegate to local
news directors, thereby reducing its local reporting staff to as few as
fifteen or twenty people, bringing local operating costs down to depths
that autonomous stations could never reach. When asked to defend the
tight reins with which Sinclair controls its local channels, Hyman mim-
icked Clear Channel's Randy Michaels. "Just like Sears tells all of its
stores, 'You will sell Craftsman tools.' McDonald's tells all of its
restaurants, 'You will have a sesame seed bun.' That's the business we're
in . . . To suggest that our TV stations are all simply stand-alone franchises and the local general manager can make any decision he wants
about the program he carries is actually factually incorrect."[2]

AT SINCLAIR, THE MOST IMPORTANT DECISIONS ABOUT LOCAL TELEVISION
have always concerned politics. And for good reason: of all the options
available to Americans, local television has long been and, despite
recent struggles, remains to this day among the most popular and
trusted source of news. Cable stations, television networks, newspapers, and radio may have dedicated followers, but none offer the warm,
familiar local faces that are always there to explain the major happenings,
issues, and events that, as meteorologist Reid put it, are "coming our
way." Sinclair tactfully established two station strongholds (or duopolies,
whereby one company owns and operates two stations) in midsize cities,
including Columbus, Pittsburgh, Milwaukee, and Las Vegas, where it
could influence swing-state voters but avoid national scrutiny.

With NewsCentral, Sinclair aimed to establish a national network
of outlets that would transform local news broadcasts into platforms
for the management's favorite conservative causes. For example, after
9/11, Sinclair forced all of its stations to have on-air personalities pledge

support for President George W. Bush and the War on Terror during their broadcasts. It forbid its Fox affiliate in Madison, Wisconsin, from airing ads produced by the Democratic National Committee during the summer of 2004. During the 2004 presidential campaign, Jon Leiberman, then the Washington bureau chief, complained that Sinclair was using its local stations to air "propaganda meant to sway the election," and that the news manager, citing pressure from the top, consistently denied requests to report on the torture scandal at Abu Ghraib. An ex-producer at Sinclair said he was ordered not to report "any bad news out of Iraq—no dead servicemen, no reports on how much we're spending, nothing." And the producer that Sinclair sent to Iraq to report on the war called the resulting coverage "pro-Bush." "You weren't reporting news," she explained. "You were reporting a political agenda that came down to you from the top of the food chain."

By far the most prominent NewsCentral segment was "The Point," a nightly editorial hosted by Hyman that Sinclair required all of its stations to broadcast. Hyman, in his late forties, is a proud navy man and former intelligence officer who decorates his walls with drawings of battleships and carries a POW-MIA bracelet engraved with the name of a U.S. war casualty from the Persian Gulf to remind himself of the cost of freedom.[3] Hyman swaggers around the office with his chest puffed high, wears his hair in a wave, and on camera spouts invective with the subtlety of a shock jock. In some typical editorials Hyman railed against the "angry left" ("the least generous people in America" or the "blame America crowd") and "clueless academia"; dismissed peace activists as "wack jobs" and Hans Blix and "his band of Keystone investigators" as incompetent; labeled the French "cheese-eating surrender monkeys" and then senator Tom Daschle the "Obstructionist-in-Chief"; charged the NAACP president with being "intent on bomb-throwing"; and blasted the networks for their "skewed news coverage and bias." As the 2004 election approached, Hyman opined that "the terrorist leaders would dearly love to see President Bush replaced by Senator Kerry." His own policy preferences? Regressive tax reforms, such as a flat tax or a national sales tax, that would take from the middle class and give to the rich. Privatizing Medicare and Medicaid. Escalating the war in Iraq.[4]

Amid the deluge of conservative political news and commentary that flooded NewsCentral's nightly broadcasts, however, Sinclair offered only a few drops of local political news. Not that this was uncommon.

In the late 1990s a group of researchers affiliated with the Norman Lear Center at the University of Southern California decided to ask a simple question: during campaign season, when citizens need to learn about their political choices, how much information is available on broadcast television from the stations that promise to serve the public interest in exchange for a license to use the public airwaves?[5]

To find the answer, they began recording and analyzing evening news broadcasts in the run-up to local, state, and federal elections. In 1998, then again in 2000, 2002, and 2004, they assessed tens of thousands of stories from dozens of stations. Audience studies typically show that consumers want their news to be entertaining, but they also have strong interest in and demand for news about local political and civic issues. According to a recent survey conducted by the Radio and Television News Directors Foundation, more than 93 percent of viewers believe that "an important function of local TV news is to inform people like you what's happening in your community," while more than 70 percent believe that "an important function of local TV news is to act as a watchdog looking over local government." Television stations that broadcast the highest-quality news programs tend to get high ratings. But how much coverage of local election issues are television stations actually supplying during political prime time?[6]

Less than you might think. Consider the Lear Center's report, *Local News Coverage of the 2004 Campaigns.* Between October 4 and November 1, a team of researchers led by Martin Kaplan observed 4,333 evening news broadcasts (from 5:00 p.m. to 11:30 p.m.) in eleven metropolitan markets reaching about one-quarter of the nation's viewers, ranging in size from New York to Des Moines, and in region from Seattle to Dallas and Miami. Sixty-four percent of the broadcasts contained at least one election story, and 55 percent had a story about the presidential race. Yet a mere 8 percent of the broadcasts ran a story about a *local* candidate race, which includes campaigns for the U.S. Congress (the subject of 60 percent of the local political stories), state senate or assembly (1 percent), mayoral or city council seats, judgeships, law enforcement posts, education-related offices, and regional or county offices. The report documented the breakdown of a typical thirty-minute news broadcast: about nine minutes of commercials; six and one-half minutes for sports and weather; three minutes for elections (two minutes for the presidential campaign, and thirty seconds for congressional, state, and local races combined); two and one-half minutes for crime; less than two minutes for both local interest and teasers; less than a minute for unintentional injury and business; and about a minute for government, Iraq, and foreign policy, combined. In total, *"eight times more coverage went to stories about accidental injuries, and 12 times more coverage to sports and weather, than to coverage of all local races combined."*[7]

Moreover, the local political stories that did air rarely provided useful information on policy matters. Only 32 percent of the stories concerned "issues," and 5 percent addressed local ballot initiatives, whereas 44 percent focused on "strategy" and the "horse race" (the competition for office). Twenty-eight percent of the local campaign stories contained a soundbite, the average length of which was twelve seconds. Local candidates got considerably more exposure from paid advertisements than from news coverage (no wonder officials are so reluctant to endorse campaign finance reform), with commercial-to-news time ratios up to 17:1 for U.S. Senate candidates and 7:1 for those running for the House of Representatives.

These patterns held even in close, contentious races. In Washington State, for example, the dramatic gubernatorial election ended in a virtual draw, with the victorious candidate winning a recount by just over one hundred votes.[8] During the last month of the campaign, 5 percent of the evening local news broadcasts in Seattle had a story about the election, while collectively Seattle television stations devoted fourteen times more airtime to teasers and bumper music than to the gubernatorial race. Perhaps surprisingly, the Lear Center detected significant variations in the ways that stations covered local politics, which they attributed to the principles and priorities of station and corporate managers. Managers at twenty of the forty-four stations in the study pledged to give candidates free airtime during the campaign, and these stations tended to provide more local political coverage, too. In Des Moines, Iowa, the Hearst-Argyle CBS affiliate KCCI dedicated 11 percent of its stories to local races, while one of the Sinclair Broadcast Group's stations, Fox affiliate KDSM, "failed to air a single story about a local race."[9]

THE LEAR CENTER'S REPORT PROVIDED RELIABLE MEASURES OF HOW little political news and civic information are available on local television;

these data have helped convince a growing number of congressional leaders that what we can't see *can* hurt us, and our democracy, too. But what we can see is equally disturbing. Civic groups have long complained about the famous formula that governs local news programming, "If it bleeds, it leads." Communications scholars routinely blast local stations for saturating broadcasts with stories about crime, accidents, and small-scale crises, all of which lose context and meaning amid the superficial happy talk that anchors and reporters perform. Professional media critics—often the same ones who slam Top 40 radio stations that substitute market research for the taste of local DJs—regularly deride station managers for letting consultants, such as Frank Magid Associates, Audience Research & Development, and the Broadcast Image Group, persuade them to place market considerations above news judgments, and to replace political and civic stories with "news you can use" and human-interest reports.[10] Even other popular media outlets—newspapers, magazines, and Web sites—revel in contempt for local TV news. One recent *Business Week* story opened, "Imagine a world in which local TV news doesn't suck . . . It's not easy. But try. Imagine an end to pointless news-chopper one-upmanship, to 'breaking' reports on trumped-up consumer scams, to the same-show-different-anchors feeling that viewers get nightly from West Palm Beach to Walla Walla."[11]

The sources of the trouble with local TV news run deeper than most citizens recognize, and they are inextricably linked to media consolidation. In the past decade the concentration of ownership among a small number of large station owners that are particularly driven by bottom-line concerns has shifted editorial resources and programming control from the local to the national level. The results—a decline in primary television news reporting, the rise of fake local news broadcasts, and an increase of canned content such as infomercials and video news releases promoting commercial products or political propaganda—are pushing viewers to change the channel, and local TV stations are struggling to maintain their status as the nation's most popular source of news.

Consider the complicated collaborative relationship between networks and their affiliated stations. The affiliates broadcast and promote network news and entertainment; but affiliates also compete with the networks, negotiating whether and how much the networks will compensate the affiliates for airing their new programs and charge them for syndicating their old ones, and whether and how much the affiliates can preempt network shows to air programs of local interest (such as political debates, telethons, parades, sports, and cultural events).[12] The balance of power between networks and affiliates has shifted since the early 1990s, first tipping toward the affiliates of the three major networks (ABC, CBS, and NBC) when Rupert Murdoch broke into the network's territory and lured affiliates to Fox News Channel with competitive compensation offers, but then falling decidedly back toward the networks once Fox was established, new affiliates were aligned, and the FCC steadily increased the number of stations any one company could own. Station ownership caps rose from seven to twelve stations (as long as they reached no more than 25 percent of the national audience) in 1984, to any number of stations reaching less than 35 percent of the national audience in 1996 (a provision of the Telecommunications Act), and finally to 39 percent of the national audience in 2004.

In the last decade networks have joined other large media companies in expanding their holdings, establishing their "owned and operated" stations ("Network O&Os") in the leading markets. As in radio, aggressive acquisitions strategies from Big Media conglomerates after the 1996 Telecom Act dramatically reduced the number of small, local station owners. According to the Project for Excellence in Journalism (PEJ), by 2005 there remained four kinds of broadcasters: First, the major networks, which collectively "owned 126 stations, mostly in the biggest cities and in all areas of the country," including all four top markets. Next, regional and speciality chains, such as Gannett, Belo, Hearst, and Tribune, which "are owned by companies with substantial investment in other media sectors" and "are often involved in business relationships with the four major networks." Then there are midlevel chains whose "involvement in the television business is limited to what they receive from local station revenue." Finally, there are small chains in minor markets, many of which are ultimately gobbled up by bigger players. "Vanishing," the PEJ reported, "were the local owners with one or maybe two stations."[13]

During the early years of the twenty-first century, network television executives insisted that their businesses were suffering from competition with cable and Internet news. But the PEJ left little doubt that television consolidation was a financial boon for big media firms. In 1995 "the ten biggest local television companies, which include the four networks and most of the major chains . . . had $5.9 billion in revenue and owned 104 stations. By 2002 those companies had doubled that revenue total and owned nearly three times as many stations," their local stations typically generated proft margins between 30 and 40 percent, and "in larger cities the profit margins could be far higher."[14]

With highly profitable O&Os in the top national markets and strong revenue streams coming from syndicated programming, the conglomerates that control networks—Disney/ABC, Viacom/CBS, General Electric/NBC Universal, and News Corporation/FOX—toughened their stance in negotiations with affiliates. By 2000, the networks were dramatically reducing compensation levels, demanding copayments for broadcasting popular sports events (such as the NCAA basketball tournament, the Olympics, and professional football), and in some cases even getting reverse compensation from affiliates. The E. W. Scripps Company, which owns ten network affiliate stations but none in the top ten markets, reported that its network compensation dropped from about $16 million to about $8 million between 1998 and 2002, for an average loss of nearly $1 million per station.[15] Alan Frank, the president of Post-Newsweek Stations, told me that his company's CBS affiliate in Jacksonville severed its ties with the network after "they offered a compensation renewal package that was at best punitive. They wanted reverse compensation for the NCAA tournament, they cut what they offered us, and they weren't giving us a rebate for the stinkers. It was a bold plan to transfer money from one side to the other. We were the second-highest-rated station in the market, so we left."

The networks assert power over the affiliates in other ways, too, such as pressuring affiliates not to preempt national shows for special local programs, and expanding their claim on prime-time advertising minutes. Frank estimated that the typical affiliate controls around 20 to 25 percent of the prime-time advertising units, with the remainder going to the networks. Hank Price, former vice president and general manager of the CBS O&O in Chicago and now president and general manager of the Hearst-Argyle-owned NBC affiliate in Winston-Salem, North Carolina, told me that "a prime-time show like ER is going to bring in a lot of advertising revenue, but [stations] don't have a lot of those minutes to keep." Popular syndicated programs also generate significantly more revenue for the networks than for the affiliates. "After payroll, syndication is the second-highest cost for most local stations," Price said. "Shows like *Oprah* and *Dr. Phil* cost so much money that you don't make much from them. *Oprah* in New York City costs about $500,000 per week. Even in Hartford you pay $50,0000 a week. But you air *Oprah* and *Dr. Phil* because they bring in viewers, and you keep them for news."

Although the networks had won the fight to lift station ownership caps in 1996, by 2000 they were aggressively lobbying for another increase, with some industry leaders pushing Congress to remove the caps outright. Yet the Network Affiliated Stations Alliance, the umbrella organization of ABC, CBS, and NBC affiliate boards, pushed back. Frank, who chaired the group, told the U.S. Senate Committee on Commerce, Science, and Transportation that "the growth in network power is remarkable and is felt in significant ways across the broadcast community . . . today local broadcasters have less independence, less ability to make sound programming decisions for their local communities."[16] He outlined the hazards of further consolidating broadcast television in a scathing editorial published by *USA Today* in 2002.

If that 35% cap is lifted, the networks will gobble up stations. What will viewers lose if this happens? Local and regional coverage, whether it's local weather or news or candidate debates or high school sports or charity events important to a community . . .

National networks have an economic incentive to broadcast all network programming, even when non-network programming would better serve a local community. That's because networks make money by selling national advertising—and those ad rates go up when TV ratings go up, which happens when the network's programs are broadcast by all of its local affiliates. The syndication value of network-owned programs also increases when they are broadcast nationwide.

Even under existing rules, networks exert economic leverage over TV stations by threatening to penalize them or terminate their network affiliation if they pre-empt more than a few hours of network programming. During the 2000 presidential election, for example, NBC demanded that its affiliates air game one of the American League baseball playoffs rather than the first presidential debate. After station owners protested long and hard, NBC backed down. If NBC had owned stations covering more of the nation, it could have gotten its way.

Abolishing the cap also would lead to fewer choices for consumers in other ways. When networks recently were permitted to enter the program-syndication business, the number of major syndicates dropped from dozens in 1996 to a handful today—most of them tied to the networks. If networks gain control of more local stations, they're apt to pressure the locals to use their own syndicated shows, further reducing regional programming variations.

The networks argue that they need to buy up their affiliated stations in order to earn a profit and compete with cable and satellite television. But even with artificial accounting practices that make them look less profitable than they really are, the networks collectively reaped profits of more than $4 billion in 2000. And despite the inroads made by cable and satellite, broadcast television retains its dominance, accounting for about 60% of total national viewership.[17]

Deprived of revenue, autonomy, and negotiating power, the affiliates have had to search for new sources of income. Broadcasting paid programming is among the most popular strategies, and today infomercials and home-shopping shows generate over $5 billion a year in sales. Deregulation is doubly responsible for spreading infomercials over the public airwaves. In 1984 the Reagan administration pushed Congress to eliminate caps on the amount of time that television broadcasters could sell to advertisers, allowing network affiliates to join cable channels in the infomercial business. Yet station managers found it unsavory and were reluctant to do so—until 1996, when the Telecom Act was passed; then networks acquired their own outlets and cut payments to affiliates, leaving local stations few options for making up the income that were easier than scheduling paid programming. Since then the number of infomercials on the air has soared; leading companies, such as Gateway Computers, Sony, Carnival Cruise Lines, and Time Life, have produced their own programs; and infomercials have entered the daytime as well as late-night schedule. In 2002 *Forbes* reported that during a typical month, "300,000 infomercial spots appear on 36 national cable stations and 1,800 broadcast stations . . . To watch them all would take you roughly 1,027 years—and it might seem longer."[18]

Most infomercials use news and talk show formats to disguise the fact that they are pure sales pitches, designed to market products such as the Ronco Showtime Platinum Rotisserie and BBQ, Slim Down Solution, the Torso Tiger, the Body by Jake Bun and Thigh Rocker, and all varieties of abdominal exercise machines (including three that require no actual exercise—just plug them in, strap them on, and they'll work your muscles for you). Occasionally local news reporters participate, drawing on their journalistic credibility to promote and legitimate the products and the programs. Some stations have found more subtle ways to integrate commercial pitches into their broadcasts, blurring the fuzzy line between news and advertisement that is supposed to separate the marketing and editorial divisions of journalistic organizations. In Tampa, for example, one broadcaster sold four-minute segments of airtime on its morning news program for $2,600. In Philadelphia, KYW-TV used a local television medical reporter to introduce a sixty-minute prime-time special, *Health Test,* which promoted cardiac specialists at the Albert Einstein Medical Center, the program sponsor, leaving viewers unsure whether the show was news or advertisement.[19] At a media reform conference in 2003, FCC commissioner Jonathan Adelstein, who has become an outspoken critic of paid programming, said, "We may be getting tighter abs, but we're also getting flabby democracy."

LOCAL NEWS, WHICH TYPICALLY GENERATES A THIRD OR MORE OF A station's revenues because (unlike network programming) stations don't have to share advertising income from news with networks, is the real profit center of affiliates. In recent years stations have responded to the economic pressures born of consolidation and the rise of national cable networks by airing more local newscasts than ever before. In the early 1990s typical affiliates in medium and large markets broadcast around three or four hours of local news per weekday. Today many of those stations have doubled their news offerings, broadcasting two to four hours of news in the early morning, a half hour or hour at midday, an hour and a half in the early evening, and another half hour late. But here's the rub: local stations, whether owned by small chains, midsize companies, or networks, have not increased their staffing levels to match the production needs of their news-heavy schedules, and in some cases they have actually reduced personnel while increasing their news offerings.

How do they make it work? By squeezing as much work as they can out of their reporters, producers, and anchors. By relying on video news releases that disguise government propaganda or commercial marketing as journalism and allow stations to customize preprogrammed content so that it looks homemade. By faking local stories in which on-air personalities perform the role of reporters while reading ready-made scripts. By broadcasting stories available from national news sources on satellite feeds. By purchasing video and, occasionally, reporting from private companies. By combining stations into one newsroom and sharing staffs across channels. And, in some companies, by centralizing news operations into a single studio where news directors dictate editorial spin to their small local staffs. If the parallels with broadcast radio are striking, it's because during the late 1990s and early years of the twenty-first century television companies looked to conglomerates like Clear Channel to learn how to make consolidation work. As the former FCC chairman Reed Hundt predicted, "Radio is the model. That's the harbinger for what's going to happen to TV."[20] By 2000, it was already happening, and nowhere is this clearer than at the headquarters for the company whose Des Moines station aired no local political stories during the 2004 election, Sinclair Broadcast Group.

WHEN I VISITED SINCLAIR'S HEADQUARTERS ON A MILD WINTER DAY IN December 2004, Mark Hyman showed off the operation with the pride of a new parent. Sinclair, he explained, set up NewsCentral so that its stations could compete with network affiliates in the advertising market for local news. "Thirty to thirty-five percent of the advertisers in any typical market only buy on local news," Hyman told me. "If you're looking at pure dollars and cents, do we want to be in a business where, at best, we're only competing for seventy percent of the dollars?" Sinclair needed that income because it was saddled with debt from its aggressive acquisition strategy in the 1990s, and its revenues, around $739 million in 2003 and $736 million in 2002, lagged behind those of other station groups.[21] But rather than spend money for a full news operation at each of its stations, Sinclair came up with a cheaper alternative: it hired skeleton staffs at local stations and integrated their light reporting with a centrally cast news program that was produced in the Maryland headquarters but designed to *look* like local news. Hyman claimed that Sinclair designed the NewsCentral model to start low-cost newscasts on stations that never before carried local news. Like his colleagues at Clear Channel, Hyman had learned the language of journalistic ethics and civic responsibility, and he was eager to testify as to the depth of Sinclair's commitment to the communities it served. Sinclair did start newscasts on the WB and UPN channels, which had not previously had them. But Sinclair also bought network affiliates with flourishing news programs, slashed the staffing levels, and converted them to the NewsCentral model despite intense local complaints. In St. Louis, Missouri, Sinclair closed the entire news division of its ABC affiliate KDNL and has not broadcast local news since October 2001.²²

As we toured the NewsCentral studios, Hyman called my attention to the main sets, especially the anchor desk and the backdrops. They were created to match those at Sinclair's affiliates, leading viewers to think that on-air personalities broadcasting from the Hunt Valley studios were actually in the same room with the handful of local news reporters it employed at each station. Josh Silver, the executive director of the media reform organization Free Press, complained to me that "there's no indication that these pieces are coming from NewsCentral in Maryland, no disclaimer. I'm a full-time media critic, I've got a Sinclair station, and I thought Hyman was local! The first week I saw him, I thought, 'Wow, they got a real right-wing wacko here in Springfield, Massachusetts.' I didn't know they were central casting."

Sinclair blew its cover in 2004, its third year operating News-Central, when it used its fleet of local stations to take center stage in the presidential campaign. Sinclair caused its first election-year scandal that April, when it forbid its ABC affiliates from broadcasting *The Fallen*, a *Nightline* special in which Ted Koppel read the names of American soldiers killed in the Iraq war. As veterans' groups and a bipartisan group of congressional leaders protested the act of censorship, *Broadcasting & Cable* editorialized that "Sinclair has simply replaced *Nightline*'s worthy tribute with its own political agenda."²³ U.S. senator John McCain, a former POW, wrote harsher words in an open letter to the company: "Your decision to deny your viewers an opportunity to be reminded of war's terrible costs, in all their heartbreaking detail, is a gross disservice to the public, and to the men and women of the

United States Armed Forces. It is, in short, sir, unpatriotic. I hope it meets with the public opprobrium it most certainly deserves."[24]

Sinclair executives brushed off the charge, and in October, just weeks before the election, they notified affiliates that they planned to preempt regular coverage with *Stolen Honor: Wounds That Never Heal,* a documentary in which former prisoners of war accused presidential candidate John Kerry of inciting additional violence against American POWs and prolonging the war through his own domestic and international antiwar campaign. Again, scores of public officials, citizen groups, and media watchdogs protested. The Kerry campaign condemned Sinclair's use of its local broadcast licenses to influence the race as "un-American," and demanded that the Federal Election Committee consider the program an illegal in-kind contribution from Sinclair to the Republican Party.[25] But Sinclair did not back down from its plans to broadcast *Stolen Honor* until after the investment firm Glickenhaus & Co. threatened to sue the company for placing its political agenda ahead of its fiduciary obligations to shareholders. Lehman Brothers called the decision to show the special "potentially damaging—both financially and politically," and Moody's Investment Service downgraded its rating for Sinclair from "stable" to "negative."[26] Ultimately Sinclair aired *A P.O.W. Story: Politics, Pressure, and the Media,* its own special on how the media influences voting, while denying that it ever planned to broadcast *Stolen Honor* in its entirety.

When I asked Hyman and Smith, the president and CEO, if the public outcry over Sinclair's apparent plans to air *Stolen Honor* had changed their editorial direction, they looked at each other incredulously, then talked to me as if I were insane. "I'd do one of those *Stolen Honor* specials every month if we could," declared Smith, an imposing man with a pink complexion, small facial features, big opinions, and a blustery, confrontational manner. "The lesson was very straightforward: that we can do this kind of content, preempt network, and make more money. There is no question in our mind now that we can do news-type specials on subject matter that is of broad interest to people and make more money, whether it's a national-interest kind of story or local-interest kind of story. We can do those stories and make more money. That now becomes a consideration for us and the whole news infrastructure that we have in place." Hyman agreed. He said the *Stolen*

Honor controversy "was ten million dollars' worth of free advertising. People who'd never heard of us before suddenly knew who we were. Now we're getting all the press releases, phone calls, and interviews that were hard for us to get before. We're on the map."

SINCLAIR WAS FOUNDED BY THE LATE JULIAN SINCLAIR SMITH, WHO obtained a UHF license in 1971 and set up WBFF, a small, family-owned broadcasting company in Baltimore. In 1986, his four sons, David, Frederick, Robert, and J. Duncan, joined Julian to build a large television company, which they called the Sinclair Broadcast Group. In 1990 the brothers took over and, as the company's Web site says, "set out to make their vision a reality."[27]

David already had experience in media—but not the kind most of his colleagues in television would appreciate. In the 1970s he was a partner in a business called Ciné Processors, which copied porn films from the basement of a building owned by another of his father's companies, the Commercial Radio Institute. "We had the lab in operation for like a year," recalled David Williams, Smith's partner in the operation. "We got videotapes copied onto film and put the soundtrack on a cassette. The first one was *Deep Throat*, which had just opened in New York and hadn't opened anywhere else. All you had to do was get the film and the sound in sync, and you had something that was not available anywhere. We'd just solicit guys in the strip joint area and tried to sell them."

Smith's media connections came in handy in 1996, when he was arrested on suspicion of soliciting a prostitute who, police said, performed "an unnatural and perverted sex-act on him" in a Mercedes owned by Sinclair. As a special form of community service, Smith arranged with prosecutors to have Sinclair broadcast televised reports on state drug courts. LuAnne Canipe, a Sinclair reporter, recalled a Baltimore judge complaining to her about the deal. "The judge was outraged," she later told *Salon*'s Eric Boehlert. "He said, 'How can employees do community service for their boss?'"

By that point David Smith had plenty of experience engineering ways to get around legal restrictions that hampered his competitors. In 1991 he wanted to purchase WPGH-TV in Pittsburgh, even though he already owned another station in town, WPTT, and federal communications policy prohibited any company from controlling more than one broadcast outlet in a market. So, following the regulatory route paved by radio entrepreneurs, Sinclair's lawyers—whom current and former FCC staffers regard as among the most aggressive in the industry—asked the FCC to break precedent and allow them to set up a Local Marketing Agreement (LMA), in which they could sell WPTT to an African American station manager and Sinclair employee, Eddie Edwards, as Sinclair continued to run it. The FCC, which had expressed interest in supporting minority station owners, agreed, and Smith was proud of the arrangement. "What an opportunity that was to give something back to the African American community!" he told me. Rainbow/PUSH saw it differently, accusing Edwards of being a front man for Sinclair, and the National Association of Black Owned Broadcasters later opposed his dealings with the Smith family.[28]

In the following years the Smiths further pushed the limits of FCC ownership rules, forging other LMAs with their friend Edwards and their mother, Carolyn Smith. With Carolyn's capital, she and Edwards created a company called Glencairn, through which they bought stations in cities where Sinclair already operated and quickly transferred control to David. Carolyn then transferred her ownership interests in Glencairn, roughly 90 percent of the company, into trusts for her grandchildren, children of the Smith brothers.

After years of lobbying by the television industry, the FCC relaxed its restrictions on ownership in 1999, allowing duopolies in markets with eight or more voices (or owners), on the condition that only one station is rated in the top four. Soon after, Sinclair replaced Glencairn as the proposed purchaser of a station in Oklahoma City, without protest from Glencairn, which had purportedly been planning the deal for its own independent interests. Next, Glencairn petitioned to sell five stations to Sinclair in cities where duopolies were now legal. This was too much for the FCC, and in 2001 it ruled that Sinclair exercised illegal control of its business partner. Yet the commission, still reluctant to regulate, chose to grant four of the five licenses to Sinclair anyway, leveling a nominal forty-thousand-dollar fine as punishment. Commissioner Michael Copps was incredulous, and, in the manner of a Supreme Court justice dismayed by his colleagues' decision, he authored a scathing dissent.

The assessment of a fine combined with the approval of the transfers at issue is incongruous. The finding that an illegal transfer of control occurred at least raises questions about the control of Glencairn on an ongoing basis, and about the independence of Glencairn from Sinclair once Glencairn is controlled by the mother of Sinclair's owners and owned in trust for their minor children . . . With each transaction over the years, Sinclair has stretched the limits of the Commission's local television ownership rules . . . The transactions before the Commission today raise issues that prompted the majority to find that there has been an illegal transfer of control and to assess a fine. But the Commission nonetheless has allowed the transaction to go through without further review. Each transaction moves the line to which all of our licenses are subject. And this decision moves it further still.[29]

Despite the ruling, David Smith told me, "[At Sinclair] we're so pristine about the way we do things, we're so black and white there's no gray on us." His mother helped clear the record by changing Glencairn's name to Cunningham Broadcasting. Today she nominally owns more television stations than any other woman in the United States.

Cunningham's official street address is on West Forty-first Street in Baltimore, which is also the home of Sinclair's local Baltimore station, WBFF. Before I visited I didn't know whether Carolyn Smith spent much time there running the operation. When I was sitting in Mark Hyman's office in Sinclair's Hunt Valley headquarters, she strolled over on her walker and delivered him the mail. "Mrs. Smith is amazing," Hyman told me. "She's here every day sorting the mail. And if you touch it before her, you're in big trouble."

DURING THE RUN-UP TO THE 2004 ELECTION, THE OTHER UNTOUCHABLE at Sinclair was Armstong Williams, the conservative African American pundit and "special analyst" to whom Smith gave many of the news division's plum assignments, including interviews with Speaker of the House Dennis Hastert and former House majority whip Tom DeLay. Williams even got an hour on camera with Dick Cheney in December 2003, at a time when the vice president was refusing all other media requests. "The news director wanted to get Williams's face on our news program as much as possible," one Sinclair veteran told me.

"Management here loves him." The feeling is mutual. "David Smith is a good friend," Williams explained to me. "I had pursued Sinclair for a long time to do stuff with them. It's a big fish. Sinclair brought me stuff that I did not have—real numbers, where you can get the Speaker of the House or the VP. I was a part of that team, man. I was there for election coverage; I covered a lot of that campaign. If there was breaking news, I'd cover it for them, too." Williams had plenty of other media work, including a television and radio show called *The Right Side,* a syndicated weekly column with Tribune Media Services, and regular invitations to appear on national news shows. But Sinclair was special, he said. "They added a real audience. On Sinclair I was talking to millions of viewers a night."

Williams had another job during the 2004 campaign. In the beginning of that year, the U.S. Department of Education paid him $241,000 of taxpayer money to promote its controversial policy agenda through his media contacts and appearances. Because of Williams, Education Secretary Rod Paige got access to Sinclair viewers, too. Williams's contract with the Department of Education required that he help Paige get airtime, and the pundit delivered, granting the cabinet member responsible for his lucrative deal a long interview that Sinclair broadcast nationally, without disclosing Williams's relationship with the government. Smith said he didn't know about the contract, and managing editor Carl Gottlieb denied anyone at Sinclair was aware of Williams's deal. But Smith also told me, "I don't have a clue if anyone at Sinclair knew about it . . . It wasn't a secret." The Sinclair producer who edited the interview remembered it regretfully. "It was the worst piece of TV I've ever been associated with. A terrible interview. A love fest. You've seen softballs from Larry King, right? Well, this was softer. I told my boss it didn't even deserve to be broadcast, but they kept pushing me to put more of it on tape. In retrospect, it was so clearly propaganda."

Williams's arrangement with the Department of Education remained unreported until January 2005, when *USA Today* obtained a copy of his contract through a Freedom of Information Act request and published a major story, headlined "Education Dept. Paid Commentator to Promote Law."[30] The FCC's Payola Rules leave little doubt that either Williams or Sinclair could have broken the law, since Williams was legally obligated to disclose his government contract to Sinclair, and if Sinclair knew about the deal, it was legally obligated to tell its viewers.[31]

As the story spiraled into a major political scandal, Tribune Media Services, which had syndicated Williams's newspaper column, claimed that it had not known about the contract and cut its ties to the pundit. Sinclair's contract with Williams expired in late 2004, but when I last spoke with him Smith left open the possibility that Williams will return, telling me, "We want to study the whole relationship and find out what the facts are. I don't think we can trust what the USA Today says." Williams is confident that Sinclair will have him back. "David Smith has stood beside me as a friend. He does not abandon you during the storm. I'm not too concerned about my relationship with Sinclair, if you know what I mean."

Most professional journalists and media watchdogs felt otherwise, as did the Government Accountability Office (GAO), which conducted a thorough investigation of the Williams case and reported that the Bush administration had used him to illegally disseminate "covert propaganda."[32] The reports of Armstong Williams's dual roles in paid politics and punditry raised questions about the prevalence of this practice, and in the first months of 2005 mounting concerns over the government's use of taxpayer dollars to disseminate propaganda through the media motivated a series of investigations.

The crass form of political payola that the Department of Education funded is unusual, yet weeks after the Williams story broke, the Washington Post and USA Today reported that the U.S. Department of Health and Human Services had paid two other syndicated columnists, Maggie Gallagher and Mike McManus, to promote a controversial $300-million marriage initiative that diverted federal funds from welfare to marriage counseling. Gallagher, whose column is distributed by Universal Press Syndicate, received $21,500 for writing her support, while McManus, whose Ethics & Religion column appears in about forty newspapers, had personally accepted up to $10,000 as well as an additional $49,000 more for his foundation, Marriage Savers. Like Williams, Gallagher and McManus had not publicly disclosed the deals in their columns or in other media appearances.[33] Once they were exposed, however, the president decided that political payola was no longer viable. Following his second inauguration, Bush announced,

"We will not be paying commentators to advance our agenda. Our agenda ought to be able to stand on its own two feet."[34]

ACTUALLY, THE BUSH ADMINISTRATION HAD ALREADY EMBRACED A MORE effective way of producing promotional material that passes as journalism: video news releases (VNRs), the prepackaged "news" stories manufactured for government agencies and businesses by commercial production companies and distributed via satellite or Internet so multiple networks and local broadcasters can air them in real time. VNRs are analogous to print press releases: they typically endorse a policy or a product; they present only one side of an issue; they often serve as provocation for independent reporting by the journalists who receive them. Yet what sets them apart from ordinary PR releases is that they are explicitly designed so that producers have the option of either customizing the content, using their own on-air personalities to read ready-made scripts that accompany the footage, or simply broadcasting them as is. Usually VNRs blend into a newscast without viewers noticing that the segments are canned. Regular viewers of local news programs have seen thousands of them. Yet networks and affiliates are loath to acknowledge, let alone report, on their own use of VNRs, so most Americans are unaware that they exist.

Businesses have always been the main users of VNRs. Pharmaceutical companies, medical equipment suppliers, insurers, automobile manufacturers, and telecommunications firms, among others, hire VNR producers to craft stories that subtly market new products. But government agencies, particularly under the Bush administration, have stepped up their use of VNRs, too. Rather than (or in addition to) paying the high costs of filming and broadcasting a commercial, businesses or governments invest around twenty-five thousand dollars for a VNR and hope that affiliates throughout the country will air them as news stories. "It's a crapshoot," said Tom DeVries, who ended his long career as a journalist and television producer at several leading network affiliates and opened his own video production company, DeVries Media, where we met in 2004. "But you may get four, five, six million impressions, from New York to Tuscaloosa to Anniston, Alabama, the smallest commercial television market in the United States." The potential audience is not only large but also a credulous one because viewers believe they are watching journalism. As one VNR maker, KEF Media Associates, advertises, "VNRs deliver specific client messages within the credible editorial content of a newscast."[35]

Leading VNR producers, such as Larry Moscowitz, the president and CEO of the industry leader Medialink, like to say that VNRs have existed since the Eisenhower administration. According to John Stauber from the Center for Media and Democracy and Sheldon Rampton of PR Watch, VNRs were not widely used until the 1980s, "when PR firms discovered that they could use film, edit and produce their own news segments—even entire programs—and that broadcasters would play the segments as 'news,' often with no editing."[36] But not that often yet. DeVries remembered how little he and his colleagues at a San Francisco station respected VNRs when they first received them. "It was 1984 or '85. The VNR was from the Israeli Embassy, and the package contained a three-quarter-inch tape and a bunch of paper. We all booed it. We thought, 'Maybe they do these in Salt Lake City, but we do not do this here.' I left the newsroom in 1993, and at that time VNRs were still treated with disdain."

By the 1990s and early 2000s, however, local stations were heightening their use of VNRs and other external sources for news, such as CNN Newsource or the Associated Press Television News service, and today one PR company advertises that "90 percent of TV newsrooms now rely on VNRs."[37] Nielsen Media Research studies conducted through the 1990s found that virtually every broadcaster used VNRs in their newscasts, and that the number of VNRs per broadcast increased over time. According to Marion Just and Tom Rosenstiel, "From 1998 to 2002, a study of 33,911 television reports found, the percentage of 'feed' material from third-party sources rose to 23 percent of all reports from 14 percent. Meanwhile, the percentage of stories that included a local correspondent fell to 43 percent from 62 percent. Local broadcasters are being asked to do more with less, and they have been forced to rely more on prepackaged news to take up the slack."[38]

Advanced technologies make the process more efficient and less expensive. Whereas in the 1980s VNR makers paid to mail cassettes to each potential outlet, today both large and small producers use digital recording tools that stations can easily manipulate as well as satellite distribution systems that make the segments immediately available to broadcasters with the right equipment. But another main reason that

VNRs are so common is that the cookie-cutter content they provide reduces stations' need for paid reporters, and affiliates can use them to reach the high profit margins their corporate owners and investors demand by filling the air with news from nowhere rather than with expensive journalists and production crews.

In addition to VNRs, stations can purchase and customize longer reports for sweeps periods from companies such as NewsProNet. According to Stanford University's Grade the News project, the result is that television stations across the United States run the same special "investigative story," using their own on-air personalities to read identical scripts or perform mock interviews with people who have already been taped. At least six local newscasts in U.S. cities broadcast their own version of a NewsProNet's exposé that warned viewers about Innovis, a "secret" credit bureau company that was collecting private information about customers and selling it without permission. But Grade the News looked into the story and found that "each claim was misleading. The company, Innovis, isn't secret. It doesn't report to those who might approve your car or house loan. And according to the story's own sources, it's received far fewer complaints than its competitors."[39] Not only had the stations failed to check these facts on their own; several framed the story to look as if they had reported it themselves.

There's nothing illegal about making, distributing, or broadcasting a VNR that promotes a commercial product or a canned news item. But it hardly counts as local journalism, especially when the audio, video, and recommended script come from a remote source, and pretending that it does violates conventional journalistic ethics. On several occasions researchers and investigative journalists have found that station managers who use VNRs publicly deny that they do so. Many say the practice has become so common that they do not make special note of it in their records.[40]

The rules for broadcasting VNRs made by government agencies are different. Federal law prohibits the use of public funds for covert publicity or propaganda. During the 2005 payola scandal, the Government Accountability Office (GAO) warned heads of federal departments and agencies that stations using prepackaged political news are obligated to provide "clear disclosure to the television viewing audience that this material was prepared by or in cooperation with the government department or agency." Government agencies that make VNRs share this responsibility. As the GAO states, "While agencies generally have the right to disseminate information about their policies and activities, agencies may not use appropriated funds to produce or distribute prepackaged news stories intended to be viewed by television audiences that conceal or do not clearly identify for the television audience that the agency was the source of those materials."[41] Making VNRs to market government programs so that citizens learn about the services available to them is acceptable. Misleading citizens by airing them without disclosing the fact that government agencies produced or sponsored them is not.

USING VNRS IS A BIPARTISAN PRACTICE. CONCERNS OVER THE WHITE House's efforts to promote policies through VNRs first emerged during Bill Clinton's presidency. In 1996 David Bartlett, then president of the Radio-Television News Directors Association, complained that "the White House doesn't want you to know that they are spending taxpayers' money peddling these phony interviews with [President Clinton.] I mean, that harms his credibility . . . members of Congress do it routinely."[42] Under Clinton, the Department of Health and Human Services (HHS) produced a series of VNRs on prescription drug and preventive health benefits that purposely deceived viewers, closing with a paid performer who used the standard journalistic sign off, "Lovell Brigham, reporting."[43]

The first public outcry over George W. Bush's misuse of VNRs came in January 2004, when HHS issued a fake news story to promote a controversial Medicare prescription benefit program. HHS crossed the line by providing a script that refers to Karen Ryan, the public relations consultant who appears in the story, as a "reporter," and then having Ryan end her praise for the policy—"This is a program that gets an A-plus!"—with the familiar send off, "In Washington, I'm Karen Ryan reporting." Neither the video footage nor the anchor scripts stated explicitly that HHS made the package.

Ryan is a veteran VNR performer who had made videos with seven federal agencies in 2003 and 2004, and many others for commercial clients. The HHS segment got special attention because the GAO discovered it while investigating the administration's use of public funds to promote the Medicare prescription plan, and because forty local stations ran the Ryan "report" as news. Although media critics and Democrats condemned the department for deceiving the public, HHS spokesman Kevin Keane dismissed the concerns. "The use of video news releases is a common, routine practice in government and the private sector," he told the *New York Times*. "Anyone who has questions about this practice needs to do some research on modern public information tools."[44]

Though Clinton and congressional Democrats used VNRs frequently in the 1990s, the Bush administration—where a top adviser famously disparaged the "reality-based community" and declared, "When we act, we create our own reality"—helped make them standard tools of governance.[45] Overall, the first Bush administration spent $250 million on contracts with private public relations firms between 2001 and 2004, nearly doubling the $128 million spent by the Clinton administration between 1997 and 2000.[46] According to a *New York Times* investigation, the Bush administration ushered in "a new age of prepackaged TV news" in which "all participants benefit . . . Local affiliates are spared the expense of digging up original material. Public relations firms secure government contracts worth millions of dollars. The major networks, which help distribute the releases, collect fees from the government agencies that produce segments and the affiliates that show them. The administration, meanwhile, gets out an unfiltered message, delivered in the guise of traditional reporting." Under Bush, the report continues, "at least 20 federal agencies, including the Defense Department and the Census Bureau, have made and distributed hundreds of television news segments . . . Many were subsequently broadcast on local stations across the country without any acknowledgment of the government's role in their production."[47] The price tag for the administration's foreign and domestic policy PR reached unprecedented levels. As the GAO, drawing on a survey of only seven of the fifteen cabinet-level departments, reported, between January 2003 and June 2005, "the Administration spent $1.6 billion on contracts with advertising agencies ($1.4 billion), public relations firms ($197 million), and media organizations and individual members of the media ($15 million)."[48]

Political agencies at all levels of government are certain to continue making VNRs until Congress formally prohibits the practice, and local television stations are certain to continue broadcasting them. The revelatory reports about VNRs and other fake TV news that the major print media (and particularly the *New York Times*) published in the spring of 2005 ended years of public silence on the issue. Predictably, by summer the covert propaganda scandals had churned out of the news cycle. In April 2006 the Center for Media and Democracy and Free Press issued a report showing that seventy-seven local televisions stations—including seven owned by Sinclair, seven by Tribune, six by Viacom, six by Fox, and two by Clear Channel—had aired VNRs as if they were legitimate news reports between June 2005 and March 2006. As always, local television news programs did not report on the practice.

Today Comedy Central's *The Daily Show* is one of the only television programs that continues to cover the story of how Americans' most popular and trusted source of information deceives viewers with VNRs. The humor show has itself become a popular source of news, especially among young adults, and faux-anchor Jon Stewart has earned the trust of a national audience that is ever more skeptical of networks and affiliates. The coverage of televised propaganda, noted the media critic Daniel Price, would be hilarious if it weren't so disturbing. "Out of TV's many journalistic outlets," he wrote, "it [takes] a fake news show to expose a real news show for passing fake news off as real."

5

OWNING IT ALL

In January 2006 Gannett Company, the nation's largest newspaper chain, closed its Hazard bureau in eastern Kentucky. For decades the small outpost had produced news about the region's coal-mining industry for the *Louisville Courier-Journal,* which won a Pulitzer Prize for public service in 1967 and an inestimable level of public appreciation for its tough reporting on issues such as occupational health and safety, mining deaths and disasters, pollution, and labor disputes. "Did the *Courier-Journal* play a watchdog role?" asked Bill Caylor, president of the Kentucky Coal Association, in an interview with the *New York Times.* "Yes, newspapers do. They force us to not become lax."[1]

Between 1918 and 1986 the *Courier-Journal* was locally owned and operated by three generations of the Bingham family, under whose direction it became the first paper in the United States to appoint an independent ombudsman. The *Courier-Journal* provided generous employee benefits and flexible working conditions, won eight Pulitzers, and became nationally renowned for its tough, probing journalism. "My grandfather said he saw the paper as a public trust, and we ran it that way," said the late Barry Bingham Jr., the daily's last family publisher. "We made a marginal profit, maybe 5 or 6 percent." But in 1986, the Binghams, mired in family disputes, sold their paper to Gannett. The Virginia-based conglomerate, which launched *USA Today* just four years before acquiring the *Courier-Journal* while already on its way to accumulating nearly one hundred dailies nationwide, "has profit-margin demands that the Binghams never dreamed of," Barry Bingham explained. By 2005, for example, Gannett's margins were around 30 percent. To reach these levels, the chain downsized reporting staffs across its fleet of papers and shifted resources to the suburbs, where there are more affluent readers and, with them, large advertisers seeking their business. According to Tony Oppegard, an attorney with experience prosecuting mining companies for safety violations, in the early years of the twenty-first century a surge of new mining companies trying to "make a quick buck" with "little dog holes" meant that citizens "need a watchdog like the *Courier-Journal* all the more."[2]

The daily paper used to be considered a necessary tool for American democracy. As Oliver Wendell Holmes famously put it, "Only bread and the newspaper we must have, whatever else we do without." If, historically, broadcast media have been especially well suited for emergency communications, print journalism has been uniquely capable of providing sustained and enterprising reporting on key social institutions— government agencies, businesses, hospitals, neighborhoods, schools, and the like—that shape our everyday lives. The demise of Gannett's Hazard bureau is merely one small act in a drama that American communities everywhere are beginning to observe in their own hometowns: in the age of consolidation, newspaper journalism is becoming a luxury good.[3]

TODAY GANNETT AND THE OTHER MAJOR NEWSPAPER COMPANIES ARE simultaneously contracting and expanding: On the one hand, newspaper chains are laying off journalists, closing bureaus, and abandoning countless small towns, neighborhoods, and city beats from Hazard to Honolulu at breakneck speed, racing to cut costs and raise profit margins. On the other hand, they are converging operations—merging production and distribution of news and information with television stations, Internet properties, and cable outlets—wherever possible, and searching for new ways to saturate local markets with products marked by their corporate brand. These opposing tendencies help explain one of the great paradoxes in today's media business: while citizens are bombarded with an apparently endless supply of media products, the shrinking supply of primary producers at the local level renders media content strikingly similar, regardless of its form.

Big Media conglomerates insist that they are pulling out of less lucrative markets because of an industry-wide financial crisis. Overall circulation levels for traditional, printed papers are stuck in a steady free-fall, and young people are turning elsewhere for news and entertainment. Alternative weeklies and Internet sites such as Craigslist are formidable competitors for classifieds. The loss of large local retailers, such as department stores and car dealers, has slowed a traditional stream of revenue. Since 2000 a spate of high-profile scandals heightened public distrust of newspaper reporters, and comparable scandals involving newspaper business managers who reported inflated circulation levels elevated the distrust among advertisers. In 2005 major shareholders at Knight Ridder, then the nation's second-largest newspaper chain, forced managers to sell the company because its profit margins were deemed insufficient. Newspaper stocks are sluggish. "At this point," wrote the financial columnist James Surowiecki, "everyone knows that news-papers are doomed."[4]

But the state of newspapers is more complicated than it appears, and even skeptics like Surowiecki acknowledge that the newspaper business generates remarkable cash revenues and is, however surprisingly, well positioned to become even more necessary in the digital age.

Newspaper journalism has never been as ubiquitous or influential as it is today, and, by the profitability standards of even the most lucrative industries, it remains robust. In 2005, for example, newspapers generated $47 billion in advertising revenues and enjoyed daily circulation around 78 million, not including the Internet. In October 2005 the Newspaper Association of America released audience surveys showing that the Web sites maintained by newspaper companies gave them greater media presence than previously believed, with 7 million people reading the *USA Today* on a weekly basis (about three times the reported Audit Bureau of Circulations figure released in September 2005, 2.3 million), along with 5 million at the *New York Times* (compared with 1.1 million), 2.65 million at the *New York Daily News* (690,000), 2.4 million at the *Los Angeles Times* (840,000), 1.8 million at the *Washington Post* (680,000), and 1.65 million at the *Chicago Tribune* (590,000).[5] Moreover, newspapers provide the core editorial content for radio, television, and Internet news sites, from those produced by major media companies to those made by solitary bloggers. Without newspaper reporting, most other news media would have little basis for their journalism.

Despite constant cries from observers who say that the newspaper is doomed, daily papers routinely generate profit levels that dwarf those in other businesses, including Fortune 500 companies, whose average margins in 2004 were around 6 percent, and even Big Oil companies, such as Exxon Mobil, whose record-setting profits in 2005 came from a margin of roughly 16 percent. According to the Project for Excellence in Journalism, in the first six months of 2003 the top thirteen publicly traded newspaper companies had average profit margins of 19 percent. Morton Research reported that the weighted average of profit margins for newspaper divisions of the largest media companies jumped from 13 to almost 21 percent between 1991 and 2004. In 2004 three of the most economically successful chains, Gannett, McClatchy, and E. W. Scripps, earned nearly 30 percent margins, compared to roughly 18 percent at the Tribune Company.[6]

Profits were lower at the publicly traded New York Times Company (16 percent), Washington Post Company (14 percent), and Dow Jones & Company (9 percent), where two-tiered stock systems allow controlling family owners to sustain large investments in journalism at the expense of revenues. Yet even these levels are far above the Fortune 500 norm. The industry is indeed changing. But newspaper reports on the death of newspapers are greatly exaggerated—particularly by the media conglomerates that have something to gain from regulatory changes that allow them to own more local outlets. What is really hurting newspaper companies is not competition but greed.

DURING THE PAST TWO DECADES THE CHICAGO-BASED TRIBUNE COMPANY, a midlevel media conglomerate with outsize aspirations to climb to the top of the nation's leading urban markets, helped lead the industry's aggressive lobbying campaign to eliminate long-standing FCC "cross-ownership" regulations that prohibit one corporation from controlling a newspaper and broadcast station in the same market—unless the arrangement is "grandfathered" into law because of arrangements that predate the restriction, or permitted through a special federal waiver.

More than any other media company, Tribune has wagered its future on repealing the cross-ownership ban. As its president and CEO Dennis FitzSimons recently boasted: "Tribune anticipated deregulation. We acquired Renaissance Communications [which owned six television stations, including WBZL in Miami] in 1997 [for $1.1 billion], giving us a cross-ownership situation in South Florida. We acquired Times Mirror [whose properties included the *Los Angeles Times*] in 2000, giving us cross-ownership situations in Los Angeles, New York and Hartford, Connecticut. We now have five markets where we own both a newspaper and television station."[7] In other words, rather than accept the standard federal cross-ownership laws, FitzSimons used the same strategy that the executives at Sinclair Broadcast Group and Capstar Broadcasting employed on a smaller scale: seeking waivers and lobbying to bring the laws into compliance with his own plans.

With a head start on other media conglomerates, Tribune became the only corporation to own and operate a major newspaper and broadcast television station in each of the top three markets, New York (*Newsday* and WPIX), Los Angeles (*Los Angeles Times* and KTLA), and Chicago (*Tribune* and WGN). It's a strong business model, as FitzSimons attested. "Those three markets have 16 percent of total U.S. population and 25 percent of households with income of more than $150,000," he boasted to shareholders. "Advertisers have to be there." "We're confident in the future of local mass media," added Pat Mullen, the president of Tribune Broadcasting.

For Tribune, no city is as important as Chicago, where it operates its flagship local newspaper; WGN-TV, which broadcasts local sports, news, and entertainment; WGN Radio-720, the region's top-rated AM radio station (which in many ratings periods beats the most popular FM station, Clear Channel's WGCI, as the top station overall); *Chicago*, the city's leading local magazine; Chicagoland's Television (CLTV), the only local cable news and talk station; Metromix.com, the city's top online entertainment and listings guide; ChicagoSports.com, a leading sports Web site; *Hoy*, the city's most popular Spanish-language daily newspaper; and *RedEye*, a weekday tabloid designed to lure young professional readers between the ages of eighteen and thirty-four.

Tribune's corporate leaders are deeply connected to the region's power elite, and the company has made major investments in Chicago's civic life. After the death of longtime editor and publisher Colonel Robert R.

McCormick in 1955, Tribune helped establish the McCormick Tribune Foundation, which makes substantial contributions to universities, schools, and other civic institutions. The Tribune and McCormick names saturate the Chicago metropolitan area, from the monumental McCormick Place convention center on the city's lakefront to the ultramodern McCormick Tribune Center on the Northwestern University campus, where many of the city's future journalists train. To top it off, Tribune also owns the city's beloved sports franchise, the Chicago Cubs.

According to Bruce DuMont, a veteran local broadcaster who once worked at WGN and is the founder and current president of the Museum of Broadcast Communications, Chicago is "a Tribune Company town" because Tribune's diverse media holdings give it "many platforms to influence what people see, hear, and read," and its "well-known and well-endowed institutions give [it] tentacles that reach far and deep in the city." Sitting in the new museum building office space, the garrulous media executive told me that being the headquarters for a giant media company benefits the city, because it gets journalistic and philanthropic attention that most cities—including those where Tribune owns other newspapers—have lost. As in nearly all U.S. metropolitan areas, DuMont said, "our banks are no longer Chicago owned. Our insurance companies are no longer Chicago owned. Our utility companies are no longer Chicago owned, whether it's electric, gas, or the phone company. Our cable system is not locally owned. The only major thing that is still owned is the newspaper and the media company."

Locally owned and operated newspapers are all but obsolete in the contemporary media market—even in major cities such as Los Angeles, Houston, and Miami, whose wealth and sophistication suggest that they could support one. "Today," said Frank Blethen, the outspoken publisher whose family has run the *Seattle Times* for five generations and is currently battling the Hearst Corporation, a conglomerate on a par with Tribune, for control of the Seattle market, "only about 250 of the nation's 1500 newspapers are independently owned and operated," and only a portion of these are locally managed. Speaking at the University of Washington's Democracy Fest just before the 2004 election, Blethen declared that "frighteningly, our nation's newspapers and media are now mostly controlled by a small group of corporations whose only value is more wealth and unbridled control."[8]

In Chicago a growing number of residents and community organizations worry that Tribune's omnipresence gives the conglomerate undue influence in local affairs, and that its multiple platforms for delivering news and entertainment result in Chicagoans seeing, hearing, and reading the same stories, in various forms, over and over during the course of a day. *Chicago Tribune* readers who turn on CLTV or WGN are likely to find print reporters or columnists repeating their accounts from the television news studio now located in the heart of the newspaper office or the radio studio on the ground floor, and are certain to get "cross-promotional" plugs for Tribune's other media products. Jack Fuller, the former president of Tribune Publishing, believes that the company should be entitled to own even more local outlets than it already has. He told the U.S. Senate Committee on Commerce, Science, and Transportation that it is impossible for any media company to dominate a market in a digital age. "In addition to newspapers, magazines, broadcast television and radio," he argued, "now Americans can get news from a proliferation of national all-news cable operations such as CNN, Fox News, and MSNBC, as well as from local cable operations . . . On the Internet they can get news from a wide variety of sites from all over the country and all over the world."[9] Fuller glossed over the problems that most concern Chicagoans: that national cable stations and Internet sites provide virtually no additional local content, and that much of their "news" is actually commentary and entertainment, not the local reporting that newspapers once provided with zeal.

When it comes to local journalism in Chicago and most other U.S. cities, finding primary reporting is increasingly difficult, whether for conventional beats (such as city hall and the neighborhoods) or special investigative projects. Consolidation and the rise of chains have reduced the number of professional news sources, and nowhere has this reduction been more dramatic than in the newspaper industry. According to the U.S. Bureau of Labor Statistics, newspaper employment dropped from 455,700 in 1990 to 381,300 in 2003, and although local newsrooms in small and midsize cities were hit especially hard, papers in major markets were not left unscathed.[10]

Such rampant downsizing only began after major newspaper companies had established monopolies in most U.S. markets, buying up or forcing out independent local owners throughout the nation. The media scholar Phyllis Kaniss wrote that "between 1940 and 1989, New York

City went from having eight to three major metropolitan papers, Los Angeles from eight to one, Boston from nine to two, Philadelphia from five to two . . . and Detroit, Kansas City, Dallas, Cleveland, and St. Louis from three to two."[11] Whereas in 1923 about 40 percent of American cities had more than two daily newspapers and nearly all were locally owned and operated, by 2000 only about 2 percent of cities had more than one paper and roughly 80 percent of all dailies were owned by chains. The legendary press critic A. J. Liebling would have been particularly disturbed by this condition. In 1960 he wrote that "a city with one newspaper, or with a morning and an evening paper under one ownership, is like a man with one eye, and often the eye is glass."[12]

ALTHOUGH CHICAGO IS ONE OF THE FEW AMERICAN CITIES TO RETAIN two major newspapers, Tribune has used its many media outlets to establish a dominant voice. When a story piques the interest of Tribune editors, it echoes through every medium, giving the company extraordinary influence in setting the local agenda. For the *Justice Derailed* series, an ongoing investigation of abuses in the criminal justice system including corruption in capital punishment cases, Tribune has generously backed a team of star journalists and published nine separate multipart series since 1999. "They offered us everything we needed," said Maurice Possley, one of the lead reporters when we spoke. "Time, space, and resources to pursue the investigation. They got us a Lexis-Nexis subscription for the legal research. They didn't demand the story right away. They let us do the reporting, develop it. They gave us full support."

Tribune promoted the series by placing the authors on its radio, television, and Internet outlets. Steve Mills, another lead reporter, explained to me: "I couldn't ask for any more support from the *Tribune*. We did a ton of local media after the report came out. We did CLTV and WGN, and that helped it pop to the national level." Steve Edwards, from the public radio station WBEZ, said that "if the *Tribune* decides something was a major story and runs front-page coverage and repeated editorials on it, you would hear that story topping many local newscasts, you would hear other reporters doing more coverage of that issue. You would hear more roundtable discussions of that most likely on WBEZ and WTTW [the public television station]. You would hear more coverage of it on WGN radio and WGN-TV and on CLTV. There's no question there would be a ripple effect. They have put the death penalty front and center on the agenda, and on that issue they've been huge."

Not only has the *Justice Derailed* project served the city's public interest; it has also helped save the lives of innocent people that the state of Illinois had sentenced to death. The Republican George Ryan, an advocate of capital punishment who was the governor when the *Tribune* initiated its series, publicly acknowledged that the paper's reporting established a compelling case for exonerating wrongfully convicted inmates, pardoning others, and commuting the death sentences of all 156 people that Illinois had condemned to die—an act Ryan committed in his last days in office. "The *Tribune* series left me reeling," Ryan explained. "Half of the nearly three hundred capital cases in Illinois had been reversed for a new trial or re-sentencing. Over half! . . . After seeing, again and again, how close we came to the ultimate nightmare, I did the only thing I could do. Thirteen times we almost strapped innocent men to a gurney, wheeled them to the state's death chamber and injected fatal doses of poison in their veins. I knew I had to act . . . until I can be sure that everyone sentenced to death in Illinois is truly guilty, until I can be sure with moral certainty that no innocent man or woman is facing a lethal injection, no one will meet that fate."[13]

Ryan's decision helped trigger a national political movement that compelled other governors and state legislatures to begin debating their own moratoria on capital punishment. The *Tribune*'s investigations sparked a small journalistic movement, too. "Newspapers in other states tried reproducing what we had done," Possley said. "Our series provided a template." Barry Scheck, a cofounder of the Innocence Project, considers the newspaper's service invaluable. "The *Tribune* reporters played a major role in the death penalty debate," he told me. "Their work made a difference immediately, and it will have a long-term impact, too."

THE DOWNSIDE OF TRIBUNE'S POWER TO SET CHICAGO'S NEWS AGENDA and shape local political debates, however, is that both stories that it ignores and stories that its rivals uncover first are significantly less likely to seize the public's attention. Steve Rhodes, who wrote a local media column for *Chicago* magazine before Tribune took over, said, "Tribune is the eight-hundred-pound gorilla, and that's where most news derives from. The first thing that TV news directors do in the morning is read the *Tribune*. The radio is rip and read. The *Sun-Times* [Chicago's second-largest daily newspaper] is always responding and reacting to the *Tribune*." Bruce DuMont told me that Tribune uses its media holdings to advance its corporate goals and political projects, and to silence its opponents. "They have clout at the local political level, the state level, and the federal political level, because of the coverage that the Tribune Company and its various media entities include. It's not only reporting, but also the editorial coverage. If you're engaged in a project that is not favorable to the Tribune Company, you could end up by not having any media coverage, or bad media coverage. It makes it very difficult to compete." Even Chicago mayor Richard M. Daley, who has enjoyed nearly unchecked personal power in the city for almost two decades, acknowledges the influence of Tribune—particularly when his favorite local sports team, the Chicago White Sox, wins the World Series but gets little attention. "How can you compete with Tribune?" he asked in the fall of 2005. "I mean, give me a break. They own the Cubs, they own WGN Radio [and] TV and CLTV. Come on. You think you are going to get any publicity for the White Sox? You can't. Let's be realistic."[14]

What Daley observed in sports and culture coverage is even more true for hard news. Take the Chicago Housing Authority's Plan for Transformation, a $1.5-billion, ten-year project announced in 2000 that involved demolishing roughly eighteen thousand units of public housing around the city, developing or rehabilitating thousands of others, and moving thousands of families into the private market. According to the city, "Under the CHA Plan for Transformation, all 25,000 leaseholders and their families are asked to relocate at least once—either to a temporary home or to a new or rehabbed permanent home."[15] This was a massive and controversial project, the largest urban-planning initiative for Chicago since the Urban Renewal programs of the 1950s, and it was led by an agency so inept that the federal government put it in receivership during the 1990s. The plan would affect a broad swath of the city, from the places that would gain or lose public housing complexes to the areas that would take in or refuse former CHA residents. In the process, the CHA plan would stir up the most sensitive and difficult urban issues: race, class, crime, discrimination, segregation, government power, and the rights of the poor. Yet local and federal agencies developed and implemented the plan without significant public input, not even from public housing residents.

Immediately, concerned citizens and civic groups began asking important questions. Why had there been so little public participation in the planning stages? Would the city government ensure that there were enough temporary and permanent units to house the relocated people? Would displaced residents have the right to return to their old neighborhoods, several of which were already gentrifying? What would happen to residents' long-standing communities and social networks? What kinds of special services would be available to them? How would the city of Chicago track the relocated people and measure the program's success? These questions were ripe for investigation, yet the *Tribune* made little effort to answer them. The newspaper lists almost fifty journalistic projects on its "special reports" Web site, yet not one concerns public housing.

Jamie Kalven, a local author and community organizer who spent years working in and writing about one of the largest CHA complexes, began our conversation about public housing by calling attention to the glaring inconsistencies between the *Tribune*'s intensive coverage of death penalty cases and its routine neglect of the city's African American neighborhoods, where chronically unemployed men are likely to be unfairly caught up in the dragnet and wrongfully accused. "The *Tribune*'s big series is great," Kalven told me. "But it can hardly compensate for its failure to do daily coverage of the ways that the city and local police are unfairly criminalizing black people and the poor. This is Chicago—the city where Amnesty International filed a report about human rights abuses by local authorities. Where is the regular beat on police violence, the devastating drug war, or corruption in the courts? What about coverage of segregation? Or poverty? You can't make up for that with a special report."

The CHA plan, Kalven argued, is far more important than the *Tribune* has acknowledged. "Chicago is indeed being transformed," he insisted. "Entire communities have been obliterated. Places have been erased. This restructuring of the city can only be compared to the period after the Great Fire of 1871. It represents a failure of various institutions. But above all it's a failure of journalism. The city's dominant journalistic institution, the *Chicago Tribune,* has provided at best intermittent coverage, nothing sustained. This has, in turn, tended to shape coverage by others. I have little doubt that had the *Tribune* inquired deeply and on a sustained basis into the dismantling of public housing, it would have created the occasion and the space for other media to follow its lead."

IN 1975 THE FCC PASSED THE NEWSPAPER-BROADCAST CROSS-OWNERSHIP ban to help ensure that citizens have access to a wide range of sources and perspectives, and that a leading local media company cannot decide which issues or positions get a public hearing and which do not. If one media company (or "voice") dominates the production and distribution of local information in a market, regulators reasoned, that organization could have an unhealthy influence on its political, cultural, and economic life. "The reasons for these rules are simple," explained former U.S. senator Ernest Hollings, a Democrat from South Carolina who said he owed his political career to laws that prevented a local media giant that opposed his candidacy from monopolizing the market and using the position to crush his first campaign. "Diversity in ownership promotes competition. Diversity in ownership creates opportunities for smaller companies, and local businessmen and women. Diversity in ownership allows creative programming and controversial points of view to find an outlet. Diversity in ownership promotes choices for advertisers. And diversity in ownership preserves localism—so individuals in towns across America are afforded access to at least several sources for their local news and information."[16] If there is a public benefit to cross-ownership, Hollings argued, neither media companies nor the FCC have identified it.

In the 1970s broadcast television stations and newspapers were the most popular sources of local news. They still are. Despite the many new sources of information available online or on cable, consumer studies, including those done for the FCC, consistently show that local TV and newspapers are where most people get their news.[17] According to Gene Kimmelman, director of the nonpartisan public-interest group the Consumers Union (which publishes *Consumer Reports*), audience research by his organization showed that "80 percent of consumers say their major source is local broadcast networks and their newspaper."

It's the journalism, not the newsprint, that makes newspapers necessary for self-governance. While our democratic culture could survive the loss of the physical newspaper, it would be endangered without the kinds of reporting that newspapers provide. Newspapers publish exponentially more news and information than TV or radio newscasts, providing greater quantity, diversity, and depth of coverage, with more human resources for proactive investigative reporting (such as the *Tribune*'s death penalty project) and a broad range of local beats. A large metropolitan daily will often run between 80,000 and 100,000 words per issue, whereas a typical thirty-minute local television news broadcast contains between 3,000 and 3,600 words.

If, however, a newspaper company also owns television and radio stations, it can easily use its stronghold on local journalism to promote its own vested corporate interests rather than acting like a news organization, particularly the kind that covers the dangerous consequences of vested interests dictating the news. Consider Milwaukee, where Journal Communications controls the *Milwaukee Journal Sentinel,* WTMJ-TV, WTMJ-AM, and WKTI-FM, all leading outlets. In 1994 and 1995 the city debated whether to support public funding for a new stadium to prevent the Brewers, the local baseball team whose games were broadcast by WTMJ-AM, from leaving town. "In late 1994," reported the Consumers Union, "the CEO of the Journal Group, Robert Kahlor, became head of the Milwaukee committee championing public financing for the stadium, and even registered as chief lobbyist." Did the company's interests affect its coverage? According to Dave Beckman, a media scholar and columnist for a local alternative weekly, "The Journal Company's newspaper, TV news shows and news talk radio station all marched lock-step supporting the public financing position," with the *Journal Sentinel* rallying support for the stadium through its sports pages, news sections, and editorials. The proposal, which after two setbacks in the Wisconsin State Senate ultimately passed by one vote, divided the region. But "the citizens of Milwaukee, despite the contentious nature of the issue, did not have antagonistic voices in the media to rely on."[18]

To prevent such situations, the FCC recommended against eliminating the restriction on cross-ownership in its 2000 biennial review of ownership rules, stating that "the newspaper/broadcast cross-ownership rule should, as a general matter, be retained because it continues to serve the public interest by furthering the important public policy goal of viewpoint diversity." The commission recognized the business efficiencies achieved by cross-ownership but explained that "this result did not necessarily advance the Commission's goal of viewpoint diversity because, without a diversity of ownership or editors, there would be no real diversity of viewpoints."[19] The commission's recommendation was a blow to the Tribune Company, but it hardly took the FCC's decision as final. Instead, Tribune doubled its spending for lobbyists between 2000 and 2003, gambling that it could use other means to persuade regulators to terminate the ban.[20]

The stakes were high for Tribune, which in 2004 owned fourteen newspapers and had an overall daily circulation of 3.6 million, placing it behind only the better-known chains, Gannett and what was then Knight Ridder, in market penetration. (In 2006 Tribune became the nation's second-largest newspaper chain.) Tribune has more outlets in major cities than its competitors, though, and its 2004 revenues, $6.6 billion, were second in the industry to Gannett, which then owned ninety-nine dailies in forty-one states, twenty-one television stations, one hundred Web sites, and dozens of media outlets overseas. Tribune is also the nation's fourth-largest owner of local television outlets, with twenty-six TV stations, including nine in the top ten and eighteen in the top thirty markets. It has extensive investments in emerging TV networks, including one-quarter of the WB and about one-third of the Food Network, and it develops and distributes first-run TV programming through Tribune Entertainment. Tribune was an early investor in AOL and other Internet ventures, and it has ownership stakes in a fleet of Web sites, including BlackVoices.com, and major classified services such as CareerBuilder.com, Topix.net, Cars.com, and Apartments.com. Combining local television, newspapers, and Internet properties is the key to its business model.

TRIBUNE AIMS TO MAKE EACH OF ITS MEDIA HOLDINGS A NODE IN ITS "synergistic" network of news, information, and entertainment makers, and it has developed a "convergence" production and distribution process that achieves an economy of scale by breaking down distinctions between print, broadcast, and Internet platforms. The conglomerate has built sophisticated technological systems for centralizing its journalistic, entertainment, and marketing resources, gaining efficiencies that allow it to keep staff levels lower and profit margins high despite falling newspaper circulation. In the course of one assignment, for example, Tribune reporters will often write a newspaper article, develop special Web content, and appear on a Tribune television or radio station, projecting the story to multiple audiences while promoting the brand. By the early 1990s the former *Tribune* editor James Squires realized that "journalism, particularly newspaper journalism, has no real place in the company's future. No one ever uses the word. The company bills itself as an 'information and entertainment' conglomerate and hopes that newspapers will become a smaller factor in its total business." Most tellingly, Tribune managers redefined their product by abandoning their rhetorical commitment to newspaper journalism and the values it represents. In 1998, when Howard Tyner was editor of the *Tribune,* he told the *American Journalism Review,* "I am not the editor of a newspaper. I am the manager of a content company."[21]

I learned about the transformation from journalism to *content*—a term that carries none of the professional status or craft standards associated with *journalism*—in the late 1990s, when I visited the *Tribune*'s remodeled newsroom and interviewed staff reporters, and again in 2001, when I spent a week at the Tampa News Center in Florida run by another corporation, Media General, a southeastern media company that owns and operates the city's leading television station, newspaper, and Internet sites from an integrated Superdesk.[22] The *Tampa Tribune,* with a weekday circulation above two hundred thousand, and WFLA-TV, the local NBC affiliate, are considerably smaller than the Tribune Company's outlets in Chicago. But Media General's News Center is one of the most technologically advanced and managerially innovative convergence complexes in the world, and media executives regularly visit the site to observe what might happen to local journalism if the cross-ownership ban is repealed.

Both Media General and Tribune have separate editorial staffs responsible for the different platforms they operate, as well as multimedia managers responsible for coordinating work and building relationships between the news teams. Although not all stories produced at the News Center are made to cross platforms, editors and reporters try to maximize newsroom productivity by remaining vigilant for convergence possibilities. Every day the editors from the print, Internet, and broadcast divisions have a fifteen-minute "convergence meeting" to discuss shared projects and evaluate the previous day's work; the company developed the digital News Bank system so that the staff for different media can easily access the news budget (the list of stories slated for the paper) and completed stories before they are published; and every month the multimedia manager compiles a report that lists successful convergence projects and praises staff for participating. "We produced nearly 200 overt acts of convergence in February at the News Center," one internal report reads. For example, "In addition to writing daily stories for the *Tribune,* Winter Olympics reporter Bill Ward appeared nightly on WFLA and wrote regularly and compiled video reports for TBO.com [Tampa Bay Online]. *Tribune* pushes readers to TBO to view postcards from Ward. His *Tribune* notebook ran daily during the Olympics."

These kinds of projects demand new skills, more time, and additional work for everyone involved. According to the managing editor, who oversees the daily editorial meetings and is most responsible for daily production of the paper, "my own job used to be a lot easier, just get out the paper. Now the matrix is a lot more complicated." A sports editor explained that convergence affects the way he makes story assignments and the techniques reporters use to produce stories. "When you cover something now, the first thing you do is write a small TBO.com piece, then you do a TV spot, and *then, finally* you do a [*Tampa*] *Tribune* story. You have to do something for each medium—but *also,* by the time you get to the paper, you have to do something different—figure out what you can add with a newspaper story. So you have to come up with something that works with print. We [also] have to think about multimedia when we make our assignments. Before we used to just send the best writer, but now we have to think about who can do multimedia. If we have one guy going to the Olympics, we need someone who can do it all," by which he meant doing TV. As print reporters in convergence companies are learning, being telegenic is becoming a necessary journalistic skill.

"Journalists' jobs have definitely changed," Media General's Tampa human resource director told me. "These are not regular newsroom jobs. Reporters are writing differently if they're asked to broadcast. Photographers are also doing more. Not only are they going on more assignments, but they're also bringing multiple cameras. Broadcast guys, some with no still background, are now stretching their skills. They now have multiple jobs rather than one, so time management and multitasking are the biggest challenges for them. Our main convergence people are really maxed. I can't imagine asking them to do more."[23]

No one questions that convergence reduces the amount of time newspaper reporters have to conduct interviews, go out in the field, research, and write. While I was in the Media General newsroom I shadowed print-based reporters who were pulled away from their desks to do short television spots or longer stories for television. The *Tampa Tribune* has a much larger business reporting staff than the sister TV station, WFLA, so business reporters regularly write one- or two-minute updates for television while sitting at their desks, then go downstairs to put on makeup and shoot several takes before a mobile television camera unit. On one day I observed that

> after writing her report, Mary comes down to the second-floor studio around 3:45. She has to wait for Graham, the convergence manager, to get ready, and she spends a lot of time standing around chatting. By 4:10 they are ready to shoot. Graham runs the teleprompter while Mary does her one-minute report. Afterward they go to the control room and watch the tape. Graham calls Mary the "one-take wonder" because usually she can get the take right on the first try. But this time there is a problem with the background noise in the newsroom, and they have to shoot it again. Mary returns, waits a few minutes for everyone to get set, and then goes again. This time it works, but she still has to wait for everyone to listen to the tape and watch the video. At 4:20 she returns upstairs to take off her makeup and resume her reporting.

While she was waiting for Graham to prepare the shoot, I asked Mary how she felt about the television work. "Well," she began, "the good part is that it's fun, it's different, it's difficult, and it's interesting for me. It's a break from my regular routine. But a few weeks ago I did TV every day for two weeks. And every day—when you spend forty minutes writing the script, twenty minutes putting on makeup, twenty to thirty minutes taping, and then taking the makeup off—it takes like two hours to do the job. That's two hours—a quarter of my day—and that doesn't help my reporting. At the end of two weeks I was going crazy." Lisa, a *Tribune* religion reporter and a convergence veteran who does more extensive television work, was most disturbed by the non-journalistic, body labor that television demands. "The main thing you spend time on with TV is putting together the way you look. I have to do my hair, and then redo it throughout the day because you know it's not going to hold when you're running around reporting the way we do for print. And I have to bring the right outfits, the right jewelry. And dealing with all this superficial TV stuff just takes a lot of time, and it gets you thinking about other things."

Managers and editors recognize that convergence journalism inevitably leaves journalists less time to report, reflect, and produce stories.[24] According to a top editor in Tampa, with the new arrangements "there's definitely think time lost, and reporting time." This is precisely what Lisa, in Tampa, and several *Chicago Tribune* reporters told me. Newspaper journalists are specifically concerned about new constraints on their work, and they fear that the norms of television news production will take over print as the media production process converges. Lisa explained: "In print I have thirty-five inches—not a huge amount of space, but not short either. When I put on my TV hat I think about what works here—the emotion, the visuals, the sound. But thank God I can then do my print job, because I can't say what I want to say in a one-minute, thirty-second TV segment." The most ardent critics in the newsroom worry not only about lost reporting time but also about how the partnership allows the forms of television news—such as the short report, soft features, and heightened attention to brand-name, celebrity journalists—to penetrate the print medium and facilitate what they disparagingly call "*USA Today*–style papers."[25]

At the *Chicago Tribune,* journalists learned about the company's emerging interest in television when managers decided to build a television news studio in the heart of the newspaper editorial space, directly outside the main editor's door. The studio, designed for the convenience of print reporters contributing TV spots, and also so that viewers would see that the station delivered up-to-the-minute news from *Tribune* journalists, both literally and symbolically centralized the role of television production in the newspaper. The Tampa News Center, which was specially designed to facilitate convergence, is organized around an open "Superdesk" staffed by print, Internet, and television editors. Television producers, along with a bank of fifteen television sets in a semicircle around the desk, dominate the space. Moving print reporters into the TV studio may well improve the overall quality of local news-casts, and in fact Big Media companies make considerable use of one study from the Project for Excellence in Journalism reporting that "stations with cross-ownership—in which the parent company also owns a newspaper in the same market—tended to produce higher qual-ity newscasts."[26] Yet the study did not examine what happens to the quality of newspaper articles under the same conditions, and it's hard to observe either Tribune or Media General without concluding that, where cross-ownership is permitted, the future of newspapers is not only on the Internet but also in television.

IN RECENT YEARS A NUMBER OF WELL-KNOWN NEWSPAPER PUBLISHERS have begun to warn the public about these trends. By the 1990s promi-nent editors and reporters who had so far refrained from addressing how bottom-line pressures had undermined journalistic values began pub-lishing tell-all commercial nonfiction books describing how accountants, marketers, and investment bankers had stormed the newsroom and hijacked its mission. The result was a veritable genre of its own: the news media disaster story. Ironically, though, the damning reports about the downfall of local journalism did not appear in the newspapers that their authors edited, leaving the millions of readers they reached on a daily basis without "news about the news"—except in their bookstores and libraries.

After retiring from an eight-year stint as editor of the *Chicago Tribune,* James Squires published *Read All About It! The Corporate Takeover of America's Newspapers,* in which he complains that "what the news media do for a living today is no longer journalism at all," and that "there no longer is even the illusion that public service is the first goal of the institution." In *The News about the News: American Journalism in Peril,* the *Washington Post* editors Leonard Downie Jr. and Robert Kaiser single out Tribune, which "wants a 30 percent margin," as a com-pany whose commitment to "protecting such high profits can easily undermine the notion that journalism is a public service." But they are equally critical of other chain newspapers that "now belong to giant, publicly owned corporations far removed from the communities they serve. They face unrelenting quarterly profit pressures from Wall Street now typical of American capitalism" and are managed by owners who "see newsrooms as money-eating cost items."[27]

Richard McCord, whose book *The Chain Gang: One Newspaper Versus the Gannett Empire* recounts the story of how Gannett, which owns *USA Today* and nearly one hundred daily newspapers, crippled competitors and shored up monopolies in small and midsize cities across the nation, begins with a publisher complaining that "They [Gannett's managers] are the devil incarnate!"—and proceeds to show why.[28] Under the direction of Al Neuharth, who was CEO from 1973 to 1986, and John Curley, who replaced him, Gannett developed a reputation for ruthless business practices designed to establish local monopolies: jack up advertising rates; downsize the editorial staff (and, where possible, break up the union); shrink the newsroom; then watch the profit margins soar. Gannett's business strategy generated extraordinary profit margins, but its ruthless cost cutting at the expense of local journalism earned it the contempt of reporters and editors everywhere, including at other chains.

In 1974, for example, Gannett bought both daily papers in Oregon's capital, Salem, the *Oregon Statesman* and *Capital Journal,* and merged them into one financial unit. Salem residents worried that Gannett would soon merge the newspapers altogether (it did, in 1980), leaving the city with only one voice. But advertisers did not have to wait this long for monopoly pricing. By 1975 Gannett had raised the rates 43 percent, and local retailers clamored for a new outlet. Encouraged by the opportunity, a Portland company called Community Publications created a new free weekly, the *Community Press,* in March 1976, and it did well enough to add a weekend edition by year's end. Marketplace competition was not part of Gannett's original plan, however, so the chain arranged with a regional company to print its papers for 10 percent below the market rate and transferred N. S. "Buddy" Hayden to serve as publisher and implement "Operation Demolition," which he described as a major initiative "to fatally cripple the *Community Press.*" How did Gannett do it? According to legal files released to McCord, it gave its local staff a list of advertisers to lure away from the *Community Press,* providing cash rewards for each client successfully won over. One memo, from Gannett's advertising executive Wayne Vann, explains: "When an advertiser is demolished from the *Community Press,* you receive a code C for credit of $10.00 per account for each week the account stays demolished. (But the $10 credit is lost for each week the ad goes back into the CP—that is, it is taken away.) The whole idea of the program is to reduce or eliminate each of the advertisers on your base list, while at the same time you keep additional advertisers from advertising in the *Community Press*." McCord found that Gannett "was providing free advertising to keep business out of the weekly"—including more than six thousand dollars' worth to a supermarket on condition that it end its relationship with *Community Press*.[29]

There is nothing unusual about competing for clients, but Community Publications considered Gannett's behavior predatory and anticompetitive, in the legal sense, and after closing the *Community Press* in 1978 it sued the chain for $12 to $18 million in antitrust violations. The two companies settled the case privately just one week before it was scheduled to go to trial. "To avoid exposure, Gannett bought its way out," McCord complains in his book. Gannett announced that the settlement payout "would have 'no material financial impact' on the company," and so "the nation's richest newspaper company could simply weasel out of trouble by writing a check."[30] Emboldened by the experience, Gannett steamrolled over competitors in other American cities in similar fashion. McCord highlights cases in New Mexico and Wisconsin where he had helped private owners win hard-fought legal and journalistic victories to prevent Gannett from taking over their markets and replacing quality local newspapers with cookie-cutter dailies. But these are exceptional stories in recent urban history, and the proof of Gannett's domination may well be visible on a newspaper box near you.

Gannett's business practices are infamous in the newspaper industry, but the chain's public reputation comes from its generic formula for mass-producing "reader-friendly" local papers: pare down news space on the page (the news hole) and cram with ads; replace hard news with wire copy and superficial local reports, how-to stories, quality-of-life and entertainment features, question-and-answer columns, and lots of "happy news." According to the company, local information is the key to market success. But the newspaper scholar Aurora Wallace argues that the industry Gannett leads "champions the local in the abstract as it commits fewer and fewer resources to its service." For example, rather than build up the editorial staff for professional local reporting, Gannett pushes populist, "civic journalism" projects, encouraging residents to write folksy tales about their community's positive features. "We're all reporters, because each of us tells stories," says the introductory film at its Newseum complex in Virginia. So who, after all, needs to pay trained journalists to do any deep digging?[31]

It's indisputable that Neuharth invented a recipe for increasing newspaper profit margins, which soared from below 10 percent when the papers were owned by families and small business to nearly 40 percent during prosperous periods of Gannett management. But the business model has degraded reporting at some of the best local dailies in America, including the *Des Moines Register,* the *Asbury Park Press,* and the *Louisville Courier-Journal.* These publications had earned their professional reputations through decades of aggressive, hard-hitting journalism focused on their hometowns. Once Gannett took over, managers from the McLean, Virginia, headquarters descended to hollow them out, stuffing the pages with gimmicky projects designed to create the impression of local engagement. "The results," wrote the columnist and former *Des Moines Register* editor Geneva Overholser, "are brittle and lifeless . . . Our newspapers do not read as if they are written and edited by people who feel the city's pulse, who've long walked its streets, who love its quirks, know its history, and care deeply about its future—because, by and large, they are *not.*"[32]

GANNETT HAS BEEN SPEARHEADING BIG MEDIA'S TAKEOVER OF LOCAL newspapers for decades, but in the late 1990s and early years of the twenty-first century it was Hollinger International, directed by the media mogul and British Lord Conrad Black and President and Chief Operating Officer David Radler, that escalated corporate aggression against dailies and their readers into an outright war on journalism—especially at its main U.S. publication, the *Chicago Sun-Times.*

Black, who was born into a wealthy family and became enamored of William Randolph Hearst during childhood, began his career in publishing by purchasing the *Sherbrooke Record,* an English-language daily in Quebec, in the late 1960s. "We like to joke that Sherbrooke is where Conrad Black learned to rape and kill," said one of the paper's veteran employees in the documentary *Citizen Black.* "This is the place he learned his operating methods." In 1971 he and Radler, his business partner, started to acquire additional papers in their native Canada through a holding company called Sterling Newspapers, and in the late 1970s they acquired Hollinger International. Soon Hollinger had become the nation's leading owner of daily papers, and it reached overseas to purchase major international publications such as London's *Daily Telegraph,* the *Sydney Morning Herald,* and the *Jerusalem Post.*[33] When speaking before a Canadian government panel assembled to address mounting fears of media consolidation in the 1980s, Radler famously quipped that his greatest contribution to journalism was "the three-man newsroom—and two of them sell ads."

In 1994 Hollinger made its most significant U.S. acquisition, purchasing the *Sun-Times* from an investment group led by Adler & Shaykin. The second paper in the Second City—and a tabloid at that—the *Sun-Times* was still one of the top ten U.S. dailies, though its reputation for gritty city news reporting and aggressive investigations that it had earned under its original owners, Chicago's Marshall Field family, had been fading since they sold the paper to Rupert Murdoch in 1984. (Murdoch flipped it two years later after buying a local TV station and coming up against the cross-ownership ban.) Black and Radler made Chicago Hollinger's corporate headquarters, acquiring a fleet of small community publishers in the metropolitan area, including Pioneer Press Newspapers, Star Newspapers, Suburban Chicago Newspapers, and the *Daily Southtown,* so that they could consolidate operations and offer special advertising packages to clients.

Once their mini-empire was in place, the duo got down to business, flushing out nonunionized journalists, refusing to replace departing staff even when top reporters on key beats left, and eventually instituting a hiring freeze that slowly bled the paper dry. One veteran told me that when he first came to the *Sun-Times* there were no empty desks in the newsroom, so he had to type out his stories when other reporters were out of the office. After a few years under Hollinger management there were empty desks everywhere. The editors and reporters worked fanatically to put out a serious daily; yet without an adequate supply of journalists it was hard to regularly produce in-depth reports on Chicago's key institutions. Morale plummeted, as did the quality of the paper.

An overworked staff of city reporters, sports writers, and sharp columnists kept the *Sun-Times* afloat, while the paper continued to receive attention for its celebrity writers, including Robert Novak, Roger Ebert, Rick Telander, and Richard Roeper. Despite the pressures that made labor-intensive reporting difficult, the *Sun-Times* managed to publish an occasional investigative piece, most notably a three-part series in 2004 called "Clout on Wheels: The Scandal of Chicago's Hired Truck Program," in which Tim Novak and Steve Warmbir revealed that Mayor Richard M. Daley's administration "spen[t] $40 million a year hiring private trucks that perform[ed] little or no work in a program corrupted by mob influence and patronage." The series, which provided the names and locations of the firms and owners in on the scheme, sent shock waves through Chicago and embarrassed Daley, who prided himself on reinventing city government so that it ran like an efficient business. In fact, the report uncovered the kinds of corruption that Chicagoans expected from the first Mayor Daley, not his son.[34]

Hard-hitting investigations such as "Clout on Wheels" were once a standard feature of the *Sun-Times,* and veterans there speak proudly about their history of digging up important local stories that the *Tribune* missed. When I did fieldwork in the newsroom during 2002, however, the journalists universally complained that all but two or three of them were too busy with daily assignments to conduct long-term projects.

Everyone at the *Sun-Times* knew that Black and Radler considered the paper a cash cow, but the extent to which they milked it did not become clear until August 31, 2004, when a special committee of Hollinger's own board of directors released a 513-page report accusing the duo of looting some $400 million from the company—about 95 percent of its profits from 1997 to 2003. The committee, which was led by the special counsel and former SEC chairman Richard Breeden but did not include the celebrity conservatives Black had handpicked for his informal advisory board (including Richard Perle, Henry Kissinger, Margaret Thatcher, and George Will), found evidence of "an overwhelming record of abuse, overreaching, and violations of fiduciary duties by Black and Radler, the two controlling shareholders," and accused them of establishing a "corporate kleptocracy . . . in which ethical corruption was a defining characteristic of the leadership team." The report alleged that in addition to "nearly $200 million in excessive and unjustifiable management fees," Black and Radler took some $15 million in corporate cash without notifying the board; paid roughly $90 million to themselves and their cronies for fraudulent noncompete agreements; spent $61.3 million on private jets that were often used "for their own prestige, comfort, and convenience"; offered Black's wife $1.1 million annually for a "no-show job"; and made major charitable contributions with Hollinger funds that resulted in named honors—the "Black Family Foundation Wing" at the Hospital for Sick Children in Toronto and the "Radler Business Wing" at Queens University—for the executives.[35]

The report in Kingston, Ontario, served as the basis for shareholder suits, such as a $540-million case against Black, Radler, and other members of their leadership team, and another against board members that was settled out of court for $50 million in May 2005. It also helped spur a grand jury to pursue criminal investigations of Black and Radler, with Radler ultimately entering a plea-bargain agreement to pay a $250,000 fine and serve a twenty-nine-month prison sentence for mail fraud in exchange for cooperation in the ongoing probes of Black by federal prosecutors and the SEC. When the investigation began, Black issued a public statement complaining that, "like all fads, corporate governance has its zealots, and its tendency to excess." He was equally defiant when it ended and criminal charges were looming, initially refusing to relinquish control of his media properties, then plotting to pin responsibility for corporate malfeasance on Radler, and finally threatening that the government would ultimately have to compensate him for its own wrongdoings. As his attorney, Greg Craig, told the *Wall Street Journal,* "There was no fraud, and the federal government will soon be paying it all back, with interest."[36]

Craig's remark made little impact on Patrick Fitzgerald, the U.S. Attorney prosecuting Black's case. On November 17, 2005, the grand jury indicted Black on eight counts of mail and wire fraud, among other charges, the maximum penalty for which is forty years in prison and a $2-million fine. "What has gone on here is the grossest abuse by directors and insiders," Fitzgerald announced. "The indictment charges that insiders at Hollinger—all the way to the top of the corporate ladder— whose job it was to safeguard the shareholders, made it their job to steal and conceal." The SEC also brought civil charges against Black for the same acts, and prosecutors sought additional penalties for Hollinger executives.

Black may go to prison if he is convicted of the criminal charges, but that is unlikely. Hollinger investors may recoup some of the losses they suffered at his hands, but not all. There may be more lawsuits, criminal investigations, and special inquiries. And the *Sun-Times,* which remains a Hollinger paper (though perhaps not for much longer), may find its way into better hands. But the citizens of Chicago cannot demand compensation for the damage Hollinger did to one of their leading news organizations, and they have no way to measure the costs Hollinger inflicted on their democratic culture. Like residents of so many other American cities, they can only imagine how many stories—about corporate fraud, government corruption, or any number of social and economic trends that affect their everyday lives—went unreported while media moguls looted their hometown.

HOLLINGER IS A SPECTACULAR AND EXTREME EXAMPLE OF WHY TREATING the news primarily as a source of revenue—and secondarily, at best, as a source of reporting—can have disastrous consequences; and there's nothing to suggest that Black's peers in the newspaper business have been similarly corrupt. Yet even when management acts ethically, the standard economic pressures that push newspapers to cut back on journalism routinely hurt cities, depriving residents of the chance to learn vital information about the institutions that help determine their fate.

Consider just a few of the issues that local papers with downsized editorial staffs missed in recent years. Today we know about Enron, but not because of the *Houston Chronicle*'s investigative journalism or even its regular business coverage. Until national publications exposed the crooked company's extraordinary malfeasance, the *Chronicle* never scrutinized the source of its wealth. Although the *Fortune* magazine writer Bethany McLean, working off a tip from a skeptical hedge fund manager named James Chanos, raised questions about Enron's financial reporting and stock valuation in a March 2001 feature story, "Is Enron Overpriced?" the *Chronicle* did not immediately follow up. In the *Columbia Journalism Review,* Scott Sherman reported that "on August 19, 2001, in response to [CEO Jeffrey] Skilling's resignation and a concurrent fall in the stock price, the *Houston Chronicle* business columnist Jim Barlow announced: 'It's still a company with innovative people who have shown they can turn ideas into profitable businesses. That's why the current problems will blow over.'"[37] Not until October 31, 2001, the day after federal regulators upgraded their inquiry into Enron's financial transactions, did the *Chronicle* begin to change its tune.

In San Francisco the independent weekly *Bay Guardian* used to run an annual feature on the top stories that the city's major papers—the

Chronicle (which is owned by the Hearst Corporation) and *Examiner* (which used to be controlled by Hearst but is now a free tabloid owned by the Denver billionaire Philip Anschutz)—failed to cover. Inspired by Project Censored, the media research group at Sonoma State University that publishes yearly lists of twenty-five domestic and international stories that didn't make the mainstream news, the *Bay Guardian* asked journalists and community leaders to identify unreported local issues. In 1999, for example, one of the weekly's panel of experts complained that the big papers had inadequately covered the sweeping deregulation of the energy industry, failing to explain a bill that helped utilities and large users but harmed residential consumers and small businesses. Two years later this issue would return with a vengeance, when an unprecedented series of rolling blackouts made residents of the Golden State wonder why they hadn't been warned that this might happen. The *Bay Guardian* also criticized the dailies for doing little reporting on the labor practices of local companies, pointing out that the San Francisco–based Gap, which leading international organizations had condemned for using child workers, deserved more serious scrutiny at home. Like Enron in Houston or WorldCom in Clinton, Mississippi, the story on San Francisco's corporate behemoth made national headlines before it was featured in the local news.

Corporate malfeasance usually begins at home, and in the 1990s American dailies had a heaping grab bag of stories waiting for them just outside the newsroom. In how many towns did Wal-Mart force employees to work overtime without pay or lock in the night staff? And how many years did it take for these practices to make the news before they were uncovered by writers for national magazines? The rise of national chain news production also helped redefine the measures that journalists use to assess the economy. Business reporters who lacked time, resources, and editorial directives to cover local companies, workers, and labor market conditions ramped up their quick and easy coverage of stock values while neglecting to examine why the average American was working more hours, taking home comparable pay, and bearing the burden of more personal debt than he or she did in 1970. When the boom cycle of the 1990s came to an end and economists warned that the bubble was bursting, most reporters failed to look at corporate chicanery in their own backyards.

Local news organizations have not adequately explained who pays the price when large corporations threaten to leave their hometowns, taking hundreds or thousands of jobs with them unless the government doles out generous subsidies and tax breaks. Nor have they reported the public risks when state agencies outsource important services, including educating children and providing health care to the elderly and poor, to private firms who offer to do it for less. These kinds of stories should be the journalistic core of local newspapers. But when the editorial staff is small, or estranged from hometown institutions, or too busy to investigate, complicated issues and hidden corporate or political practices don't make it into print until the damage has been done.

ACCORDING TO THE *AMERICAN JOURNALISM REVIEW,* WHICH IN THE late 1990s initiated an investigative series on the state of American newspapers, consolidation and editorial downsizing in the industry have resulted in a dramatic loss of state-level political reporting at the very moment when it is most necessary. Since the Reagan presidency, a series of New Federalist social policies have delegated more power from Washington to the states, while the declining political power of city governments—whose base of affluent residents fled to the suburbs and formed a new suburban power bloc—has made statehouses the key sites of local decision making, even in states such as New York, California, and Illinois. The kinds of crucial decisions that are in the hands of state government include whether and how to use capital punishment, mandatory minimum sentencing, and juvenile justice systems; how to regulate the energy and utility sectors; how to allocate public education spending; and how and where to use funds from the Department of Homeland Security. With rare exceptions, stories about state-level politics are the exclusive province of local news organizations—or, as is increasingly the case, they are not covered at all. As Charles Layton and Mary Walton reported, "A survey of capital press rooms shows that most have fewer reporters today than in the recent past . . . In capital press rooms around the country, there are more and more empty desks and silent phones. Bureaus are shrinking, reporters are younger and less experienced, stories get less space and poorer play, and all too frequently editors just don't care."[38]

The absence of political reporters is even more striking in small towns, where lesser-known chains such as Liberty Group Publishing and Community Newspaper Holdings acquired scores of community papers across the country, pared down the editorial staff, pumped up the pages with news from wire services, consolidated printing operations, even merged editions with other publications nearby. According to Aurora Wallace, "Community weeklies were once indispensable sources for coverage of local events which no other news outlets would cover: town council meetings, school board decisions, youth sports . . . and all the assorted activities of local citizens . . . The owners of such newspapers have historically been residents of the places where the newspapers were printed and had vested interests in the health of the communities where they operated."[39] Consolidation at this level of the market usually happens silently, however, because in small towns there is rarely anyone outside of the community paper who reports on local news.

Big-city political reporting has not been spared, either. In the late 1990s and early years of the twenty-first century, for example, San Francisco's daily papers failed to report on an issue that directly affects much of the city's population: a financial crisis generated by the clumsy, corrupt, and incompetent commercial development of the Presidio, a former army base that is now San Francisco's "crown jewel" and was recently declared part of the National Park Service. The Presidio is home to many threatened plant species and is an ecological treasure on coastal land adjacent to the Golden Gate Bridge. In 1996 the U.S. Congress established the Presidio Trust, charging it with the novel task of making the park financially self-sufficient by 2013. Originally, the trust hoped to raise funds by refurbishing and renting out the eight hundred army buildings remaining on the premises as residential units, but it soon expanded its scope. In 1999 its board began negotiations to lease the park's decrepit Letterman Hospital to the filmmaker George Lucas for $5.8 million annually (about 14 percent of the park's yearly operating costs); Lucas has since built the Letterman Digital Arts Center on the grounds. Initially, local activists raised fears that a full-scale sell-off would soon turn the precious parkland into the city's next Fisherman's Wharf, complete with tourist hotels, cheesy amusement parks, and chain restaurants. A few city reporters pursued the story of preservationists and environmentalists battling the trust's plans for growth. But none of the major local news organizations dug deeply into the issue.

A freelance journalist named Kerry Tremain began to uncover the
story that they missed: In 1998 the trust hired the former air force pilot
James Meadows as its executive director, but if the board asked for
references, it must not have read them carefully. The highlights of
Meadows's job history include wildly overspeculating on real estate
projects around Phoenix, Arizona, eventually bankrupting his corporation, Cardon Meadows, and leaving taxpayers the bill. While the
company was failing, Meadows cut off payments to his suppliers, threatening never to pay them unless they continued working without immediate compensation. According to one local attorney representing a
plumbing firm, "many small companies here lost everything" because
of Cardon Meadows's shady practices, and Meadows was named in
thirty-five lawsuits against his organization. After another failed partnership, this one with Gordon Hall (who would later be convicted of
illegally paying stock promoters associated with the mob to increase
his company's share values), Meadows himself filed personal bank-
ruptcy. And in 1990 Meadows tried to start a home-building division
at Castle & Cooke in Bakersfield, California, yet he left in 1994 when
the company's weak performance resulted in significant layoffs and
neighborhood groups filed suit against the firm. One can only imagine
how many realtors dreamed of spearheading development on the Presidio project. But, with no one looking closely and no watchdogs in the
newsroom, Meadows's record earned him the job.

It didn't take long for Meadows to repeat his business history.
Tremain, who began investigating the trust at his own expense after
reading local news coverage and feeling dissatisfied with its reporting, wrote that in only a few years "Meadows has wreaked havoc with
the trust's finances and reputation. The agency's building program is
stalled, and its plans to achieve self-sufficiency are leaking badly . . .
He is widely distrusted and has created an organization saddled with
egregious cost-overruns, cover-ups, a disgruntled real estate community,
and staff turmoil . . . The park's future is already in financial peril."
How did he do it this time? Meadows hired an old friend, Bruce
Anderson, who had worked with him in Denver, to run the trust's facilities department, which employed over 300 of the trust's 460 workers;
Anderson's wife ran the procurement department, which handled bids
from the private contractors who competed for park projects. The
work crews that the Andersons hired for renovations consistently billed

twice as much as they initially estimated, with cost overruns reaching the millions. The trust failed to demolish the extant structures that it had to clear for Lucas to begin his project, so the expected revenues from the lucrative lease arrangement didn't materialize. Meadows did make sure that the Officers' Club was ready for a Russian art exhibition, even though the fast-paced project required so much overtime that the final bill, for $2 million, was almost four times the estimate. Tremain reported that the invitation-only opening party featured "Russian caviar, giant ice sculptures, champagne, and fine California wines, paid for with trust funds." Indeed, Meadows indulged in the perks of his post, driving a BMW convertible, flying first-class, and living rent-free in a six-thousand-square-foot mansion overlooking the park—but only after the trust spent eighty thousand dollars to renovate it.

None of this was public knowledge before tiny *San Francisco* magazine published the results of Tremain's six-month investigation, for which they paid him six thousand dollars. ("About the same amount I would have gotten if I had interviewed a celebrity chef instead of doing investigative work," he told me.) Tremain's reporting, which earned him a nomination for the National Magazine Award in the Public Interest category, made a major impact, ultimately prompting follow-up coverage from San Francisco's large news organizations and pressuring the trust's board to urge Meadows to resign and to replace him with a more qualified developer. We can only speculate how much damage to the trust's finances could have been prevented if the local newspapers had looked more closely at the issue that was hidden before them in plain sight. For now, though, the park's future remains uncertain, with Congress threatening to increase the scale of commercial development in the Presidio if the trust does not make progress toward its goal of self-sufficiency by 2013.

In the heyday of city newspapers one of San Francisco's dailies might have hired Tremain to conduct investigations similar to the Presidio report full-time. But there is little support for an investigative reporting staff in contemporary papers, especially in cities where there is no serious local competition. Despite the success of his story, Tremain could not continue the Presidio project and regretted, he said, that [he] wasn't able to adequately explore perhaps the bigger issue in any depth—the very uncomfortable trade-offs involved at the nexus of private and public interests that the park's development raises." San Francisco, Tremain admitted, actually gets significantly more journalistic attention than its neighbors in the region. "I'll tell you a giant black hole of reporting," he offered. "Oakland. Nobody is interested in Oakland. You have a local newspaper, the *Tribune,* that used to be the center of power in the city. The fact that it had the largest tower in Oakland meant something. Now they demand quick turnover and quick stories but don't cover the city well. At the magazine level, *Diablo* and *San Francisco* are two big regional magazines. But I've never seen a story on Oakland in *San Francisco,* and you couldn't sell an Oakland story to *Diablo* to save your life."

With no market in Oakland, and the local issues involving San Francisco's park system fading away, Tremain looked beyond the region and wrote about President Bush's drive to privatize national parks. That wasn't professionally viable, either. As Tremain put it, cities may pay a price for losing investigative reporters, but for journalists "doing investigative reporting freelance is an almost guaranteed way to go broke."

THE TRIBUNE COMPANY INSISTS THAT LOCAL JOURNALISTS WILL CONtinue to disappear from the media landscape unless the FCC allows cross-ownership, helping newspaper companies convert to convergence and thereby make its business even more profitable. During the media policy debates of the past decade, Tribune lobbyists and executives threatened that the company could not afford strong editorial staffs if it was prohibited from combining a newspaper and television broadcast station to achieve an economy of scale in a single market. Yet residents of Los Angeles, New York, and Hartford, cities where Tribune had already established cross-ownership of a television station and newspaper, had cause to doubt the company's commitment to maintaining robust journalism staffs under any conditions. They had experienced firsthand the reality that, contrary to its rhetoric, after acquiring new newspapers Tribune makes deep cuts to the editorial division, eliminates foreign and domestic bureaus, and replaces them with content from its hubs, the *Chicago Tribune* and *Los Angeles Times.*

Editors and reporters worry that the kind of investigative reporting and intensive local coverage that the company now supports in its top markets is threatened by the expansion of its business, and that, for instance, the *Tribune* and *Times* bureaus will not provide local perspectives on national and international issues that affect their readers. In Los Angeles, the *Times*'s highly regarded editor John Carroll resigned because Tribune—reeling from a judicial ruling that it was liable for paying the federal government roughly $1 billion in back taxes and interest owed by Times Mirror—imposed a series of sweeping layoffs, reducing the editorial staff from more than 1,140 to 940. Local civic leaders in Los Angeles are particularly anxious about the absence of a locally owned and operated newspaper whose management has a special commitment to the community. The *Times* continued winning Pulitzers once Tribune took over, but newsroom morale deflated when managers in Chicago hardly acknowledged its success.[40]

After the transition critics complained that the *Times* lost its connection to Los Angeles, where issues such as immigration and the international entertainment business could make the city an ideal laboratory for journalism that explores global issues in a local context, circulation at the *Times* plummeted at a rate more than twice the industry average, falling from over one million to 851,500 by March 2006, partly as a result of its editorial estrangement. The former *Times* book review editor Steve Wasserman wrote that "there is a strong feeling within the newsroom . . . that its Chicago masters regard Los Angeles as an alien planet whose denizens are made of different DNA." Moreover, he argued, "There is no consensus within the paper as to who it represents or what, if anything, it should stand for. It has no voice; it lacks gravitas." The editors did make one major decision, however. In October 2005, the *Times* announced it would attempt to regain readers by running shorter articles and more celebrity stories.[41]

In Baltimore editors and reporters complain that the *Sun* has lost much of its staff because, as its Newspaper Guild representative Michael Hill said, Tribune "has decided that this city can't afford the kind of paper that the *Sun* has been for a century and more."[42] Tribune's response: in fall 2005 it offered a voluntary employee buyout plan, with the goal of reducing the staff by another 75 people. Weeks later Tribune announced similar plans for its papers in Hartford, Connecticut; Orlando, Florida; Newport News, Virginia; and Allentown, Pennsylvania. Ultimately, Tribune added its big-city papers to the chopping block, too, paring 45 newsroom staffers from New York's *Newsday,*

85 journalists from the *Los Angeles Times,* and about 220 employees from the *Chicago Tribune.*[43]

Tribune's cutbacks to its local newsrooms continued through 2006. But that fall Los Angeles civic leaders began to fight back. On September 12, a group of twenty prominent citizens, including former U.S. Secretary of State Warren Christopher, wrote a public letter to Tribune management, calling on the corporation "to keep the *Los Angeles Times* a vibrant paper." The authors, responding to rumors that additional layoffs to the reporting staff were imminent, declared that "we have watched with concern as our newspaper has repeatedly reduced the size of its staff, cut the space given to news and declined in circulation . . . All newspapers serve an important civic role, but as a community voice in the metropolitan region, the *Los Angeles Times* is irreplaceable. We are not quite sure this is fully understood by those outside our community." If Tribune was unwilling to make "an even larger investment in the *Times,*" they concluded, "perhaps a different mode of ownership would better serve Los Angeles."[44]

The growing campaign to defend journalism at the *Times* got an unexpected boost the next week, when Dean Baquet, the *Times* editor, and Jeffrey Johnson, the publisher, openly defied Tribune's orders to impose another round of newsroom layoffs while keeping operating expenses flat. Baquet and Johnson were immediately summoned to Chicago, and before they left neither man knew if he would remain a Tribune employee for long. In October, Tribune ousted Johnson but said it would retain Baquet, at least for the time. Dennis FitzSimons, the CEO, announced that Tribune would begin to consider selling off some of its properties and unwinding its troublesome partnership with the Chandler family. Investors reacted enthusiastically, yet the citizens' response—like so many other unreported stories in the age of media consolidation—is news we'll never know.

6

CHAINING THE ALTERNATIVES

It's 1977. The Bronx is burning, Son of Sam is on the loose, and a two-day blackout cripples New York City. Yet one of Manhattan's most dramatic surprises comes when the archconservative media mogul Rupert Murdoch buys the nation's most famous alternative weekly news publication, the *Village Voice*. The paper's notoriously outspoken and politically progressive editorial staff had already accused the previous owner and editor, *New York* magazine's publisher Clay Felker, of dulling the *Voice*'s editorial edge, reining in writers' freedom, and displacing serious news stories with soft features and lifestyle reporting. But Murdoch, who acquired the *Voice*, *New York*, and the *New York Post* to establish beachheads in the U.S. media market, threatened these values even more, and his takeover nearly inspired an insurgency. According to a column by the staff writer Alexander Cockburn, Murdoch could be treated the way unwanted chieftains once were in New Guinea: "they would take [him] out to the mountainside, stretch him out, and smash his testicles flat with a rock."[1] Only an "alt weekly" (as the genre came to be called) would print such a threat to its new owner, and only an alt weekly editor would fight to protect the author who made it. Despite Murdoch's efforts to have Cockburn fired, the writer's byline returned in subsequent issues. The Australian magnate gradually learned that an antiestablishment attitude and a license to print what the respectable dailies suppressed were the sources of the *Voice*'s popularity. Keeping his hands off the paper, Murdoch let it line his pockets instead.

Had they known this would happen, the three men who founded the *Voice* in 1955 might never have printed the first issue. Dan Wolf, forty, his upstairs neighbor, Edwin Fancher, thirty-one, and the writer Norman Mailer, thirty-two, had great literary ambitions but modest expectations about the scope of the *Voice*'s coverage and the size of its audience. After all, another Village weekly, *Caricature,* folded just a few years before, and the area already had the *Villager,* a paper stuffed with ads, announcements, apartment listings, and light news."[2] Fancher and Mailer each put five thousand dollars into the project, Wolf agreed to become editor in chief so long as he could be an equal partner, and they rented a two-room office at 22 Greenwich Avenue. In the first issue, published October 26, 1955, and featuring a front-page photograph of folk musicians in Washington Square, they printed an introductory article proclaiming that the *Voice* "will serve not merely the Village proper but also the Cooper-Stuyvesant, Gramercy Park, Lower East Side, and Chelsea areas. Its editors expect it to have a wide circulation in uptown New York and elsewhere, since it is in part intended to provide thoroughgoing coverage of the special entertainment and other features of this unique neighborhood. They foresee a net paid circulation for the Voice of at least 10,000."

For a nickel, readers received twelve pages of surprisingly boilerplate local news reporting, bold social and political commentary, edgy humor, extensive cultural coverage, and serious arts criticism from a roster of eclectic writers. Readers also became part of a happening, helping to support a countercultural movement that would speak to and stand for a growing number of young Americans who did not find their concerns reflected in the daily newspapers. It took a while. Only about 2,500 people bought the first issue, and the publishers lost one thousand dollars per week for the first few months of operation. Yet the letters from readers, so witty and well written that they soon became a featured part of the paper, signaled that the paper was hitting one of the city's central nerves. Mailer's columns, which began in January 1956, boosted the *Voice*'s public profile, and Wolf attracted a number of distinguished contributors by offering them a chance to bare their souls with intensely personal and brutally honest writing that would infuse the page with attitude. But he couldn't keep Mailer, whose frustration with the project proved uncontainable. After four months as a columnist, the temperamental writer alienated many of his colleagues and editors, complained that as a minority owner he had "no real voice in the control of anything except [his] column," and left the city for Europe. Mailer would ultimately return to the paper, yet as he made his first dramatic exit he huffed that the *Voice* had become "remarkably conservative for so young a paper."

From today's perspective, however, what's striking is that the early issues of the *Voice* were remarkably local, with news and cultural reporting that consistently featured the West Village. Photographs of Washington Square appeared regularly on the front page, as did news stories about New York University, neighborhood development, the housing crunch, and conflicts over the public culture of bohemians. The paper localized city and national stories, using Village characters or institutions as pegs for reports about the arms race or the civil rights movement. On May 11, 1960, for example, the main page-one story on civil disobedience to protest air-raid drills featured a demonstration at the Women's House of Detention on Greenwich Avenue, and on July 23, 1964, the lead story on the "weekend riots in Harlem" commented on its effects, or lack thereof, in the Village. Its regular features, such as the Village Square, Saloon Society, On Campus, the lengthy letters section (which identified the street where each writer lived), and the Press of Freedom (where readers could pen their own articles) also kept a tight focus on the neighborhood, as did its political coverage. Its ads promoted small retailers, movie houses, hotels, and nightspots, and its classifieds, both the Public Notices and Village Bulletin Board sections, were full of local offers and humorous communications. Although the editors continued reaching for a national audience, they were not shy about their parochial commitments, and by the end of their first successful year they had changed the front-page header from "A Weekly Newspaper Designed to be Read" to "A Weekly Newspaper of Greenwich Village."

By 1958 the *Voice* had earned the header "A Weekly Newspaper that Helped to Save Greenwich Village," though it never printed such a boastful claim. In its first years, the *Voice* emerged as a galvanizing force in the fight to prevent Robert Moses, New York's legendary "power broker" and modern planner, from lowering the wrecking ball on the neighborhood in order to build a four-lane highway, twelve feet for each lane, straight through Washington Square Park. (One reason for the project, Moses insisted, was that developers south of the park had been "formally, officially, and reliably promised a Fifth Avenue address," and to do this they had to bisect the park with a road.) As local publishers with a deep interest in preserving the Village's unique charms, Wolf and Fancher joined with organizers such as Shirley Hayes and Jane Jacobs to lead the campaign for preservation and self-determination. The highway, Wolf wrote, would be "the beginning of the end of Greenwich Village as a community . . . Washington Square Park is a symbol of unity in diversity . . . It brings together Villagers of enormously varied interests and backgrounds." Wolf devoted the prime real estate he controlled—the *Voice* front page and news sections—to the cause. Leading urban critics such as Jacobs and Lewis Mumford authored important articles, Charles Abrams proclaimed the "revolt of the urbs," and the staff writer Mary Perot Nichols reported on the backdoor politics driving the city's development. When the battle moved from the streets to city hall, wrote the *Voice* historian Kevin McAuliffe, "the *Voice* was the paper of the movement against Moses."[3] On this issue, at least, the countercultural weekly provided a platform from which neighborhood residents and preservationists could speak louder than the ultimate insider and power broker. In 1959 the Board of Estimate killed the highway proposal, ruling instead that Washington Square Park would be permanently closed to traffic. It remains that way today.

Yet the *Voice* would not stay a Village paper much longer. After winning the neighborhood battle, the editors staked out journalistic territory in the rest of the city, mounting a case against corruption at Tammany Hall and becoming a beacon of urban reform, supporting Republican candidates such as John Lindsay rather than the Democratic machine. The *Voice*'s cultural coverage broadened as well, and by the 1960s it had become a vital organ for the nation's many emerging social movements and cultural experiments. The Village, as its editors liked to say, had already become a state of mind rather than a place. The paper expanded, giving news reporters and even art critics the space to write long-format articles, adding high-profile columnists, and opening its pages to sustained battles over the most divisive issues of the time, from feminism to black power, abortion to the Cold War. It continued to feature local issues, and its most prominent columnists engaged in fierce debates over the Village's unions, public schools, political representatives, community organizations, and, of course, cultural activities, many of which had national significance. But the balance of coverage gradually shifted as the paper expanded, with metropolitan, national, and international coverage outweighing the neighborhood offerings. By 1968, the paper's header was changed to "The Weekly Newspaper of New York," and cover stories were less likely to feature the Village. The paper's circulation grew, as did its influence. Prominent magazines such as the *New Yorker* began mimicking the *Voice's* style and tone, occasionally even hiring away its best writers. Cultural entrepreneurs in cities from San Francisco and Seattle to Chicago and Boston created new weeklies based loosely on the *Voice's* model, providing both news about alternative ways of life and alternative news about issues that the daily papers were ignoring or covering poorly. The weeklies expressed the free-spirited, antiestablishment sentiment that blossomed in places like Haight-Ashbury in San Francisco and Old Town in Chicago, helping a rising generation of young people who questioned the authority of political leaders and journalistic institutions to find its voice.

THE ALT WEEKLIES ALSO HELPED ADVERTISERS FIND A MARKET, ONE that would ultimately be more lucrative than anyone at the *Voice* imagined. Wolf and Fancher began to recognize this during the 1960s, when they unleashed their sales team from the confines of the Village, selling enough ads to quadruple the length of the paper, raise the newsstand price to fifteen cents, and pay writers better wages. Then, in 1970, Carter Burden, a Democratic city councilman and former adviser to Robert Kennedy, offered to buy the paper for $3.2 million, so much more than the ten thousand dollars the publishers originally invested that they couldn't turn him down. Wolf and Fancher remained involved in the paper, but four years later Burden entered into a merger with Clay Felker, who paid $2.5 million and purchased six hundred thousand shares of stock for controlling interest in the paper, fired the two founders, and took over as editor. Mailer joined Wolf and Fancher to sue over alleged violations of their contract with Burden. They won $485,000 in the settlement, but control of the paper remained decidedly out of their hands. When Murdoch took over in 1977, they could do little more than scream.

At least they had good company. By the late 1970s alt weeklies were gaining popularity in cities throughout the nation, and about thirty publishers—a motley group of rabble-rousers, bohemians, small business owners, and aspiring baby barons—began planning their own trade group. They formed the Association of Alternative Newsweeklies (AAN) during their first meeting, in Seattle, in 1978. Calvin Trillin, who covered the event for the *New Yorker,* wrote that "just about everyone wanted to talk about taking market surveys and collecting accounts receivable and figuring out the hideous problems of distribution."[4] They must have had some good ideas. In the 1980s and 1990s ads for alcohol, tobacco, fashion, music, and movies became standard features of the alt weekly genre, as did a conventional format featuring local news in front, heavy coverage of big-label bands and Hollywood films in the middle, classifieds and sex ads in back, and national columnists sprinkled wherever space allowed. Weeklies in major markets fattened up until they were too thick to fold and too heavy to carry in a purse.

Not that the publishers minded. By 1992, the AAN papers reported $174 million in revenues. The booming economy of the late 1990s sent revenues soaring to more than $500 million, where—despite major losses in income from classified ads, which are moving to Web sites such as Craigslist, competition from "faux alternatives" put out by daily newspapers, and a spate of online publications dedicated to cultural coverage—they currently remain.[5] According to a 2004 survey commissioned by the AAN, readers of alt weeklies are not bohemians but *Influentials,* "the 10% of the population that tells the other 90% where to shop and dine, how to vote, and, most importantly, how to spend their discretionary time and income."[6] *American Demographics* adds that the average age of an alt weekly reader is forty-six, the average annual income is more than $60,000 ($64,000 by 2004), and about half of all readers are over thirty-five.[7] The audience, in other words, is not so alternative anymore. And neither are the papers' owners.

Murdoch held on to the *Voice* until 1985, when he sold it to the pet products scion Leonard Stern for $55 million. Stern Publishing held the paper for fifteen years, during which it acquired six other major alt weeklies, including the nation's second largest, the *LA Weekly.* In 1980 the investment firm Weiss, Peck & Greer bought Stern's holdings for $170 million and changed the publishing group name to Village Voice Media (VVM). A brand name was necessary because the firm had a major competitor, New Times, encroaching from the other side of the country.

In 1970 a small group of Arizona State University students and antiwar activists led by Michael Lacey and Jim Larkin started their own alternative weekly, the *Phoenix New Times,* when campus administrators refused to fly the flag at half-mast after the Kent State massacre, in which the Ohio National Guard shot four student protestors dead and injured nine others. "It reflected a frustration not just with the war but with American society in general," Lacey, who is also an accomplished investigative reporter, told the *Nation.* "It was an indictment of the entire culture, a repudiation of capitalism."[8]

But Lacey and Larkin, who became chairman and CEO of New Times, gradually learned to commodify their dissent and invest it in chains, acquiring the *Denver Westword* in 1983, moving into Florida in 1987, Texas in the early 1990s, California in the mid-1990s, and the Midwest (Missouri and Ohio) in the late 1990s. In early 2005 New Times owned eleven alt weeklies, more than any other company, and also owned the Ruxton Media Group, a marketing consolidator that sells ads for twenty-eight weeklies, including the *Chicago Reader,* the *Washington City Paper,* and the *Austin Chronicle,* and more than 1,500 college papers. Yet the company wanted to control more papers, and everyone in the industry knew it. In October 2005 the New Times and VVM announced plans to merge, with the New Times managers taking controlling interest of the company's shares and the majority of seats on the corporate board. The new group would control seventeen of the largest alt weeklies, reaching about a quarter of the AAN audience, and enjoy a level of market domination that, as the *Boston Phoenix* noted, would "establish what both chains are supposed to despise."[9] Adding insult to irony, the new group would claim the industry's leading antiestablishment brand name, Village Voice Media.

Years before, at the 1997 Media and Democracy Conference in New York City, Lacey had responded defiantly to requests for New Times to respect the editorial autonomy of so many local outlets by declaring his managerial philosophy: "I'm going to run these papers the way I want, and if you don't like it you can kiss my pink Irish ass."[10] At the *Village Voice,* where editors and writers worried that New Times managers would destroy their tradition of politically loaded criticism that reaches for a multicultural readership, Lacey promised that "we're going to come in and we're going to pay a lot of attention to content and to editorial. That's what we've done in every city that we've gone into." As for those editors and media scholars who warned that consolidation would homogenize the alt weekly market: "They are," Lacey proclaimed, "the sort of armchair critics that life passes by."[11]

But it was VVM's and New Times' market allocation agreement, not Lacey's incendiary rhetoric, that compelled the U.S. Department of Justice (DOJ) to review their proposed merger. Three years before, the federal government cracked down on the two companies when New Times closed *New Times Los Angeles* to give VVM a monopoly with *LA Weekly,* and VVM killed the *Cleveland Free Times* so that the *Cleveland Scene* could enjoy the same. Their CEOs put out a joint statement explaining, "Through this transaction we have been able to strengthen our respective competitive position in two important markets. As a result, both *LA Weekly* and *Cleveland Scene* will better serve the needs of the readers and the advertisers in their communities." But the DOJ and the states of California and Ohio disagreed, immediately filing antitrust suits. In 2003, just three months after the deal, the DOJ announced in a consent decree that it was "requiring the companies to terminate their illegal market allocation agreement," which was necessary "to restore competition in those markets." R. Hewitt Pate, the acting assistant attorney general in charge of the Antitrust Division, declared that "rather than letting the marketplace decide the winner, these companies chose to corrupt the competitive process by swapping markets, thereby guaranteeing each other a monopoly and denying consumers in Los Angeles and Cleveland the continued benefits of competition." It was a historic occasion: the Bush administration, and Attorney General John Ashcroft's office in particular, were reprimanding leaders of the alternative media for acting as monopoly capitalists. Two years after the announcement, the DOJ had to decide if it could entrust the two companies to legally operate as one.

ALT WEEKLY PUBLISHERS HAD BEEN SPECULATING ABOUT THE NEW TIMES' ambitions to take over VVM since the 2003 antitrust scandal exposed their collusive relationship, and by the summer of 2005 the editorial divisions of VVM papers were getting anxious about their future. They were, of course, *already* working inside a chain company. But, with some notable exceptions, VVM had proven to be a hands-off owner, even in valuable markets such as Los Angeles and Seattle, allowing editors enough independence and control over formatting and design to maintain the local flavor of each paper. When I visited the *Seattle Weekly*'s funky downtown office space, the former editor, Knute "Skip" Berger, told me that VVM managers "are strong believers in having local editors who love what they're doing and know the markets and are really into it. They've given us tremendous freedom." "Seattle isn't afraid of New York City," said David Brewster, a Yale graduate who founded the *Weekly* in 1976 with hopes that sophisticated cultural coverage would attract young professional readers, and remained actively involved until his partners persuaded him to sell to VVM in 1997. When we met in Seattle, Brewster explained, "David Schneiderman [the CEO] makes no public appearance here. The *Weekly* runs no Voice writers. It's not a generic or formula paper. It's not even widely known that the Voice is the owner here, and there's no desire to make it otherwise." In fact, VVM's silent control of the paper disturbed Brewster, who stayed active in Seattle's civic life by starting another new community project, Town Hall Seattle. "The readers ought to know who the owners are," he insisted. "It's kind of a public trust and a public utility, so it bothers me that it's sort of concealed."

Brewster's overall satisfaction with VVM's former management was not surprising, since he, Berger, and the key *Weekly* partners carefully evaluated offers from a number of leading media groups, and were courted by the New Times, the *Chicago Reader*, and a subsidiary of Hollinger International, the company controlled by Conrad Black. "There was tremendous interest when we were selling the *Weekly*," Berger explained. "David and I wanted to keep the ownership local, but most of the people interested were not local and we weren't successful. Then we went through this process of being romanced by all these different chains."

The meeting with Hollinger's speculators was particularly memorable. "They took our management group out to dinner and were talking about how great their company was, wining and dining us and asking questions about the *Weekly*. And I asked the guy, 'Well, why are you interested in alt papers?' He said, 'Well, alt weeklies are the last uncon-solidated niche in publishing in America.' And I was like, 'Wow . . . we're the last unconsolidated niche.' Needless to say, I did not recom-mend that we sell to them."

Berger also recalled meeting with New Times, whose abrasive jour-nalistic style clashed with the *Weekly* group's journalistic commitment to community building and high-minded criticism for cultural elites. "Lacey and Larkin came from New Times. We had this lovely dinner, and everybody was talking shop. Then there was this silence after din-ner, and I can't remember whether it was Lacey or Larkin, but I think Larkin said, 'Is there anything you guys want to ask us?' And I said, 'Well, why would a booze and testosterone fueled company like New Times, why would you guys be interested in running a matriarchy like the *Weekly*?' Most of our managers were women. David ran the paper in a very sensitive way, very civil and courtly. We were kind of a matri-archy. There was a stunned silence, and then everybody roared with laughter. It was a hilarious mismatch. Even now, when I run into Lacey or Larkin, they always come up to me and say, 'Hey, how's the matri-archy?' They wanted us quite badly. They made a bid, and they were very disappointed when we went to the Voice."

"The Voice was a good fit for us," Berger claimed. "The only thing I didn't like was that they weren't local. They understood the papers. We spoke the same language. And they're a company with a great track record on editorial independence, as opposed to somebody who was going to apply a cookie cutter, or somebody who was going to come in and make cost cutting their first priority." Not that VVM refrained from all cost cutting or formatting changes in its new investment. Since 1990 Brewster's group had been publishing *East Side Week*, a subur-ban alt weekly targeting the affluent professionals working for local technology companies such as Microsoft, Concur, and GeoEngineers. Although it was not yet generating major revenues, the *Week* was help-ing to create a distinctive regional voice and public culture in a place full of innovative young people. The editorial staff was deeply commit-ted to the project, as was Brewster, the publisher, and his investors, who recognized the potential to profit by targeting the resource-rich commu-nity. VVM owned and operated similar papers, the *Long Island Voice* and *Orange County Weekly*, which made it an especially attractive suitor. Yet VVM, which lacked an institutional interest in Seattle's edge cities and suburbs and had a strong incentive to boost the bottom line, folded the *Week* within a year of the acquisition.

VVM also made substantial changes to the *Weekly,* albeit not in the news hole so much as in advertising, where national companies and the sex industry (escort workers, private dancers, phone sex services, and the like) established an unprecedented presence in the paper, decisively changing its look and feel. The *Weekly* was always a relatively prudish, high-brow publication, especially before competition with the *Stranger,* an upstart weekly started by the *Onion*'s cofounder Tim Keck, pushed the *Weekly*'s board to expand its pop culture coverage and convert from a paid subscription-based circulation model to a free paper in 1995. Brewster, who said that his ideal reader was "a thirty-five-year-old lawyer who was married," and whose main concern was that the paper "was read by people who had graduated from college," did not mind ceding the younger audience of rock fans and sex column devotees to a competitor. He was not even embarrassed by the *Weekly*'s legendary failure to cover Sub Pop Records, the pathbreaking independent music label that first recorded Nirvana, Soundgarden, and many other Seattle bands and helped to launch grunge rock into the stratosphere—even though the two companies were in the same office complex. Brewster preferred his 40,000 loyal subscribers to 120,000 people who picked up the paper for nothing.

Yet the success of other free weeklies and the threat from the outrageously funny and increasingly popular *Stranger* convinced Brewster's partners that the model worked, and he reluctantly agreed to go along. When VVM took over, the paper that once refused to print personal ads that mentioned any body parts between the neck and the knees lost its inhibitions. "Lady Aurora. The Sweetest Bitch You'll Ever Meet," says one ad in the Fetish classifieds of a recent issue, listed next to "HellHouse Dungeon," and across the page from a few dozen color photographs of women—"Busty Blonde!" "Sexy Student!" "Asian Dream!"—thrusting out from their thongs, bikinis, and lingerie. The impact of these graphic images was enormous, Mike Crystal, the former *Weekly* publisher who is now the publisher of the *Chicago Reader,* told me. "The body sculpting stuff that goes over so well in LA, sex ads in the back, explicit pictures that work in New York—those things had been successful for the Voice group. Although they may appear to be business matters, they have a huge impact on the way the paper feels as an editorial product. You get people who say 'I like what you've got up front, but I don't want it around the house.' When those decisions are made at a corporate level, you can no longer control your own marketplace. You might think, 'Oh, that isn't going to really work for us,' but suddenly that's not your decision."

THE *WEEKLY*'S EDITORIAL STAFFERS LEARNED TO LIVE WITH A RAUNCHIER version of their paper, but along with their colleagues at other VVM weeklies, they grew nervous when rumors about a New Times takeover circulated through the industry. Although both companies were chains, only New Times had a reputation for using a standard formula— deride activists and reformers, hammer the local government, focus the cultural coverage on national bands and Hollywood films while doing smaller pieces on local acts, and refuse to endorse political candidates— wherever it went, flattening the differences in cities as distinct as Phoenix, Miami, and Cleveland. Mike Lacey, the New Times cofounder with spiked gray hair and a tongue sharpened for lashing, found such anxiety predictable but misplaced. The man responsible for the chain's journalism has long insisted that hard-hitting, locally focused, and objective investigative reporting is the hallmark of New Times publications, and he takes special pride in the hundreds of awards that his papers have won. In interviews, Lacey insists that New Times grants editors considerable autonomy, provides writers with good salaries and working conditions, and delivers a fresh and fierce paper to readers in each one of its markets. As he recently wrote: "The disgrace of the serial rapes at the Air Force Academy in Colorado first saw the light of day in our Denver paper. In Cleveland, we recently published grand jury documents that the daily sat on. In Phoenix, our writers broke the polygamy scandal in the Mormon sect on the Utah/Arizona border, as well as the stories about poor people submitting to unnecessary surgery so that doctors and patients both—but particularly the doctors—could swindle insurance companies."[12]

New Times reporting has impressed some of the toughest critics in the business. The *Slate* press critic Jack Shafer, who edited the *Washington City Paper* for a decade before serving briefly as the New Times' first editor at the *San Francisco Weekly*, told me that "Lacey and

Larkin are engaged, savvy, and good newsmen," and that "every one of the papers that they've started is ten times better than it was before they took over." Mark Jacobson, who authored a long profile of Lacey for *New York* magazine after VVM announced the merger, reported that there is "a consensus that New Times often published excellent local investigative stories," even if there is "the sense that Lacey and Larkin's papers were vicious corporate sharks." Not that this would bother Lacey, who called himself "this year's Visigoth, the new asshole in charge," and complained about the staff's civility on his first visit to the *Voice* after the merger. "Someone could have at least told me to fuck off," he joked.[13]

Although no writers were imprudent enough to flip off their prospective employer in person, in private many feared that they would either be downsized or defanged if the Department of Justice let Lacey and Larkin seize control. Editors at the most venerable VVM papers, the *Village Voice* and *Los Angeles Weekly* (which, like the *Seattle Weekly*, had rebuffed an earlier bid from New Times and been sold to VVM instead), were notably concerned. The *Weekly* group had competed with the short-lived *New Times Los Angeles* (*NTLA*), and veterans such as Harold Meyerson and Marc Cooper had assailed the company for bluntly applying its signature cynicism, libertarianism, and knee-jerk contrarianism to a city that had no interest. "Isn't it possible," Meyerson wrote after *NTLA* closed, "that one reason the New Times never made money in Los Angeles is that it was out of sync with L.A.'s politics—or, at least, the politics of the people who pick up alternative weeklies in this city? In the best tradition of the alternative press, *New Times* was an inveterate establishment basher, but its view of who was the establishment and who the outsider was classically neocon. In the world according to *New Times,* a beleaguered, largely white middle class was set upon by a slew of false messiahs claiming to represent the city's nonwhite, downtrodden poor. Not that this doesn't happen in L.A., but the majority of the city truly is nonwhite and poor, and some of the *New Times'* purported demagogues were actually the people most responsible for helping that new majority."[14]

Cooper, who was careful not to denounce his prospective employer, expressed concern that the New Times' policy of refusing to endorse political candidates or campaigns masked its strong ideological orientation. "The *Voice/L.A. Weekly* papers are stolidly liberal-lefty and continue to keep a finger or two dipped into some nebulous conception of a counterculture," he claimed. "The New Times chain, by contrast, takes pleasure in poking fun at P.C. liberalism and by refusing to take partisan stands, fancying itself as a group of lone libertarian lone-shooters. Sometimes the results are refreshingly unpredictable, hard-hitting exposés of politicians both conservative and liberal. Other times the product is sophomoric and snarky, lacking in any serious analysis."[15]

In addition to their editorial concerns, the staff at VVM papers worried that New Times would eliminate journalists, substitute syndicated columns written from corporate headquarters for locally written film and music reviews, and redesign the format to create a homogenized big-brand identity. Editors responsible for cultural coverage were anxious that the New Times' standard packages would necessarily limit the space for coverage of small bands and local film events. Mark Athetakis, who was the *San Francisco Weekly*'s music editor from 1998 to 2000 and a staff writer until 2002, said that the New Times dictated the shape of cultural coverage much more than his current employer, the *Chicago Reader*. "I was given a strict mandate when I started at the *Weekly*," he told me. "New Times has a specific format, not just in terms of what gets reviewed, what fills the features, but also the tone you're supposed to strike. There was a sense that central command was there and there were certain marching orders. Andy Van De Voorde [the executive associate editor for the chain] had separate meetings with every music editor and gave them some sort of advice."

Athetakis admired the journalistic ambitions of New Times cultural reporting, but he was convinced that the chain's editorial style, which usually emphasizes long stories about national acts making local appearances, leaves little room to cover emerging music scenes. "The *Reader* is designed to make as much space for interesting local music as possible," he explained. "For example, we have something called the Treatment, which previews about twenty to twenty-five upcoming shows. Some will be big arena shows, but most of the previews are covering smaller acts, with a special interest in smaller local acts. Writers know they are not just encouraged but also responsible for keeping tabs on what's interesting in the local scene. In the *Weekly* it didn't shake out that way because you would be picking one or two bands that would be given the big push. There was not a whole lot of space for reviews, maybe one or two concert previews. There was impatience for the extended music essay. So much weight was put on the feature that there was less interest in criticism."

VVM's news and feature writers feared that, even if they kept their jobs, the New Times would place them on its infamous five-week reporting cycle. The chain, as industry insiders knew, kept its profit margins high by employing fewer full-time editors, writers, columnists, and critics than other major companies in the business, and the editorial divisions at the *Los Angeles Weekly* and *Village Voice* were significantly larger than any outlet in the New Times stable. Journalists competed for special permission to do longer investigative stories that the New Times could nominate for prizes, for which they would get generous reporting budgets and be exempted from the relentless publishing cycle. But these opportunities were rare, and in general Lacey and Larkin made their business model work by imposing strict production demands on each of the company's writers, demanding a full-length feature story every five weeks (about ten per year) as well as a number of smaller articles. "It may sound okay compared to what newspaper reporters do," one New Times writer told me in confidence, fearing professional sanctions from the industry's main employer. "The problem is that they want to do a city magazine, and they expect us to write magazine-style stories without giving us enough time. We had three weeks to report, one week to write, and one week for edits. I started to feel like a hamster in a wheel."

Not only does this tight production schedule drain reporters and drag down newsroom morale; it also reinforces the decidedly antigovernment political slant of New Times papers. According to staff writers, the five-week cycle pushes them to report often on public institutions and individuals, for whom it is easier to gather information, rather than on private-sector firms for which investigative reporting requires more time and effort. Writers also learn to gain time in the cycle by adopting the chain's standard slash-and-burn tone with stories designed to do damage. Jeremy Mullman, a former *San Francisco Weekly* writer, told me that "the paper had a reputation for throat slitting." Yet when the communications scholar Rodney Benson conducted a content analysis of the chain's reporting in San Francisco and Los Angeles, he found a distinctly political pattern to its choice of whose throat to cut. "Journalists at the two New Times papers cover government aggressively, ever on the lookout for corruption, dishonesty, or hypocrisy from politics,"

Benson found. Yet "more typical of the New Times approach to business and economic issues is a focus on the colorful, controversial entrepreneur or the off-beat enterprise . . . Just as often, business stories are stripped entirely of politics, focusing instead on the amusing and bizarre."[16]

To be sure, the New Times has printed important investigative stories about corporate corruption and profiteering, but the thrust of its coverage is so focused on discrediting local public figures that New Times critics accuse the company of "anticommunity" reporting that stands against everyone and everything, from small theater companies to neighborhood organizations and, especially, activist groups. "They're wary of people who protest for a living," Mullman told me. "A professional activist is someone they're inclined to roll their eyes at and make fun of." "The editor humiliated me in a staff meeting when I pitched a story about some local activists with a good cause," another former New Times reporter confided to me. "So I quickly learned to censor myself and stick with stories he liked."[17]

During the late 1990s and early years of the twenty-first century, one of the *San Francisco Weekly*'s pet projects involved criticizing critics of gentrification, even though they were on the losing end of a furious development process driven by the dot-com boom and the soaring Bay Area real estate values. In May and June of 1999, the *Weekly* editors summoned up the spirit of the genre's founders and planned an elaborate hoax. The paper printed a prominent ad announcing a "Stop the Hate" rally for YUPPIE rights in response to a series of attacks by vandals in the Mission district, where young professionals and hip commercial establishments were displacing working-class residents at an alarming rate. In a dramatic reversal, the *Weekly* had turned the countercultural movement from which it had arisen into the primary object of its scorn.

"The ad," explained John Mecklin, the *Weekly* editor at the time, "was written entirely in the gooey vocabulary of underdog leftist social protest; at the same time, the ad's content clearly called for the masses to rally and rescue professionals who had used six-figure salaries and Silicon Valley stock portfolios to buy homes in the Mission District." It listed a phone number and a contact person, named "Bradley," for press inquiries. A number of local media outlets called immediately, only to get a recorded message or, in the case of a *San Francisco Examiner* reporter named Emily Gurnon, a returned call saying the organizers were too busy for an interview. Mecklin was thrilled when Gurnon wrote a story about the fake event anyway, and he was delighted to see some 250 counterprotestors show up to oppose a group that did not exist.

"Bradley," Mecklin wrote, "did not appear. But that didn't stop the demonstration. This is, after all, San Francisco. No need for reality when protesting is in the air." The paper's prank did not amuse the neighborhood's Latino, blue-collar, and elderly residents, many of whom were struggling to keep their homes and maintain their communities. Nor did it help the *Weekly* writers, who earned the distrust of both local sources and colleagues at other papers. Yet such concerns have no place in the world according to New Times, where the young professional readers they target are encouraged to enjoy a good laugh at the expense of the do-gooders and the downtrodden. According to Mecklin, "If a couple of hundred people in the Mission are so focused on neighborhood politics that they cannot recognize absurdity staring them right in their faces, is it not the clear duty of SF *Weekly* to bring humor back into their lives?"[18]

NOTHING ABOUT THE NEW TIMES' REPORTING IN THE BAY AREA HUMORS Bruce Brugmann, the founder and publisher of the *San Francisco Bay Guardian*. Brugmann, whose burly, six-foot-five-inch frame and bushy gray beard can barely contain his roaring contempt for chain weeklies in general and New Times in particular, has been the industry's strongest advocate of locally owned and operated publications committed to defending urban underdogs against the power elite. The *Guardian* has a special place in the universe of alt weeklies. It was the first alternative paper explicitly designed to challenge the local dailies, the *Chronicle* and *Examiner*, which were locked in a Joint Operating Agreement, and it won the funding to become a weekly (about $500,000) by settling an antitrust lawsuit against the "Chron-Ex" in 1975.[19]

The *Guardian*'s mission statement—"It is a newspaper's duty to print the news and raise hell"—has stayed constant since Brugmann and his wife, Jean Dibble, printed the first issue on October 27, 1966, when they were both thirty-one years old and lacked the resources to publish on a regular basis. So has the editorial style, which dedicated readers appreciate for the unwavering progressivism of its reporters and critics, including some whom the industry justifiably ridicules for their predictability and occasional myopia. "You tell me the issue," taunted Mecklin, when we met during his last months as *Weekly* editor. "I'll tell you what the *Guardian* is going to say."

The *Guardian's* editorial team insists that predictable criticism is exactly what principled journalists *should* produce when the institutions they cover make predictably dangerous decisions. Whether the issue is unchecked urban development or an unsound rationale for military aggression, the *Guardian* is not shy about reporting a story with a frame that reinforces its politically progressive editorial line. The New Times publications revel in their rival's apparent misjudgments, and the *Guardian* staff is eager to spit back. During a two-hour conversation in his large but cluttered office, Brugmann recounted that before President Bush announced plans to invade Iraq, "we came out and said that the war is wrong. It's preemptive. It's immoral. It's based on lies. It has no exit strategy." After the U.S. military toppled Saddam Hussein's regime and took over Baghdad, the *San Francisco Weekly* gave Brugmann a mock "Best Local Psychic" award. "We came out early and gave their editors a special award for 'Best Premature Ejaculation,'" Brugmann gleefully exclaimed. "And now they've regretted it ever since, because guess who was right!"

"We're an activist paper, a paper that has a point of view," said the *Guardian's* executive editor, Tim Redmond, during my visit to the *Weekly's* two-level, lofted office space in the Portrero Hill neighborhood. "We think that a good newspaper should be out to change the world, not just to make money. We energize and promote progressive activism in San Francisco—to be useful to people, and to provide intelligent, insightful arts and entertainment coverage that also supports the local arts community. While we are critics, we are not boosters. At the same time, we feel like it's partially our responsibility to give the little guys a break. We do it because we care. That's really our editorial mission, to try to make San Francisco a better place." Thirty years ago many other alt weeklies shared this editorial philosophy, though others—the *Seattle Weekly* and the *Chicago Reader*, for example—aimed for the sophisticated literary style associated with the *New Yorker* or *Atlantic Monthly* rather than the activist model associated with the underground press. The *Guardian's* activist voice is exceedingly rare in today's market, yet it expresses something essential in the spirit of the "left-coast city" it covers. It is utterly San Franciscan, and although Mecklin, the *Weekly* editor, told me that "unless you're an idiot, if you're a reasonably intelligent person, this [the *Weekly*] is what you read," the *Guardian* remains the more popular local paper.

Unlike Seattle, no one in the Bay Area is confused about who runs the leading alt weekly, especially once the *Guardian* began stamping the phrase "Locally Owned and Operated" on every newspaper box. And as the battle between the *Guardian* and the *Weekly* turned into a bloodbath, San Franciscans had a rare chance to witness a newspaper war over competing visions of the future of local media.

Like the *Voice*, the *Guardian* started with a small staff that let the city's young literary aspirants and muckrakers use the paper to launch their writing careers. They had plenty of juicy subjects, from San Francisco's summer of love, corrupt local draft boards, and the booming music scene in the Haight-Ashbury neighborhood in the late 1960s to the fledgling movement to curb high-rise development on the waterfront and the fight to increase public input for the city's new public rail system, Bay Area Rapid Transit District (BART), during the early 1970s. The *Guardian* has always featured strong coverage of the city's dynamic cultural environment, with bracingly open and honest discussions about sex and drugs. But the paper's greatest initiative, which to this day Brugmann calls "the granddaddy of all civic scandals," involves reporting the story of how the for-profit company Pacific Gas and Electric (PG&E) maneuvered to block a municipal electric system that, in the paper's view, would save San Francisco residents hundreds of millions of dollars each year. A biochemistry professor at the University of California, Berkeley, named Joe Neilands broke this story for the *Guardian* on March 22, 1969, and since then it's become an unspoken rule that "almost every editor and reporter on the staff at one time or another . . . investigates or reports on the story."[20]

No one has ever called the *Guardian* a writer's paper, and even its editors will say that literary quality is relatively unimportant because they aspire to be a "reporter's paper" instead. The weekly earned this title in 2005, when its staff writer Adam Clay Thompson's "Forgotten City" series on public housing problems in San Francisco won the prestigious George Polk award for best local reporting. Unlike the *Voice* (before it merged with New Times), the *Guardian* has let go of veterans and retained a predominantly youthful reporting corps, it rarely publishes the kind of political feuding among columnists that made the

New York paper so feisty, and its news section rarely contains a story that's not driven by a progressive political line. Mecklin told me that "nobody writes anything that Bruce Brugmann doesn't say is okay," while the paper suffers because he insists on "paying people like shit, treating people like shit, and running them off the lot."

Guardian staffers acknowledge that they don't get the financial support that the *Weekly* offers reporters when they're working on major investigative pieces. Yet they receive roughly the same starting salaries as their equals at the *Weekly* (between $35,000 and $42,000 a year, depending on experience), and they were spared from the downsizing that New Times imposed on its papers after 9/11. "There's just not a sense of security working there," said Athetakis. "Back in 2001–2, NT was laying off reporters throughout its papers. And nobody in the office was hearing a damn thing about it except secondhand from the people who were getting fired. There was no explanation from Lacey or Mecklin saying, 'We're sorry we're doing this because . . .' It was just sort of like, 'Okay, well, it's happening, and this is the kind of corporate culture that exists here.'"

IN MARCH 2002 REDMOND PUBLISHED AN ARTICLE ANNOUNCING THAT A *Guardian* advertising executive who resigned without notice on a Saturday night in August 2000 and began working for the *Weekly* the following Monday had "printed out more than 1,000 pages of confidential *Bay Guardian* account records on her last day in office . . . Among those records was detailed account information for every single *Bay Guardian* advertiser, as well as contracts and related information for the Alternative Weekly Network, a cooperative organization that sells national ads for alternative papers." Although the former employee settled with the *Guardian* for ten thousand dollars, this was small compensation for the theft of information whose potential value Brugmann estimated at "tens of millions of dollars." Redmond also reported that the *Guardian*'s attorneys sent a letter to the *Weekly* citing evidence that the paper "offered music retailers discounts of 40 percent off published rates and free half- and full-page four-color ads; offered clubs and club promoters discounts of as much as 70 percent and told smaller clubs that they'd only get a price break if they agreed not to advertise in the

Bay Guardian; [and] offered resort, casino, and travel-related advertisers 13 weeks or more of free full-page ads, and run free ads for real estate and housing clients without the knowledge of the advertisers."[21]

Mecklin, the *San Francisco Weekly* editor, responded the next week with an article written in the New Times signature style.

> The *Bay Guardian* is failing, but the roots of the failure lie not in evildoing by SF *Weekly* and/or New Times; most everything Redmond claims in that regard is either untrue or a real distortion of reality. No, the *Bay Guardian* is headed down because Bruce Brugmann and the *Guardian* have abused the paper's readers and advertisers at length. On the editorial side, the paper has trampled journalistic standards and bored readers with a stream of repetitive and predictable ideological lectures. On the business side, among other things, the *Guardian* has failed to maintain the type of basic circulation auditing that would assure advertisers they are getting what they pay for. Yes, the *San Francisco Bay Guardian* seems to be suffering—from self-inflicted wounds.
>
> . . . A huge portion of the *Guardian*/Redmond claim that SF *Weekly* has engaged in anti-competitive behavior appears to rest on the *Guardian*'s shocking—shocking!—discovery that the *Weekly* sometimes offers discounts to attract new advertisers. People on the *Weekly* ad staff tell me that the *Guardian* is itself a past master at bartering, giving away, and discounting ad space. And public records prove that the paper has given away tens of thousands of dollars of ad space to a favored political cause. But you know what? It's OK with me if the *Guardian* discounts or gives away its ad space, because discounting is a fairly ordinary part of the newspaper business. Our business side sometimes discounts ads to gain new business—within the context of making profit. That's called enterprise, and the last time I looked, even here in San Francisco, enterprise and profits were still allowed.[22]

Mecklin's article achieved its intended effect, bringing the *Guardian*'s steaming publisher to a furious boil. The New Times' *Weekly* and the *East Bay Express,* amid high-level reports that they were losing money in the tight Bay Area market, continued their standard business practices.[23] On October 19, 2004, the *Guardian* filed a lawsuit in a San Francisco superior court, charging the New Times with predatory pricing by selling advertisements either at or below cost, and of offering secret deals to clients willing to stop advertising in the independent paper. The *Guardian*'s complaint argues that "the defendants . . . knew that by offering and selling advertising space at below-cost prices, they could cause the *Guardian* to lose money on its advertising space and eventually be forced out of business, while defendants would be able to subsidize their own losses caused by that practice through profits derived from other newspapers in the New Times publishing chain that do not face significant competition."[24] Once again, Mecklin replied immediately in the *Weekly.*

> Of late, you may have noticed (or been unable to avoid) some elements of a smelly BS-offensive emanating from Brugmann-land (or would that be Brugmania?). As usual, in this offensive, the *Guardianistas* have depicted *SF Weekly* and its parent company, New Times, as conscienceless violators of all norms of civil society. Think of Col. Gen. Grubozaboyschikov of SMERSH in the old James Bond novels, crossed with John D. Rockefeller, Osama bin Laden, and the grand vizier of the Ku Klux Klan, and you've got an understated notion of the *Guardian*'s take on New Times . . .
>
> I am not intimately involved in the business operations of *SF Weekly.* After years of enduring it, however, I think I know enough about the smell of *Guardian* bullshit to be pretty sure the same analysis of that newspaper's problems is applicable now . . . The *Bay Guardian* stink machine runs 24/7/365, and its output is prodigious. Even so, I think its smelly distortions of reality will be even less enchanting to a court of law than they have been persuasive in the court of San Francisco public opinion. Excuse me. I have to go buy some cologne.

The war of words would only intensify during the next twelve months. In May 2005 Redmond wrote that "opponents of newspaper consolidation—including me—are starting to worry about the flurry of rumors and unconfirmed reports that there's some sort of merger in the making between the nation's two largest alternative newspaper chains." The *Guardian* warned that a New Times takeover would affect the industry's advertising market as well as its editorial content because the VVM's papers would likely join Ruxton, the New Times' national sales group, depriving the other major alt weekly marketer, the Alternative Weekly Network (AWN), of its most valuable clients. With the leading alt weeklies in New York, Los Angeles, Chicago, Houston, Miami, Denver, Seattle, Phoenix, San Francisco, Washington, D.C., and Dallas, Ruxton would control access to most of the major alt weekly markets, and the remaining papers in the AWN group would have less to offer national advertisers. Redmond noted that the DOJ would have to approve a merger, but he also quoted an "industry insider" who said the takeover was "pretty much inevitable."

The *Guardian* turned up the heat in late August, announcing that "several reliable sources have told us they've spoken to senior executives at New Times and have been told a deal is imminent," and speculating that recent cuts in VVM's freelance pay rates were designed to achieve parity with New Times compensation levels.[25] The next week Redmond found his smoking gun, reporting that the *Guardian* had obtained documents from "a May 27, 2005, draft of a merger agreement . . . The draft calls for the creation of a new company controlled by a nine-member board. Five of the members would come from Phoenix-based New Times and its primary venture-capital firm, the Boston-based Alta Communications. New Times . . . would have 62 percent of the equity in the new venture, and VVM . . . would have 38 percent."[26] The deal was on, and the *Guardian* called for both state regulators and the DOJ to block it.

On October 24, 2005, the New Times and Village Voice Media announced their plans to merge by early 2006, pending approval from regulators. According to their press release, "Village Voice Media will have a combined weekly audited circulation of 1.8 million papers and 4.3 million readers weekly when the merger is completed. Village Voice papers will join New Times' national advertising sales agency Ruxton Media Group. Ruxton will represent 35 weekly alternative publications from coast to coast with audited circulations of 3.1 million weekly. The merger also will bring VVM online classifieds into New Times' backpage.com, which combines the popularity of free classified online bulletin boards with new revenue opportunities for affiliated papers. The addition of the six Voice papers means backpage.com is now licensed to 37 newspapers in major American markets."[27] The press release did not explain that the merger would give the new company control of about 25 percent of the Association of Alternative Newsweeklies market, consolidating the industry to a level that no other media—radio, television, or daily newspapers—had yet reached. Nor did it say that other members of the AAN were clamoring to have the new company, which had lost any serious claim to being "local" or "alternative," kicked out of the group.

Back in Phoenix, where the new Village Voice Media would be headquartered, the company's future CEO, Jim Larkin, declared that "together, New Times and Village Voice Media create a truly national media company with highly desirable demographics, geographic diversity and a unique print and Internet platform that is poised for tremendous growth."[28] Meanwhile, in San Francisco, the *Guardian* tried to reverse the spin. "Stop the merger," it pleaded. "If this merger goes through, [the new company] will be in a strong position to increase media concentration, damage competition, hurt readers and advertisers . . . It would also add to the homogenization of media in the state and damage the vigorous marketplace of ideas envisioned in the First Amendment."[29]

The Department of Justice and the Federal Trade Commission (FTC) did not agree, and it didn't take them long to decide, either. On November 23—less than a month after the merger announcement—the FTC Web site listed the deal among a number of cases that the federal government would not challenge. The merger was legal, and all that remained was the paperwork. Days later, VVM CEO David Schneiderman, who got a $500,000 bonus for completing the deal, e-mailed his employees to say, "I am pleased to inform you that the Department [of] Justice has approved our merger with New Times. We expect to close in about a month or so." The *Guardian* would not give up, calling upon California attorney general Bill Lockyer to request a public review before approving the merger in his state, and suggesting that the aggressive office of New York attorney general Eliot Spitzer "also has a good case here."[30] But most others in the industry were resigned to the outcome. On December 5 Dan Forst announced that he would step down after nine years as the *Village Voice* editor in chief, and although he publicly stated that he was not leaving because of the merger, few of his colleagues believed him.

The new VVM management took control of the *Voice* on January 31, 2006, a dark and blustery winter day. One staff writer, who asked to be quoted anonymously so as not to risk reprisals from the company that now dominates the alt weekly labor market, reported that Lacey immediately began meeting with individual employees, and within days called a meeting with the full editorial staff.

It was forty people in a conference room, and the meeting did not go very well. Lacey is a no bullshit kind of guy, which is a good thing. But he came across as a bully and a blowhard.

He quickly started attacking [Washington Bureau correspondent] Jim Ridgeway and [staff writer] Nat Hentoff, saying their work was subpar. While Lacey may have had legitimate critiques of their work lately, or a particular piece, they're both highly respected people and to call out those two people grated on people. Hentoff and Ridgeway represent the old ideal of the *Voice*. It's obvious that Lacey does not like the political side of things. He says we're overly obsessed with Bush.

He made these broad proclamations about what he wanted to change. Some of these things, there was no disagreement. He wanted better writing. He ended the health column. He got rid of the essay in the front of the book, and that was good because none of us could ever figure out what it was. Lacey also says he wants more "impact stories." But at the same time, he says he doesn't want us to touch hard news like the dailies. He says he [doesn't] want wonky stuff. It had us worried that he was changing what the *Voice* does.

The annoying thing about Lacey in that meeting, and which he had [previously] admitted, was that he hadn't read the paper very much. It's like he picked up the most recent two issues and read them and all his comments were based on that. It seemed like he walked into that meeting to set us on our heels. It had that effect. We left the meeting shaken up and angry.

That May, Lacey announced that Erik Wemple, the editor of the *Washington City Paper,* would take over as the Village Voice's editor in chief in July. Wemple is a widely respected journalist with ample alt weekly experience, yet he had never lived in New York City, and critics questioned how the decision to hire him squared with Lacey's professed commitment to improving the paper's local coverage. It turned out not to matter, however, because within weeks Wemple, after telling *Voice* staffers that working under Lacey's heavy-handed command would be a challenge for everyone, himself included, realized that he was not up for the struggle. He resigned, citing disagreements over newsroom managements, and promptly returned to the *City Paper* in D.C.

As editors and writers at the VVM papers in Los Angeles and Nashville pondered their future and the *Voice* scrambled to find a new editor, Knute Berger resigned from the *Seattle Weekly,* ending his short-lived relationship with Lacey. In California the former *Voice* and *Guardian* music contributor Jeff Chang published "Eulogy for the Alt Weekly." "Competition in the 'alternative weekly' sector has been all but eliminated," he wrote. "There is no longer anything 'alternative' about the alternative. The long goodbye to an oppositional politics and aesthetics begins now."[31] Chang's article, which included the requisite barb that VVM "is now the Clear Channel of alt-weeklies," was notable not so much for what it said as for where it was published. Not in a daily newspaper, nor in a weekly. Not in a magazine, nor even in print. Chang wrote it for his personal blog, and it was available to anyone with an Internet connection from the very moment he hit the "Enter" key. In a completely consolidated media marketplace, perhaps the future of "alternative alternatives" is online.

7

THE NET AND THE NEWS

Joel Dinerstein has always been an avid consumer of alternative media. Yet he never needed it as urgently as in the late summer of 2005, when he evacuated his home in the Uptown neighborhood of New Orleans just hours before Hurricane Katrina hit. Dinerstein, a former rock critic who is now on the faculty at Tulane University, shuttered his doors and windows and said good-bye to his neighbors before driving to Austin, Texas, to take refuge with friends. Though safely out of Katrina's deadly reach, Dinerstein was emotionally unmoored and gripped by a need to know what was happening to the people and places that anchored his life. New Orleans was no Minot, of course—the hurricane was the world's biggest news story. Dinerstein listened to radio reports on the long drive to Austin and watched the continuous television coverage from his hosts' living room. The national news coverage, he told me from back home in the bayou, was visually powerful yet also misleading and incomplete. "I didn't trust the coverage. It seemed like the reporters were just hanging out in the French Quarter and taking helicopter rides. It was clear that the national media knew nothing about New Orleans—culturally, socially, racially. I didn't believe a lot of the stuff they were reporting—the looting, the violence, the idea that most people here were turning on each other."[1]

Like most Americans, Dinerstein appreciated the aggressive political journalism coming from the networks and cable news outlets, and he understood why they focused so heavily on the spectacular scenes at the Superdome, the Convention Center, the Ninth Ward, and the French Quarter. Like most New Orleanians, however, he was frustrated by how difficult it was to get reliable information about the other parts of the city, including his own. "The images were weird because they never showed Uptown," his neighborhood. "And there was no reporting about it on TV either." Calling his friends and neighbors who had stayed was not an option, because they all had lost cell phone service when the towers were knocked out, and their land lines were dead.[2] Most of his e-mail contacts were unreachable, too, since many local servers were down (Tulane's would be out for about six weeks), making messages to local addresses undeliverable. "There was no way to get in touch with other people from New Orleans. I couldn't get news about them, and they couldn't get news about me. That was really disorienting."

Lacking information about the fate of his friends, Dinerstein sought out primary news reporting from journalists who knew New Orleans and personal testimonies from people around Uptown and Tulane. Had the hurricane hit ten years earlier or in a less developed part of the world, it might have been impossible to get anything like this. But in 2005 Dinerstein could connect to the Internet, where the *Times-Picayune*'s Nola.com published both a frequently updated, online version of the daily newspaper—rich with local journalism that would ultimately win major national awards, including a Pulitzer—and a digital bulletin board where anyone could post or retrieve information.[3] With a few keystrokes, Dinerstein could download streaming video from WWL-TV, the only New Orleans station that offered continuous broadcasting and webcasting of its news coverage, staffed by local anchors with familiar faces and street-level knowledge that made for more dependable reporting about different neighborhoods and communities. Here, for example, is an exchange between Eric Paulson, a twenty-eight-year veteran of New Orleans news television, and Sally Ann-Roberts, who sat in a Baton Rouge studio and described images shot from a helicopter on a webcast around 10:00 a.m. on August 31.

"There's Reverend Green's church. It was under water."
"Oh my!"
"Now we should be coming up on that agricultural center."
"We're by city park, we're by the stables."

"There's two condo developments, the Lake Marina Tower, and then
that new one."

"There's the Joe's Crab Shack, there's the Southern Yacht Club."

"There's the Orleans Marina. I used to have a boat there."

"A very good friend of mine lives in one of those boat houses there."

"Oh my."[4]

Although it's unclear how many New Orleanians were watching this
exchange online, those who did must have felt a little closer to home.

The Internet allowed traditional media such as WWL-TV and the
Times-Picayune to maintain operations when other broadcast towers
were down and printing presses inaccessible, and to reach audiences far
outside the city limits. But the Internet's more innovative role involved
providing an outlet for new communication platforms, such as blogs,
digital bulletin boards, and listservs, which ordinary people could use
to post or receive vital information, much of it hyperlocal and intensely
personal. Hours after the hurricane touched down in the Gulf region,
Craigslist became a central hub for offers of housing assistance and
calls for information about missing persons: "Share House in NH for
Hurricane Katrina Family." "Any info on Biloxi High—Missing Mom."
"Looking for Brenda or Brad Kava." "I can call your friends/family
and let them know you are safe." The blogosphere lit up with several
thousand posts about Katrina, some containing little more than short
comments or links to major media reports, others providing more of
the firsthand observations and raw images that Dinerstein was seeking.

Soon after the hurricane hit New Orleans, NOLA.com became the
major clearing house for accounts of ground-level conditions in all parts
of the flooded city, as well as photographs, desperate requests for information about missing people, celebratory reports of loved ones found,
and offers of assistance from California to Vermont. The Web site featured reporting by the *Times-Picayune* staff at its center, while on the
margins it provided links to discussion forums for twenty different
neighborhoods and special pages for "Missing Persons," "Survival Stories," "Pet Rescue," "Reach Out," "I'm OK Forum," "Homes Available," "Volunteer," "Sound Off," and "In Memoriam." The site
attracted interest from all over the world, providing possibilities for
human connection to those who might otherwise have experienced the
disaster as a distant event. Yet its major impact was local. As Dinerstein

explained, "NOLA.com operated as something of a public forum for New Orleanians through September and October, and it continues in that capacity as people decide whether and when to return." By December 2005 there were roughly 6,700 original posts, and thousands more responses, on the Uptown section alone.

For the large community associated with Tulane University (students, parents, faculty, staff, and alumni), a new site called Tulane Student Blog emerged as the primary place for debating the immediate and long-term future of the institution. Brett Hyman, a rising senior with unusually fierce enthusiasm for his school, began the blog on August 31, two days after the hurricane made landfall, by posting photographs of Uptown and imploring fellow students to take caution before enrolling in other universities. Hours later, he produced an entry headlined "Don't Transfer!!" "Tulane needs us," he wrote. "If too many of us transfer, they'll lose tons of money and it will bring them down, significantly." For those worried about the security of their homes near campus, Hyman provided a report from his brother, who had stayed in the area. "During his walk he saw no looted buildings anywhere. No evidence of vandals or roving gangs. Increased presence of National Guard and police. Uptown seems quiet and peaceful. Drew cannot stress highly enough how on his walk through major and side streets he has not seen any looting or suspicious activity. Perhaps if somebody left a 12-pack of cold beer on their front steps, it would go missing, but other than that, there has been no looting of residences that he has observed. Drew expects that looting is probably happening in some places, but it is grossly exaggerated by the media."

LONG BEFORE KATRINA PROVED ITS VALUE, EXECUTIVES AT BIG MEDIA companies and their allies on Capitol Hill insisted that the Internet was the source for so many novel sources of news and information that it rendered most policies regulating ownership of old media—television, radio, and newspapers—absurd. How could any one media company— even if it did own the local newspaper, one of the four network affiliates, and eight radio stations—monopolize the news market when the Internet offered consumers countless additional options? As NBC vice president R. Robert Okun argued when asked about whether the FCC should cut ownership restrictions on television stations in 2003, "There's so much competition out there, so many choices you could probably take the cap off."[5] Senior Research Fellow James Gattuso of the Heritage Foundation went a step farther, arguing that ownership caps actually harm the public. "Rather than media monopolies," he wrote, "consumers face a bewildering and unprecedented amount of choice. Instead, the real danger to Americans is that outdated and unnecessary FCC restrictions will limit improvements in media markets and technologies, limiting the benefits that they can provide."[6] This position inspired the ambitious policy agenda of then FCC commissioner Michael Powell. As he told the USC Annenberg's *Online Journalism Review,* "Contrary to the popular discourse about media I actually think we're awash. I say to my staff, 'I guarantee you with all the stuff that we have that no significant news event can happen in the world and we're probably less than 20 minutes from hearing about it.' . . . It's pretty remarkable that I can go to Google News and immediately have 4,000 sources of news from all around the world. The breadth of access gives me a perspective that's pretty fascinating."[7]

Thanks to digital technologies, satellite services, and the extraordinary range of content available online, Americans with home Internet access enjoy unprecedented levels of diversity in the global marketplace of ideas. Policy makers would be irresponsible if they did not carefully consider how the smorgasbord of content available online has changed the way traditional media works. But the matter is not so simple. One problem is that the digital divide between those who have and those who do not have access to the Internet is deeper than we generally recognize. According to the Center for the Digital Future at the University of Southern California, about 21 percent of the population did not use the Internet at all during 2005; 33 percent of U.S. households lack a home Internet connection, and among those that do, less than half have a high-speed connection that facilitates easy access to video and audio streams. It is common knowledge that wealthy and highly educated citizens are more likely than others to have Internet access, and that whites and Asian Americans are more likely to have home access than African Americans and Latinos. They are also more skilled at using it, and thereby more capable of accessing the news, information, and services available online. According to recent communications research, the educated and affluent are more likely to find new sources of information and entertainment on the Net, whereas less educated and affluent users tend to restrict their visits to Big Media and commercial outlets.[8]

While it is apparent that the Internet is not as ubiquitous as media chiefs claim, neither is it as rich and reliable a source of local news as its enthusiasts often say. The Net, after all, is designed to transcend terrestrial distance so that users can connect to faraway people and places, and for that reason many communications experts have defined it as an "antilocal" medium. The Katrina crisis helped to reveal how some of the extraordinary innovations in new media content can contribute to the vitality of civil society, and even in noncrisis situations there are countless examples of new Web sites that enrich local offerings. Yet the celebratory rhetoric about the rise of grassroots journalists, bloggers, and the revolutionary potential of the Internet threatens to obscure the fact that Big Media companies are harnessing the Web to amplify their voices as never before. Despite the recent emergence of exciting online local projects, the idea that new technology has rendered the dangers of consolidation obsolete is the greatest and most dangerous media policy myth of the digital age.

BIG MEDIA DOMINATES THE WEB. ACCORDING TO THE PROJECT FOR excellence in Journalism's (PEJ) *2006 State of the Media* report: "The Internet has long been known for a seemingly unlimited number of news sites from across the political spectrum. The most popular sites, however, are generally associated with the media establishment. Of the top 20 Nielsen/NetRatings sites in 2005, 17 were associated with traditional news companies—those that produce most of their content offline for newspapers, television, or magazines." The top ten news Web sites for December 2005, as measured by the number of unique visitors, were as follows: Yahoo News, 24.6 million; MSNBC, 22.9 million; CNN, 20.9 million; AOL, 14.7 million; Internet Broadcasting Systems (which webcasts television segments from network affiliates and other major broadcast companies), 12.9 million; Gannett, 11.5 million; *New York Times,* 10.9 million; Tribune newspapers, 10.5 million; Knight Ridder Digital, 9.9 million; *USA Today,* 9.9 million.[9] New media giants such as Yahoo, AOL, and IBS join the major networks, cable stations, and newspaper chains on the list, but they don't supply much original content. As Gene Kimmelman, the director of the Consumers Union, explains, "The internet is a wonderful source of news and information. A small percentage of consumers rely upon it. When the FCC asked them where do they go? More than half go to broadcast.com. The next largest segment go to newspaper.com. It's the same sources of news and information using a new technology, a new medium, but it is not more diversity of viewpoints, it's not more competition in the media."[10]

Even Big Media moguls and fiercely libertarian publishers are concerned about the way conglomerates are establishing dominance on the Net. Barry Diller, the executive who helped create Fox Broadcasting Company, ran ABC Entertainment, Paramount, and Vivendi Universal, and went on to become the chairman and CEO of USA Interactive (whose holdings include the Home Shopping Network and Ticketmaster), predicts as much. "The same thing is going to happen in the Internet that has happened essentially to our other mass-communications pipelines. You can already see at Comcast and others the beginnings of efforts to control the home pages that their consumers plug into. It's for one reason: to create a toll bridge or turnstile through which others must pay to go. The inevitable result of that, without any question, is that every domino will fall."[11]

Although Big Media companies have developed elaborate plans for channeling Internet traffic to their Web sites, most have not made major investments in original reporting, particularly at the local level. The majority of online news content consists of repackaged wire service articles and syndicated newspaper stories, and most daily newspapers use the Web primarily to republish print articles rather than offering interactive or multimedia products. New media giants such as Yahoo, AOL, and IBS rely almost entirely on news supplied by other organizations, while bland, brief stories from wire services such as the Associated Press and Reuters constitute about three-fourths of the content at ABC.com and three-fifths of the content at both Fox.com and MSNBC.com. Even top newspaper companies, such as the New York Times and the Washington Post, make heavy use of wire services for their Web sites so that they can provide up-to-the-minute content, effectively publishing lower-quality news that they would never print on paper.

Major media companies have transformed the vast open space of the Internet into an enormous echo chamber, with the same stories reverberating in site after site without a significant uptick in original journalism. Lacking a strong business model for Internet news, media managers at leading Web sites actually reduced the professional staffs for editing, rewriting, and localizing wire copy between 2003 and 2004. The result: roughly three of every five wire-service stories posted on the sites studied was unedited by the sites' own employees. The PEJ, which analyzed 1,903 news articles published by nine leading online news sites, concluded that "the content they offer on the Web, while improving in volume, timeliness and technological sophistication, remains still significantly a morgue for wire copy, second-hand material and recycled stories from the morning paper."[12]

THE LACK OF PROFESSIONAL JOURNALISTS WHO FACT-CHECK, EDIT, OR add reporting to the prepackaged stories that circulate through the most popular Internet sites is a key source of the central problem with news published online: its unreliability. So much news first reported on the Internet is inaccurate that readers are reluctant to trust it unless it comes from a proven, and usually "old media," news company. Of course, the Internet does not have a monopoly on fabricated or misleading journalism. The scandals involving errant or outright fake reporting by Jayson Blair and Judith Miller (of the *New York Times*), Stephen Glass (of the *New Republic*), and Jack Kelley (of *USA Today*) proved that the highest-profile and most respected American news outlets are vulnerable to gross violations of journalistic ethics. These cases remain exceptional, however, and the dramatic internal investigations and severe punishments for faulty or fabricated reporting reflect the industry's commitment to enforcing professional norms.[13]

Americans' reluctance to trust Internet news sources, especially those that come from individuals, bloggers, and less established brands, is not unfounded. Anyone who has surfed to the fringes of the Web knows that most small sites offer more opinion than reporting and conform only vaguely to contemporary journalistic standards. Where did Wal-Mart and its public relations firm, Edelman, go to find outlets willing to print, sometimes verbatim, the controversial company's promotional copy as if it were straight news or opinion, or to republish scripted self-praise for the chain's role in Katrina relief projects? Where did the self-proclaimed new media journalists spread the story about Jews planning

September 11 and warning four thousand members of their faith to avoid work at the World Trade Center that morning? The Web, of course, which is why even Dan Gillmor, whose book *We the Media* champions the revolutionary capacity of "grassroots journalism," recognizes that "for manipulators, con artists, gossips, and jokesters of all varieties, the Internet is the medium from heaven."[14]

In countless cases, even professional reporters have been duped, taking inaccurate stories from Internet sources and republishing them in the mainstream media. In December 2005, for example, a *Los Angeles Times* reporter named Julie Cart found a story about Wyoming governor Dave Freudenthal, who apparently reversed a successful effort to reintroduce endangered wolves into the state by refusing to respect the Endangered Species Act, declaring that the state "now considers the wolf as a federal dog," unprotected by law. The *Times* published a report on the wolves on its front page, only to learn that the Internet story about Freudenthal's decree was a hoax, posted as an April Fool's joke by someone who never expected it to reach journalists in one of the nation's most esteemed publications, let alone appear on page one. In its "For the Record" section the next day, the Tribune Company–owned paper that had eliminated so much of its editorial staff acknowledged that "an article in Tuesday's Section A about tensions over the federal effort to reintroduce wolves into parts of the West wrongly attributed to Wyoming Gov. Dave Freudenthal a statement that Wyoming considered the Endangered Species Act no longer in force and 'now considers the wolf as a federal dog.'"[15]

The *Los Angeles Times* was hardly the first major organization to be duped. False Web reports about issues that affect the economy, from the assassination of Bill Gates to product updates for pharmaceutical companies such as Cel Sci and fake reports of an SEC investigation into the accounting practices of Emulex Corporation, have shaken up stock markets after credible television and Internet news sources repeated them.

Sometimes the hoaxes enter U.S. elections. During a debate between U.S. Senate candidates Hillary Rodham Clinton and Rick Lazio in October 2000, New York's WCBS-TV reporter Marcia Kramer demanded that they both declare how they stood on "Federal Bill 602P." Clinton, dumbstruck, said, "I have no idea." Then Kramer responded: "I'm going to tell you what it is. Under the bill that's now before Congress, the U.S. Postal Service would be able to bill e-mail users five cents for each e-mail they send even though the post office provides no service. They want this to help recoup losses of about $230 million a year because of the proliferation of e-mails. But if you just send 10 e-mails a day, that would cost consumers an extra $180 a year. So I'm wondering if you would vote for this bill." Both Clinton and Lazio opposed the proposal, with Lazio denouncing it as "an example of the government's greedy hand in trying to take money from taxpayers that, frankly, it has no right to." The candidates had good reason to be disturbed—but not about Bill 602P, which was a complete fiction, and in fact one of the most popular urban legends spread online. In one common version of the hoax, the bill is supposedly sponsored by a mythical congressman named Tony Schnell, endorsed by a *Washingtonian* editorial that was never written, and opposed by a nonexistent law firm at a fictitious address.[16] Although countless e-mail messages and Web sites exist to warn readers about the hoax and inform them that there is no Bill 602P, no one let WCBS know.

Government agencies have proven credulous, too, resulting in unnecessary health scares that undermine trust in public officials and media alike. In March 2004, officials in Aliso Viejo, California, grew so concerned about an Internet report on the dangers of dihydrogen monoxide that they debated banning Styrofoam cups, which use the chemical in production. The Web site that presents the report offers dire warnings about the compound: "Dihydrogen monoxide is colorless, odorless, tasteless, and kills uncounted thousands of people every year . . . Most of these deaths are caused by accidental inhalation of DHMO, but the dangers of dihydrogen monoxide do not end there. Prolonged exposure to its solid form causes severe tissue damage. Symptoms of DHMO ingestion can include excessive sweating and urination, and possibly a bloated feeling, nausea, vomiting and body electrolyte imbalance. For those who have become dependent, DHMO withdrawal means certain death."[17] More than 3 million people have visited the site, where they can read about DHMO and cancer, the Enviro Impact of DHMO, and use of DHMO in the dairy industry. The messages are alarming—"Found in every lake, river, and ocean"; "It's a major part of acid rain"—until one realizes dihydrogen monoxide is, in fact, H_2O (or water) and that the Web site is an educational satire, designed by the Villanova University computer science professor Tom Way. Officials in Aliso Viejo learned that they had been duped before they voted to limit the town's use of water, and today they know to treat news on the Net more skeptically.

Even the most fervent Web enthusiasts believe that the suspicions generated by fake Internet stories drive browsers looking for "real" news to the Web sites produced by major media brands, thereby amplifying their voices. As Gillmor, the grassroots journalism advocate, conceded, "The flood of unreliable information on the Net could have the ironic effect of reinforcing the influence of Big Media, at least in the short term."[18]

IN MOST CITIES, WEB SITES RUN BY NEWSPAPER COMPANIES ARE THE most popular sources of online local news and information, and they will remain so as long as they provide access to print journalism for free. Yet innovative Internet journalistic projects are beginning to pave new ground in city reporting, covering stories not treated in traditional news outlets, and sometimes even beating daily papers on routine local stories that they now lack the staff to get. In New York City, for example, a nonprofit research, education, and advocacy organization called the Citizens Union Foundation (which is connected to the Citizens Union, a good-government group founded in 1897) launched the *Gotham Gazette*, a Web site "that would provide one-stop shopping for persons interested in the public policies and civic life of New York City," in September 1999.[19] Jonathan Mandell, its tireless editor and a third-generation New York journalist, joked that the site, which is animated by cartoon graphics, is "named after the newspaper that Batman reads."[20] With a five-person editorial staff and an annual budget of around $500,000, which comes from grants and pledge drives, the *Gazette* publishes a daily digest with links to key stories from the city's unusually rich supply of local news outlets (dailies, weeklies, monthlies, and Internet publications); original reporting on a broad range of civic, cultural, and political issues; guest columns from prominent public officials, scholars, and journalists; a city calendar; a book club page; a classifieds section; links to popular local Web sites and blogs; and many special features, such as a budget explainer, interactive city maps, and educational computer games that simulate city planning problems.

The *Gazette* is a remarkably rich publication, which is why about
seventy thousand unique users visit its site each month and more than
ten thousand subscribers signed up to receive "The Eye-Opener," a daily
e-mail that highlights the morning's biggest stories, including those covered by the major commercial media and some that the top outlets
miss. The Web site began winning accolades and online journalism
awards soon after it began publishing, but the *Gazette* really proved its
value during the most difficult year in New York City's recent history,
2001, before September. As Mandell explained in an e-mail, "We offered
the most comprehensive coverage of the local races in 2001, a year in
which term limits kicked out three-quarters of the elected officials in
New York City, and a new campaign finance formula attracted hundreds of 'citizen-candidates,' most of whom had never run for office
before."[21] As usual, local television stations did not offer sufficient airtime for the four hundred or so aspiring candidates who wished to publicize their positions, while the major newspapers and magazines offered
sporadic, uneven coverage of the seventy city races. The *Gazette* created "Searchlight on Campaign 2001," which blended its digest model
with issue-driven original coverage, links to political parties, government offices, nonpartisan policy organizations, and columnists, as well
as district-level information pages and a separate page for each individual race. The public-service project won an Innovator Award from the
Pew Center for Civic Journalism, became a regular feature during election
years, and emerged as a model for community Web sites in other cities.

When terrorists attacked the World Trade Center on 9/11, *Gazette*
staffers heard the impact from their office, which was close to the Twin
Towers. Although everyone was forced to evacuate, the producers managed to post some original coverage by 4:30 p.m., and by September
12 they built a message board where visitors could check on the status
of friends and relatives or express their concerns. Because most of New
York City retained electricity after the disaster, residents used the Internet to get news and communicate with others, and the *Gazette* operated
much like NOLA.com would four years later. The *Gazette* played
a key role in consolidating information about New York City after
9/11, when city residents and officials began debating difficult questions about how to rebuild. According to Mandell: "From the beginning, when New Yorkers talked of rebuilding, they were defining it in

many different ways. Some meant the physical reconstruction just of the 16 acres known as Ground Zero; others, the economic recovery of Lower Manhattan or of all of New York City. Still others were talking about the spiritual and psychological recovery of the city's residents, or the efforts at restoring the feeling and the fact of safety and security, or the process of memorializing and of creating a memorial. We organized Rebuilding NYC to help New Yorkers understand these distinctions, with what have now grown to be 10 different topic sections."[22] In 2002 the *Gazette* won the Online News Association's award for service journalism by an independent organization for its Rebuilding NYC project (it had been a finalist for the Searchlight 2001 project), and the next year it won the top prize, for general excellence in online journalism.

CIVIC WEB SITES MAY BE ESPECIALLY USEFUL DURING CRISES, BUT A growing number of citizens and political officials are finding that they can also make government more effective in normal times. Today the overwhelming majority of elected local officials—about 73 percent—regularly go online to communicate with their constituents and learn about public opinion, and the majority of adult Internet users—some 97 million Americans—e-mail officials or go to government Web sites to participate in civic affairs.[23] Citizens have good reason to take advantage of "e-government" Web sites. Done well, the sites offer a level of information about public services, programs, and issues that has never before been so easily available. In Washington, D.C., for example, the www.dc.gov site gives residents, prospective business owners, and tourists a comprehensive overview of city life and works as a portal into civic affairs. The clearly written site features vital information about local schools, crime issues, taxes, and transit conditions; allows residents to make important and otherwise time-consuming transactions, such as renewing a driver's license, requesting an identification card, or paying a parking ticket; offers a special service request center, an emergency center, an education center, and interactive programs through which users can make personalized maps or get driving and Metro directions to any part of the Capitol.

Not that www.dc.gov provides citizens with a full toolbox for civic participation. E-government sites usually contain no direct links to critical local journalism or to reports by independent organizations, and they do more to promote than to check the power of local agencies and officials. If the mayor is investigated for a felony crime, police officers abuse a private citizen, city council members make backroom deals with developers, or the school system fails to educate children, www.dc.gov is hardly the place to learn about what happened. Some official government sites provide links to the personal sites of elected officials, where, as New York voters recently discovered, politicians can use their Web sites to alter news stories about their record. During William Weld's short-lived run for New York governor in 2006, the *New York Times* reported that his staff republished "sanitized" versions of two newspaper articles in the "News" section of his site, "removing all negative phrases about him, like 'mini-slump' and 'dogged by an investigation,' and passages about his political problems." When questioned, a Weld spokesman justified the practice by "comparing it to selecting positive blurbs to run in movie advertisements."[24]

In Washington, D.C.'s middle-class and affluent neighborhoods, dozens of organizations have developed hyperlocal Web sites and discussion forums for sharing information and reinvigorating collective participation around every conceivable neighborhood issue and event. More than one thousand residents in Mount Pleasant, an ethnically diverse neighborhood of thirteen thousand in the central north part of Washington, D.C., known for its architect-designed row houses and apartment buildings, go to their neighborhood site, www.mtpleasant dc.org, to find services (from baby-sitting to computer consulting), learn about city schools, search for housing, plan opposition to unpopular development plans, or simply gossip about parochial concerns. Registered participants drive the action on the discussion forum, which has become a main artery for civic engagement. In 2005, for example, residents posted thirty-nine messages in a debate over a controversial ban on single sales of beer in local liquor stores, forty-six about new parking regulations, fifty-four about a private club in a neighborhood house, fifty-seven about a proposal to build a bikeway to Rock Creek Park, and eighty-three about cars running through red lights at a busy intersection. Sometimes the debates are more urgent. When Greg Shipe, a thirty-four-year-old resident, was killed in a drive-by shooting while walking his dog, the online discussion—about gun control, local policing tactics, public drinking, and neighborhood community ties— attracted about ten thousand total visits from concerned participants.

NEIGHBORHOOD WEB SITES HELP TO ENCOURAGE CIVIC PARTICIPATION, but citizens searching for something that resembles original journalism are more likely to find it in the blogosphere, where, among the thousands of sites dedicated to politics, professions, and all matter of personal subjects, a small but active set of independent publishers are posting intensely local content—firsthand observations, neighborhood stories, critical reports, and candid photographs—from their PCs. In New York City, where some residents brag about spending most of their time and money within a few streets around their apartment, there are blogs covering microneighborhoods that span a block or two.

A weblog, write the blogging political scientists Daniel Drezner and Henry Ferrell, is "a web page with minimal to no external editing, providing online commentary, periodically updated and presented in reverse chronological order, with hyperlinks to other online sources."[25] But Gothamist, a metropolitan blog covering all of New York City, is expanding the meaning of the term. Gothamist was founded by Jake Dobkin, a Park Slope native who told me he had "never left New York for more than ten weeks at any one time," and Jen Chung, who manages the site when not working in an ad agency. The pair became close friends as Columbia University undergraduates and then began instant-messaging each other with stories about the city when they joined the network of the bored at work—young professionals who surf the Web while putting in long hours on the job.

"Jen is a media maven," Dobkin, a hipster with an MBA from New York University, told me while sipping mint tea in a SoHo café near his apartment. "She absorbs everything, especially about culture and the arts, and she's a local news junkie, too. I'm interested in weird things: signage, graffiti, alt culture, and stuff in the paper that just seems quirky. We were sending way too much of this to each other on IM and e-mail, and in 2002 we started putting some of it on my Web site. Our friends would comment on it. Then we realized that what we were doing was interesting to more people. Blogs weren't big in New York, but I knew about them from work I had done in San Francisco, and I found some lightweight content management software that a company called Blogger gave away for free. I created a site called Gothamist and moved our content there in February 2003. There weren't many local blogs anywhere then, but Jen and I were interested in the kind of local stuff that would go into a metro paper, and we just started posting."

Gothamist took off, attracting young, highly educated readers who liked the quirky commentary and edgy cultural coverage Chung and Dobkin offered, and getting boosts from other blogs, such as Gawker, which linked to the site. "Gothamist has three main elements," Dobkin explained. "One-third is metacoverage, where we aggregate stories from the mainstream media and amplify the most interesting or overlooked items. One-third is original content. And one-third is user-generated content, stuff we get from reader tips and comments." Although neither Dobkin nor Chung has a background in journalism, Dobkin said, "We're serious newspaper readers, and that helps us, because we have an appreciation for what stories and issues are important for our readers. We're filling a void, especially for people our age, whose issues and interests weren't being addressed by the dailies."

They also have a good eye for cultural activities as they first surface on local streets. In June 2005 Gothamist began praising an unknown Brooklyn and Philadelphia band called Clap Your Hands Say Yeah!—even inviting them to promote their self-produced, eponymous CD in Gothamist's "Movable Hype" concert series. When the band broke out later that year, making the *Rolling Stone* Hot List, landing a feature story on NPR, selling twenty-five thousand copies of their album, and filling up concert venues wherever they played, they cited Gothamist's attention as a major boost.[26] "We've always been able to spot small stories that blow up into citywide or even national news," Dobkin told me. "Look at the Sony graffiti ad campaign story. I was walking in my neighborhood and I saw these spray-painted ads for PlayStation all over the place. I shot it and posted it as an editorial."

"This week," wrote Dobkin, "Sony PlayStation graffiti pieces have been popping up like cancer all over Manhattan. The pieces are sometimes drawn by hand—others are wheat pasted to walls all over SoHo and NoLita. It's clearly a large campaign, and deserves a thoughtful, measured response. Here's mine: corporate graffiti sucks. Sucks! Sucks! Sucks! It sucks for a variety of specific reasons: 1. It's exploitive . . . 2. It's fake . . . 3. It's deceptive . . . 4. It is not positive brand association . . .

5. Neighborhoods don't like it . . . 6. It's illegal . . . In conclusion: please cut this crap out."[27] The message resonated. Within a month, the local, national, and even international media were covering the issue, with *Wired,* the *Washington Post,* and the BBC among the many outlets filing reports. It turned out that Sony had launched the graffiti ad campaign in cities throughout the country, and, once it became public, officials and residents demanded that the company take the ads down. Not only did Sony ignore the complaints; it pushed the campaign even deeper into New York City life. On January 26, 2006, Gothamist reported that "*Sony is now advertising on human skin,* by co-opting those little stamps they use at clubs . . . Nothing classier than getting branded with some marketing company's artwork! This is definitely worse than the graffiti. At least there they were only messing with our neighborhood walls. Now they are using your skin as their advertising substrate. Disgusting, Sony—just really, really gross."[28]

Gothamist also covers local politics, from the mayoral election to the transit worker strike, by summarizing and editorializing about news stories, and by linking key reports from the major media. "Our site doesn't work well unless there is a lot of mainstream local media in town, because our metacoverage depends on it," Dobkin said. "Some people think that we'd be worried about competition from newspapers and other blogs. But this is not a zero-sum game. The more good stories there are, the better we can serve our readers." Gothamist readers can always comment on a story. Yet as the site became popular, many aspiring writers wanted to do their own original posts, too. The publishers, who had been doing about seven stories a day, were eager to grow. Since both had other full-time responsibilities, they welcomed new contributors. The site expanded, reaching about twenty-five new posts per day by 2005, taking on a part-time staff of two dozen (whom they pay, on average, under ten dollars per post), and attracting roughly one hundred thousand unique users each month. Today, Dobkin explained, "Gothamist has tentacles everywhere. Every neighborhood in New York City has at least one Gothamist reader, and in most places we have people who send comments and tips. If a fire starts in Manhattan, we'll have photos online within minutes. Our readers play a big role in content production. They send us story ideas and pictures, and they have fun doing it." Advertisers also want to participate. "At first they approached us," Dobkin explained. "We didn't really know how to handle the business, but we learned fast. After I finished business school I decided to work on Gothamist full-time, and I'm trying to get Jen to join me, too."

By 2006 Chung had a real incentive to make Gothamist her regular vocation: She and Dobkin had created Gothamist LLC, and in the previous two years they had used the New York model to start fourteen other local blogs, in cities from San Francisco (www.sfist.com) to Toronto (www.torontoist.com), London to Shanghai. Dobkin said he never intended to create a local blog brand, but in late 2003 Rachelle Bowden, a friend of theirs who was moving to Chicago, asked if they would help her start Chicagoist. "There weren't many costs for us," Dobkin said, "so we agreed to support her and pay the operating costs. Rachelle would be responsible for the content, and we would split the advertising revenues fifty-fifty. Although Chicago had a few local blogs, there was nothing like what we did, and Chicagoist became a hit." From there the expansion unfolded quickly. "There are a lot of cities with young people who want good local content, and we were getting requests from writers and editors who asked if they could work with us. We started LAist, which was rough because the editor soon left to work on John Kerry's campaign and we had to search for a replacement. But in D.C. and San Francisco it worked smoothly from the outset, and in London, Paris, and Shanghai it's going well, too."

For now, Dobkin and Chung are hands-off managers. Local editors are fully responsible for content on the cityist blogs they publish; they need only guarantee that all the content is locally relevant, and that contributors do city coverage rather than the kind of personal writing that is so common online. Yet Dobkin understands the media business, and he recognizes the potential value of an Internet publication with a proven record of reaching the young, well-educated, and upwardly mobile professionals whom the newspaper industry cannot attract. "We'll never be able to do the long-form reporting that the mainstream media does," he acknowledged. "No one is going to do a five-thousand-word piece for Gothamist. We're not going to cover all the big local institutions, city hall, the schools, businesses, and the like. But the short, quickly written stories work much better for us than they do for the dailies and the alt weeklies. Soon every major publication is going to be blogging.

That's just a fact. They won't be able to take the risks we take. They won't have our authenticity. So I wouldn't be surprised if they came to us and asked if we'd be willing to sell our business."

LOCAL BLOGGERS CAN MAKE AN IMMEDIATE IMPACT IN SMALL TOWNS and suburbs, where self-publishers with deep community ties are beginning to cover news and publicize issues that thinly staffed, chain suburban weeklies fail to see. In suburban New Jersey, a novelist, freelance journalist, and former newspaper columnist named Debra Galant started Baristanet, a blog about the towns of Bloomfield, Glen Ridge, and Montclair. (Galant chose the web address www.baristanet.com in an effort to create a virtual coffee bar.) She came up with the idea after learning about local blogging at a "meet-up," a social event organized online. Initially she partnered with Glen Ridge mayor Carl Bergmanson, with each investing three thousand dollars, Galant taking all editorial responsibilities, and Bergmanson handling the business. The arrangement didn't work, though, and Bergmanson sold his interest to Laura Eveleth, who threw herself into the project, selling ads and registering the site as a limited liability corporation. Soon they took on another partner, the Montclair resident and freelance journalist Liz George, and then hired a part-time writer, Annette Batson. The three content producers, all of whom work from home, take responsibility for updating the site and monitoring content on different days of the week. Along with the main content, they added a "Happenings" page with highlights of local cultural events, a food section with restaurant listings and reviews, a classifieds section, and a popular real estate page. Although Montclair and Bloomfield have well-regarded weekly newspapers, Glen Ridge actually has two, and all three towns have established Internet discussion forums, Baristanet has found its niche, especially among the more urbane residents who get most of their news from the *New York Times* or *Wall Street Journal* and appreciate the blog's approach to local affairs.

When we met at Montclair's Café Eclectic on a crisp January afternoon, the stylish mother of two teenagers was waiting patiently, cloaked in a fur-trimmed jacket with her cell phone, car keys, and designer notebook displayed on the table. Were it not for her slightly mischievous smile, I would not have identified Galant as the keen observer and biting social critic who has shaken up Essex County, where she has lived for seventeen years, with incisive posts about the mismanagement of municipal services, misbehavior in the schools, and speculation and fights over development in the local real estate market that are the open secrets of suburban life.

In 2005, for example, Baristanet caused a stir by reporting that the manager of the local public swimming pool had been taking the lifeguard staff to the movies instead of opening the facility on a day when storms gave way to sunny skies, leaving flustered parents calling town hall from behind the closed gates. "In December we broke a story that came from my daughter, who goes to Glen Ridge High School," Galant told me. "It's the same school that had the famous rape case in 1989, when a bunch of guys raped a mentally retarded girl."[29] Some students formed a hip-hop group called Porno Hate Train. They circulated one song with insults and sexually explicit lyrics naming other kids, and another with outrageously racist remarks about the victims of Katrina. Baristanet's brief post, published on December 2, included lyrics from the eponymous "The Hate Train" song.

It's gross that people in your city smell like baboons
You're living in shit and mad disease
and you all blame the President
Bitch nigger please[30]

The report shocked local residents, including parents of Glen Ridge students who had not learned details about the hateful raps that some of their children had written before reading about them online, and sparked an outpouring of comments about the state of the town. The *Star-Ledger,* New Jersey's leading regional daily newspaper, picked up the story after Baristanet because the beat reporter Phil Read checks the site regularly. "The kids involved threatened us," said Galant. "They posted a comment on the blog that they would find out where we live and come after us. They egged our house, too. My daughter, who's seventeen, threw herself into the argument. But my son, who's thirteen, asked me to stop because one of his friends told him that her mother didn't like me. I told him that we had to stand up to bullies, though, and he accepted that."

If on occasion Baristanet breaks a big story, with news from traffic accidents or photographs from crime scenes taken after readers provide tips, more often it depends on the mainstream media for its news reports. "We get Google News alerts for all three towns," Galant told me. "The local newspapers cover the town council and Board of Education meetings. We could never do that. We actually have a "Scooped by Phil Read" page, with a link to his stories in the *Star-Ledger*. We might be able to compete if we had resources to have a real news staff. But that's not my goal."

Neither does Galant aim to practice pristine, by-the-book journalism. Baristanet plugs local businesses whose proprietors give its producers free products and services, and doesn't disclose whether the message is a paid advertisement or an independent review. "What could be better than a hot stone massage at Harmony Day Spa?" says a post from May 2006. "They let us try one for free, and though a massage fan, the Barista had never indulged in hot stone before. It felt like hot wax pouring down our back, in a good way. The atmosphere is elegant, clean and slightly New Age . . . Tell them you heard about them on Baristanet."[31] The site indulges in small-town gossip, whether about home sales or prominent personalities. Galant explained: "We get Google News alerts for all the local celebrities: Bobbi Brown, Michael Strahan, Tom Cruise [who's from Glen Ridge]. We wanted to make the site like a small *Village Voice,* something that would be lively and culturally useful. Now the site lights up whenever something happens. It has news, entertainment, and a discussion board. And we have enough income to give the grunt work to other people and focus on content. Some people gave me a hard time when I started this. My brother, who's very successful, told me that I was wasting my time doing something so local. But people like it. I'm having fun. And at this point I don't think I could give it up."

WHAT BARISTANET AND GOTHAMIST HAVE IN COMMON IS THAT THEY ARE supplemental sources of news and information for communities that are already well served by the mainstream media, and they succeed as businesses because they attract advertisers looking for new ways to reach young or affluent consumers. For the rest of the country, the more pressing problem is that the communities that have the most to gain from Internet news sources are the least likely to have them. Until Internet access and computer literacy are distributed more equitably, there is real danger that local Internet sites, from e-government tools to neighborhood forums and blogs, will—contrary to the intentions of their founders—exacerbate inequalities among American communities, adding new resources for advantaged citizens to participate in democratic institutions or assert their claims to services, while letting the disadvantaged sink deeper into the digital divide.

Consider the uses of Internet discussion forums, which have proven to be especially valuable for citizens during moments of crisis. Approximately forty-five minutes after Greg Shipe was murdered in Mount Pleasant, a thirty-two-year-old African American named Michael Lanham was killed on the streets of Southeast Washington, a poor and segregated neighborhood just a few miles away. Coverage of the two killings was dramatically different in the major local newspaper. As the *Washington Post* ombudsman Michael Getler noted, a 528-word story about the Mount Pleasant homicide "went on the front page of Monday's Metro section. There were quotes from neighbors, from a classmate at Vanderbilt University's business school, and from D.C. council member Jim Graham (D-Ward 1), who said it was a 'horrible event' and the first fatal shooting in Mount Pleasant in almost two years." For the Southeast Washington murder, however, a 56-word, "three-sentence story appeared in the Metro in Brief column."[32] Few readers would be surprised by such disparate treatment by the major media, yet the story does not end here. Southeast Washington has neither the density of local bloggers one finds in more affluent neighborhoods, nor a popular Internet forum where residents can organize vigils, demand better services, communicate directly with local police officers, or debate how to better protect themselves on the streets. While their neighbors in Mount Pleasant used the Internet to discuss how to improve conditions in their traumatized neighborhood, the residents of Southeast Washington had nowhere to go on the Net.

The D.C. story is no anomaly. Four months after Katrina hit, Joel Dinerstein could learn about Uptown and the neighboring Garden district by reading any one of the 9,120 original posts, not to mention the even greater number of responses they generated from participants in their collective NOLA.com neighborhood forum. Yet there was far less information for displaced or returned residents interested in learning about conditions in the city's less prosperous communities. As of late May 2006, for example, there were only 2,506 original posts in Treme and the Sixth through Ninth Wards combined, and a mere 709 in

Gentilly. Michael Tisserand, who was the editor of the *New Orleans Gambit Weekly* at the time of the hurricane and had to evacuate with his family, told me, "We learned how much easier it was to get assistance from FEMA by filing claims on the Internet rather than on the telephone, which was almost impossible. Lots of government services that were hard to line up in person or on the phone were available online. Those of us who had Internet access had a huge advantage."

Most Americans, regardless of neighborhood, city, or region, agree that the Internet is a remarkable technology, one that has already changed the media ecosystem and is certain to continue transforming it as more television and radio programs are transmitted online. But the Internet's echo chamber effect, its susceptibility to misinformation, and the deepening digital divide illustrate a point that media historians have made repeatedly through the generations: new technologies do not eliminate the need for carefully crafted regulations that prevent a small number of giant companies from dominating the marketplace.[33] In fact, they make such regulations all the more urgent. Today the challenge is doubly daunting, because not only are policy makers responsible for creating conditions that promote a wealth and diversity of local content, but they must also ensure that all Americans have equal opportunity to participate in their community's political and civic life. Increasingly, this means treating Internet access as an essential public utility, tantamount to delivering water, gas, and electricity. As a growing number of citizens are arguing, the future of democratic citizenship depends on it.

8

FIGHTING FOR AIR

On a hazy Saturday morning in June 2005, meteorologists reported that Chicago was about to endure the "warmest weekend since last summer," with temperatures hovering around ninety and unseasonable humidity making the city air feel swampy, like Florida in August. Ordinarily the midwestern metropolis would welcome an early summer hot spell, yet this year marked the tenth anniversary of the great 1995 heat wave, when 739 Chicagoans died in brutal conditions. The weather took its greatest toll in the city's poorest and most segregated neighborhoods—places like North Lawndale, an African American community on the West Side where decades of economic deterioration, population loss, and political neglect resulted in a landscape of empty lots, shuttered storefronts, and abandoned buildings, the kind of depleted neighborhood conditions that discourages visitors and potential investors from outside the area and fosters social withdrawal as a survival strategy for vulnerable residents. North Lawndale, like so many other shunned and stigmatized urban areas, was decidely cut off from the public goods and amenities that most city dwellers take for granted. The people who lived there not only were at risk of suffering in silence during treacherous weather but also were missing opportunities afforded to those with easy access to the greater city's economic and cultural life every day.

I first learned about the particular dangers of social disconnection in North Lawndale during the late 1990s, when I did fieldwork in the community to understand why there were nineteen heat-related deaths there during the 1995 disaster. I have subsequently followed the neighborhood's modest upward trajectory as developers experiment with new housing and commercial projects. Rebuilding was a frustratingly slow and often halted process, but on this warm weekend morning something special was happening: a coalition of civic organizations was planning to install a "wireless mesh" or "point-to-point network," with a signal emanating from the original Sears Tower and going out to a series of small antennae placed on the roofs of local buildings. The mesh network would produce an "invisible cloud" of coverage, providing free Internet access to North Lawndale families who signed up for the service. About twenty-five people gathered to kick off the project by activating live connections at four residences and holding open computer workshops at a new community center. "Most of our families don't have access right now," said Carol Merrill, who grew up in North Lawndale and now works a few blocks from home at the Carole Robertson Center for Learning. "Affordability is a deterrent, because a lot of people are struggling just to do the basic things in living. But it's so much easier to do things here if you have the Internet. It puts you in a whole different place."

Her neighbor, Derrick Mack, had just returned to his family's house in North Lawndale after graduating from Eastern Illinois University that May, and he was so excited about having high-speed Internet in the community that he volunteered to help build the network. Mack and I joined a small team of sweaty workers who drove through the neighborhood that morning, stopping at places in the network to attach cables to the antennae and drilling holes through walls made of brick and stone before connecting the lines into the PCs of local residents. "I always wanted to do something in the neighborhood," Mack told me, his soft features and puppy eyes conveying earnest enthusiasm and hope. "I don't want to abandon it. I want to be a young black man here with a college degree."

Back at the community center, Mack narrated North Lawndale's history with a bare-bones story that could apply to hundreds of African American ghettos across the nation, from the crowded period in the 1950s and '60s when there were "lots of shops and busy streets" to the apocalyptic 1970s, '80s, '90s, when factories closed, banks and grocery stores shut down, the streets emptied, and "things just went down." Today, he explained, black professionals and some well-meaning foundations are leading efforts to revitalize the neighborhood, and community wireless is emerging as an essential tool. "Internet access is crucial for North Lawndale, especially for the kids here, and also for seniors. There's so much they can do online—shopping, services, getting things you can't find in stores. It's so convenient. We can network, start up a North Lawndale Web site. And it will help us stay connected, to meet other people in the community. It'll be great."

For the Center for Neighborhood Technology (CNT), which led the project, it was an important initiative, part of a broader effort to connect about 250 households in four low-income neighborhoods to the Internet, offer classes on how to conduct online job searches and contact service providers, and demonstrate the value of high-speed access as a tool for economic development and social integration for those on the wrong side of the digital divide. The North Lawndale campaign grew out of a nationwide movement to promote media access. Chicago is just one of hundreds of U.S. cities where grassroots organizations, many working with public- and private-sector partners, are building affordable broadband networks to help underserved communities access and use the Web.

U.S. taxpayers funded the research and development that produced the Internet, making American citizens among the first to enjoy the benefits of Web technology. Although the United States remained a leader in Internet innovation through the 1990s, by the end of the first Bush administration it had fallen to thirteenth place in national broadband usage, with service that was "the slowest, most expensive and least reliable in the developed world."[1] As *Foreign Affairs* reported, in 2005 the United States was "the only industrialized state without an explicit national policy for promoting broadband." But rather than passively accept this condition, citizens throughout the country have begun demanding better access to the service that their tax dollars helped to create, mobilizing to turn public spaces into free "hot spots," where anyone with a mobile device can get online. Cities such as Atlanta, Austin, Seattle, and San Francisco are already saturated with public access points. Moreover, as Michael Calabrese and Matt Barranca from the New America Foundation observed, "dozens of United States municipalities long ignored by wireline providers because their markets were considered too small to justify laying cable or DSL have deployed unlicensed wireless networks ... with rapid returns on their investment." The successful early projects were in places as diverse as St. Cloud, Florida; Owensboro, Kentucky; Franklin County, Washington; and the Pala Indian Reservation in San Diego County.[2]

By 2005 support for municipal wireless service had spread from small underserved towns to major metropolitan areas, with Philadelphia, Minneapolis, and Portland announcing plans to contract with private-sector firms to provide citywide broadband access for reasonable fees because the major commercial services had failed to provide affordable service to disadvantaged citizens. The decision was particularly controversial in Philadelphia, where Verizon Communications, the dominant telephone company, and Comcast, the locally based cable giant, protested that the program would undermine commercial companies that already offered high-speed connections at market rates. "If you think this through for a second," said Verizon spokesman Eric Rabe, "you realize that the city is taxing us, to some degree they are regulating us, and now they're a competitor of ours. And I think you have to question whether that's a really genuinely fair situation."

Mayor John Street was more concerned about another fairness issue. In his view, the for-profit Internet providers had demonstrated their indifference to the city's poorest neighborhoods and residents: with Internet access in private hands alone, more than 90 percent of households in Philadelphia's affluent areas had home Internet access, compared to less than 25 percent of households in poor neighborhoods. Street found this unacceptable, and he declared: "I believe the day will come when having access to the Internet will be just as common as having water in one's house or having, you know, some form of electricity or some form of heat ... Wireless Philadelphia will allow low-income families, families that are on the cusp of their financial capacity, to be able to be fully and completely connected. We believe that our public school children should be—their families have to be connected or else they will fall behind, and, in many cases, never catch up."[3] In the program Street envisioned, broadband access would cost Philadelphia families between ten and twenty dollars per month, less than half the rates at the time.

With their market domination threatened in Philadelphia, leading cable and telephone companies rushed to the Pennsylvania statehouse, urging their legislative allies to ban publicly subsidized municipal wireless projects in cities where there is a private-sector provider. There was little public support for the state senate's Act 183, which critics dubbed the "Verizon Bill" due to the widespread perception that the company played a prominent role designing the bill. But for telecommunications and cable companies, which controlled more than 95 percent of the national broadband market, the stakes were high. Anticipating competition for Internet service, since 1996 the industries had invested heavily in state-level lobbying and made major contributions to local officials, exerting extraordinary influence in the state capital, Harrisburg. It didn't hurt that David Cohen, Democratic governor Edward Rendell's former chief of staff and a regular atop surveys of the state's most powerful people, was Comcast's executive vice president, or that Verizon alone had spent more than $3 million on state-level lobbying in the previous two years.[4] To call the cable and telephone companies "well connected," as the Center for Public Integrity did in its major report on state-level political lobbying by the industry, was to understate their power.

After a rancorous debate that made the pages of the *Wall Street Journal* and the *New York Times,* the Pennsylvania state legislature passed a measure requiring any municipality interested in building a public wireless service to give the primary local phone company the right to do it instead, unless the municipality could complete the job within fourteen months. Calling the bill "a victory for Verizon Communication," the *Times* reported that "if the phone company proceeds, the city must drop its plans to build a broadband network."[5] To make the bill politically acceptable, Verizon agreed to exempt Philadelphia from the requirement, and the city moved forward with its public plan. "While it may be good news for Philadelphians, it doesn't bode well for the rest of the country," said Jeff Chester, of the Center for Digital Democracy. "This is just an exception for Philadelphia, placing the rest of Pennsylvania, and indeed the other 49 states [where the cable and telecommunications lobbyists would turn next], off limits to municipal networks."[6]

Chester was prescient. Telecommunications and cable lobbyists would storm local governments and statehouses throughout the country, and within months fourteen states passed laws restricting the development of municipal wireless projects. The effort reached Congress in May 2005, when U.S. representative Pete Sessions, a Texas Republican who had been a senior executive at the giant telecom company SBC Communications (which later in 2005 would acquire AT&T) before coming to Congress introduced HR 2726, the "Preserving Innovation in Telecom Act."

Alongside the three other telecommunications giants, Verizon, Bell-South, and Qwest Communications, SBC had already established itself as an industry leader in the fight against public access projects. According to the Center for Public Integrity, a nonprofit research organization in Washington, D.C., "The San Antonio–based company is the most prolific spender on both lobbying and campaign contributions at the state level among telecommunications companies . . . SBC employees and political action committees spent $10.2 million on campaign contributions on state races from 1999 to 2004. The company also spent a minimum of $16.3 million to lobby state governments across the nation in 2003 and 2004."[7] The Sessions bill, which proposed a blanket prohibition on any municipal telecommunications service, information service, or cable service in markets where private firms offered similar products, was especially restrictive. Yet it was not until the public disclosure of the congressman's industry ties that the proposal began to be deemed politically unpalatable, and it stalled in committee. This power grab by the private sector may even have backfired. Inspired by strong public interest in municipal access programs, in June U.S. senators John McCain and Frank Lautenberg introduced the "Community Broadband Act of 2005," a proposal that, if it ever became law, could override state-level restrictions and allow local governments to provide wireless service.

By 2006 the political debate over Internet access expanded into another realm. Leading telephone and cable companies lobbied Congress to grant them rights to discriminate among Web sites, providing faster connections to the sites of corporations that pay a premium for high-speed service, and even to block access to selected sites altogether. Civic organizations quickly mobilized to preserve Internet freedom (or network neutrality), calling for legislation that would obligate telephone and cable companies to run any devices and applications that consumers choose, and to offer all users equal access to all available content. By summer the campaign to promote faster, cheaper, and open broadband access was attracting grassroots organizations and political officials from red and blue states, crossing right over the nation's class and color lines.[8]

The fight to preserve Internet freedom and expand Internet access for the disadvantaged is just one part of a growing media reform movement that is unifying citizens concerned about problems stemming from consolidated ownership of radio, television, and newspapers, from the loss of local broadcasters to the loss of local content, along with those worried about issues such as broadband access, payola, propaganda, and copyright. Consolidation is the movement's bedrock. In May 2003 CNN's *Lou Dobbs Moneyline* (now *Lou Dobbs Tonight*) polled its viewers on whether "too few corporations own too many media outlets." Although the audience for Dobbs's program is neither liberal nor progressive, 80 percent said yes. Finding consensus on media policy issues is by no means uncommon. After the FCC announced its 2003 decision to relax ownership caps, Wayne LaPierre, the executive vice president of the National Rifle Association, declared that "groups as diverse as the National Rifle Association, the National Organization for Women and the National Council of Churches oppose the FCC's sellout to monopoly-minded media giants." U.S. senator Barbara Boxer, a Democrat from California, said, "In all the years I've been [in Congress], I've not seen such deeply held feelings across ideologies." Americans may be politically polarized and mired in the culture wars, but when they are fighting for air they are on the same side.[9]

TODAY AN UNPRECEDENTED NUMBER OF AMERICANS HAVE TAKEN UP THE cause of media reform, in hopes of reining in the local media outlets that slipped into the hands of distant corporate overseers. In the last decade ordinary people who—of all the things to fight for—never thought it would be access to local news and culture, have begun to engage in activities as diverse as volunteering to assemble wireless networks, teaching classes on "media literacy," forming watchdog groups to monitor news and entertainment content, producing independent journalism about under-reported topics, and simply writing letters to express concern about proposed media policy regulations. After the 2004 elections, both MoveOn.org and True Majority polled members to ask what issues are most important for the future. "In each poll," wrote the communications scholar Robert McChesney and the journalist John Nichols, media reform ranked second, ahead of peace, health care, education, and social justice."[10]

The project of challenging media conglomerates, demanding content that serves the public interest, and restoring more public and democratic control of the airwaves has become the fastest-growing bipartisan social movement in the United States. "Today, for the first time in U.S. history, the issue of corporate control over the media is a political issue," U.S. representative Bernie Sanders, an Independent from Vermont, told me in May 2005. "There is no issue more important than this because it touches upon all political issues. Millions of people are now thinking about this issue. This is one of those areas where there is fire taking place all over the country." If Big Media outlets do not cover the conflagration, it's only because they have so much to lose.

Reporters understand the stakes better than anyone, as I learned during my interviews with countless journalists who complained about how consolidation had hurt their profession and undermined their working conditions but told me that they couldn't produce stories about the issue because it might damage their career. FCC commissioner Jonathan Adelstein made the same point when discussing his staff's research on media ownership: "We've heard from a lot of journalists who said they felt very intimidated doing this story, sometimes explicitly, and sometimes it's implicit. It's clear to them that it's not a career advancing move to write a story that challenges the policy that is being promoted by their boss . . . I think it'd be helpful if people could speak to us and be able to have their identity protected, so that they can say, in an unfettered way, what their concerns are, without having any concern about that hurting their career. I feel right now that journalists in particular are feeling intimidated about it. Which raises a real question about the independence of journalism in this country."[11]

There is no reason to think of the nation's media ecology as a natural, inevitable, or unalterable system, in which powers on high set the conditions and citizens have no capacity to clean up the polluted airwaves. Today media activists are organizing media reform campaigns in their hometowns while building a spate of national organizations— including the Media Access Project, American Federation of Television and Radio Artists, Communications Workers of America, Fairness and Accuracy in Reporting (FAIR), the Future of Music Coalition, the Center for Digital Democracy, Free Press, the United Church of Christ, the Parents Television Council, and Youth Media Council—that are fighting to revive the vital organs of American democratic and cultural life.

• • •

A DECADE AGO, NO ONE PREDICTED THAT MEDIA REFORM WOULD become such a galvanizing social issue—not even leaders of the largest media watchdogs and advocacy groups. As recently as 2001, Congressman Jesse Jackson Jr. remarked, "The case for media reform is not being heard in Washington now . . . I hear people everywhere around the country complaining about the media, but we have yet to figure out how to translate those complaints into some kind of activist agenda that can begin to move Congress."[12]

Two years later, more than two thousand people turned out for the first national media reform conference at the University of Wisconsin-Madison, an event that its organizers originally expected to draw about two hundred and had to expand when registrations poured in. Sitting with me in the large cafeteria of the student union building, FAIR's founder, Jeff Cohen, scanned the crowded room in search of friends, then squared his long frame in my direction and offered a look of amused bewilderment. "Fifteen years ago people thought I was nuts," he explained. "There were no protests of media institutions. Media was something you grumbled about, not something you fought. Eight years ago we didn't have a media reform movement. Proposals got hashed out while we were on the outside and in the wilderness, and we got the 1996 Telecom Act. Now we have the movement, and what we need is the political opening to make things happen."

Historically, such openings have been unusual. Since the turn of the twentieth century, Americans who wanted to shape media policy had to mount relentless, well-organized campaigns against industry groups and government agencies that preferred to act without public input. Citing threats to the nation's democratic process, citizen groups persuaded legislators to block monopolies in the newspaper and broadcasting industries during the 1900s and 1930s, and to connect concerns about competition and diversity in the media market to broader reform movements of those eras. Yet the Communications Act of 1934, which established the FCC, essentially ended the brief period of public participation in media policy making. After the commission opened, citizens would not even win the right to be heard in regulatory debates and take actions in courts until 1966, when the Office of Communications

of the United Church of Christ (UCC) won a landmark case against the
FCC in a U.S. court of appeals.[13]

The UCC's campaign had deep roots in the civil rights movement.
In the 1950s, Reverend Martin Luther King Jr. complained about the
way southern broadcasters treated African Americans. Radio and television stations rarely invited blacks to speak over the airwaves, perhaps because of the stations' support for discriminatory policies and use
of hateful speech. King's concerns helped move Reverend Everett C.
Parker, a member of the Broadcast Pioneers and the director of the
Office of Communications of the UCC, to travel through the South and
survey broadcast content. The research, not surprisingly, showed that
"stations typically broadcast hard-line segregationist views, and very
little attention was paid to civil rights issues, except with extreme dispar-
agement." Parker presented his findings to a group of church leaders,
and together they decided to ask the National Association of Broadcasters to demand that each broadcast licensee "pledge itself to air diverse
programming, to use courtesy titles (Mr., Miss, Mrs.) for blacks, to provide blacks the opportunity to present their views on the air, particularly
in cases where they felt they'd been attacked or when their views were
not represented at all, and to accord blacks equal opportunity to buy
air time." According to the communications scholar Robert Horwitz,
who conducted an extensive interview with Parker for his article about
the UCC case, "The [NAB] board voted it down quickly and unani-
mously."[14]

Civil rights activists were accustomed to preliminary setbacks, however, and although communications attorneys in the Capitol warned
them against it, Parker and his colleagues decided to press the issue by
legally charging a broadcaster with violating the public-interest provisions of the Communications Act. In 1964, Jackson, Mississippi,
television stations WLBT (an NBC affiliate) and WJTV were scheduled
to come up for license renewal, a process whose success was (and
remains) virtually guaranteed unless the broadcaster has blatantly violated FCC rules. WLBT was a notoriously discriminatory station, with
no African American employees despite an audience that was about 45
percent black. Parker persuaded Aaron Henry, the president of the
National Association for the Advancement of Colored People's (NAACP)
Mississippi chapter, and Robert L. T. Smith, a local politician and small-
business owner who had filed complaints against WLBT with the FCC

because the station refused to sell him airtime during his unsuccessful run for the House of Representatives in 1962, to join him in challenging its license. They filed a "bill of particulars," claiming that WLBT "had failed to serve the public interest, convenience, and necessity."

According to Horwitz, the UCC's petition "charged that WLBT had discriminated against Negroes in the presentation of news and announcements and the selection of program material. The station had failed to serve the interests of the substantial Negro community in its viewing area and had further failed to give a fair presentation of controversial issues, especially in the field of race relations. In addition, WLBT provided a disproportionate amount of commercials and entertainment, with very little attention devoted to public affairs, education, or information." To establish its case, the UCC organized a team of white monitors, none of whom were UCC members ("so that," as Parker explained, "the Commission couldn't say that blacks were doing something to (sic) their own interest and not telling the truth"), to review one week of WLBT's offerings.[15] Among their key findings were that, except for fifteen minutes of spirituals broadcast at 6:45 a.m., the station's four hours of religious programming on Sunday morning originated out of white churches; that almost all the live local performers were white; that there were no black entertainers in the local offerings; that the only local children's program banned black children from participating; and that the rare local public-service announcements that the station did run did not mention events in the black community or efforts to oppose segregation. WLBT's attorneys claimed that national network programming offered material for black audiences. Yet the UCC had also checked the station's logs, which revealed that the station had often substituted local coverage for NBC's national stories about race relations, and introduced those it did run with warnings such as "what you are about to see is an example of biased, managed, northern news. Be sure to stay tuned at 7:25 to hear your local newscast."[16]

The UCC petititon offered "overwhelming" evidence of the flaws in WLBT's coverage, and the FCC staff recommended that the commission consider revoking its license. Yet the petition was the first license challenge by a group that had neither an economic interest in the station nor a problem with electrical interference from the station's signals, and, after a year of delaying, the commissioners ruled against the UCC, saying that it did not have standing to protest the license. The FCC announced that, by a four-to-two ruling, it was dismissing the petition on grounds that the signers had no legally legitimate interest in the matter. Although the FCC renewed the WLBT license, the station's refusal to acknowledge any wrongdoing, coupled with the scathing comments from two dissenting commissioners, compelled the commission to limit the renewal to one year instead of the standard three. Angered and emboldened, the UCC immediately filed an appeal with the U.S. Court of Appeals for the District of Columbia Circuit, whose chief justice was the conservative Warren Burger (whom President Richard Nixon would later nominate as chief justice of the U.S. Supreme Court). In a surprising decision, *Office of Communication of United Church of Christ v. FCC,* Burger's court ordered the FCC to conduct hearings on WLBT's license renewal. "After nearly five decades of operation," the chief justice wrote, "the broadcast industry does not seem to have grasped the simple fact that a broadcast license is a public trust subject to termination for breach of duty."[17]

The court-ordered hearing took place in Jackson the next year in a room that, according to Horwitz, "was overflowing with Confederate flags." Earle K. Moore, the lead attorney for the Office of Communication, remembered that local African Americans were particularly nervous. At the beginning of the hearing, Moore could persuade only one black person, Robert L. T. Smith, to sit at the counsel's table. Moore also had a hard time lining up witnesses."[18] The hearing examiner, who oversaw the case, showed "solicitude for the station's witnesses and animosity toward the Intervenors," the UCC. After refusing to apply the burden-of-proof recommendations of the court of appeals, which had in fact been placed on the station, and blocking some of the UCC's testimony, the hearing examiner ultimately ruled that the UCC had "woefully failed . . . to come forward and sustain their serious allegations" against WLBT, and recommended that the FCC renew the station's license for three years. In a five-to-two decision, the conservative commission registered its agreement. Once again the UCC appealed, and once again the U.S. court of appeals took the case. This time, however, they would convene in the ceremonial courtroom, a clear signal that something significant was at stake.

In fact, the stakes were even higher than the litigants imagined. In an unexpected ruling, the appelate court blocked WLBT's station renewal and opened a new process in which civic groups could apply for the license and seize a slice of the airwaves for their own use. But the decision had even greater consequences for the public's relationship to broadcast media. The court used the UCC case to establish a new precedent, extending to citizens the "right to stand" before regulatory agencies that ruled on matters of public interest, and requiring broadcasters to recognize and address the concerns of local populations and minority groups. The decision opened the floodgates for civic groups that wanted to diversify content and improve community programming, forced broadcasters to hire minorities for their on-air staffs, and turned *access to the airwaves* from an abstract concept into a concrete cause. It also taught civil rights advocates and other activists an important lesson: whether the ultimate cause was racial segregation, quality education, fair representation, or the democratic process itself, demanding an open and accountable media would be an essential if frustrating part of the fight.

CIVIC GROUPS LEARNED ANOTHER IMPORTANT LESSON FROM THE UCC victory: media reformers could monitor and record broadcast content to establish whether and how media companies are polluting the nation's public airwaves, turning watchdog techniques into the primary and most popular tools of the media movement.

Consider the problem of indecency and the campaign to make broadcasters respect community standards. Conservative Christian groups mobilized their constituents around the issue in the early years of the twenty-first century as radio conglomerates such as Clear Channel and Cumulus replaced local programs with nationally syndicated shock jocks whose crude banter offended their sensibilities, and their campaign reached a fever pitch after Janet Jackson exposed a nipple on the 2004 Super Bowl halftime show. The Parents Television Council (PTC) and the Family Research Council (FRC) pressured the Bush administration, Republican members of Congress, and the FCC to dramatically increase fines for offending media companies that, as the PTC's president, L. Brent Bozell, put it, "would pollute . . . the public's airwaves," and liberal groups such as the American Civil Liberties Union warned about the potentially chilling effect of censorship and threats to free speech resulting from the FCC's vague definition of *indecency*. "Because of the vagueness," its executives wrote in a letter to congressional leaders, "speakers must engage in speech at their peril, guessing what the FCC will determine to be prohibited. Increasing fines merely exacerbates the problem, particularly for small broadcasters. Rather than face a potentially ruinous fine, smaller broadcasters are more likely to remain silent."[19] Although ultimately Democrats and Republicans supported more onerous penalties for indecency, resulting in heavy fines for Clear Channel, Infinity, and high-profile personalities such as Howard Stern and Bubba the Love Sponge, the issue remains divisive today.

Americans do agree that as consumers, we should not have to pay for content that we don't want, particularly not when it offends us. Yet that is precisely what we have to do when we purchase cable television, because programmers, such as Disney and Viacom (which own cable channels), demand that providers, such as Comcast and Time Warner (which own cable systems and sell home connections), offer bundled packages that combine unpopular channels with the ones we really want, and cable companies pass the costs on to us. As Dan Isett, PTC's director of corporate and government affairs, told me, "If a local cable company wants Nickelodeon, Viacom says that they have to carry lots of other things that they own, like MTV and VH1. They not only have to carry them, but often they have to put it in their basic package, too." Senator McCain, who has been a steady advocate for cable consumers, used his opening remarks at a March 2004 hearing on escalating cable rates to complain that "when it comes to purchasing cable channels beyond the basic tier today, consumers have all the 'choice' of a Soviet election ballot. One option—take it or leave it. You want ESPN? You must buy 40-plus channels of expanded basic. You want CNN? You must buy 40-plus channels of expanded basic. You want Comedy Central? Well, you get the idea."[20] Once it was technologically impossible for cable companies to offer each household an individual menu of choices. Yet today it is not only feasible but economically beneficial— albeit for consumers, not providers and programmers, who stand to lose subscription and advertising revenue if they cannot force-feed channels into the box.[21]

Cable companies provide limited flexibility with their tiered packages and "video-on-demand" marketing campaigns, but their prices, particularly since the 1996 Telecom Act, never waver. Average cable rates have risen nearly three times the rate of inflation since 1996, when industry leaders convinced Congress that by deregulating the business they could keep costs down. In some markets cable prices have skyrocketed. U.S. Public Interest Research Group (PIRG) reported that "the larger the cable company and the greater the dominance of a region through clustering of systems, the higher its rates." That helps explain why after deregulation nearly all cable subscribers experienced rate increases above 50 percent, with Cablevision customers in New York City getting a cumulative increase of 94 percent that essentially doubled their monthly bills. The price hikes do not stem merely from an increase in the number of channels offered, because today consumers pay more *per channel* than they did ten years ago—even though cable companies have downgraded the quality of basic packages by moving popular stations, such as HBO and ESPN, to the expensive premium and digital tiers, and letting service levels fall low enough to rank among the worst-rated businesses in the history of the American Customer Satisfaction Index. "These increases defy logic," complained Senator McCain during one recent regulatory conflict. "The cable industry has risen to new heights in their apparent willingness and ability to gouge the American consumer."[22]

There is a simple reason that cable companies get away with these practices: they enjoy monopoly power, leaving consumers, no matter how much they dislike their local cable provider, with nowhere else to get the service. Cable providers say that satellite services offer real competition, but the U.S. General Accounting Office has shown that this is not true. Satellite services have many competitive disadvantages: The satellite dishes require direct exposure to the southern sky, which many city dwellers lack. They sometimes do not offer local broadcast stations that carry popular local news and sports programming. They cannot deliver high-speed Internet access. The result is that satellite television is most attractive to sports fanatics and residents of remote rural areas without access to cable. The proof is in the pricing: in a typical market, the presence of satellite television service brings down the cost of cable television by about twenty cents per month, whereas the rare presence of a second cable provider results in monthly consumer savings of around five dollars.[23]

According to Gene Kimmelman, the director of the Consumers Union (which publishes the popular *Consumer Reports* magazine): "The fact is large cable operators simply do not compete with one another. Not one of the incumbent cable operators has ever expanded its infrastructure into an already-wired community and competed head-to-head. Instead, the major cable operators have through mergers and acquisitions become national firms, operating in regional clusters . . . In markets where 98 percent of Americans live, a single cable operator dominates multi-channel video distribution with a market share exceeding 80 percent." These numbers actually understate the extent of the large providers' presence. As U.S. PIRG reported, big cable operators, or companies with substantial investments in cable operators, own (wholly or in part) about 40 percent of the top cable channels; and "of the top 26 channels in terms of subscriber and prime-time ratings, all but one (the Weather Channel) is affiliated with either a principal cable operator or a broadcast network." In other words, much of the money that cable providers "spend" on programs is actually boosting their own bottom line.[24]

The top cable operators generated record-setting revenues in 2000–2004—precisely when representatives of the industry such as James Robbins, then president and CEO of Cox Communications, testified during the Senate hearing on escalating cable rates that the industry faced "formidable competition." Robbins and Cox chairman of the board James Kennedy (who soon after became the CEO) struck a different note in the "Letter to Shareholders" that they included in the company's 2003 annual report, published around the same time as the Senate hearing, boasting of some of the "more than 22,000 reasons we're so confident in Cox's prospects for prosperity." "Although Cox's phenomenal performance in 2002 was a tough act to follow," they wrote, "2003 was another remarkable year. Revenue grew 14% to $5.8 billion, operating cash flow increased 19% to $2.1 billion, operating cash flow margin improved significantly and, for the first time, we generated free cash flow for the full year, at $306.6 million."[25]

The picture was even rosier at the largest cable operator, Comcast, where Chairman and CEO Brian Roberts gushed that the company had "record operating and free cash flows," and exclaimed, "We are delighted to report terrific results for 2004 that include surpassing $20 billion in revenue for the first time in our history."[26] The astounding figure was an 11 percent increase over the $18.3 billion in revenue Comcast generated in 2003, which was itself 9 percent more than the $16.8 billion it earned in 2002. During the 2004 Senate hearings on cable rates, industry leaders insisted that they were doing everything possible to keep consumer costs down, yet the financial tables that Comcast published in its shareholder reports told another story. The "monthly average video revenue per basic subscriber" had jumped 6 percent between the final quarters of 2003 and 2004, and the "monthly average total revenue per basic cable subscriber" had gone up more than 10 percent. Put these numbers next to a cable bill and you can see that misinformation from Big Media is not limited to what you see (or don't see) on television.

IN THE EARLY YEARS OF THE TWENTY-FIRST CENTURY, PUBLIC FRUSTRATION with the cable industry's three core problems—cost, content, and local control—inspired another unusual alliance for media reform. The Parents Television Council (PTC), a conservative nonprofit organization whose base of one million members and three dozen local chapters calls for strict decency standards and heightened corporate accountability in media, and the populist Consumers Union (CU), led their constituents in a campaign to demand à la carte service from cable providers, so that Americans, who on average watch only seventeen of the many score stations they receive, would not be forced to pay for the ones they didn't want. As a letter to Congress circulated in June 2005 by a coalition including PTC, CU, and the AFL-CIO (the leading coalition of labor unions) put it: "Why can you pick up the phone, order and pay for HBO if you want it, but can't pick up the phone, cancel and stop paying for MTV if you don't? When you visit your local convenience store to purchase milk and bread, should you also be forced to take and pay for a carton of cigarettes, too?"

To defend the system, cable providers and programmers argue that bundles help them offer a wider variety of channels, since big packages support niche channels that might not otherwise get enough subscribers to stay in business. But both providers and programmers have a more fundamental reason for taking this position: not only can cable providers charge higher subscription fees for multichannel bundles than they can for à la carte services, but cable programmers that own several stations in a bundle can offer advertisers their own big packages, giving them slots across their empires. "When the CU and PTC aligned," said Ben Scott, the Free Press political director, "the industry got a bunch of corporate money, hired a high-end PR firm, and developed a brilliant strategy. They went around to the civil rights groups and said that à la carte would reduce the number of people who will get ethnic television, that it would destroy BET, TV One, Oxygen. And a bunch of congressional Black Caucus members came out against it." The irony, Scott told me, is that "for years minority programmers were saying that the big cable companies were shutting them out. But they didn't want to alienate them and risk losing the chance for a contract." Media reform organizations insist that a mandated "free tier" not only would help minority-focused and public-interest stations to flourish in an à la carte system but would also encourage competition in special-ized markets, such as foreign-language or ethnic programming, that are now quietly dominated by Big Media. (Viacom, for example, has con-trolling interest in BET, while Time Warner and Charter are major investors in Oxygen Media, and Comcast has operational control of TV One.)[27] "By setting aside twenty slots for qualifying independent, minority-owned channels," Scott argued, "you'd get more channels competing for ethnic niches. À la carte paired with the free tier solves any diversity problem."

The groups involved in the Cable Choice initiative, which called on cable providers to offer all consumers à la carte service options, had distinctive but overlapping concerns. Speaking at a U.S. Senate hearing on indecency in January 2005, PTC president Brett Bozell claimed that PTC represents "the vast majority of Americans sick and tired of the sewage pouring out of their airwaves, or on cable programs they are being forced to underwrite." His colleague Dan Isett told me that "you can't make an affirmative choice. And you also can't make a negative choice and stop supporting a channel like MTV. Even if you block the channel with the V-chip, you're still paying for it, and you're support-ing the company that makes it."

"Let me tell you why Cable Choice must—I repeat, must—happen," Bozell testified.

> In recent weeks and months, a number of the so-called expanded basic tier networks have aired some of the most graphic and shocking con-tent imaginable . . . I'm talking about advertiser-supported basic and expanded basic cable; what familes are given to take when they sub-scribe to this service. Several weeks ago the FX network, owned by the News Corporation, aired a program featuring a storyline wherein a funeral home worker preserved his deceased sister's head. He assembled

various body parts from cadavers and stitched them together, adding his dead sister's head. And then he had sex with his Frankenstein-like creation. Call it incestuous necrophilia.

Not long ago that same network also aired a different program with an episode featuring a police captain who broke into a house to arrest two gang members. There was a struggle for a gun, and when the gang members prevailed, one of the gang members held the gun to the head of the kneeling police captain and forced him to perform oral sex on him . . . Mr. Chairman, it would be one thing if these networks were supported by subscribers who wanted to watch such filth. It is wholly another thing for you, me, and 80 million other American families to be forced to subscribe to these networks—to underwrite the production of this material—in order to watch the Disney Channel, the Golf Channel, the History Channel or a football game on ESPN.[28]

PTC's relentless criticism of the News Corporation bothered political conservatives who expected more allegiance to the company that produces Fox News. But Isett told me his organization is convinced that "media consolidation as a rule yields bad results for consumers. Big companies put out much more indecent material than the smaller groups. It's not the mom and pop broadcast stations whose owners and personalities you see in the grocery store every day." Rupert Murdoch may be a hero to Isett's allies, but PTC treats the media mogul just as it does Hollywood executives. During our conversation Isett mentioned scholarly and official studies that establish a link between Big Media companies and indecency, but he has other ways of making the connection. "It's intuitive that executives in Los Angeles are not going to know what local community standards are, or how to respect them," he explained, before establishing a connection between the methods used by PTC and the United Church of Christ decades earlier. "That's why we believe in local control. We also do our own content analysis. We have about ten analysts in Alexandria who watch broadcast and cable channels all day and log TV shows. And our grassroots chapters around the country send us content. They're incredibly active. You'd be surprised how much we get."

Christian conservatives are by no means the only Americans who are outraged about the levels of graphic violence, profanity, and sex on daytime and prime-time television. Parents of all political and religious persuasions, and even a surprising number of civil libertarians, have been so upset about irresponsible programming decisions by Big Media groups that they have supported tough penalties against companies that violated decency standards. On its Web site, PTC proudly reprints a *Seattle Times* article stating that "U.S. Rep. Jim McDermott, D-Wash., is one of the few legislators with 100 percent on the ACLU's 'scorecard,' voting along the organization's lines on its key issues. He bucked the ACLU, however, on the decency bill. 'I think we have a responsibility to protect our children. This is not a First Amendment question,' McDermott says. 'God knows I'm a First Amendment guy. But there is a need for us to be responsible for what our kids are exposed to, and I think it's the FCC that ought to make those kinds of decisions.'"[29] Jonathan Adelstein and Michael Copps, the two most liberal FCC commissioners, have taken a similar stance. Weeks after the Janet Jackson incident, Copps testified to the U.S. House of Representatives Subcommittee on Telecommunications and the Internet: "We open the door to unprecedented levels of media consolidation and what do we get in return? More garbage, less real news and progressively crasser entertainment. Should we really be surprised that two of the very biggest media conglomerates—Viacom and Clear Channel—alone accounted for more than 80 per cent of those fines that were proposed for indecency?"[30]

While PTC's campaigns focus on improper content, CU is principally concerned about unfair charges from cable providers. For example, CU points to a 2006 USA Today/CNN/Gallop poll showing that only about 30 percent of consumers would pay to buy sports programming that included ESPN, while the majority of households, some 53 percent, probably would not if they had the choice. Without à la carte pricing, however, they don't. And ESPN, which generates about half of Disney's $54-billion market value, is one of the most expensive channels in expanded basic cable service for providers and, ultimately, consumers, at two to three dollars per subscriber, compared to others that are twenty-five cents or less.[31]

Whether the problem is what goes into the cable box or what goes onto the cable bill, both PTC and CU share a fundamental commitment to local control, and a deep conviction that the industry's monopoly leverage, with one dominant provider in nearly every market, has weakened it. "For consumers, the appeal of choosing which cable channels to buy is undeniable," wrote Bozell and Kimmelman, the CU director, in a joint editorial. "And for parents who care about what their kids watch, the option is indispensable . . . There is one thing that everyone can agree on: Regardless of what programs consumers find objectionable and why, they should not have to pay for channels they don't want."[32]

Facing both intense public pressure and heightened scrutiny from the FCC, in 2005 cable giants Time Warner, Comcast, and Echostar tried to head off legislation on Cable Choice by offering consumers a "family tier" package that excluded controversial channels such as MTV and VH1. Yet Time Warner's package also excluded many popular channels that cultural conservatives prefer, including the History Channel, Animal Planet, Turner Classic Movies, ESPN, the Learning Channel, the Game Show Network, MSNBC, Fox News, CNBC, Inspiration Network, Trinity Broadcasting Network, and Eternal Word Television Network. Bozell denounced the package as "a very bad joke," saying that "it is perfectly obvious Time Warner is deliberately offering a product designed to fail . . . According to Time Warner, no family should want to watch sports. According to Time Warner, no family should want to receive any news channel other than Time Warner's CNN. According to Time Warner, classic movies are not appropriate for families. And neither is religious programming."[33] Instead of appeasing its critics, the cable industry riled them.

The industry also failed to mollify the FCC, and in February 2006 the commission issued a stunning reversal of its position on Cable Choice. Just two years earlier, the commission had paid the consulting firm Booz Allen Hamilton to study the feasibility of Cable Choice options, and together they concluded that such a system would result in higher prices for customers who ordered more than nine channels. After further review, however, the FCC's Media Bureau announced that with à la carte pricing "a subscriber could receive as many as 20 channels, including six broadcast signals, without seeing an increase in his or her monthly bills. This is more than the 17 channels that the average household watches. The corrected calculations also show that, in three of the four scenarios considered in the Booz Allen [Hamilton] Study, consumers' bills decrease by anywhere from 3 to 13 percent." The commission explained that it had identified "a number of errors in the Booz Allen Hamilton Study" and acknowledged that the 2004 report "relied upon unrealistic assumptions and presented biased analysis." Moreover, it concluded, "The current industry practice of bundling programming services may drive up retail prices, making video programming less affordable and keeping some consumers from subscribing."[34]

Reversing its published findings is uncommon for the FCC, because doing so invites suspicion that the commission's research is pliable to political interests. But Kevin Martin, who replaced Michael Powell as chairman in early 2005, had publicly expressed his sympathy for the PTC's position on Cable Choice and indecency, and he boldly challenged his predecessor's position. "I was surprised by the results of (the 2004 report)," he told the press, "which is why I wanted to look at the issue further." The *New York Times* called the FCC's about-face "a frontal assault on business as usual," and *USA Today* reported that the study "undercuts a bedrock principle of the cable industry—that big bundles of channels deliver the best value for consumers." Senator McCain immediately announced his intention to introduce legislation that would reduce franchising restrictions for new video providers willing to offer Cable Choice (though he did not follow up on it), and major telephone companies, seeking to take advantage of the bandwidth built into their networks by their industry's lobbying of state legislatures for state-level television franchises, began to enter the TV service market. Although à la carte was not yet a fait accompli, PTC and CU were confident that the service would soon be available. "I think this will invigorate policymakers to pressure the cable industry and programmers to deliver the kind of channels consumers want, and at a lower price," said Kimmelman. "The cable industry," Bozell declared, "no longer has any arguments left."[35]

CAMPAIGNS FOR CONSUMER CHOICE IN PRICING AND CONTENT ARE A popular form of media activism for middle-class parents and families. For an emerging generation of younger activists who have taken up the cause of "media justice," the major challenge is not to silence Big Media but to expose its irresponsible use of damaging misrepresentations and discriminatory imagery, and to establish a place for their own voices on the air. Taking inspiration from the environmental justice movement, which sprang up to call attention to the fact that poor and minority communities are unfairly exposed to dangerous pollutants such as industrial waste, media justice activists have declared themselves the primary victims of toxic representation. "It's not just an issue of fairness," the activist Malkia Cyril told me. "For people of color, what the media does is literally a matter of life and death. I come from a family that was torn apart by inaccurate coverage of what we were doing. The media dehumanized us, which made violence against us, from killings to incarceration, seem legitimate."

Raised in New York City by Black Panther members, Cyril moved to Northern California in 1996, at age twenty-one, in search of a more tolerant and diverse youth culture. In 2001, she helped to start the Youth Media Council (YMC) in Oakland, a historically African American and increasingly Latino and Asian city that was a key target for California's crackdown on juvenile crime. "The War on Drugs. The War on Crime. These became wars on young people of color, especially in California," Cyril told me, in a soft, almost muffled voice that barely rose above her large and powerful frame. "We're the enemy. And since the local media have made us out that way, we decided to do something about it, to hold them accountable."

Using techniques honed by the United Church of Christ and also employed by the Parents Television Council, the YMC trained a group of seventeen teenagers to conduct content analysis, then had them monitor three and one-half months of coverage from KTVU-TV, a Fox affiliate whose evening news had recently been named "the best local newscast in the United States" by the Project for Excellence in Journalism. "They were extremely good compared to other stations," Cyril explained, "but we had the impression that this A+ station was doing a C- job on youth issues." In 2002 the YMC published the results of its study as *Speaking for Ourselves: A Youth Assessment of Local News Coverage.* The report documents a spike in local coverage linking young people to crime at the very moment that local youth crime rates dropped precipitously. Among the key findings: "In the period from March 1 to June 15, KTVU reported 55 stories about pets or animals and only 12 stories about youth and poverty. For each KTVU story about youth and poverty, there were 11 such stories about youth and crime. In stories about youth, law enforcement and politicians were quoted more often than any other sources. Only one story mentioned the declining rate of juvenile crime, and only two stories mentioned that school shootings are rare. When solutions to problems were offered, more than 83 percent focused on punishment, increased policing, or incarceration." Of the roughly five hundred quotes in the stories, 70 percent were from adults, mostly from police, prosecutors, and politicians. Young people, in other words, were usually spoken for or spoken about, rather than given a chance to speak.[36]

According to the YMC, these patterns reflected broader trends during the 1990s and early years of the twenty-first century, when misleading news coverage that denied young people the microphone helped whip up public support for more punitive social policies for juveniles. "In a 1996 California poll," the report explained, "60% of respondents reported believing that juveniles were responsible for most violent crime, although youth were actually only responsible for approximately 13% of violent crime that year." But such misunderstandings are not limited to California, and during the 1990s local politicians throughout the country cited public opinion, doubtless built by sensational reporting of youth crime, as the basis for pulling back on long-standing juvenile protection programs. Since 1992, forty-five states have loosened criteria for charging children as adults in criminal cases. In California the incarceration boom resulted in a dramatic reversal of state spending priorities, and by 2000 more taxpayer dollars were going to jails and prisons than to its public universities.

Cyril said that the YMC was not interested in simply documenting the extent to which young people were misrepresented, nor in merely castigating the journalists and news agencies who portrayed youths as criminals. Instead, she issued the report along with an invitation to news organizations to become partners in conversation, if not coproducers of better youth coverage. As the YMC report put it:

> We can transform media bias into media justice by building strong relationships between news outlets and youth organizations, and increasing the dialogue between journalists and youth community members . . . We continue to live and die on the word of experts and reporters. It is therefore critical to our survival that journalists and communities work in partnership to report on public policy issues that frame the contours of our conditions and draw the boundaries that define our lives. The organizations of the Youth Media Council want to establish relationships with news outlets to ensure that news coverage fairly and accurately represents our communities, thoroughly explores our issues, and brings our voices to the center of policy debates about youths.

"We did a press release announcing the findings," Cyril recalled, "and then we had a delegation visit to KTVU, where we brought about fifteen of our young people and asked to speak with the news director." Local station managers, not accustomed to such requests from viewers, misinterpreted the nature of YMC's visit. "At first they didn't understand that the kids weren't interested in a tour. But these were kids from the streets, and they were serious."

Ultimately, KTVU allowed the YMC delegation to meet with the news director, who agreed to disseminate *Speaking for Ourselves* to every reporter on staff. "They were defensive at first," Cyril explained. "But they were willing to work with us eventually. They hosted a roundtable for all reporters in the area, and they helped legitimize the report and our other work." A few months later, local community organizations that were protesting Clear Channel's decision to fire the popular DJ and community affairs director "Davey D" Cook asked YMC to do another study, this time on KMEL, the Bay Area's leading radio station for young listeners. "We didn't have any money," recalled Cyril. "But I said, 'Who cares? Let's do it.'"

The report, titled *Is KMEL the People's Station?* showed that the station had become a steady advocate of both the war in Iraq and the local war on crime, effectively blocking out voices from grassroots peace and social justice organizations that had formerly contributed to Davey D's shows. Clear Channel had also standardized the playlist so that "the Bay Area's strong community of popular local artists was practically unheard," while also shutting off the channels through which listeners could provide meaningful feedback on the programming changes. "KMEL only encourages audience participation through on-air contests and games," the report states.[37]

"It was a very small project," Cyril told me. "But that study has circulated everywhere, all the way up to the FCC." It was also surprisingly effective, at least for the short term. "Right after our campaign KMEL initiated more local artist programming. They hosted an on-air broadcast about the war and 9/11, with young people talking. As far as we know, it's the only broadcast like that that Clear Channel has done anywhere in this country." Once YMC let up the pressure, KMEL let go of this programming style. Before long, the Bay Area music writer Jeff Chang reported, "KMEL was back to its old tricks, and it sounded like a regular Clear Channel station again." Worse, in 2005 its sister station, "Wild 94.9" KYLD-FM, hired Rick Delgado, the controversial producer whom Emmis Communications Corporation fired from its "Hot 97" station in New York City for his role in writing, recording, and broadcasting the infamous "Tsunami Song," which featured the lyrics:

> *There were Africans drowning*
> *Little Chinamen swept way*
> *You could hear God laughing "Swim You bitches, swim."*

That fall, YMC announced that it would challenge the licenses for four Clear Channel stations in the Bay Area, all of which expected to have their renewal applications rubber-stamped, as usual, by the FCC. "We know we're not going to win," Cyril confided to me, an ironic smile and gentle laugh breaking up her reserved demeanor. "But we're saying it's wrong to do hate radio. We're trying to rebuild the idea of the public interest. We're trying to create standards that will be the foundations for future rules. Maybe we won't succeed in our lifetime. But we had lost a lot of fights before *Plessy v. Ferguson* and *Brown v. Board of Education*. And I know that someday we'll prevail."

9

THE MEDIA AND DEMOCRACY

Josh Silver has spent the last decade working as a full-time activist for a cause that every American supports. "What I want is to have a real, working democracy here in the United States," said the energetic young executive director of Free Press, the organization he cofounded in late 2002 and has quickly turned into the nation's most prominent media reform group. "We now have a political system run by big money and a media controlled by big corporations that are happy to keep Americans uninformed about the bread-and-butter issues that affect us most. You can't have democracy without an educated public, and you can't have an educated public with the media ownership structure we have today." What compounds the problem, Silver added, "is that there are few major issues where the policy-making process is as decidedly undemocratic as it is for media. And that's what Free Press set out to change."

The media was not always Silver's primary concern. In 1997, when he was approaching thirty and his friends were settling into families and careers, the political junkie let his civic interests take over, packing everything he owned into his car and moving from Washington, D.C., to Arizona to become the campaign manager for the Clean Elections ballot initiative. "We wanted to make the electoral system more open and competitive," Silver told me. "That meant giving candidates a way to run without relying on special-interest money. Arizona had experienced a bunch of campaign finance scandals, and—after a lot of work—we

won the initiative there. I really believed that the clean election movement could catch on in national politics, too. But after we won in Arizona
similar efforts in other states got hammered. It was devastating. But the
parties who oppposed it spent a ton of money on the media, and they
convinced people to support a system that actually shut them out."

Yet Silver knew that this was not the only lesson to take from his
experience with the Clean Elections movement, and he returned to
D.C. in search of a deeper explanation for the forces that were driving
American politics. "Someone recommended that I read *Rich Media, Poor
Democracy,*" by the prolific communications scholar Robert McChesney.
"I was thinking about the book one night before turning on the evening local newscast, and the top story—I kid you not—was the rising
cost of lobsters. There it was, lobsters with a big graphic saying TOP
STORY stamped on the TV. And I said to myself, 'Damn, if more than
sixty percent of Americans say local TV is their main source of news,
and rising costs of lobsters is what they learn about it, no wonder we're
in such bad shape.' After that I looked up McChesney online and cold-
called him. I knew what he had written, but I wanted to know what he
was going to do. He asked me some questions, and I told him about my
background. Then he said, 'Josh, I've been waiting for you to call for
years.'"

Months later, McChesney and his collaborator, John Nichols, a
progressive journalist, traveled to D.C. for meetings on media policy.
They made time to visit Silver at his home, where they launched Free
Press over dinner. By January 2003 they had raised about $100,000. Sil-
ver moved to Northampton, Massachussets, because he was convinced
that a grassroots organization could get trapped in a Beltway bubble
and lose touch with ordinary citizens. He also opened a small Free Press
office in Washington—and his timing was perfect. In September 2002
the FCC had initiated the "biennial regulatory review" required by Congress, which also indicated that it would soon schedule a formal vote
on new ownership rules. Just a few months later, lobbyists, civic groups,
and consumer organizations were stepping up their public campaigns
to preserve or roll back existing limits on how many broadcast outlets
a company could own, and the House and Senate were holding formal
hearings on media regulation in anticipation of the FCC's upcoming
vote. A heated debate about media policy was breaking out in the
Capitol, reaching an unprecedented pitch when the FCC announced

that its vote would take place on June 2. "The ownership fight launched us," said Silver, a mischievous smile breaking out across his face. "We had just started, and suddenly we were in the center of the ring."

CONGRESS AND THE FCC WERE ACCUSTOMED TO MAKING MEDIA POLICY without public scrutiny. In the two years before the Telecommunications Act of 1996, media and telecommunications companies doubled their lobbying investments on Capitol Hill.[1] The proposed legislation, which included expanding ownership caps for broadcasting, cable, telecommunications services and giving away digital spectrum, would have far-reaching consequences for both the media industry and citizens, and it attracted considerable attention in the trade publications and the national business press. Yet, as the media policy scholar Patricia Aufderheide wrote in her book about the political process behind the act, despite its "broad social significance," the issues raised by the proposed legislation "rarely . . . made the front pages of newspapers . . . and exceedingly infrequently made TV news . . . By and large," she concluded, "the American public perforce ceded the argumentation over terms of the Act to experts."[2]

This may be overstating the role of the commission in dictating the terms of the 1996 act, since many of its proposed regulations were supported and in some cases actually written by industry leaders, and political officials from both parties also aggressively advocated for the act. Fresh from their sweeping electoral victories in 1994, Republicans made relaxing ownership caps the key part of their national media policy proposals, drafting a bill in 1995 that allowed newspapers to own and operate television stations, and television stations to own and operate as many radio stations as they liked in the same market. Then president Bill Clinton threatened to veto such sweeping measures but, determined to push through laws that would encourage private-sector interest in developing the "Information Superhighway," and facing the reality that the 1996 act passed the House by a vote of 414 to 6 and the Senate by 91 to 5, he ultimately supported most of the congressional majority's deregulatory agenda.

Clinton's closest Democratic colleagues were more enthusiastic than he about the virtues of loosening the federal government's reins on Big Media companies. Vice President Al Gore called passage of the act "a historic event that will change forever the way every American lives, works, learns and communicates." Reed Hundt, who went to high school with Gore and studied law with Clinton before the administration picked him to chair the FCC ("I owe this job to lots of hard work and to fortunate seat assignments," he once said), pledged that "this bill creates the promise of good, high-paying jobs for millions of Americans and the promise of competition and its benefits of lower prices, higher quality and better service to us all." Upon signing the Telecommunications Act of 1996 into law, Clinton declared: "My administration has promoted the enactment of a telecommunications reform bill to stimulate investment, promote competition, provide open access for all citizens to the Information Superhighway, strengthen and improve universal service and provide families with technologies to help them control what kind of programs come into their homes over television. As a result of this [act], consumers will receive the benefits of lower prices, better quality and greater choice in their television and cable services, and they will continue to benefit from a diversity of voices and viewpoints in radio, television and the print media . . . Today with the stroke of a pen, our laws will catch up with the future."[3]

That future began immediately, ushering in a golden age for Big Media, if not for consumers. Just one year after its implementation, the industry had been dramatically consolidated through an unprecedented series of mergers, acquisitions, and new partnerships. Relaxed ownership caps in radio and television resulted in a feeding frenzy, with giant companies like Clear Channel, Viacom, and Disney gobbling up small broadcasters and minority-owned stations while showing little interest in local content, whether it be news reporting or music programming. Cable television rates soared. Not only did Internet service go up in price; it also went down in speed and service quality compared with what was available in other nations. Local phone service remained uncompetitive. And broadcast companies acquired $70 billion worth of digital spectrum—with which they planned to expand the number of radio and television stations that they operated—for free. The FCC neither provided a compelling rationale for the giveaway nor specified any meaningful public-service obligations that it would impose on the corporate beneficiaries, so it's no surprise that citizens were the biggest losers in the deal. According to a report published in 2005 by the nonpartisan citizens advocacy group Common Cause, "Over ten years, the legislation was supposed to save consumers $550 billion . . . Industries supporting the new legislation predicted it would add 1.5 million jobs and boost the economy by $2 trillion. By 2003, however, telecommunications companies' market value had fallen by about $2 trillion, and they had shed half a million jobs."[4]

FALLOUT FROM THE 1996 TELECOM ACT WAS NOT THE ONLY REASON THAT the FCC was in the spotlight. In previous years the commission had been directed by men of scant renown, such as Alfred Sikes (1989–93), Reed Hundt (1993–97), and William Kennard (1997–2001), none of whom attracted much interest outside of the media industry. But President George W. Bush selected an unusually prominent chairman: Michael Powell, a military veteran and then thirty-seven-year-old son of Secretary of State Colin Powell, was given a mandate to clear away the so-called regulatory underbrush that impeded market activity, and to do so with what industry analysts considered "unprecedented authority" from the White House. Powell, who first came to the FCC as a commissioner in 1997 after serving in the U.S. Department of Justice Antitrust Division, had already established his reputation as a free-market fundamentalist who, as even the venerable libertarian William Safire put it, "never met a merger he didn't like."[5] "Monopoly is not illegal by itself in the United States," Powell told *Wired* magazine. "People tend to forget this. There is something healthy about letting innovators try to capture markets." On January 23, 2001, the day after Powell's official nomination, *USA Today* announced that Powell would take a "hands-off approach to communications regulation," with Priscilla Hill-Ardoin, senior vice president of the telecommunications giant SBC, calling the new chairman "a consistent voice advocating market competition over regulation."[6]

Powell bears a strong physical resemblance to his father, but his utopian faith in a better world shaped by new communications technology and open markets places him ideologically closer to President Bush, for whom he quickly set to work. On March 29, 2001, the new chairman told the House Subcommittee on Telecommunications and the Internet that "suddenly, the Commission finds itself blown into a position in which its decisions have far-reaching impact, not only on the industry, but increasingly on the whole of the American national economy and that of the world." Powell explained that he was "humbled and priv-ileged, and some days daunted" to have responsibility for such an impor-tant set of policy issues, and he assured the House subcommittee that he looked forward to working with them in a democratic manner.

Yet the agenda he would go on to outline was comprehensive and radical, particularly with respect to changing ownership limits. Accord-ing to Powell, under his control the commission would end its long-standing practice of forcing the industry to prove that regulations were harmful to consumers or unnecessary to promote the public interest. Instead, the FCC would bear the responsibility of justifying any own-ership rules that it wished to continue imposing. "Deregulation," he declared in his opening remarks, means "validate the purpose of a rule in the modern context, or eliminate it. As simple as that. Resist interven-tion, regulatory intervention, absent the evidence of persistent trends that can be understood, or evidence of clear abuse."

"That, my friends, is not the law," said veteran Democratic senator Fritz Hollings, who called a hearing on media consolidation for July 2001 in response to Powell's pledge. Even the former FCC chairman Reed Hundt, whose support for the 1996 Telecom Act helped initiate an unprecedented wave of broadcast media mergers, condemned Powell's actions. "No one self-polices antitrust," he explained. "What Powell is doing is abdicating the responsibility Congress has given him. It's extra-ordinarily lawless, and it deserves the country's interests. He proposes to allow the creation of the greatest, most prodigiously sized media conglomerates that have ever bestrode the planet. And he seems mas-sively indifferent to whether markets are competitive."[7]

The chairman didn't flinch, turning his "validate or eliminate" credo into policy, and immediately putting it to use. On July 25, just days after the Senate hearing on consolidation, Powell cast a decisive vote in the FCC's three-to-two decision to grant a waiver to Rupert Murdoch's News Corporation, allowing the major Bush backer's media company to acquire ten television stations from Chris-Craft Industries, a move that put it in conflict with national ownership limits, the cross-ownership ban, and the duopoly restriction—all of which the FCC is supposed to enforce. "This decision . . . shows the lengths the Commission will go to avoid standing in the way of media mergers," wrote Gloria Tristani, one of the dissenting commissioners. "The transfer of these television sta-tion licenses violates the Communications Act and raises serious concerns

regarding the ongoing concentration in the ownership of television stations and other media." Moreover, she argued, "today's decision effectively eliminates the requirement that merger applicants demonstrate to
the FCC that their license transfer would serve the public interest. The
majority fails to identify a single public interest benefit resulting from
this merger."[8]

Powell, however, had long before registered his conviction that the
commission could not effectively protect the public interest—mostly, he
had infamously said, because he did not know what the phrase meant.
"When I first became aware that I might be nominated to a seat on the
Federal Communications Commission," Powell told an audience in Las
Vegas in 1998, "I was thrilled that I might be one of those charged with
protecting and promoting the public interest. I had long known that the
public interest was a pivotal part of communications regulation, but
realized I was unsure what it really meant . . . Having read the scriptures
of [former Harvard Law School dean James] Landis and [U.S. Supreme
Court justice Felix] Frankfurter suggesting that I would just know the
right thing to do, I expected some sort of revelation, for I did not feel
particularly enlightened after being confirmed by the United States Senate. The night after I was sworn in, I waited for a visit from the angel
of the public interest. I waited all night, but she did not come. And, in
fact, five months into this job, I still have had no divine awakening and
no one has issued me my public interest crystal ball. But I am here, an
enlightened wiseman without a clue."[9]

WHEN POWELL BECAME CHAIRMAN, CIVIC ORGANIZATIONS AND CON-
sumer groups reached out to the commission with offers to help
it develop a more robust concept of public interest. Others mocked
Powell in protest, dressing up as angels of public interest and requesting a visit with him. Powell forged ahead without engaging any of them,
intent on replacing fuzzy notions of the public interest with what he
considered "hard science," mostly in the form of technical papers
developed by FCC staff economists or outsiders commissioned for the
job. "Powell started with a real and arrogant belief in the so-called
economic science," the attorney Harold Feld told me. (Feld is senior
vice president for the Media Access Project, a nonpartisan telecommunications law firm in Washington, D.C., that is actively involved in

national media policy.) "But he and Ken Ferree [chief of the FCC Media Bureau, which manages policy for broadcast, electronic media, and cable television] had a clear idea of what theories they believed, and they expected the evidence to show that deregulation works."

Their confidence was not wholly unfounded. "Public-interest advocates traditionally had not relied upon either empirical evidence or sophisticated economic theory to prove their points," reported Feld, who brings a scholar's mind and an activist's energy to his legal work. "They persuaded policy makers and the courts through the gut instinct that when one firm owns two outlets those firms do not genuinely compete. In 1978 the Supreme Court found it self-evident that if one company owned two outlets that those two outlets would not compete and would likely share common views. This was a rationale for blocking cross-ownership. But the neoclassical economics school put a lot of energy into showing that this intuition was wrong. In media economics, the bulk of published articles, especially in theory, but some with a little evidence, argued ownership rules were not necessary and may even inhibit the production of better news products."

Yet there were serious problems with the commission's "scientific" method. Much of the FCC's research was founded on questionable assumptions, including the fact that its economic models were based more on highly disputable market predictions than on actual market data about media use, resulting in hard data built on soft foundations. Sometimes the research results were downright comical. "The commission tried to make a diversity index that would justify deregulation," Feld recalled. "And they did it in about two months, without much outside help. But the thing made no sense whatsoever. In New York City, the index gave the same market share to the Dutchess Community College low-power television station and the ABC station. It also weighted the impact of different media with a multiplier, and since television is more popular than newspapers, the index claimed that the Dutchess Community College station made more impact than the *New York Times*. The amazing thing is that they actually used the index anyway. It was a core part of their case for loosening the ownership caps."

Moreover, on the whole FCC researchers did not operate according to standard rules for scientific research. "They used proprietary data that the commission would not release to other researchers," Feld explained, with an incredulous laugh. "No one could replicate their studies or validate their findings. The FCC was actually surprised when the Consumers Union asked for the primary data on which their studies were based so they could reanalyze them."

Feld, a composed and eloquent speaker, sped up his pace furiously as his case against the commission's approach to policy making unfolded. "The truth," he exclaimed, "is that the FCC doesn't do real social science. They spend too much time listening to Heritage [Foundation] and Cato [Institute], and all the free-market ideologues who do 'research' to prove what they already believe. Then they misrepresent their own findings, because they don't appreciate the complexity of economic models, nor even of the questions they ask. And I've seen them distort the research to support the results they wanted."

The staff of the Media Access Project, which would ultimately lead a legal challenge to Powell's most ambitious deregulatory initiatives, was convinced that preserving any meaningful consumer protections required not only defending the concept of public interest but also producing persuasive theories and solid empirical research that challenged the chairman's predetermined positions. "Powell didn't think that supporters of regulation could make anything beyond the usual appeals to democracy and the need for diversity," Feld recalled. "He didn't think there could be a substantive, quantified case made for the sake of diversity, or localism. In point of fact, there was plenty of theoretical and empirical evidence proving not just that further consolidation was a phenomenally bad move, but that existing consolidation had already produced what economists call inefficiency and what the rest of us call monopoly control of information. We went out and began rounding up whatever good research was out there. We got real research from university professors. We read the studies by the Consumers Union. We learned what was wrong with the FCC's papers. And we stunned Powell when we produced this. He didn't know what to do."

AS HE LED THE FCC TOWARD THE 2003 RULING ON OWNERSHIP LIMITS, Powell must have been even more surprised by the attack on his policy agenda mounted by economic libertarians and fellow-traveling free-marketeers who, after witnessing the consequences of the 1996 Telecom Act, were so convinced that gutting ownership limits had produced uncompetitive media markets that they opposed the chairman's plans to further relax the caps. The most devastating public argument against Powell's deregulatory agenda came from William Safire, the legendary Republican speechwriter-turned *New York Times* columnist whose series of articles about the perils of media consolidation captured the attention of political conservatives in the Beltway and media moguls in New York. The poignant and politically influential critic delivered his opening remarks in a March 7, 2002, op-ed.

> In the world of telecommunications, the urge to converge has led to the creation of worldwide media empires that promised the happy marriage of news and entertainment content with the computer, wireless telephone and video—all supposedly lowering prices to consumers with no restraint of trade or news. Does anyone believe that is what has been happening? In the real world, intimidating "mere size" has become, when not sin itself, the occasion of sin. Today's any-merger-goes regulators permit cross-ownership of content and distribution while encouraging corporate titans with swollen egos to gobble up competitors or suppliers. Where does this power grab leave the innovative entrepreneur, the small business, the individual talent and the consumer?

Though Safire took a shot at liberals, it was Powell he singled out for bungling his managerial responsibilities. Safire challenged Republicans to stop supporting the relentless expansion of Big Media groups.

> With the roundheeled Michael Powell steering the Federal Communications Commission toward terminal fecklessness; with the redoubtable Joel Klein succeeded at Justice's antitrust division by an assortment of wimps; and with appeals courts approving the concentration of media power as if nothing had changed since President Taft's day, the checks and balances made possible by diverse competition are being eradicated. The longtime anti-business coloration of liberals reduces their ability to take on the convergence con. It is for conservatives to ask ourselves: Since when is bigness goodness?[10]

The column stirred up conservatives, but not for long, so in January 2003 Safire fired off another salvo. "You won't find television magazine programs fearlessly exposing the broadcast lobby's pressure on

Congress and the courts to allow station owners to gobble up more stations and cross-own local newspapers, thereby controlling information residents of a local market receive. Nor will you find many newspaper chains assigning reporters to reveal the effect of media giantism on local coverage or cover the way publishers induce coverage-hungry politicians to loosen antitrust restraints," he commented, writing the words that so few of his peers had the courage or security to type. But the dangers of consolidation, as Safire explained, were most evident in local radio.

> Take a listen to what's happened to local radio in one short wave of deregulation: The great cacophony of different sounds and voices is being amalgamated and homogenized. Back in 1996, the two largest radio chains owned 115 stations; today, those two own more than 1,400. A handful of leading owners used to generate only a fifth of industry revenue; now these top five rake in 55 percent of all money spent on local radio. The number of station owners has plummeted by a third. Yesterday's programming diversity on the public's airwaves has degenerated to the Top 40, as today's consolidating commodores borrowing public property say "the public interest be damned."

Safire was well aware that his position on media policy would confuse readers who were accustomed to his assault on excessive government intervention in the marketplace. "Does this make me (gasp!) pro-regulation?" he asked.

> Michael Powell . . . likes to say "the market is my religion." My conservative economic religion is founded on the rock of competition, which—since Teddy Roosevelt's day—has protected small business and consumers against predatory pricing leading to market monopolization. One of the Democrats on the FCC, Michael Copps, is concerned that "we're relying on institutions to cover this debate which have interests in the outcome of the debate." Republicans in the House, intimidated by the powerful broadcast lobby, don't admit that some regulation can be pro-business . . . Perhaps Commerce Chairman John McCain will see T.R.'s trust-busting light and start heavy granulating in hearings—before merger mania afflicts TV and film the way it is debilitating local radio.[11]

As, in Safire's words, an "unprecedented torrent of e-mail came roaring in" to his *Times* mailbox, the crusading columnist continued to elaborate his argument.[12] "Aren't viewers and readers now blessed with a whole new world of hot competition through cable and the Internet?" he asked on the morning of a Senate ownership hearing in May 2003, previewing the "shucks-we're-no-monopolists line that Rupert Murdoch will take today [when he testifies]."

> The answer is no. Many artists, consumers, musicians and journalists know that such protestations of cable and Internet competition by the huge dominators of content and communication are malarkey. The overwhelming amount of news and entertainment comes via broadcast and print. Putting those outlets in fewer and bigger hands profits the few at the cost of the many. Does that sound un-conservative? Not to me. The concentration of power—political, corporate, media, cultural—should be anathema to conservatives. The diffusion of power through local control, thereby encouraging individual participation, is the essence of federalism and the greatest expression of democracy. Why do we have more channels but fewer real choices today? Because the ownership of our means of communication is shrinking. Moguls glory in amalgamation, but more individuals than they realize resent the loss of local control and community identity.[13]

Safire's columns, circulated widely online and in syndication, generated thousands of letters—"You should see this stack," he wrote—and helped to persuade conservative and liberal citizens and policy makers that the FCC was now actively working against the interests of anyone who did not own a major media company. Republican senator Trent Lott, for example, had vigorously supported Powell's nomination to the commission in 1997, but as both his party's intellectual leaders as well as rank-and-file supporters registered their disdain for Big Media, the Mississippi leader became a vocal critic of consolidation. "With too much concentration," Lott warned, using language inspired by Safire's essays, "companies no longer have to be competitive with rates or product. There would be less incentive to produce something fresh, something different, something priced reasonably or something that caters to another point of view. Already in some markets, advertisers and customers have no choice but to use one particular media outlet . . . Big national print chains in particular already have virtual monopolies in some places . . . Expanding concentration of media ownership may be in the best interest of huge Washington or New York–based media giants, but it would not be in the best interest of . . . media consumers like you and me."[14]

While fiscal conservatives complained about the loss of market competition, cultural conservatives charged that consolidation had deprived communities of the chance to control their own broadcast stations, resulting in a glut of nationally syndicated programs that threatened to drive off the air local religious shows, sporting events, and other local programming that Big Media companies were reluctant to program in place of their own content. In North Carolina, Senator Jesse Helms and Representative Richard Burr (who succeeded Helms as senator in 2004) cowrote a blistering editorial insisting that "conservatives recognize the danger of nationalizing broadcast television content" and claiming the "right of local viewers to influence programming." The southern legislators endorsed the media activism of the Parents Television Council, the Christian Coalition of America, and the National Religious Broadcasters. "Local stations must be empowered to make programming decisions based on community concerns, not forced to march in lockstep with network mandates," they exclaimed. "We are not willing to silence the voices of local viewers in favor of a single voice from New York or Los Angeles. Are You?"[15]

Among conservatives, the loudest response to the possibility of further consolidation came from the National Rifle Association (NRA), which in 2003 called the U.S. media system an oligarchy and mobilized hundreds of thousands of its members to write Congress and the FCC with a simple demand: save American democracy by stopping media consolidation and restoring local control. Wayne LaPierre, the NRA's executive vice president, led the grassroots campaign, stirring members' fears that conglomerates would crush local voices and calling for all citizens to "speak out vs. FCC while you can." The NRA conveyed its primary concern in an "Urgent NRA Bulletin" titled "Media Monopoly Alert," warning that "gun-hating media giants like AOL Time Warner, Viacom/CBS, and Disney/ABC . . . could literally silence your NRA and prevent us from communicating with your fellow Americans by refusing to sell us television, radio or newspaper advertising at any price." (In the next year liberal groups would complain that Clear Channel refused to sell them airtime to advocate Democratic causes.) "Minority or unpopular causes—think of women's suffrage in 1914 or civil rights in 1954—would be downplayed or dismissed to keep viewers watching and advertisers buying," LaPierre warned. "That's no way to run a democracy . . . The only way to stop this is to denounce it from the highest rooftop now, while you still have a voice . . . Tell everyone the airwaves belong to the American people, and the FCC's job is to protect the public interest—not big media barons who want a monopoly on public discourse."[16]

LAPIERRE HAD GOOD REASON TO SUGGEST THAT AMERICANS DELIVER their message to the FCC from "the highest rooftop"—there were few other meaningful ways to participate in the policy-making process. The FCC was legally obligated to seek public review before eliminating the ownership laws. Yet Powell, who continued to believe that media policy was the domain of technical experts, economists, and the industry, purposely ignored public opinion and grassroots input on his proposed rule changes—refusing to attend some of the FCC public hearings held before the vote. Powell did, however, keep the FCC's doors open to Big Media companies and their trade organizations, leaving the unmistakable impression that the commission had been captured by the industries it was supposed to regulate. According to a report published in May 2003 by the nonpartisan Center for Public Integrity (CPI), during the eight months leading up to the commission's June vote, "the nation's top broadcasters have met behind closed doors with FCC officials more than 70 times to discuss a sweeping set of proposals to relax media ownership rules," whereas the two leading public-interest groups working on media policy, Consumers Union and the Media Access Project, "have had only five such sessions." In the view of CPI's founder, Charles Lewis, these contributions left little question that "the FCC is in the grips of the industry," captured by the very companies it was supposed to regulate.[17]

SURPRISINGLY, TWO COMMISSIONERS, MICHAEL COPPS AND JONATHAN Adelstein, shared the CPI's view that from the beginning of Powell's tenure the FCC had embarked on a disturbingly antidemocratic policy-making process. After December 2002, when Adelstein, a South Dakota native, amateur musician, and legislative aide to Senator Tom Daschle, joined the commission on which Copps had served since May 2001, the two Democrats had allied to launch a populist campaign promoting public participation in the ownership debate with the ultimate goal of slowing down Powell's fast-tracked proposal for shredding the remaining strands in the regulatory net. Copps, a former U.S. history professor who served as assistant secretary of commerce for trade development at the U.S. Department of Commerce during the Clinton administration, publicly expressed his concerns about the FCC's race to deregulate in September 2002, when Powell issued the Notice of Proposed Rulemaking that signaled his intention to conduct an expeditious biennial review. "I don't know of any issue before the Commission that is more fraught with serious consequences for the American people than the media ownership rules," said Copps, in a somber but urgent formal statement worth quoting at length.

> There is the potential in the ultimate disposition of this issue to remake our entire media landscape, for better or for worse. At stake is how radio and television are going to look in the next generation and beyond. At stake are old and honored values of localism, diversity, competition, and the multiplicity of voices and choices that undergirds our American democracy. At stake is equal opportunity writ large—the opportunity to hear and be heard; the opportunity to nourish the diversity that makes this country great and which will determine its future; the opportunity for jobs and careers in our media industries; and the opportunity to make this country as open and diverse and creative as it can possibly be.
>
> The Nineties brought new rules permitting increased consolidation in the broadcasting industry, on the premise that broadcasters needed more flexibility in order to compete effectively. These rules paved the way for tremendous consolidation in the industry—going far beyond, I think, what anyone expected at the time. These changes created efficiencies that allowed some media companies to operate more profitably and on a scale unimaginable just a few years ago. They may even have kept some companies in business, allowing stations to remain on the air when they otherwise might have gone dark. But they also raise profound questions of public policy. How far should such combinations

be allowed to go? What is their impact on localism, diversity and the availability of choices to consumers? Does consolidation always, generally or only occasionally serve the interests of the citizenry? How do we judge these things?

... I hope we might even consider, as a Commission, holding hearings here and around the country, to speak with Americans and better gauge what the reality of particular media markets is. I don't want to vote on final rules—and I would be reluctant to vote on final rules— unless and until I feel comfortable that we have the information and the analysis needed to inform our votes. We need as many stakeholders as we can find to take part in this proceeding. I want to hear more from industry, from labor, from consumers, from academe, from artists and entertainers, from anybody who has a stake in how this is resolved. And I think just about everyone, if he or she stops to think about it, has an interest and a stake . . .

Because the stakes here are so incredibly high, it is far more important that we get this done right than that we get it done quickly. I keep coming back to the high stakes involved in what we are doing. Suppose for a moment that the Commission decides to remove or significantly change current limits on media ownership—and suppose our decision turns out to be a mistake. How do we put the genie back in the bottle then? No way.[18]

As a result of pressure from the dissident commissioners, Powell organized an FCC ownership task force and invited formal comments on the dozen expert research reports that the FCC published on the issue. Yet critics immediately complained that the terms of the debate were at once excessively technical for ordinary citizens and insufficiently transparent for professional analysts, because the commission would not release the original data and outsiders had no choice but to accept the findings at face value. Public pressure forced the commission to release "parts of the data" in October, but Copps, declaring that he was still "disappointed and alarmed" by the FCC's feeble effort to include citizens' voices in the debate, continued "banging the drum for a national debate" through town hall meetings throughout the country. Powell was openly hostile to what he considered an antiquated democratic practice. "In the digital age," he insisted, "you don't need a 19th century whistle-stop tour to hear from America."[19]

Continued opposition to meeting with the public was untenable, however, and finally Powell gave in, agreeing to hold a hearing in nearby Richmond, Virginia, in February 2003. The five-hour event, however, was not exactly what Copps had in mind. Powell framed the forum by asserting his controversial notion that "unless we can re-justify each broadcast ownership rule under current market conditions, the rule goes away," and for the first few hours prominent experts, including executives from Fox and Clear Channel as well as consumer groups, lectured the audience with prepared statements, relegating citizen comments to the late last hour. But the audience waited patiently for the rare chance to formally express its opposition to cutting ownership limits. "Oligopoly in the fourth estate is a real threat to diversity and the democratic ideals that form the philosophic core of this nation," said Dr. Allen C. Barrett, then president of the local NAACP chapter. Rain Burroughs, a child-care worker, added, "We don't want Fox and Viacom owning every station we turn to on the dial," while Nathan Long, an English instructor, complained that "there are fewer and fewer options and opinions in the news. If you have a corporation saying they are going to represent diversity, and you hear citizens saying, 'No, they're not,' I ask you to seriously consider which you should listen to."

Concerns such as these might have moved the three Republican commissioners who were leaning toward relaxing the ownership rules to solicit more public opinion on the issue. But, as McChesney, the scholar and cofounder of Free Press reported, "Powell immediately announced that the Richmond hearing provided 'enough' input from the public and that it was imperative to get the process completed as quickly as possible . . . Powell, [Kathleen] Abernathy and [Kevin] Martin would not attend any of the subsquent public hearings on media ownership."[20]

The Republicans' refusal to hold additional open meetings with the public did not deter Copps and Adelstein, who announced that they would conduct their own hearings, independently traveling across the country to hear firsthand how ordinary Americans wanted the FCC to define and protect the public interest. Between March and May, the commissioners attended most of the twelve public hearings on media ownership hosted by civic groups and universities from Los Angeles, California, to Burlington, Vermont. The events were extraordinary, with hundreds of citizens in each city pouring into community centers in a torrent of democratic activity that few other issues could inspire. Yet the ever-vigilant Copps, informed of a survey showing that three-quarters of the American people had not heard about the impending media policy changes, worried that the commission had still failed to reach millions of those who would be affected by its decision. "It's like a state secret," he told a capacity crowd at the University of Southern California. "It's amazing. We will have a new or substantially changed system in place before most people even know it's up for grabs. And 'up for grabs' is the right term, because as I travel around the country holding my own hearings and attending forums like these, I hear about deals in the making, like newspaper-broadcast cross ownership agreements, where the terms are already decided, the deal is done, and all that remains is to fill in the signature blocks after the Commission votes on June 2."[21]

Having castigated his colleagues for neglecting to do appropriate outreach, Copps also blamed the media for avoiding the story of its own political controversy.[22] Not only had Big Media companies purposely kept Americans in the dark about the social and political stakes of media concentration; they had also established a "climate of fear" among their employees, making journalists, editors, and producers aware that critical coverage of consolidation could cost them their jobs. "It has been a revelation to me that there are media professionals with strong feelings about the downsides of consolidation for the American people who are afraid to speak for fear of retribution," Copps reported. "I hear privately that speaking out on this issue would cost many people their careers." "Sometimes it's implicit," added Adelstein. "It's clear to them that it's not a career advancing move to write a story that challenges the policy that is being promoted by their boss."[23]

AS THEY CROSSED THE COUNTRY, COPPS AND ADELSTEIN LEARNED THAT ordinary Americans were less inhibited about voicing dissatisfaction with their local offerings and opposition to further consolidation. "Of the hundreds of citizens I heard from," Adelstein reported, "many extremely articulate, not one of them stood up to say, 'I want to see even more concentration in our media ownership.' Not one."[24] When the commissioners returned from their "whistle-stop tour," they heard again from a purple coalition of grassroots organizations that had delivered their demands for *deconcentrating* the media to Washington, D.C., with approximately 750,000 e-mails and letters arriving at the

FCC before its June 2 vote. "Judging from our record," said Adelstein, "public opposition [to relaxing the ownership caps] is nearly unanimous, from ultra-conservatives to ultra-liberals and virtually everyone in between." Even Chairman Powell acknowledged that he had heard the nation's democratic wish. "I will concede the point that we had strong amount of e-mail and news that expressed concern," he said on national television. "If you pulled any one of these postcards out of our bins, what you would have read is that there's a general anxiety or concern about consolidation."[25]

Liberal media reform groups such as Free Press, the Center for Digital Democracy, and Fairness and Accuracy in Reporting (FAIR) made sure that progressives were leading the letter-writing campaign. "We were just a little fish at the time," recalled Josh Silver, of Free Press. "But we got our Web site up in time to do a petition before the FCC vote, we were sending out press releases, and we were doing outreaches all over the place. We needed a partner with real constituents to get the letters out, though, and I thought MoveOn would be perfect. I called Eli Pariser [executive director of MoveOn.org Political Action] and had McChesney call Wes Boyd [cofounder of MoveOn.org and MoveOn.org Civic Action]. We all met at a restaurant in New York and worked things out over coffee. MoveOn didn't really have a media policy agenda at the time, but they understood that their constituents cared about this, and they were immediately receptive."[26]

On May 8, 2003, MoveOn.org launched the "Stop Media Monopoly" petition, its first campaign on media ownership issues. "On June 2, the Federal Communications Commission is planning on authorizing sweeping changes to the American news media," the group's solicitation letter explained. "When we talk to Congresspeople about this issue, their response is usually the same: 'We only hear from media lobbyists on this. It seems like my constituents aren't very concerned with this issue.' A few thousand emails could permanently change that perception. Please join us in asking Congress and the FCC to fight media deregulation." The response was overwhelming. "So many people responded so quickly that we could tell this was a hot issue," Pariser told me. "Our members sent the letter on to friends, they signed the petition, and then joined MoveOn. The strength of that petition drove us to get more involved. It totally surprised us. The FCC rule making was not where we thought the energy was going to be. We thought it was going to be a side issue with a few respondents. But it turned out to be a core issue for our constituents, one of the biggest petitions we'd done." Although MoveOn.org had only been organizing around media ownership for a few weeks, its petition generated around 250,000 letters in one week. "We sent so many comments to the FCC that we crashed their server," Pariser recalled. "They're not used to receiving hundreds of thousands of e-mail comments at a time."

The unprecedented outpouring of bipartisan opposition to more deregulation undermined the legitimacy of Powell's determined push to cut the caps. For the chairman could not deny that he was ultimately accountable to the American people, as he had gone on record saying that when the FCC makes policy decisions, "the input of individual citizens is invaluable. They can file comments and express those views on the record. And we can use them. Part of what they have to count on is for us to be their surrogate."[27] Yet Powell showed no signs of the conflict in his own position as he kept the FCC racing toward the scheduled June 2 vote. After keeping Copps and Adelstein in the dark for months, he released the proposed rule changes to the other commissioners—but not to the public, which again was kept out of the process—on May 12, giving his colleagues the absolute minimum time for review required by law. McChesney wrote that "Copps and Adelstein immediately asked for a delay of the vote, a 'traditional right of commissioners,' which had never been denied in anyone's memory. Powell rejected the request, citing counsel by his Republican colleagues on the Commission, Abernathy and Martin."[28]

As the date of the decision approached, public demands for a more democratic media policy-making process reached a din. "Let's debate this out in the open, take polls, get the president on the record and turn up the heat," wrote William Safire in his May 22 column. Copps sounded a similarly desperate note. "We are on the verge of dramatically altering our nation's media landscape without the kind of national dialogue and debate these issues so clearly merit," he warned. "If FCC Chairman Powell continues to insist that the roll be called on June 2 . . . the FCC will have voted on this, changed the rules, reconfigured the media landscape, and told the world that, sorry, there's no opportunity or time for public comment on what has been voted into place. Right after that, prepare to see a veritable gold rush of media company buying and selling . . .

I just wonder who is going to be America's broker in all this? Somehow I had the quaint idea that maybe the FCC was supposed to pay some attention to that."[29]

The decision Copps feared turned out much as he predicted: on June 2 the FCC issued an order that bore not a single mark of the public's input. Voting along party lines, Commissioners Martin and Abernathy joined Chairman Powell to form a three-to-two majority over Copps and Adelstein, recommending that Congress eliminate the ban on cross-ownership, raise the national cap on television station ownership from 35 to 45 percent of the national market, and allow one company to own three television stations in one town. That evening, PBS reported that the proposed laws represented "the most sweeping changes in the nation's media ownership rules in a generation," allowing "a single company [to] conceivably own up to three television stations, eight radio stations, the cable television system and cable TV stations, and the only daily newspaper in a single city." North Dakota senator Byron Dorgan, who had became an outspoken critic of media consolidation after observing Clear Channel's role in the Minot disaster, complained: "This is a big deal. It's going to affect what the American people can see, can hear, can read . . . Seldom have I seen a regulatory agency cave in so completely to the big economic interests." Trent Lott, his Republican colleague, simply stated that "this is a mistake."[30]

Copps and Adelstein issued bitter statements on the decision. "I'm afraid a dark storm cloud is now looming over the future of the American media," wrote Adelstein. "This is the most sweeping and destructive rollback of consumer protection rules in the history of American broadcasting . . . This plan is likely to damage the media landscape for generations to come. It threatens to degrade civil discourse and the quality of our society's intellectual, cultural and political life. I dissent, finding today's Order poor public policy, indefensible under the law, and inimical to the public interest and the health of our democracy." Copps also condemned the order as an act of "radical deregulation" that ignored the public will. "I dissent to this decision," he wrote. "I dissent on grounds of substance. I dissent on grounds of process. I dissent because today the Federal Communications Commission empowers America's new Media Elite with unacceptable levels of influence over the media on which our society and our democracy so heavily depend . . .

Where are the blessings of localism, diversity and competition here? I see centralization, not localism; I see uniformity, not diversity; I see monopoly and oligopoly, not competition."

But Copps knew that the order had to clear several hurdles before becoming law, and he had faith that the public calls for regulatory protection would lift the bar for final approval. "This Commission's drive to loosen the rules and its reluctance to share its proposals with the people before we voted awoke a sleeping giant," he declared. "American citizens are standing up in never-before-seen numbers to reclaim their airwaves and to call on those who are entrusted to use them to serve the public interest . . . The media concentration debate will never be the same. The obscurity of this issue that many have relied upon in the past, where only a few dozen inside-the-Beltway lobbyists understood the issue, is gone forever."[31]

COPPS WAS PRESCIENT. LESS THAN FORTY-EIGHT HOURS AFTER THE FCC announced its deregulatory order, all five commissioners assembled before the Senate Committee on Commerce, Science & Transportation, which had demanded that the agency explain its decision. The committee chairman, John McCain, opened the meeting by reminding the commissioners that despite his "long voting record in support of deregulation" and general belief "in letting markets, not government, regulate the way businesses operate," he was skeptical about their proposal. "The business of media ownership, which can have such an immense effect on the nature and quality of our democracy, is too important to be dealt with so categorically. And I have come to believe that there must be some limits on media ownership to avoid what we have seen happen in radio." Commissioner Martin, whom some conservative critics of consolidation had pressured to dissent, defended the order as "our best attempt to respond to the courts' admonitions and our Congressional mandate by recognizing the availability of new media outlets, evaluating their impact on these core goals, and modifying our rules as appropriate."

Such bureaucratic language could not calm Senator Ernest Hollings, the committee's ranking Democrat, who called Powell a "fraud" and accused the three Republican commissioners of turning the FCC into an "instrument of corporate greed." Nor did it impress Senator Ron

Wyden, who said the order "rings the dinner bell for the big media conglomerates who are salivating to make a meal out of the nation's many
small media outlets." Again, Free Press and MoveOn.org rushed to the
Hill to remind congressional leaders of the widespread opposition to
deregulation, impressing the representatives with their heaping bags of
letters from citizens. "We lobbied every committee that was working
on media," said Silver. "We had to be aggressive, because so much was
on the line." Surprsingly, their work paid off immediately. In late July
2003, the U.S. House of Representatives, in a 400-to-21 vote, backed an
appropriations bill that would preserve the national television ownership limits. Without this intervention, quipped Democratic representative Edward Markey, the FCC's rules would "make Citizen Kane look
like an underachiever."[32]

Big Media companies have powerful allies, however, and Powell's
order was not dead yet. Whereas President Bush, during the previous
year, had quietly supported a rollback on ownership restrictions, now
he spoke loudly, threatening to use his executive veto power for the
first time if Congress did not restore the FCC's decision. The stakes were
high, and Bush used the threat to instruct fellow Republicans where
they should stand. Both Viacom and Rupert Murdoch's News Corporation, the right-wing conglomerate that had consistently backed his
administration, were already broadcasting to more than 35 percent of
the national audience, and they would be legally obligated to sell off
many stations if the caps were not increased or their waivers were not
extended. The Tribune Company had also received waivers to operate
beyond the standard ownership limits, and if Congress upheld the cross-
ownership ban it too would have to sell off some of its properties or
renew its waivers. On the other side, media reformers and civic organizations were invested as well, with Free Press, MoveOn, the Parents Television Council, and the NRA rallying their constituents for another round
of letter writing. By the fall, American voters had sent another 1.5 million letters to the FCC and Congress, demanding that they withstand
executive intimidation and preserve the ownership restrictions.

A dizzying series of political chess moves followed. The Senate moved
the FCC rules into an omnibus appropriations bill that was already
packed with other contentious issues, making it unlikely to pass; then,
under heavy pressure from the White House, congressional Republicans
brokered a late-night "compromise" in which the television cap rose to

39 percent—raising suspicions that it was specially made for Viacom and the News Corporation, which conveniently would not have to let go of any stations. Congress appeared headed for an about-face when Senators Lott and Dorgan pushed through a rarely used "resolution of disapproval" under the Congressional Review Act, in a 55-to-40 vote that effectively overturned the FCC order. But the House leadership refused to bring the resolution to the floor, and the issue stalled.

Then the media reform movement made its move. On behalf of a small, Philadelphia-based low-power radio collective called the Prometheus Radio Project, the Media Access Project had petitioned the U.S. Court of Appeals for the Third Circuit to review the FCC's decision. "The Commission's Order is arbitrary and capricious in a number of respects," the petition states. "It also violated both the Communications Act and the Administrative Procedure Act's public notice requirements. Petitioner respectfully requests that the Court reverse and remand the FCC's Order to the extent that it unlawfully repeals the prior ownership rules and adopts new ownership regulations, reinstate the prior ownership rules, and grant all other relief as may be just and proper."[33]

On September 3, 2003, the Third Circuit Court announced that it would issue an immediate stay on the FCC order, blocking implementation of all proposed rule changes until it reached a verdict. Major media companies, industry trade associations, and civic organizations immediately began drafting briefs for the federal appellate court that would decide the matter—at least until the next regulatory review process or an appeal to the U.S. Supreme Court. No one questioned the significance of the outcome. "In one motion," said Blair Levin, a media analyst for the firm Stifel, Nicolaus and a former FCC chief of staff, "everything that the FCC approved could be completely wiped out."[34]

10

LOW POWER TO THE PEOPLE

The Prometheus Radio Project may have been the lead plaintiff in the media industry's most important legal dispute, but the collective of West Philadelphia progressives with a do-it-yourself spirit and a principled belief in noncommercial programming had long operated without explicit permission as it challenged Big Media for a piece of the airwaves. Prometheus's roots were planted a few months after the implementation of the Telecommunications Act of 1996, when the group's founders grew upset enough about the lack of local content and diverse programming in their city's radio offerings that they went underground to start the West Philadelphia Pirate Radio (WPPR) station, 91.3, from a secret location in the economically impoverished but culturally rich neighborhood near the University of Pennsylvania campus.

Calling themselves Radio Mutiny, the collective aimed to provide West Philadelphia with news, commentary, and music that had no other outlet. They had a greater purpose, too, connecting with the emerging community media movement that helped ordinary people get their stories, ideas, and voices into a city whose airwaves were increasingly dominated by a small number of huge companies. Radio Mutiny members wanted to forge an open and free-spirited space on the dial, but they had no broadcast license, few resources, limited technical skills, and zero experience when they began. Participants put their own money into the project and, since they declared Radio Mutiny an "antiprofit" organization, harbored no hopes of recovering the costs. Pete Tridish (petri dish), a long-bearded, impishly charismatic young carpenter and self-described anarchist who invented his playful pseudonym for the radio project, recalled: "All of our friends thought that we were, like, total losers" for trying to start a homemade media outlet. "People thought we were crazy, and were just really dismissive, which makes sense. They said, 'You can't just build a radio station.'" Yet Radio Mutiny did, right in Pete Tridish's house. Getting it up and running took about nine months, and on several occasions the project stalled when the collective rubbed up against the limits of its abilities. "We blew up a number of amplifiers trying to set up the studio," he told me. "But we made it."

Not that Radio Mutiny's equipment was especially powerful. Whereas the major commercial radio stations in cities such as Philadelphia commonly broadcast with 50,000- to 100,000-watt signals strong enough to reach listeners in distant suburbs, WPPR operated with 20 watts and rarely breached the neighborhood borders. While Clear Channel and Cumulus aggressively marketed their nationally syndicated programs and touted their sophisticated systems for transmitting clear signals across the large metropolitan region, on its Web site Radio Mutiny boasted, "We have been heard: As far in the northwest as Lower Merion and the West River Drive just before Germantown; On Delaware Avenue to the east, up near the Torresdale el in northeast." WPPR's signal did not interfere with others in the area, nor did its programming provide real competition for the big radio stations in the market. What Radio Mutiny did was offer a rhetorical challenge to the media industry at every possible opportunity, proclaiming on its Web site that "Radio Mutiny has set out to prove that in this era of corporate dominance and political backlash, this era in which a large portion of our society's culture and consciousness is industrially produced by media conglomerates driven by fantastic profit margins . . . volunteers with a passion for culture and with vital, direct interest in civic affairs can make better programming than the mega-corporations controlling the majority of media outlets."

Just what kind of content did Radio Mutiny offer? Music, of course, including jazz, zydeco, classical, folk, punk, funk, indy rock, and a range of international styles. Unconventional news, talk, and community programs, such as a show hosted by a former prison inmate who critically examined the criminal justice system, life behind bars, and the vast dragnet that captured thousands of Philadelphia residents during the 1990s incarceration boom; the *Africa Report,* hosted by a former member of the African National Congress and antiapartheid activist who was part of the growing African immigrant population in West Philadelphia; and a safe-sex show produced by the "Condom Lady," who interspersed her advice and commentary with classic disco tunes. These are not the formats that media consultants are likely to recommend to commercial clients, yet they reflected the concerns of WPPR's hyperlocal audience. Soon West Philadelphia was buzzing with excitement about its new station, and more than forty-five amateur DJs were participating regularly. The same friends who had teased the Radio Mutiny collective for trying to make a do-it-yourself media outlet now wanted their own shows.

WPPR'S GROWING POPULARITY PLACED THE PIRATE STATION IN DANGER, though, because the National Association of Broadcasters (NAB) was actively pressuring then FCC chairman Reed Hundt to crack down on unlicensed operators. Although amateurs pioneered American radio, since 1927, when the Radio Act was passed, federal regulators have favored commercial operators and forced nonprofessionals onto the margins of the dial or off of it altogether. "Noncommercial radio virtually disappeared between 1927 and 1934," wrote the media activist Greg Ruggiero, "shrinking to barely two percent of all radio airtime by 1934."[1] Amateurs would remain on the fringes of the dial until 1948, when educational institutions persuaded the FCC to grant them low-power "Class D" broadcast licenses, not to exceed 10 watts on the low range (between 88 and 92 MHz) of the FM band (though they were later allowed to reach 100 watts), for noncommercial stations that would serve as both training grounds for future programmers and laboratories for the medium. The stations were never in high demand, but by the early 1970s the spectrum they occupied would be. In 1972, the Corporation for Public Broadcasting (CPB) petitioned the FCC for control of more space on the "educational band," arguing that the quality and availability of Class D operators was so inconsistent that they failed to serve the public interest, and that the spectrum could be more effectively used for high-power public radio. The FCC complied in 1978, ordering Class D stations to upgrade their power above 100 watts or lose their spots on the dial. The ruling effectively outlawed low-power stations, turning all microradio operators into pirates, forever doomed to sail the airwaves without license.[2]

For years the pirates operated below the FCC's radar screen, and the commission made little effort to monitor their work. That changed in 1993, when an unlicensed operator named Stephen Dunifer started Free Radio Berkeley (FRB was 25 watts at 104.1 FM) from a secret location, and used the station to challenge the authority of the FCC. Dunifer took inspiration from Mbanna Kantako, a legally blind public housing resident in Abraham Lincoln's hometown, Springfield, Illinois. In 1987 Kantako founded Human Rights Radio to air his community's concerns about police discrimination and racial inequality that commercial stations failed to cover. The commission raided FRB in November 1993, fining Dunifer twenty thousand dollars for broadcasting without a license. Dunifer solicited help from the National Lawyers Guild on Democratic Communication, which challenged the fine on grounds that the FCC's ban on low-power radio violated his First Amendment protections and undermined the public interest. A five-year legal battle ensued, during which FRB, which became a magnet for radio enthusiasts and volunteers, stayed on the air, and Dunifer crusaded for microradio, traveling widely to promote local projects. Although a federal judge shut down FRB's broadcast station in June 1998, Dunifer refashioned the project as FRB IRATE (International Radio Action Training Education), and, as a media educator and activist, he is now more effective than ever.

BY THE MID-1990S THE FCC'S ENFORCEMENT DIVISION BEGAN CRACKING down again on low-power stations throughout the country, and Radio Mutiny went on the air at a moment when dramatic stories of station busts were circulating through the independent media network. In July 1996, the aspiring dance music programmer Alan Freed began operating Beat Radio, FM 97.7, at 20 watts and 110 feet, from downtown Minneapolis. One year later, two U.S. marshals joined FCC agents to raid the station, seizing its equipment and taking it off the air. In October 1997, another group of U.S. marshals assisted the FCC in a raid on the Community Power Radio station in Sacramento, again confiscating its equipment and forcing the station to shut down; later the next month the FCC took down two stations in Florida. When William Kennard replaced Reed Hundt as FCC chairman in November 1997, he signaled that he would heighten the campaign against pirates.[3]

Pete Tridish remembered Radio Mutiny's predicament. "Nine months after we got on the air, we're getting really psyched about it. Then we start hearing that the new chairman of the commission has gone out busting pirates. So we were getting a little nervous. If you don't let the FCC in, and they don't have a warrant, they can't really do anything. They'll often go back and get a warrant, come back a couple months later. But they can issue a ten-thousand-dollar fine for each unauthorized broadcast that they cite. If you do let them in, they can confiscate the equipment and anything that's attached to it." As they gained prominence in West Philadelphia, members of the collective began planning for a possible raid. "We had tried to stay out of the mainstream media," Tridish said, "because we heard that one of the main ways the FCC enforcement works is by searching the mainstream media, just reading articles. If a pirate comes up, that's where they send people. But then an article showed up about us in the local city paper. And a week later, we got our first visit from the FCC."

The core Radio Mutiny members were meeting across the street from the building that housed WPPR's studio and broadcast equipment, and they saw the agents at the door. An eighteen-year-old woman who was staying there answered the bell, yet she refused to let the men in suits enter. Lacking a warrant, the agents had no choice but to leave the premises and return another time. Initially, the visit produced conflict inside the Radio Mutiny collective, deepening the divisions between those who wanted to stay underground and those who wanted to steer the pirate station into the spotlight and stage a public confrontation. After a few hours of debate, though, they came up with a plan that everyone liked. Radio Mutiny would mobilize its members and listeners for a march to the site of Benjamin Franklin's printing press. They would carry the transmitter with them, daring the FCC to make a public show of force in the symbolic capital of the American free press. Tridish explained:

I made these really fun press calls. I'd say, "Hello, my name is Pete Tridish, from the Radio Mutiny collective. Until three days ago, we refused all contact with the commercial media, but the other night, the FCC came and threatened to bust down our door and take away our radio station. So we are challenging the chairman of the FCC, William Kennard, to come on down, in front of Benjamin Franklin's printing press, and bust us for bringing a community radio station to Philadelphia." We made a big banner that said, "1763, Benjamin Franklin challenges the Stamp Act and refuses to pay taxes to King George. 1996, Radio Mutiny defies the FCC for Freedom of Speech." It was kind of corny, but it was Philadelphia, so why not?

A lot of the press came. It was great. We were trying to imitate Thomas Paine, and we put forward our seven-point platform for how we were going to make the FCC's life really suck if they did not legalize community radio. The main thing we said was that for every station like ours that they tried to harass or intimidate or shut down, we were going to travel around the United States and teach people how to build pirate radio stations and make sure that for every one, we would build ten in its place. We wanted to create a law enforcement situation that they could never keep track of or understand.

The FCC refused to take the bait. Yet Radio Mutiny's spectacle of defiance, aimed to publicly humiliate the commission, only strengthened the enforcement division's determination to take it off the air. FCC agents returned to WPPR five times in the subsequent months, but Radio Mutiny eluded them by moving the studio or finding ways to hide its equipment. Members of the collective railed against the commission during their broadcasts, making sure to taunt Richard Lee, chief of the FCC's Compliance and Information Bureau, for his personal role in muting community voices. "He was a weirdo," Tridish said, "but he also had a good sense of humor. He would send me these e-mails saying, 'Resistance is Futile. I'll be seeing you soon.'"

On June 22, 1998, Lee finally tracked down the station in a West Philadelphia apartment building, and, in an unusual move for a division director, he personally accompanied a team of agents to bring Radio Mutiny down. The crew arrived late on a Monday afternoon, not long before WPPR was scheduled to begin its evening broadcast, and waited for the show to begin. This was amateur radio, though, and that night's DJ, a former member of Free Radio Santa Cruz, was woefully late. No one was there to let the agents in, and nothing was on the air. Frustrated, the FCC agents rang a neighbor's bell and got through the entrance, then forced their way into the studio by breaking the door lock. In a routine pirate radio raid, the FCC issues a citation for broadcasting without a license to the operators in the studio and confiscates the equipment. Lee was out for revenge, though, so he and the agents turned on the station signal, powered up the sound system, and put themselves on the air. "This is Richard Lee, chief of enforcement for the Federal Communications Commission. Radio Mutiny is an unlicensed broadcaster, and we are proceeding to take this station off the air!" Lee and his colleagues then pulled the plug, packed up the equipment, and brought it back with them to Washington. West Philadelphia Pirate Radio has been dead ever since.

FOR RADIO MUTINY'S CORE MEMBERS, THE STATION'S DEMISE MARKED the beginning of a national campaign to resurrect low-power radio that Pete Tridish had boldly announced at Benjamin Franklin's printing press. That summer, the collective embarked on a pirating expedition up and down the East Coast, stopping wherever there was interest to show community groups how to start unlicensed stations. The trip marked a turning point for the West Philadelphia activists, several of whom decided to concentrate on particular grassroots media projects when they returned. Pete Tridish, however, redoubled his commitment to the national effort, and in the fall of 1998 he joined with three collaborators, Greg Ruggiero, Sara Zia Ebrahimi, and David Murphy, to found the Prometheus Radio Project. Again based in West Philadelphia, Prometheus would provide legal, technical, and organizational support to groups struggling through the complicated process of creating a low-power station from scratch, and would also sponsor educational tours, conferences, and other events to generate public awareness about low-power stations.

Along with a group of media educators and youth radio activists in Washington, D.C., Prometheus planned its first event: a two-day conference, demonstration, and party in the shadows of its greatest adversaries, the National Association of Broadcasters, National Public Radio, and the FCC. The event would culminate in a spectacular demonstration that Prometheus planned to broadcast live with its portable equipment. Pete Tridish stepped up his defiant rhetoric. "They wouldn't bust us in Philadelphia, in front of Benjamin Franklin, so now we dare them to bust us right in front of their own offices!"

In October, more than 150 pirate operators arrived in Washington, D.C., to debate media policy, teach radio skills, protest the federal war on community stations, and dance to the music of local bands. The participants made what they called giant metapuppets—a string of enormous marionettes with a monstrous, machine-age General Electric puppet controlling a giant gorilla representing the National Association of Broadcasters, which in turn controlled a Pinocchio puppet, complete with nose extension, representing the new FCC commissioner, William Kennard. They marched directly to the main FCC office and then on to the NAB headquarters nearby. When they arrived at the FCC, the protestors chanted, "FCC, go away, microradio is here to stay!" The FCC security staff did little more than watch the spectacle, so after this first stop the march moved on to its final destination, the NAB, where the pirates pulled off their greatest symbolic coup yet. With the giant puppets leading the way, the demonstrators pushed their way past the security guards and onto the NAB plaza, which held two flagpoles, one with the American flag, the other with the NAB flag. The group leaders had scouted the site before the rally, and they had arranged to have a pirate radio operator from New Hampshire capture the NAB flag and replace it with a Jolly Roger flag. The NAB security staff, focused on the raucous demonstrators, failed to notice what Radio Mutiny pulled off. "It was the big joke in Washington," Tridish exclaimed. "The NAB got their flag captured."

By waging a symbolic battle with the agencies and professional organizations that shape national media policy—the puppets, the flags, the defiant broadcasts, and the bold chants—Prometheus dramatized its sweeping strategy for promoting low-power radio stations during the same years that Big Media companies were spending billions of dollars to capture the commercial spectrum. Not only did these stunts and spectacles energize the community groups and radio operators who had so many reasons to feel dispirited after the Telecommunications Act of 1996 and the FCC started cracking down on pirate stations in the mid-1990s; they also attracted the attention, and ultimately the sympathy, of an unlikely coalition of policy analysts, think tanks, foundations, and federal officials who learned about the issue because activists forced it into public view. Pete Tridish even received an invitation to participate in a policy briefing at the Cato Institute, the influential libertarian think tank whose leadership had begun to grow concerned that Big Media's stranglehold on the public spectrum was suffocating local democracy and silencing dissenting voices. The young pirate didn't know much about Cato, so he was surprised when he arrived in casual attire, portable transmitter in hand, to find that the audience of over one hundred suits included a staff member for the FCC chairman, William Kennard, representatives from the NAB, and several heavy-hitting lobbyists.

TRIDISH WAS EVEN MORE SURPRISED WHEN THE FCC STAFFER, WHO WAS an attorney, approached him after the presentation. "I know you don't believe me," Tridish remembered him saying, "but Chairman Kennard really likes community radio and we're going to try to legalize it." The lawyer explained how the process would work. In January of 1999 the FCC would initiate a Notice of Proposed Rulemaking, requesting that members of the public and the media industry submit formal comments, their own requests and recommendations for how the federal government should regulate low-power operators. Under Kennard's leadership, the FCC was willing to consider a number of controversial proposals, such as permitting low-power transmitters up to 1,000 watts, allowing new FM stations to exist without third adjacent channel separation requirements (which, for example, would prohibit a low-power station from a frequency between 89.9 and 92.1 if there were a station at 91.5), and licensing low-power commercial stations for groups that were underrepresented on the rest of the dial. Kennard had concerns about station interference, though, and his staff member instructed Tridish that the future of community radio depended on whether its advocates could formally submit credible engineering studies demonstrating that low-power signals would not cross into other broadcasts.

The invitation to participate in the regulatory process put Pete Tridish in unfamiliar territory. He had established himself as a leading activist in the pirate broadcast movement, and he believed there was political value in encouraging ordinary citizens to openly violate media policies that they considered undemocratic and unjust, most notably restrictions on broadcasting over the public spectrum. Yet Tridish knew he could not continue promoting unlicensed broadcasting if he was going to work with sympathetic FCC staffers to win legal status for community radio. "We were entering a relationship with the FCC where we would have to start negotiating, and we just couldn't do pirate radio work at the same time. They didn't want to be proposing rules that we thought were fair, and then at the same time find out that we were encouraging people to break them."

The choice was both controversial and consequential, since it contributed to an emerging division within the microradio movement. By cooperating with the FCC, Prometheus, a newcomer in the battle over low-power broadcasting, found itself opposed to pirate leaders such as Dunifer of Free Radio Berkeley and Kantako from Human Rights Radio. Dunifer and Kantako accused Kennard and the FCC of using a modest low-power radio-licensing proposal, one that they believed corporate broadcasters would weaken further once it reached the legislative stage, to appease their critics and deflect attention from the crisis of democratic communication wrought by consolidation.

Pete Tridish had his own concerns about the FCC's proposal, and he was wary of entering a working relationship with the same federal agency that had just shut down Radio Mutiny. But he also understood that Kennard was going to push for some form of licensed community broadcasting regardless of whether or not its advocates participated in the policy-making process, and he believed that Prometheus could help to improve the outcome.

They would need new partners, though, so Tridish established ties with the Media Access Project, a leading public-interest legal firm whose talented staff had a long history of challenging the FCC and the largest media firms; the National Lawyers Guild, which had done pioneering work on community radio; and the Minority Media and Telecommunications Council. Together, they raised grant money to support the engineering research on signal interference that the FCC had requested. The study, conducted by Broadcast Signal Lab and released in June 1999, showed that low-power FM (LPFM) signals caused only minimal interference with other stations, and only within the "blanketing area," a few hundred feet from the point of transmission. (The blanketing area for a 100-watt LPFM station is 401 feet, compared with 9,150 feet for a typical 50,000-watt station.) Low-cost filters, which all radio stations were already required to provide to listeners who had interference problems and lived in the blanketing area, solved the problem. Alan Korn, an attorney with the National Lawyers Guild, claimed that the findings left little doubt that the FCC could relax its restrictions on community radio: "The National Association of Broadcasters has consistently used buzzwords like interference to scare the American public and hide their opposition to increasing the number of voices available over the airwaves. Our study shows that opening the airwaves to the public with LPFM will cause far less interference than that caused by existing full power stations. These results confirm that the only interference the NAB is really concerned with is interference with their monopoly over the radio dial."[4]

Prometheus drew on research from its allies to reach out to established media policy organizations while also continuing to conduct outreach to community organizations and radio operators in hopes of generating public participation in the rule-making initiative. The response was tremendous. Whereas in the days before media reform groups like Free Press began mobilizing citizens, a typical rule-making initiative generated a few dozen letters, mostly from the companies whose interests were directly at stake in the policy, now roughly 3,500 people and organizations, including churches, civic groups, musicians, and listeners, wrote to the commission with suggestions about how the agency should regulate low-power radio.

Even the FCC was impressed. Bruce Romano, a member of the FCC's Mass Media Bureau, told Tridish that the deluge of input inspired the bureau's staff, many of whom had originally been drawn to media policy because they cared about public-interest issues and communications, only to find that they spent most of their time evaluating the competing claims of giant media companies vying to dominate the market. "Bruce told me that when the low-power ruling came along, and they saw all of these real regular people with bad grammar and weird schemes, they just saw so much hope in it that a lot of them couldn't help but be moved. It gave some meaning to their work and created a context where people actually cared about the decisions they made." (Staff members confirmed that the LPFM letters had inspired them.)

On January 26, 2000, the FCC officially authorized the creation of two new classes of radio—10-watt and 100-watt noncommercial stations, though not the 1,000 watt-stations nor the low-power commercial stations for which many activists had pushed—intended "to provide opportunities for new voices to be heard . . . in a manner that best serves the public interest."[5] Initially, the FCC would give strong prefer-ence to local organizations interested in serving their own communities, so long as the organizations were not already invested in another broad-cast station. Yet there were few geographic constraints on the appli-cants, and the commission's plan would effectively open up space for thousands more stations. LPFM advocates, including most of the 3,500 or so who sent formal comments to the FCC, were largely pleased with the outcome. Kennard was especially excited. He called the FCC's decision an "antidote to consolidation" and promised to begin repair-ing the damage to the dial wrought by consolidation. "When hundreds of stations are owned by just one person or company," he said in a press release, "service to local communities and coverage of local issues lose out."

Many of the FCC's fierce critics were skeptical about Kennard's motivations. Soon after the FCC's announcement, Dunifer sent a sting-ing e-mail to the community radio movement, part of which stated, "Congress does not give a rat's ass about what any of us think or want. And neither does the FCC, it's all about damage control on Kennard's part. He knows that the government does not have the resources to deal with thousands of folks taking back their airwaves. So he had to come up with a strategy that would fool folks who somehow still believe the system has a degree of legitimacy and credibility and would participate in the process—just a charade really in the final analysis."[6] Dunifer and Kantako had additional motivation to reject Kennard's proposal for regulatory reform. The FCC insisted on refusing licenses to "organizations that broadcast without a license in the past, or indi-viduals serving as officers or directors of organizations which broad-cast without a license . . . unless they certify that they promptly ceased operations when notified of their violation by the FCC and, in any case, ceased operations as of February 26, 1999."[7] This policy meant that the activists who had led the pirate movement during the previous decade would be excluded from the future of low-power broadcasting that they had made possible.

Dunifer's criticisms, however stinging, would prove far less conse-quential than those of two unlikely groups that allied to oppose the FCC's low-power radio initiatives, the National Association of Broad-casters (NAB) and National Public Radio (NPR). These powerful media organizations viewed LPFM as a threat to their established positions on the dial, and they both lobbied aggressively to scale back the licensing proposal. The NAB's campaign came as no surprise. The eighty-four-year-old trade association exists to promote and protect the interests of professional broadcasters and its executive boards are packed with the presidents and CEOs of companies like Cox, Citadel, and Tribune. The NAB's influence over the FCC and Congress is a fundamental force in the media field, and while its largest members, such as Clear Channel, reaped enormous benefits from the deregulation, the Texas media conglomerate grew so much, and so quickly, that by 1999 it had lost many of its professional connections and shared interests with the smaller broadcasters that also belong to the NAB.

Just as the NAB's Radio Board found itself pulled in different directions, the fight against LPFM emerged as a common thread that could bring them back together again. Small and large radio corporations could at least agree that they did not want the FCC to open the door to new competitors, and, just as established broadcasters had done in the first battles over who could use the spectrum, they rallied around the threat of signal interference. The NAB issued a statement arguing that "the Commission's reasoning for creating these new services was to 'enhance community-oriented radio broadcasting,' but in doing so they are actually condemning radio stations across the U.S. to dealing with levels of interference that many listeners will find unacceptable." To make its point, the NAB distributed a compact disc to members of Congress that purported to demonstrate the kind of cross-station interference that would be caused by LPFM broadcasters.[8] And the NAB made special efforts to convince the leadership of National Public Radio, the nonprofit media institution revered by many of the liberal organizations and community groups that supported microradio, that LPFM signals threatened its status, too. On March 30, 2000, NPR complained that "the FCC took inadequate steps in adopting its LPFM decision to protect the signals and transmissions of public radio stations and radio reading services," and formally asked the FCC to delay implementation of its LPFM decision, "pending further testing and the adoption of suitable additional safeguards."[9]

Where Pete Tridish might once have reveled in an occasional fight against the giant media association whose flag he had captured, now he and his allies in the community media movement were dispirited when NPR allied with the NAB. Tridish claimed that "top management of

NPR went all out against LPFM" in congressional testimony and backstage lobbying, even while its leaders publicly voiced support (if weak) for the concept of microradio.[10] Along with most other low-power radio advocates, Tridish now has an abiding contempt for NPR's leaders. "They just suck," he told me, disdain all over his face. "NPR always claimed that they were completely in favor of low-power FM, and that they just had a couple of technical quibbles. But the technical quibbles were big enough that they lobbied against us in Congress. I've never met a more imperious bunch."

Although federal cuts to the Corporation for Public Broadcasting budget had forced it to solicit private sponsors (a practice it continues even after Joan Kroc, the widow of McDonald's founder Ray Kroc, left NPR $200 million in late 2003), NPR remained a genuine alternative to the commercial giants that have taken over the radio dial. Promoting diversity and helping community voices get onto the airwaves are among NPR's core values. Despite its limited political clout in the Capitol, NPR has enormous symbolic power when it aligns with the NAB, since commercial broadcasters can use NPR's reputation to fend off accusations of reputed financial motivation. In the microradio debate, the NAB aggressively exploited its support from NPR, insisting that mutual concerns about interference, not aversion to competition, brought them together. The two organizations began lobbying Congress to write alternative legislation, the Radio Broadcasting Preservation Act of 2000, that would override the FCC's decision on LPFM and dramatically reduce the supply of licenses. In an interview with *Wired* magazine, Chairman Kennard acknowledged his disappointment. "I can only conclude that NPR is motivated by the same interests as the commercial groups—to protect their own incumbency. That these people see LPFM as a threat is sad. They've done much in the past to promote opportunity and a diversity of voices."[11]

Emboldened by Kennard's interest in low-power radio, the FCC pushed back against the big broadcasters. The commission, which had already determined that the low-watt stations would not cause serious disruptions to incumbents, published strongly worded challenges to the NAB and NPR's technical arguments against LPFM. The FCC had a powerful case, in part because its engineers had discovered that the NAB's prime lobbying device, the CD distributed to show what two adjacent radio stations would sound like with LPFM, was in fact a mix of two audio tracks merged in a studio, not an actual recording of station interference. On March 24, 2000, Dale Hatfield, chief of the FCC's Office of Engineering and Technology, and Roy Stewart, chief of the FCC's Mass Media Bureau, issued a press release that blasted the NAB for using a "misleading disinformation effort [involving] a compact disc . . . that purports to demonstrate the type of interference to existing radio stations that NAB claims will occur from new low-power FM radio stations. The CD demonstration is both misleading and wrong."[12] On March 29, the FCC published a fact sheet, "Low Power FM Radio Service: Allegations and Facts," that directly refuted a series of inaccurate claims made by the NAB and NPR, once again emphasizing that the CD distributed to Congress had faked the evidence of signal interference as a way of mobilizing legislators to overrule the FCC. "The type of 'crosstalk' interference suggested by the NAB in its misleading CD demonstration on Capitol Hill, where you can intelligibly hear portions of both transmissions, is not likely to occur from actual LPFM stations operating on 3rd adjacent channels when the receiver is properly tuned to the desired station: Any such interference that might occur from an LPFM station would nearly always appear as noise or hissing, as shown in the FCC's own CD demonstration on Capitol Hill. The NAB 'crosstalk' demonstration therefore does not represent actual FM radio performance and thus is meaningless."[13]

The opponents of LPFM were undeterred. After the commission exposed the NAB's use of mock interference, the NAB removed the recording from its Web site and replaced it with other studio recordings, now manufactured to better replicate the hiss of cross-talk. Trounced by proponents of community radio, the powerful broadcast lobby took its campaign to restrict the LPFM licenses to the back rooms of Congress, where it remained influential. The stealth operation succeeded. In December 2000, Congress attached the Radio Broadcasting Preservation Act to a spending bill that the Republican leadership was determined to push through, and it passed with little public debate. The act mandated station channel separations far beyond what the FCC had recommended, a move that effectively closed off thousands of potential open frequencies for community stations in metropolitan areas, reducing the number of available licenses from five or six to one or two in many markets. Congress's decision effectively banned low-power licenses altogether in the top fifty urban markets, which meant that many of the strongest LPFM advocates would be unable to get on the air. In January 2001, newly elected President George W. Bush announced that Commissioner Michael Powell would replace Kennard as FCC chairman, leaving the low-power radio advocates without their greatest ally in Washington. According to Tridish and fellow activist Kate Coyer, "LPFM was alive, but eviscerated."[14]

After reluctantly agreeing to work with the FCC, Tridish couldn't help but question whether community radio advocates had lost more than they had won. But with Powell and the Republicans now running the commission, he'd no longer be collaborating with the FCC's leadership, anyway. The altered legislation generated thousands of license applications from community groups, religious organizations, schools, and radio enthusiasts, all of whom were eager to get on the air. Tridish knew that many of the applicants would need help starting their stations, and that Prometheus, with its technical expertise, policy knowledge, and strong ties to media activists, could play a key role in the process. It was time to return to the grass roots, and Tridish had another dramatic plan to get there.

PROMETHEUS ANNOUNCED IT WOULD BEGIN ORGANIZING BARN RAISINGS, based on the frontier tradition of collective home building. Locals and volunteers would join to build a studio, assemble the tower, raise the antenna, and begin broadcasting, all in a weekend. As a young carpenter, Pete Tridish had volunteered on Habitat for Humanity projects, and he remembered how building a house from scratch could generate powerful emotional attachments between the participants. His plan was to adapt the model, using the construction process as a forum for teaching basic radio engineering and production skills to new operators, and parlaying the energy won through collective labor to forge a community that would last beyond the event. "I thought that with building a grassroots movement, what better thing to do than to have people able to come and learn skills at the same time that they're helping. Obviously, there's easier ways to build a radio station than to have a bunch of people who haven't built one before help. But actually the model has been really good. It's a focal point for the public debate, a focal point for the movement, and it's a great excuse for everyone to come together."

Prometheus organized its first barn raising in spring 2002, when it traveled to Churchton, Maryland, to help the South Arundel Citizens for Responsible Development (SACReD) set up the 100-watt station WRYR (We aRe Your Radio) 97.5, the fifth licensed LPFM station to go on the air since the FCC enacted its new policy. In Maryland, SACReD had established its reputation by fighting to restrain runaway development in the Chesapeake Bay region, including one notable project preventing builders from replacing sixteen acres of forested wetlands with a large strip mall. Michael Shay, SACReD's founder, applied for a radio station so that the group could diversify and "[shine] a flashlight" on local government and help other activists "preserve community history."[15] More than 150 volunteers turned out for the barn raising, during which Prometheus led workshops on topics such as "using a minidisc recorder," "the fine art of deejaying," and "introduction to radio engineering," while others labored to put up the station.[16] WRYR made its first broadcast at the end of the three-day event and initiated its regular schedule a few months later. WRYR's program offerings include local talk and news shows such as *A Neighbor, Parents Journal, Local Lowdown,* and *Community Folk;* funk, country, musical memories, rock, and gospel hours; plus *Free Speech Radio News* and *Clean Power and Fresh Air.*

In December 2003, Prometheus went to Immokalee, Florida, to help the Coalition of Immokalee Workers (CIW), a group of some 2,500 Mexican, Haitian, and Guatemalan immigrant farm laborers, start their own station, WCIW, 107.9 FM. The Immokalee project was especially challenging, as CIW core members work collectively but do not have a common language, requiring organizers and workers to mediate between Spanish, Quiche, Zapotec, Creole, and English. The coalition, which had led successful campaigns against brutal labor practices in the Southwest Florida agricultural industry, was in the midst of a contentious struggle with Taco Bell. The fight involved a high-profile boycott of Yum! Brands, which also owns Kentucky Fried Chicken, Pizza Hut, and Long John Silver's, until it agreed to pay workers a penny more for each pound of tomatoes they picked. Some Southwest Florida politicians were unhappy about the negative attention generated by CIW's activities, and when Prometheus organizers began working with the coalition to plan the station, they learned that several local officials were reluctant to give the farmworkers a building permit for the tower.

According to Prometheus member Dharma Dailey, a communications failure during a public health crisis helped the CIW make its case. "During the debate there was a water advisory because a chemical contaminant had gotten into the water. Town officials used the mainstream radio to issue a warning, but none of the Immokalee had heard it. This came up at our meeting, because the officials learned that their public health warning hadn't gotten through. The farmworkers said that they needed media that could reach their community, too," and the local board finally gave in. The coalition got its building permit, Prometheus helped rally another group of volunteers, and, after another three-day barn raising, WCIW was on the air. About fifteen months later, Taco Bell ended the three-year boycott by consenting to the penny-per-pound pay raise that its tomato pickers demanded. The U.S. Congressional Hispanic Caucus called it "a truly historic agreement, marking perhaps the single greatest advance for farm workers since the early struggles of the United Farm Workers."[17] WCIW broke the news—live, and in every language its members speak.

IN RECENT YEARS ANOTHER KIND OF LANGUAGE BARRIER HAD OPENED A cultural chasm in Nashville, Tennessee, a vibrant city that is at once the buckle of the Bible Belt and a pocket of liberal voters in an important swing state. Disaffected residents there say that since the Telecommunications Act of 1996, talk radio in Nashville has become less local, more conservative, and unresponsive to its citizens, most of whom are Democrats. As of 2005, Clear Channel owned five stations, Cumulus owned three, and the Moody Bible Institute of Chicago ran two more in the area. A Vanderbilt University professor who showed me around town complained: "Radio here is just unbearable. It seems like Clear Channel owns eighty percent of the stations. Most people I know have just turned if off." According to Cecily Letendre, a radio enthusiast in her early thirties whom I met at the barn raising, "Nashville is similar to the rest of the country. Talk radio is dominated by the right wing: Rush Limbaugh, Sean Hannity, Mike Savage. There aren't liberal voices being heard in middle Tennessee. Memphis has Air America now. We don't have anything like that." Even music radio, in the town famous for its recording studios and live-music venues, began losing its local flavor when commercial broadcasters adopted the standard formats they played in the rest of the country.

As early as 1997, Ginny Welsch, a veteran radio personality in town, had grown so concerned about the rising corporate pressure to standardize content, replace DJs with voice-tracked shows, cut civic-affairs and public-interest programming, and reduce the number of records in rotation that she thought about leaving the business. She told me: "Nashville radio is terrible for local bands, terrible. They've cut down how many records they play to like nothing. There's nothing local about it. You'd think it would be hard to decide what to play in a specific market. I'm not from Nashville. I grew up in St. Louis, lived in New York for a long time, in Washington, D.C., and in Austin, Texas. None of these cities are alike, at all, and yet the big radio companies decided that people's tastes and sensibilities are the same in every single city. They've gentrified American radio, and we've lost the things that give texture and context and make it interesting."

Welsch decided to keep her day job on commercial radio, where, like many others in the industry, she used a stage name while also establishing a side business doing voice-overs. In her spare time, Welsch began recruiting friends, including her brother Greg, as well as Beau Hunter, a former San Francisco musician and radio contributor, to join her in planning a community radio station, Radio Free Nashville (RFN). Their first meeting was at a restaurant, after which news about the project spread through the city's active arts and culture networks, spurring an eclectic mix of supporters to begin participating in open sessions at the Nashville Peace and Justice Center. Ginny Welsch defined a simple mission for the project. "We believe democracy cannot function if only a few have access to the media, and we want to be the forum for the voices, the viewpoints, the people, and the music that have historically and consistently been denied access to the media or misrepresented by the corporate media. That's really our only policy."

It was an appealing message. The *Nashville Scene* reported that "by 1999 they'd grown to include college-radio hosts, teenage punks, a certified public accountant, utility workers, and a labor activist. Meeting twice monthly, the proposed RFN began drawing 20 and 30 people each time."[18] The group had virtually no funds, making even a small

AM station out of reach. Members closely followed the debates on low-power FM radio in the Capitol, hoping to land one of the new licenses proposed by Chairman Kennard. Yet when Congress diluted the FCC's policy, Nashville became ineligible for an LPFM station. RFN members became despondent, and many stopped attending the planning meetings. Even Ginny Welsch and Beau Hunter began to lose hope.

Then they got lucky. Powell, newly installed as FCC chairman, followed Kennard's precedent by approving a new spate of LPFM licenses to signal support for local operators even as he pursued an aggressive campaign to deregulate other media industries. Again, critics slammed the FCC for giving away a handful of LPFM as a way to legitimate the massive benefits it was poised to offer the conglomerates. But Welsch and Hunter were determined to exploit the opportunity. They found a ham-radio operator who was willing to give RFN a spot on the tower he had built on his land in Pasquo, a semirural, suburban area outside Nashville, and they pledged to the FCC that their 100-watt station would not interfere with any commercial outlets. In May 2002, the FCC tentatively approved the license for 98.9 FM, a prime spot on the dial, and suddenly RFN—without a budget to build a studio, raise a tower, or pay a staff—began scrambling to get the station up.

It was a false start. Within days, a radio station in Lebanon, Tennessee, filed a petition to deny RFN its license because, its owners claimed, the microradio broadcast would interfere with its own signal. Although the claim was ruled to be specious, it took the FCC sixteen months—until the end of October 2003—to say so. When it did, RFN faced an imposing deadline. If the station wasn't on the air by April 30, 2005, the license would be revoked.

Enter Prometheus. By the end of 2003 the organization had become a key player in national and local media politics. Yet it still had only four employees working in a church basement, all for less than ten dollars an hour, and it was getting so many requests to help set up LPFM stations that it had to turn down invitations. Almost immediately after hearing from Welsch and Hunter, though, Pete Tridish knew that RFN was a perfect match. "We wanted to do a barn raising in a red state. LPFM is not just something that liberal East Coast professors think would be a good idea. All kinds of people want to do it. There are important senators here, too. Bill Frist and Fred Thompson. Radio Free Nashville would help us to tell the story of LPFM; it's a station we could showcase and talk about." Prometheus organizers traveled to Nashville and began helping the group meet the technical and bureaucratic challenges involved in opening the station. The official license approval proved to be a boon for membership, and soon some seventy volunteers, including a group of twenty-five to thirty regulars, were contributing to the project. Confident and excited, they scheduled a barn raising for the first weekend in April 2005.

MY FLIGHT FROM NEW YORK CITY TO NASHVILLE WAS HARROWING. Fierce storm clouds lined the skies from the Eastern Seaboard to the Deep South, and the small jet carrying me bounced its way through an airborne sea of thick, gray cumulus, landing into a downpour. The trip to Pasquo was not much smoother for RFN. Less than a year before it planned to go on the air, the radio enthusiast who donated a spot on his tower for the LPFM station died suddenly. His heir, finding no mention of the station in the will, refused to cooperate with the group. This was no small crisis, since the FCC had given RFN a narrow range of places to base its signal, and the organization had not identified an alternate site, nor did it have the money to purchase land if something came on the market. But once more, an unlikely source helped the group avert disaster.

April Glaser is a pink-haired teenager with a passion for obscure music and sparkplug energy that bursts out of her compact frame. She graduated early from high school, started an internship at the American Civil Liberties Union, volunteered with Food Not Bombs, and, at age seventeen, became the youngest member of the RFN executive board. April earned her way into the position by working relentlessly as a fund-raiser and organizer, and by inspiring confidence that the community station would attract a generation of Nashville residents that finds little compelling content on the dial. She was living with her father, Ed, a podiatrist who owns Sole Supports, a successful orthopedic insert company, when one day she mentioned to him her disappointment about the station's loss of the tower. Ed, who describes himself as a run-of-the-mill Democrat, was annoyed by the extreme right-wing talk shows that saturate the airwaves but too busy to do anything about it. He is also an exceptionally proud parent who was moved by April's commitment to RFN. After watching April and her collaborators search in vain for land, he surprised them all with a radical proposal. He had been thinking about moving out of the city. What if he purchased an open tract of land in the hills of Pasquo, where RFN's license allowed the station to operate, put in a portable prefab home to share with April, and then built a studio and tower alongside it? Welsch, Hunter, and the other board members could hardly believe the offer. But Ed was serious, the land was available, and days later the station had a new life. All they had to do was build it.

Together, Prometheus and RFN recruited a record number of registrants for the barn raising, and a week before the event Pete Tridish led a large group of staff and volunteers from the East Coast down to Nashville to prepare. But they still weren't in the clear. Supporters canceled a benefit that would have provided desperately needed funds; a local agency ruled that the designated signal tower was unsuitable for the land; and RFN had to put off the final, mandatory electrical inspection so it could get the proper equipment.[19] In the meantime, torrential rains poured down on the land surrounding the Glaser home, transforming the grounds where visiting volunteers were supposed to camp into a soupy mud field, and gale-force winds unmoored the tents where workshops were scheduled to meet. The Prometheus staff reassured RFN members that they would be able to assemble and raise the delicate tower—provided, of course, that the rain stopped and the winds calmed. Yet the forecast was ominous, and Friday, the official opening of the barn raising (and, for good measure, April Fool's Day), brought the week's most severe storms. The event began anyway, in the bedrooms and common areas of the Glasers' house rather than in the tents.

When I reached Pasquo on Saturday morning, one hundred people—high school and college students, engineers, young professionals, anarchists, techies, LPFM operators from other towns, aspiring programmers, and scores of RFN members—were scattered around a camper, a van, and the unfinished studio, bracing themselves against wind gusts up to forty miles an hour and a rare April frost. But caterers nearby had donated gallons of coffee, and the volunteers were exchanging warm introductions. By 9:30 everyone was ready to work.

The day began in a workshop on reporting, held in April's bedroom. Eighteen people who hoped to produce their own segments for RFN squeezed around a folding table, teenagers and senior citizens cramped beside each other to hear experienced radio journalists explain how to conduct interviews ("Let the person talk. It sounds bad if you say 'uh-huh' a lot") and find decent equipment ("Don't skimp on the microphone—it's important!"). A man in his sixties interrupted to ask if he was in the right place. "I'm not a man of many words. But I'm here because I like old-time rock and roll, Little Richard, Elvis, the Beatles. And I like humor. Is this for me?" Another large group huddled together in the back of a moving van for a seminar on radio transmitters and antennae, which I joined on the tail end for a hands-on demonstration of how to assemble RFN's new equipment.

Pete Tridish toiled in the background for most of the morning, occasionally peering into a small engineering project to remind the trained instructors to let the amateurs try building things themselves. By afternoon the winds had died, and the growing crowd of volunteers was busy at work. Small groups formed around the information booth that the Prometheus staff had set up outside of their camper. Others gathered near the tables of food delivered by local restaurants and residents or participated in various construction projects that were under way around the house. In the side yard, about two dozen people took hammers and wrenches to the seventy-foot radio tower, crouching to assemble it section-by-section, piece-by-piece, as it lay sideways on the muddy terrain. Indoors there were more seminars, on underwriting and pledge drives, station governance, and writing for radio. RFN's reporting staff, fresh from their lessons, circulated through the site to conduct their first interviews for a show about the barn raising. That evening, after a massive buffet dinner, Prometheus staffers called out for help placing a device for the tower lift near the top of an enormous tree. A college student named Liz Arnold calmly approached the tree, then scrambled some sixty feet up by hand to do the job while a large crowd gathered beneath to marvel. "She says she's a climber, and I know she's going to be fine," Tridish told me as we stared up into the dark branches. "But this makes my stomach turn." Arnold completed the task to a burst of hooting below, and after landing she joined the late-night celebration by the campfire that closed the night's work.

On Sunday a blazing sun brought spring to the hilly region, drying the land enough to hold the tower base before the midday raising, which would be done by hand and pulley rather than by crane. As the volunteers congregated for breakfast, Ginny Welsch leaned back against a table at the end of the driveway, her face flush, eyes lost in a long, incredulous daze. "I can't believe this is happening," she kept saying, as she hugged volunteers and squeezed the hands of everyone who stopped by. "We started this eight years ago. *Eight years!* It was a pipe dream. And tonight we're actually going on air."

Around her, work crews raced to finish the final projects, connecting the sound board and mixer, wiring the Emergency Alert System, securing the tower, writing and rehearsing for a radio theater story on RFN's founding, while the seminars continued indoors. At noon, everyone stopped their work to help hoist the tower. Three teams lined up to brace the heavy ropes of the pulley system that they would tug on command; one group stabilized the tower; and another, led by Pete Tridish, climbed up to the roof to balance the top and direct the process. A local engineer gave us the signal. "One, two, three, heave!" And we pulled, one side at a time, shifting back and forth to maintain balance, until the tower locked into the base. We cheered, slapped hands, and smiled in anticipation. Just a few more hours to go.

By 6:00 p.m. the studio was ready for testing, and April Glaser gathered with a few friends and volunteers to pick the first songs she'd play when she had her turn to go on the air. "I think it's got to be Kraftwerk, that would be so rad," she said. "You listen to Kraftwerk?" a friend replied. "I thought I was the only one, alone in my room."

Dozens of new RFN programmers and on-air personalities had similar conversations as the final countdown to first broadcast began. Some were predictable: liberal talk, an environmental hour, Nashville and Tennessee politics, and a variety of music that rarely makes it onto the commercial dial. Others were utterly idiosyncratic: "fire safety," "health at any size," "Christian dissent," "vulgar music," and "pulp country," to name a few. No one knew just how much time it would take to program the station, nor how many listeners they would attract in the small, semirural area that the 100-watt signal would reach. But they couldn't wait to get started making just a piece of the airwaves their own.

As broadcast time approached, everyone crowded together on the patch of open land in front of the studio and passed around bottles of cold beer. We all watched as Ginny and Greg Welsch climbed the short stairway up to the studio doorway landing, where a microphone was set up. We shouted in support and counted down the final seconds until the clock hit seven, when someone called out, "Flip the switch!"

Though she had imagined opening the station by announcing the call letters and triumphantly proclaiming that Radio Free Nashville was on the air, Ginny found that impossible. Overwhelmed by joy, she broke down instead, crying in her brother's arms. RFN's first broadcast opened with several seconds of blissful silence, followed by the whooping hollers of the volunteers who had helped build the station. When Ginny regained her composure, she grabbed the mike and pulled herself up. "From Pasquo, this is Radio Free Nashville, 98.9 FM." Greg leaned in over his sister and yelled out the barn-raising theme, "Low Power to the People!" More cheers. The DJ cued Jimi Hendrix, and everyone kissed and embraced like it was New Year's Eve. RFN soon got its first phone call, from a listener who was getting the signal some twenty-two miles away. Ginny broke out in an enormous smile, and her eyes fixed on the open sky above us. "This could be bigger than we thought."

THE DIGITAL FRONTIER

On February 11, 2004, the U.S. Court of Appeals for the Third Circuit convened in Philadelphia to hear oral arguments from Prometheus Radio Project and its fellow citizen petitioners in their challenge to the FCC's order of June 2003, which recommended eliminating the cross-ownership ban and raising the television ownership caps. The Big Media companies that had invested so much to lobby for the relaxed regulations that the FCC had historically delivered were well represented: Clear Channel, Sinclair, Tribune Company, the National Association of Broadcasters, and the major television networks had all sent attorneys to defend the new ownership rules. "It was quite a spectacle," Pete Tridish, the Prometheus organizer, recalled. "They said that normally these cases last less than an hour in court. But there were so many interested parties there, and so much at stake, that it lasted a full day."

The lawyers for Prometheus, who included Andrew Jay Schwartzman from the Media Access Project, Glenn Manishin for the Consumers Union and Consumer Federation of America, and the Georgetown University law professor Angela Campbell, were first to argue before the panel of three judges, Thomas Ambro, Julio Fuentes, and Anthony Scirica. The stakes were high, Manishin explained, because under the terms of the new order, "We go from a system in which cross-ownership prohibitions, with the exception of a few waivers, are prohibited almost nationwide, to a rule that allows broadcast-newspaper combinations in markets serving up to 98 percent of the American public."

"Not only are the number of television station owners going to be reduced dramatically" with the proposed rules, argued Campbell, "but one company can also own the only daily newspaper in a community, or all of the daily newspapers in the community. They can also own a large number of radio stations, up to eight stations in larger markets. And they can of course have unlimited websites, they can own the cable system. So there's truly potential here for one company to have a very significant dominance of public discourse within their community." The FCC, she continued, counted print and broadcast media owned by the same company as if they were separate outlets: "It's like giving one person two megaphones and saying that's diversity," even though "they're now providing the same news and it's the same editorial viewpoint . . . The public is hurt by that, even if the stations can make more money as a result of these efficiencies."[1]

In its order, the FCC had justified relaxing the ownership caps through a quasiscientific analysis purporting to show that, despite the recent wave of consolidation, local media markets remained diverse and competitive. According to Manishin, however, the evidence that the commission used "is so fraught with internal inconsistencies and is so beyond the pale of reasonable exposition and empirical support that it fails under any standard." Manishin attacked the foundations of the FCC's decision, the new diversity index (DI), which the FCC—ignoring complaints from Commissioners Michael Copps and Jonathan Adelstein—"created and promulgated in secret without any public notice," to prove that many "voices" competed in local markets. "The diversity index," Manishin explained, "says nothing directly about the quality, quantity, or vibrancy of local information," and so it is a useless tool for assessing the state of local media. "We believe the Commission acted arbitrarily and capriciously," added Campbell, who asked that the court remand the FCC's decision. "The record does not support their conclusion."

Jacob Lewis, an FCC attorney, struggled to defend the agency's decision during his presentation. As for the Duchess Community College station, which the FCC weighted as more important than the *New York Times,* he allowed that "it turns out that that was improperly included in the database." But, he continued, "for present purposes I'll concede there are stations that are not as significant, as a matter of audience share, [as] other stations." Judge Ambro pushed the matter. "The New York *Times* under your diversity index goes less far than Duchess Community College. We all know that's not the case." Lewis's response hardly clarified the matter. "The diversity index is an explanation about how the Commission came to the judgments it made that are embodied in the rule," he stated. "The Commission needed information, got information in the record about how people used media, then it needed information and it looked at information about the average DI."

"At about that point," Pete Tridish told me, "everyone on our side was trying hard not to bust out laughing. And we knew we had a chance to win."

Surprisingly, some of the attorneys representing Big Media companies seized the opportunity to discredit the FCC's rule-making process, though in their view the "arbitrary" and "capricious" decisions came from the commission's efforts to defend the remaining ownership caps. Clear Channel's lawyer, Miguel Estrada, made by far the most brazen claim of the hearing, arguing that the FCC's "avowedly deregulatory statute, the 1996 [Telecom] Act," legally prohibited the commission from "impos[ing] additional regulatory burdens." The 1996 act required the FCC to review ownership rules every two years and to "modify" or "repeal" laws that did not promote the public interest. "I think 'repeal' or 'modify' in the context of this statute is more naturally read to say either get rid of it or get rid of part of it," Estrada contended, "but it's not repeal and reregulate. That would make no sense in the context of this statute." The judges, skeptical to the point of bemusement, pressed Clear Channel's attorney to clarify this position. "You're saying . . . that it's a one way street, that you can only go down the street called deregulation," prodded Judge Ambro. "Even if things change, you cannot elect to go down the street of some increased regulation in a particular area?"

Judge Fuentes posed the question directly: "So 'modify' to you means in a sense eliminate?" Estrada massaged out an answer. "It means— no, it means 'change to make less regulatory' . . . I think the Commission could not modify by saying that the highest [radio] cap, instead of being eight will be seven." Fuentes probed deeper. "So [in] your definition of 'modify,' the FCC cannot modify simply to, let's say, fix an irrational policy. Modify is only appropriate so long as there is further deregulation?" Estrada confirmed this interpretation. According to Clear Channel, from now on changes to media ownership policy can only be legal if they relax or eliminate the caps.

ON JUNE 24, 2004, THE U.S. COURT OF APPEALS ISSUED ITS OPINION. IN A two-to-one decision, the Third Circuit judges upheld the elevated national television ownership cap of 39 percent passed by Congress, because the petitioners, who were entitled to contest the FCC's order, had no legal standing to challenge a congressional decision. But the court forcefully dismissed Big Media's arguments that ownership caps were unconstitutional, as well as Clear Channel's claim that media policy making had become a "one-way deregulatory ratchet." The court also rejected the commission's proposal to eliminate the cross-ownership ban, because the arbitrary diversity index used to justify the change "requires us to accept that a community college television station makes a greater contribution to viewpoint diversity than a conglomerate that includes the third-largest newspaper in America," and therefore "requires us to abandon both logic and reality." Echoing the language of the public-interest attorneys, the court ruled further that "the Commission gave too much weight to the Internet as a media outlet . . . There is a critical distinction between websites that are independent sources of local news and websites of local newspapers and broadcast stations that merely republish the information already being reported by the newspaper or broadcast station's counterpart. The latter do not present an 'independent' viewpoint and thus should not be considered as contributing diversity to local markets." According to the opinion, the FCC's diversity measure should be based on media outlets that promote democratic and civic engagement, not on Internet sites that "may be useful for finding restaurant reviews and concert schedules," but fail to offer "the type of 'news and public affairs programming'" that public policies are supposed to promote.[2]

The decision was a devastating blow to FCC chairman Michael Powell and a setback for the Bush administration, which had pushed hard to eliminate ownership caps. Powell, who had consistently dismissed public concerns over media concentration, nonetheless issued a warning that the Third Circuit's ruling "perversely may make it dramatically more difficult for the Commission to protect against greater media consolidation," because it forced the FCC to establish sound guidelines for regulating local broadcasters. The defeated chairman complained that the court's intervention "is deeply troubling and hampers the flexibility of the agency to protect the American public, as this agency is charged to do." Yet Powell's record on protecting the interests of the American public, whose millions of letters he had ignored outright during the policy-making process, undermined his credibility. The commission's reputation suffered, too, since the court's decision helped publicize the sad fact that the FCC would go to great lengths to satisfy the industry it was supposed to regulate, but would refuse to serve citizens and communities unless the judiciary compelled it to do so.

Seven months later Powell announced his resignation from the commission. He exited via the FCC's revolving door and walked into a senior position at Providence Equity Partners, an investment firm that manages $9 billion in equity commitments from media and telecommunications companies. "Mr. Powell is not worried about now doing business with some of the same people he once regulated and perhaps frustrated," the *New York Times* reported. *BusinessWeek,* however, speculated that "Providence wants Michael Powell to ensure approval of some gigantic future purchase that will need to be reviewed by the FCC," and consumer groups feared that the former chairman would capitalize on his political influence at the public's expense. Powell "didn't make it easy for his successor," the *Los Angeles Times* asserted, because "he pushed more hot-button issues to the forefront at the FCC than he was able to resolve."[3] Kevin Martin, the ambitious young Republican who replaced Powell as chairman in 2005, would have to direct the FCC with caution.

Powell's main adversaries on the commission, Michael Copps and Jonathan Adelstein, were emboldened by both the court ruling and the uproar of public criticism for the chairman's agenda. "We have now heard from the American people, Congress, and the courts," Copps announced on the day of the Third Circuit Court's decision. "The rush to media consolidation approved by the FCC last June was wrong as a matter of law and policy. The Commission has a second chance to do the right thing. We must immediately move forward and redesign our media policy. This time we must include the American people in the process instead of shutting them out. We must rediscover our respect for core values of localism, diversity, and competition. We must protect and work to expand the multiplicity of voices and choices that support our marketplace of ideas and that sustain American democracy and creativity."

THE COMMISSIONERS HAD ALREADY ESTABLISHED A FORUM FOR ENCOURaging public participation in media policy debates, one that appeared strikingly similar to the town hall meetings that Copps and Adelstein had been conducting on their own. In August 2003, just two months after releasing its ill-fated order on the ownership rules, the FCC announced that it would set up a "localism task force" and hold a series of open "localism hearings" in cities across the country. "Powell explicitly stated that the localism task force and the hearings were not going to address the ownership issue," said Josh Silver, the executive director of Free Press. "He thought the commission could appease its critics without actually addressing their core concerns."

Powell soon learned that neither citizens nor policy makers would accept the false separation between the ownership and localism debates, and that the FCC could not plausibly deny that the issues were inextricably linked. At the first public hearing, held on October 22 in Charlotte, North Carolina, a capacity crowd of citizens embraced the rare opportunity to tell the commissioners about the hazards of consolidation in their hometowns. "To try to talk about localism without discussing media ownership is avoiding the issue," said Tift Merritt, a musician from Raleigh who had appeared on *Late Night with David Letterman* and been designated "a major new artist" by *Billboard,* but had been shut out of the playlists from local radio stations owned by consolidators. Mary Klenz, copresident of the League of Women Voters of North Carolina, claimed that only one commercial TV station in Charlotte broadcasts a local public affairs program. "We are concerned that business concerns have taken precedence over the public interest."[4]

"The hearing was humiliating for Powell," Josh Silver explained to me. "He had just forced the deregulatory order on the public, and now he was seeing how democracy works." The next hearing was scheduled for January 2004, in San Antonio, Texas, where Clear Channel is headquartered, and Big Media companies that had lobbied for raising or eliminating the ownership limits asked their own representatives to participate so that the public complaints would not dominate the event.

"A standing-room-only and often intense crowd packed into the City Council Chambers to testify," the *San Antonio Express-News* reported. Approximately five hundred people packed the hearing, some waiting in line for more than twelve hours to ensure a spot in the audience. More than one hundred people waited through the five-and-a-half hour event for a chance to make a two-minute statement before the commissioners. Almost everyone spoke out against consolidation and the proposed rule changes. "Many spoke out against profane, violent and sexually explicit information being broadcast on the TV and radio," the *Express-News* explained, "and others blasted corporate ownership of local media."[5]

I traveled to Rapid City, South Dakota, for the next hearing, in May 2004, for which there was so much advance interest that organizers issued tickets on the morning of the event, giving those who could not skip a day of work to wait in line a chance to participate. Both citizen groups and local media owners sent troops to the South Dakota School of Mines and Technology, which hosted the hearing, and Native American tribes from the long-standing reservations and sacred sites surrounding Rapid City brought members, too. An enormous crowd arrived that evening, and to accommodate the public the commission had to set up an overflow area where more than one hundred people could watch the proceedings on closed-circuit television. The meeting was full of conflict, as Native American leaders accused the FCC of disrespecting their communities by excluding them from the introductory panel, and citizens complained that Powell, who had been in town for other meetings, decided to return to Washington and skip the public hearing. Free Press, which had learned of Powell's intentions before he left town, released a public statement declaring that the chairman, who had attended several events organized by lobbyists in the previous months, "doesn't have time for his own 'localism and diversity' public hearing to listen to the American people." "This is an insult to every American and to democracy itself," Silver said.

During the open-comment session, radio listeners complained, "There used to be local talk shows, now there is none," and echoed the criticisms of media consolidation that citizens voiced whenever they were asked. Commissioner Adelstein, a Rapid City native, said, "We sensed a real frustration about the state of the airwaves," and he vowed to challenge the FCC's rush to relax the ownership caps.[6]

The public events were going so badly for Powell that the commission, which had already announced that it would hold hearings in Portland, Maine, and Washington, D.C., stopped organizing them, leaving the dates "To Be Announced" for years. Rather than wait for the commission to act, Copps and Adelstein repeated the process they had initiated in the run-up to the FCC's 2003 order, setting up their own hearings on the future of media in cities and towns throughout the country. Copps routinely thanked the citizens who participated in the forums for airing an issue that needed a public hearing. "What a difference you have made," he told a gathering of media reformers in Wisconsin that I attended. "Because of your efforts, Americans know that having media giants is inimical to the interests of Americans and is just plain bad for America. You built an unprecedented army of Left and Right, Democrats and Republicans, who know that our policy was wrong and want to do something about it. The coalition didn't splinter. It went to court together, went to Congress together, and it is getting results."

Adelstein, growing into his role as a populist regulator, solicited public input on media ownership rules from everyone he addressed. "I want your perspective on how well broadcasters are meeting the needs of your community," he said to an overflowing audience in Iowa. "Are they providing sufficient coverage of issues of local concern, including local elections? Do you have enough choice in news sources? Are broadcasters providing sufficient family friendly programming? Are you hearing local artists played on the radio? We need your input on these vital issues. This is an opportunity for all members of the community to give their perspective on how issues of concern to them are treated. I encourage you to speak out and become part of the solution in this new media landscape."[7] Although they received little support from the FCC, Copps and Adelstein continued to hold public hearings wherever possible, and capacity crowds greeted them everywhere they went.

Powell, who had turned his back on the public once it expressed strong opposition to his policy proposals, now began to suppress his own agency's research findings when they contradicted his personal beliefs. The chairman, searching for scientific verification of his belief that relaxing ownership caps would not adversely affect news coverage, commissioned an FCC study to determine whether locally owned television stations broadcast more local news than chains that controlled stations in multiple markets or companies that owned newspapers and television stations. Keith Brown and Peter Alexander, economists from the FCC Media Bureau, studied 4,078 individual news stories from five different days and sixty stations across twenty designated market areas. Their findings, reported in the working paper "Do Local Owners Do More Localism? Some Evidence from Local Broadcast News," challenged the core of Powell's case for loosening the caps. "Our study suggests that locally owned television broadcast stations air more local news than network owned-and-operated stations and non-locally owned stations," the authors wrote, noting that the difference in local coverage was dramatic. "We find that local ownership of television stations adds almost five and one-half minutes of local news and over three minutes of local on-location news. . . . [T]his finding may have implications for broadcast ownership rules."[8]

According to Adam Candeub, who was an attorney at the FCC's Media Bureau in 2004, once the paper began circulating to high levels of the agency the FCC ordered the authors to stop their research and destroy "every last piece" of the report. "The whole project was just stopped—end of discussion," Candeub told John Dunbar, of the Associated Press. The report was never released to the public, and the FCC commissioners, including Copps and Adelstein, were unaware of its existence. The study did not surface until September 2006, when, as a Congressional staffer explained, "someone within the FCC who believed the information should be made public" gave it to Senator Barbara Boxer and she produced it during Kevin Martin's reconfirmation hearing. Boxer questioned whether the report was "shelved because the outcome was not to the liking of some of the commissioners and/or any outside powerful interests," and called for an investigation into the process. "This is not a matter of national security, for God's sake. This is important information about issues that are key to the people. So I don't understand who deep-sixed this thing." Dunbar phoned Powell to ask what happened with the study, but Powell did not return his call.[9]

ENCOURAGED BY COPPS, ADELSTEIN, AND CIVIC ORGANIZATIONS INCLUDing Free Press, the National Rifle Association, MoveOn, and Common Cause, American citizens continued to write e-mails, letters, and faxes reiterating their demands to Congress and the FCC that the federal government do something to curb media consolidation. As the 2004 election campaigns intensified, members of both major political parties reported that, after the war in Iraq, media reform was the issue that their constituents cared about most. Congressional leaders who were not up for reelection called for making media consolidation part of the nation's political agenda. House Democrats, led by Maurice Hinchey (New York), Louise Slaughter (New York), David Price (North Carolina), Jay Inslee (Washington), and Sherrod Brown (Ohio), began planning to organize a Future of American Media Caucus, so that, Hinchey told me, they can "make sure media policy issues are front and center in the minds of Members."

In January 2004 Democratic presidential candidate John Kerry told the *Hollywood Reporter:* "I think [media consolidation] is a serious problem in the country, and I was against the FCC decision and efforts to narrow the ownership of media outlets in America. I think the consolidation of information is a dangerous trend in America because it has the ability to shape our Democracy and shape the flow of information. I believe you need real competition, and you need limitations on that ownership . . . I serve on the (Commerce) committee, I have actually voted on these issues, and my record is very clear about favoring real competition, being smart about transitions in the industry that you have to take into account. But I am not going to be hoodwinked into believing that we are in a place today where there is sufficient competition in some of these areas, where we should lift the rules and consolidate, and I am against it."[10]

Kerry's statement generated considerable buzz among activists and policy analysts, and the Internet hummed with speculation that the Massachussetts senator would make a populist appeal for media reform. But Kerry, like Franklin Delano Roosevelt in the 1930s and virtually every major political figure since then, was all too aware of the influence and power that Big Media companies exert during national electoral campaigns, and he stayed mostly silent on the issue for the rest of the campaign. Bob Shrum, his campaign manager, told me: "We didn't really talk about avoiding the media concentration debate. Presidential candidates just know that they can't talk about it in a campaign, because everyone in politics knows that if you upset the networks they can hurt you—not just in coverage and framing, but in contributions too." A senior adviser to the Gore campaign, who requested anonymity because he feared media repercussions for his ongoing work (nicely illustrating his own point), offered another reason that contemporary candidates avoid discussing consolidation. "There's a story that people tell in Washington," he reported. "I don't know if it's true [and a network executive denied it], but the fact that people say it helps you understand why candidates are reluctant to go after the media companies. Jack Welch, the former CEO of General Electric [which owns NBC], was in the NBC news studio on the night of the 2000 election. People say that Welch was actually screaming at the numbers guys, telling them to call the race for Bush as soon as Fox News did, so that they could settle it. That's the kind of thing that no political candidate can afford in a close race."[11]

IF HISTORY REPEATS ITSELF, AND MEDIA ISSUES DISAPPEAR FROM THE political agenda during future presidential campaigns because neither candidates nor conglomerates have any interest in raising them, Americans will be deprived of a major opportunity to issue their democratic wish for a communications system that serves their needs and interests. That would be especially unfortunate, because today—after the Third Circuit Court decision, the public outcry over consolidation before the FCC's 2003 order, and the beginning of a new presidential election campaign—Big Media companies, federal regulators, and citizen groups are battling to shape a digital frontier that may not remain open for long. The media ecosystem is at a decisive turning point, and political decisions—about ownership, openness, access, and local control—will continue to determine its future composition, diversity, and vitality. The future of our democracy and culture lies in the balance.

Not that Big Media companies are waiting patiently for their moment to further claim and develop the digital frontier. In the radio industry, Clear Channel continues to press the case its attorney Miguel Estrada made before the Third Circuit, demanding that Congress and the FCC raise the local ownership caps to ten or twelve stations, if not eliminate them altogether. In 2005 Clear Channel accelerated its rollout of digital radio stations that will ultimately allow it to multiply its broadcast fleet. On the satellite side, Clear Channel's investment in XM Satellite Radio gives it the right to operate big-brand, commercial-laden formats—such as KISS, MIX, Nashville, and Sunny—on five XM channels (XM is otherwise commercial-free, but its managers failed in their efforts to block Clear Channel's paid advertisements), as well as to provide content on several of its talk channels, allowing Clear Channel to maintain a strong presence on the service against which it competes.[12]

Clear Channel is hardly the only broadcaster plotting out terrain for the future of radio. When satellite providers such as XM and Sirius Satellite Radio announced plans to offer local news, traffic, and weather services in select locations, the National Association of Broadcasters objected, citing the fact that when satellite companies initially requested a share of the spectrum they had promised not to run local programming that would compete with traditional radio stations. "It's an absurd case on its face," wrote Radley Balko, who publishes the *Agitator* blog. "Satellite radio has taken off because traditional broadcast radio is so darned dreadful. That means the NAB is forced to argue that the government must prevent satellite providers from offering localized programming because allowing them to do so might drive local broadcasters out of business. But at the same time, NAB must argue that the service local broadcasters currently provide is of high enough quality to merit that kind of protection in the first place . . . If FM and AM radio broadcasters were really giving consumers worthwhile local content, they wouldn't need government protection from XM and Sirius."[13]

In 2004 American radio stations began using digital technology to promote a station format that sheds both local content and the pretense of live broadcasting. "JACK," which Big Sticks Broadcasting developed (selling exclusive U.S. licensing rights for the format to SparkNet Communications in 2005) after witnessing the success of a similar format in Canada, has no DJs, no call-in segments, no request lines, no local news, and no weather. Instead, market programmers reproduce the iPod "shuffle" effect by playing songs from a large list of some 1,200 pop hits recorded over the past forty years. From a studio in Toronto, Howard Cogan does the voice-overs for all JACK stations, and his signature tagline is "playing what we want." JACK clones, including a country version called HANK, popped onto the dial as other broadcasters adapted the low-cost production style for their own market niches. Yet Tom Carpenter, from the American Federation of Television and Radio Artists, told me that the stations have trouble retaining listeners, and saw the radio industry's interest in JACK as "a sign of desperation." CBS Radio has converted more stations to the JACK format than any other company, including outlets in major markets such as Los Angeles, Chicago, and New York City, where it cut costs—and quickly lost listeners—by using JACK to replace veteran DJs and programmers at famous stations like WCBS-FM. "When they did that," Carpenter told me, "listeners called us at AFTRA and wanted to know what the union was going to do to bring back the live announcers. It's unheard of that audiences would call the union to find out what's happening with talent." But with digital programming, JACK style, citizens have no other place to communicate their concerns.

TELEVISION BROADCASTERS DID HEAR FROM CONSUMERS AND OFFICIALS in 2006, when they slowly began to acknowledge that their prepackaged programming was pushing away the audiences that they needed to attract, and that the VNRs they were airing violated journalistic standards, if not the law. The most dramatic reversal came from the Sinclair Broadcast Group, whose executives had boasted that NewsCentral—the high-tech project through which affiliates would broadcast canned segments in a central Maryland studio—would establish a new model for television journalism. In March, Sinclair announced that it would scale back the NewsCentral system, killing the live newscasts that featured "must carry" editorials, partisan political packages, and weather reports, by converting it into a feed service that would supply specials, packages, and live shots from Washington, D.C., to its stations and any partners interested in "news shares."

I spoke with a Sinclair staff member on the day of its last live News-Central broadcast, and he reported that because of low ratings the company was shutting down the news operations and laying off the entire news staff at several of its stations, including those in Las Vegas, Tampa, Milwaukee, Buffalo, and Raleigh/Durham. "Once Mark Hyman [the vice president whose nightly editorial segments proved so controversial] took off like a crazy man with his right-wing views and made them must-runs, it put off the management. They were getting complaints about diversity, balance, and fairness. And that hurt their ratings." Sinclair planned to replace NewsCentral with other, even less expensive standard programming, and to open new channels as it converted to digital broadcasting. "They're going to roll out a second digital channel in Baltimore," the Sinclair staffer told me, "and then they're going to do it in Columbus. It'll be reruns, financed by paid programming from Sunday-morning religious shows. It's going to look like Airport Television, with no there there."

BOTTOM-LINE PRESSURES COMBINED WITH THE EMERGING POPULARITY of digital publishing technologies to make 2006 a tumultuous year in the newspaper industry, where anxieties about the sustainability of quality local journalism made editors and reporters tremble. Their concerns spiked in 2005, when Bruce Sherman, a Florida money manager who is the chairman, CEO, and chief investment officer of Private Capital Management, publicly urged the board of directors at Knight Ridder, the nation's second-largest newspaper chain, to "aggressively pursue the competitive sale of the company." Along with other newspaper companies, Knight Ridder stock had been slumping since 2004. Despite the industry's extraordinarily high average profit margins and steady cash flows, investment bankers worried that Internet publishing and the decline of print circulation made newspaper companies a bad long-term bet, and they tried leveraging their investments to demand operating strategies, such as eliminating expensive editorial staffers, that maximized short-term profits. Private Capital Management owned 12.8 million shares of Knight Ridder (19 percent of the company), and although during 2005 the chain's thirty-two papers generated $3 billion in revenues and $471 million in net income (up 44 percent from 2004), Sherman was dissatisfied with its 16 percent profit margin, which lagged behind chains such as Gannett and E. W. Scripps. Industry insiders looked to the battle for control of Knight Ridder to learn about their own collective fate. "The outcome," said the *Los Angeles Times*, "could write the future of print journalism."[14]

The pressure from Private Capital Management was particularly troubling to advocates of print journalism, because Knight Ridder had already made aggressive moves to downsize its local editorial divisions, centralize its national and international bureaus, and invest in online content and advertising services. Yet the shareholder demands were in fact predictable, and they will soon be repeated by investors in other media companies, because they express the inevitable logic of a market-based media system in which the primary responsibility of publicly traded firms is to maximize returns, and supporting quality news reporting is wasteful unless it directly generates revenues.[15]

Ironically, *Knightfall*—a book about the company's aborted journalistic mission by David Merritt, a former editor for a Knight Ridder paper—was published just months before Sherman pushed for the company's sale.[16] Knight Ridder's margins were lower than chains like Gannett partly because it maintained its investments in local journalism in places with sluggish adversing markets, including Philadelphia, where it owned and operated the *Inquirer* and the *Daily News*. Increasing profit margins in Philadelphia would mean even further downsizing, and as news about the possible sale circulated, citizens expressed fears about what would happen to the TV stations, radio stations, and local Web sites—let alone to their city—that depended on newspaper reporters, if their best-trained watchdogs were kicked out of town.

As journalism professionals rallied to defend Knight Ridder's newspapers, Sherman organized other institutional investors into an unbeatable coalition, and in December 2005 the board began considering expressions of interest. In March 2006, Knight Ridder announced that the McClatchy Company, a Sacramento, California, corporation that owned twelve major dailies and seventeen community newspapers, had made a successful $4.5-billion acquisition bid. "McClatchy is a dolphin swallowing a small whale," quipped one financial analyst, whose colleagues believed that a proven consolidator such as Gannett would have made a more reliable owner.[17] Yet Knight Ridder's papers expressed relief because McClatchy, which had achieved profit margins around 23 percent by publishing in growing towns and cities, was a family-run company with a strong record of supporting local journalism, and Gary Pruitt, its president and CEO, pledged that he would be committed to "good journalism being good business" in his new publications. "We plan to maintain, sustain, and further the journalism at these papers with no across the board layoffs," Pruitt told a CNBC anchor who questioned the future of the newspaper business. "Ultimately, we're competing locally, and when you look locally, our lead has actually never been larger . . . In each of these markets we have the leading local website, and the last mass medium with newspapers . . . That combination can't be matched locally. When you look at the audience of our newspaper and our website on an unduplicated basis, our audience is actually growing, which is hardly the profile of a dying industry."[18]

Not every Knight Ridder paper would be part of McClatchy's new empire, however. Upon announcing the deal, Pruitt declared that McClatchy would immediately put up for sale the twelve Knight Ridder papers located in less lucrative markets, including the *Philadelphia Inquirer* and *Daily News,* the *San Jose Mercury-News,* and dailies in Akron, Aberdeen, Grand Forks, Fort Wayne, Monterey, Contra Costa County, and Duluth. "Today is a sad day in the life of the *Akron Beacon Journal* because the *Akron Beacon* is the original Knight newspaper," said Debra Adams Simmons, its editor.[19] The mood was darker in Philadelphia, where residents worried that they would lose the *Daily News* altogether and journalists at both papers feared for their jobs. Yet the *Inquirer* staff had grounds for hope. The Newspaper Guild–Communications Workers of America, which had been actively seeking a way to manage its own dailies, and the Yucaipa Companies, the private equity firm cofounded by the California billionaire Ron Burkle and known for its socially conscious investments, partnered to make a competitive bid for all twelve of the orphaned newspapers.[20] According to Henry Holcomb, an *Inquirer* reporter and the head of the local Guild, the union was "in an even stronger position to create a new privately held company," and its proposal "would prove best for [its] members, advertisers, readers, and the regions that these newspapers serve."[21] If successful, the venture would result in the first major chain of employee-owned newspapers, giving Guild members the chance to wager their futures on their own journalism.

They never had a chance to put their money down. In April, McClatchy announced that it would sell four newspapers—the *San Jose Mercury News,* the *Monterey County Herald,* the *Contra Costa Times* (all in Northern California), and the *St. Paul Pioneer Press*—to MediaNews Group, which already owned nine newspapers in the San Francisco Bay Area, for $1 billion. The deal, which MediaNews made with two other investors, Gannett and the Stephens Media Group, was financed by exchanging assets with the Hearst Corporation, giving MediaNews the fourth-highest circulation of all U.S. newspaper companies, with fifty-three dailies reaching 2.7 million readers on weekdays and 3 million on Sundays. The news did not go over well at the four newspapers, where staff favored either prospective local bidders or Yucaipa. MediaNews CEO William Dean Singleton was known as a "merciless cost-cutter," wrote one of his new employees, the *Mercury News* reporter Mike Cassidy. "[He is] a man who strangles quality journalism by cutting staff and salaries and by closing news operations," but who can also save papers by making them more profitable. The Newspaper Guild denounced the deal as "bad news for newspaper workers, readers, advertisers, and for our communities," and called for the U.S. Department of Justice to investigate whether it met legal standards of fairness, transparency, and fiduciary responsibility to shareholders. "The newspaper industry is dominated by a small circle of ownership groups," explained Newspaper Guild president Linda Foley on the day after the sale was reported. "Yesterday's news drew that circle even smaller."[22]

Industry analysts believed that Singleton's interest in the Bay Area properties stemmed from the opportunities it presented to consolidate operations. The *Los Angeles Times* reported that the acquisition bore two "hallmarks" of Singleton's investment strategy: "It allows him to save money by combining resources at newspapers that are close to each other, and it has the potential to soften the competition from a well-financed neighbor." Had it not been part of the deal, Hearst, which owns the *San Francisco Chronicle*, would have been the prime candidate to charge MediaNews with antitrust violations in the Bay Area market, where, the *Chronicle* wrote, it now holds "a commanding position."[23]

The bidding for Philadelphia's two newspapers lasted until the last week of May 2006. Early in the month, the city's journalists and civic groups expressed outrage at a proposal from Onex, a Toronto investment firm that asked local Teamsters to promise that its drivers, pressmen, and mailers would accept massive layoffs in the *Inquirer* and *Daily News* newsrooms in exchange for preserving their own jobs. The Teamsters not only refused but publicly denounced the offer, and Onex backed off. On May 23, McClatchy announced that it would sell the papers for $515 million to Philadelphia Media Holdings, a group of local investors led by the public relations enterpreneur Brian Tierney, restoring locally owned and operated newspapers to the city. Joe Natoli, the publisher of the *Inquirer,* immediately e-mailed an enthusiastic message to his staff. "Now, we know who our new owners will be.

They are local people who care about our city and region. They believe in our future and in the future of quality journalism . . . They also know full well that we are about to become a laboratory for newspaper local ownership that will be watched intently by others. It's a terrific opportunity for us to show what we can do."

IN THE ALT WEEKLIES MARKET, NO LONGER "THE LAST UNCONSOLI-dated niche" in American media, a new giant has already emerged, and the *Village Voice* was its first major conquest. Between November 2005, when Michael Lacey and the former New Times management announced that they would take over the Village Voice Media chain, and April 2006, seventeen *Voice* employees (out of sixty editorial workers listed on the masthead) either resigned or were fired in what some staffers called a purge. The list of the departed includes some of the *Voice*'s most celebrated journalists, including Editor in Chief Don Forst, the media critic-columnist Sydney Schanberg, and the Washington correspondent James Ridgeway, who had worked more than thirty years at the paper before being fired in April. Twenty staff members protested Ridgeway's dismissal with an open letter calling for his reinstatement, and others charged that Lacey was clearing out the political progressives whose commentary and reporting, which had long defined the *Voice,* was out of sync with the libertarian, antiactivist philosophy that had defined the New Times. Lacey publicly insisted that the changes were designed to increase the amount of local reporting in the *Voice*—an admirable goal that won him praise from some media critics, even though they noted, ironically, that the publication that helped pioneer media criticism and political commentary might soon lose both. Yet *Voice* staffers questioned whether Lacey would back up this rhetoric, since New Times had a reputation for maintaining small, overworked editorial staffs and Lacey showed no signs of hiring a wave of new journalists to replace the departed writers. "I hate to be blunt about it," said former *Voice* editor in chief Karen Durbin. "[Lacey] wants to cut the budget and fatten profits." When he fired the *Voice*'s three fact-checkers and two of the five copy editors, Lacey's commitment to local journalism looked all the more suspect.[24]

As he did in San Francisco, Lacey entered the New York alt weekly scene prepared to do battle—only this time he would be fighting his own employees. Speaking on the independent radio news program *Demcoracy Now!* Schanberg described how the conflict with Lacey unfolded once he took control. "Mr. Lacey came in and very quickly told the staff that he was disappointed and appalled by the fact that the front of the book was all commentary and that he wanted hard news . . . He was insulting to the staff. He figuratively or in effect called them stenographers. He said they had to stop being stenographers . . . I objected to that, because that was so insulting, and I said that you can criticize any news staff in some ways, but the one thing that you couldn't call the *Village Voice* staff was a staff of stenographers . . . And he said, 'So, I'm unfair.' And then he added, he said, 'Look, I don't care what rouses you, even if it's getting pissed off at me.' And I said, 'I'm not pissed off at you. I don't even know you.' And he really had this huge one-ton or two-ton chip on his shoulder . . . he was totally insecure. And he gave the impression that he didn't understand the *Voice* and he didn't understand New York, and he didn't want to . . . And he said a lot of other things. He told the staff that they better prepare themselves to say goodbye to some of their friends."[25] Sure enough, on August 31 the *Voice* fired eight more people, including senior editor and veteran music writer Robert Christgau, who began working at the paper in 1969; theater editor Jorge Morales; dance editor Elizabeth Zimmer; book editor Ed Park; and art director Minh Uong. Tom Robbins, the *Voice*'s union steward, said that the spate of terminations "cuts the heart right out of the paper," and media critics declared that the wave of downsizing left the paper "gutted." The *Voice*'s iconoclasts had survived Clay Felker, Rupert Murdoch, and a revolving group of investment bankers, but the new chain management appears to have succeeded in crushing their spirits.

BY 2006 THE NATION'S LARGEST TELEPHONE AND CABLE COMPANIES WERE using all their political muscle to crush "Internet freedom," lobbying to pass federal legislation that would allow Internet providers to block, slow down, or charge extra for access to goods, services, and content from their competitors and critics. In most democratic societies, Internet service providers maintain the "pipes" but do not control what goes into or out of them. "The superabundance of content in the Internet's ecosystem is best explained by its organizing principle," writes the historian of technology Randall Stross, in which "rather than having network operators select content providers on our behalf—the philosophy of the local cable company—the Internet allows all of us to act as our own network programmers, serving a demographic of just one person."[26] In 2006, however, major cable and telecommunications companies such as Verizon Communications, Comcast, BellSouth, and AT&T (the latter two companies proposed a $67-billion "megamerger" in March 2006) lobbied Congress to pass legislation allowing them to offer customers faster access to their own sites as well as to those from companies willing to pay for high-speed delivery. In such a system, commercial companies, nonprofits, political organizations, bloggers, and civic groups that are unwilling or unable to pay providers a premium fee would have no choice but to offer a degraded, slower service. Moreover, they would face the threat that any given provider could block access to their sites altogether, without cause.

"The phone and cable lobbies have deliberately gone to the FCC to remove the fundamental regulations, which were the foundation of the Internet," said Jeff Chester, the executive director of the Center for Digital Democracy. "The Internet was required to operate as a nondiscriminatory medium. The Internet, as we knew it, grew up over telephone lines. Those lines were regulated by the FCC. Phone companies had to treat all content equitably. That's why you could have start-ups like Google or Amazon. Anybody could create a website, create a service, put their content out there. The fact that you would have to treat all content equitably was a serious threat to the plans of cable and telephone companies, because their business is based on a monopoly . . . So they went to the Bush FCC, first under Michael Powell, now under current chair Kevin Martin, and they eliminated the prohibition . . . so they can discriminate."[27]

"Let's say Comcast develops its own music downloading service to compete with Apple's iTunes," said Tim Karr, the campaign director for Free Press, when we met in Manhattan. "Without network neutrality they could effectively make their service so much faster than iTunes that no one on Comcast would buy Apple's product again. They could do the same thing with video-on-demand services. It's not just media. A cable or telecommunications giant could use its position to partner with other companies or expand its business by providing its own Internet services—for travel, shopping, books, you name it. It would make competition a joke."

The end of network neutrality could also slow innovation on the Internet, where many of the most powerful business, educational, and social applications—including sites such as eBay, MySpace, Friendster, and Skype—were developed by amateur inventers and independent entrepreneurs who tested their experiments in the open digital network. "Think about something like video-blogging," said Karr. "It's a new, exciting source of independent media, a way to make local news and original entertainment. We're just starting to see the best of them circulate to millions of people through the Net. It could develop into something big. But if Internet providers charge content producers extra for posting videos, that would likely kill independent v-blogging before it has a chance. We'd never know what it could do." In the near future more consumers will use broadband Internet services to access programs they used to watch only on television, blurring the lines between the media. Whether the World Wide Web of the future operates more like current cable television systems, in which the provider chooses the menu of consumer choices, or the current Internet, in which the consumer is free to choose whatever content she can find, will be determined by the outcome of the debate on Internet freedom.

Community organizations and political action committees across the spectrum are even more concerned about discrimination by Internet services. "Our ability to be effective depends on our grassroots organizing," said Craig Fields, the director of Internet operations for Gun Owners of America, the nation's second-largest gun rights advocacy group. During a news conference call in February 2006, Fields explained: "The Internet has been a boon for us. There used to be issues we couldn't get into because we didn't have time to do a mail campaign. Now we can organize huge campaigns online." Fields worried, however, that there are only "a handful of telecommunications companies, all of which have antigun policies," and therefore might "shut out people and organizations" whose projects they oppose. "We're on the far right," Fields reported, "but we need government intervention to ensure the freedom of ideas. What Congress is getting ready to do [by legalizing discrimination among Internet providers] is basically un-American." Gun Owners of America has little in common with MoveOn.org Civic Action, yet its members are happy to work with the gun owners if it helps keep the Internet free. "People who have never been politically involved before are signing up for this fight because the free and open Internet as we know it is under attack," said its executive director, Eli Pariser.[28]

Fears of political censorship on the Internet are not hypothetical, and China is not the only place where Internet providers seal off sites that challenge their interests. In Canada, where there are no network neutrality protections, the telecommunications giant Telus blocked its subscribers' access to a Web site maintained by the Telecommunications Workers Union when its workers went on strike in July 2005. The British Columbia Civil Liberties Assocation issued a public statement calling for Telus to stop the heavy-handed practice: "The merits of the labour dispute are not our issue. We are concerned about freedom of expression. The media report that there is acrimony on both sides of the fence on this issue. But as always, we advocate fighting speech with speech."[29] Yet Telus was under no legal obligation to do so, and if U.S. cable and telecommunications giants have their way, American service providers will be able to discriminate as they choose, too.

In April 2006 civic organizations including the Gun Owners of America, Free Press, the Parents Television Council, MoveOn.org Civic Action, National Religious Broadcasters, Consumers Union, Afro-Netizen, the American Library Association, and the Center for Digital Democracy formed the SavetheInternet.com Coalition to mount a campaign for legislation ensuring Internet freedom. During its first week, more than 250,000 people signed a petition calling for the House of Representatives Committee on Energy and Commerce to pass an amendment sponsored by the Massachussetts Democrat Ed Markey, which would add network neutrality protections to a proposed communications bill. The committee, voting largely along party lines, rejected the proposal. "The major telephone and cable companies are too powerful in the House," wrote Josh Silver, of Free Press, in an e-mail announcing that the group would soon mount a larger campaign in the Senate. "They have spent hundreds of millions of dollars in lobbying, campaign contributions, and advertising to pass this legislation."

"It's shocking that the House continues to deny the will of the people on an issue that affects everyone so directly—protecting the free and open Internet," added Pariser, from MoveOn, who was already preparing for the next round. "Our bipartisan coalition will rally the online community like it's never been rallied before, and together the public will overturn today's enormous blow to the freedom principle that's made the Internet great."

The SavetheInternet.com Coalition got its biggest boost when the Senate Commerce Committee debated network neutrality in June 2006. Ted Stevens, a Republican from Alaska, cast a decisive vote that prevented the committee from writing network neutrality provisions into its proposed telecommunications bill. Yet the explanation Stevens gave for his vote revealed such a fundamental misunderstanding of how the Internet works that it backfired, generating unprecedented publicity and support for the Internet Freedom campaign. Speaking on the Senate floor, Stevens declared: "I just the other day got, an Internet was sent by my staff at ten o'clock in the morning on Friday and I just got it yesterday. Why? Because it got tangled up with all these things going on the Internet commercially. . . . They want to deliver vast amounts of information over the Internet. And again, the Internet is not something you just dump something on. It's not a truck. It's a series of tubes." Bloggers and late night comedians had so much fun cracking jokes about this comment—which would have been even more humorous had it not come from a man responsible for regulating the Internet—that within days millions of citizens had learned about the public benefits of network neutrality legislation, and members of Congress who had previously opposed it began changing their position.

THE FIGHT OVER INTERNET FREEDOM BROUGHT EVEN MORE CITIZENS into the media reform movement and renewed the alliance between conservative, liberal, and progressive groups. Eli Pariser said that he sees an extraordinary spike in activity in his organization, MoveOn.org, whenever it takes up a media policy issue, and members pushed the organization to launch the Media Action caucus in 2005. "We have fifty thousand core members in Media Action," said Noah Winer, its twenty-eight-year-old director, who joined MoveOn.org when he was twenty-three and working as an environmental science teacher in East Brooklyn. "They're the ones who always want to get involved," he told me. "Then there's a bigger circle of people who have taken action on one of our media projects—the ownership fight at the FCC, getting one of our political ads aired on the Super Bowl [CBS said it had a policy against accepting advocacy advertisement], our Fox Watch campaign, our Sinclair campaign—and that's close to five hundred thousand."

The Media Action campaign is special because its mission is to promote vigorous watchdog journalism at the local and national level, and to protest when it is threatened. "Because of the debates about media bias," Winer explained, "grassroots media reform groups tend to come across as antijournalism—they want different coverage of their own issues and are really trying to work the refs. We believe in good journalism. We want to stand on the side of journalists, to protect them." One of the project's first major campaigns involved the Tribune Company, which announced plans to lay off employees in eight cities during 2005. "They kept saying that they had to fire people, that it was inevitable because of the Internet. They contend that they can cut jobs and preserve the same quality. It's just an absurd claim; it means that the employees they were firing had no impact, none. Our frame was not job loss; it was journalism loss. Losing their jobs would undermine the quality of local reporting. We did eight petitions, one for each city. We drafted letters for each place, listing how much money the company was making. Tribune had actually increased their profits from the year before by $93 million! And we delivered the petitions at the Credit Suisse media investment meetings in New York. I asked [Tribune's president and CEO] Dennis FitzSimons if he would meet with his customers to talk about this, and he said no. But this is not just about Tribune. We're looking ahead."

SO ARE THE MAJOR MEDIA CONGLOMERATES AND THE FCC. KEVIN Martin, who spent his first year as FCC chairman clamping down on indecency in broadcasting and even exploring ways to sanction cable and satellite companies for violating government standards, began to publicize his support for eliminating the cross-ownership ban and entrusting consolidators to serve the public interest on their own volition. In April 2006 Martin told publishers at the Newspapers Association of America conference in Chicago that he was committed to repealing the restrictions, but that they had to do a better job persuading the American people. "The failure to implement these rule changes is not our fault alone," said Martin, who surprised industry leaders by lobbying for better public relations support. "The public is not convinced of the need to change these rules, and if you can't convince the public, our chances to do that are dim."[30]

On June 21, 2006, Kevin Martin announced that the FCC would begin considering rule changes to the nation's media ownership policies. The chairman promised to hold six public hearings and commission studies of local media markets over a four-month period, pledging to "begin this dialogue in a neutral and even-handed fashion." Copps and Adelstein, all too aware that Martin had been rallying media executives to publicize their arguments for eliminating the newspaper-broadcast cross-ownership caps, were skeptical, and they warned that, without public pressure, the FCC would issue a fast and nondemocratic decision once again.

Immediately, leaders in every major media industry stepped up their entrepreneurial political efforts to shape the cultural landscape. They were well prepared, since the previous year Eddie Fritts, who headed the National Association of Broadcasters for twenty-three years, predicted that the FCC's new review "has the potential to re-shape every communications company on the globe. Because of the complexity and enormity of this endeavor, many predict it will take months, if not years to finalize a package. I happen to believe we have both challenges and opportunities, but make no mistake . . . This could be 'the mother of all legislative battles.'"[31]

Citizens and civic groups will have to be more active and better organized than ever to influence the political debate over the future of media. Before the 2006 debate began, the last time that the FCC had formally invited the public to speak out on the state of local media was July 2004 in Monterey, California, and—as usual—neither then chairman Michael Powell nor the current chairman, Kevin Martin, showed up to listen.

More than three hundred people did appear, and many of them waited for hours as they assembled into a long column that extended around the block of the local convention center and then surged forward to fill the town hall. The hearing began slowly, as a large panel of invited officials issued formal statements, and a select group of media owners, scholars, and activists had their say. Then the public commentary began, each call for reform louder than the next, and the room began to buzz. The *Monterey Herald*—whose journalists were unaware that it would soon become part of the MediaNews chain—called the event "a bad night for Big Media . . . as two commissioners [Michael Copps and Jonathan Adelstein] and a crowd of hundreds excoriated broadcasters for being generally unresponsive to local issues."[32]

Copps seized the moment, encouraging the boisterous crowd to redouble its efforts to demand the media they need and deserve. "I believe in my bones that few priorities our country confronts have such long-term importance to our democracy as how America communicates and converses with itself and how this process has deteriorated," Copps declared. His voice was gravelly from years of crusading for media democracy, but his face was beaming, and his body pushed forward against the podium, as if preparing to launch. "After traveling the length and breadth of this country, I believe we have the best chance in our generation to settle the issue of who will control our media and for what purposes, and to resolve it in favor of airwaves of, by, and for the people of this great country. Let's make it happen."[33]

WANTED: "a newspaper journalist based in India to report on the
city government and political scene of Pasadena, California, USA."

This advertisement, placed on Craigslist by a community Web site called
PasadenaNow.com in May 2007, was no Internet hoax. Within days,
editor and publisher James Macpherson announced that he had hired
two Indian journalists to cover local news and culture for the city best
known as the host of the Rose Bowl parade. One employee, based in
Mumbai, would be paid $12,000 a year to report on Pasadena's city
council, whose meetings he would watch online in streaming video. The
other, based in Bangalore, would make $7,200 a year to write about
business and lifestyle issues. "Both writers are responsible for producing
two 500-word [news] articles a day, six days a week," said Macpherson, "plus two feature stories each week, which will be a little bit
longer."[1] Macpherson, who had been in the garment industry before
starting PasadenaNow and was confident that outsourcing would
work in his new venture, promised that the staff in Pasadena would
provide editorial assistance. "I'll be sending them information packets
on the subject [of each article], JPEG photographs and, as we go along,
probably video, as well as transcripts of the interviews," which would
be conducted in Pasadena and transcribed overseas.

Six-day workweeks are uncommon in U.S. news companies, as are weekly quotas of fourteen stories. But had Macpherson been willing to pay more than $3 to $5 per hour, PasadenaNow could easily have found local journalists willing to take the jobs. In 2007 the region's leading newspaper, the *Los Angeles Times,* continued to hemorrhage reporters. In May—the same month that PasadenaNow searched for staffers in India—the *Times* pushed out another fifty-seven newsroom workers, leaving it with about a quarter fewer journalists than it employed before the Tribune Company took over in 2000. Nancy Cleeland, a Pulitzer Prize winner and ten-year veteran of the *Times* who was among those taking the Tribune's buyout offer, wrote that "like hundreds of other mid-career journalists who are walking away from media institutions across the country, I'm looking for other ways to tell the stories I care about." Frustrated that the *Times* had slashed coverage of local economic life, "which holds tremendous potential for interacting with readers," while adding a "celebrity justice reporter" and other fluffy features, Cleeland hoped to find an Internet publication that would sponsor reporting on jobs, immigration, and inequality in Southern California. "The world of online news is maturing, looking for depth and context," she explained in an op-ed for the *Huffington Post.* "I think the timing couldn't be better."[2]

Five months later, Cleeland was still unemployed. "I was optimistic when I wrote that," she told me. "I thought that Internet news sites would replace what the newspapers had cut. But right now I'm pretty discouraged. I've been looking for a way to make a living as a reporter, and there's not much. There are some jobs in business outlets, but you can only get them if you're pro-business and want to basically promote the kind of economy we have now. The blogs that hire are just hiring young kids who come cheap, and they mostly want opinions anyway." The day we spoke, Cleeland was trying to find a publisher for what once might have been a big story: The National Labor Relations Board had issued a major decision that would help businesses decertify unions, and California workers were sure to be affected. "There are virtually no labor writers left here, so no one knows the significance of the decision," she pointed out. "It's like a tree falling in the forest. I see this happening. I have to find an outlet for it." Perhaps she would do it for free, or for a small magazine that pays pennies per word, but in the long run such options would not allow Cleeland to continue as a professional reporter. "I'm mid-career. I've got a twelve-year-old daughter and a mortgage. I'm looking at having to sell my house. Eventually, I think I'll find a way to make a living. What I don't know is whether the kinds of news stories I did are going to be done again. I mean, who's going to do it?"

THERE HAS NEVER BEEN A GOLDEN AGE OF LOCAL MEDIA, A TIME WHEN news corporations covered all important issues and always lived up to the highest professional standards. But we need not cling to myths of an idyllic past to recognize when and how our current media system falters, and in the year since *Fighting for Air* was first published the signs of trouble have become even more glaring.

Over the course of 2007, some Big Media companies, including Clear Channel and Tribune, got new owners—in part because of business strategies that led managers to devalue their core content, driving away consumers. Others, such as the New York Times Company, the broadcaster Emmis Communications, and the media conglomerate Belo, sold parts of their business or spun them off into separate entities. A few pundits predict that these deals augur an age of deconsolidation, but that forecast is hard to square with the dramatic expansion of the world's largest media corporations. Rupert Murdoch's News Corporation now controls the *Wall Street Journal* and operates a national cable channel for business news. AT&T acquired BellSouth for $67 billion and is now the nation's leading provider of wireless services and broadband access. Google, becoming a media giant in its own right, gobbled up YouTube; if regulators approve, it will do the same with DoubleClick, one of the biggest online advertising companies. The media market remains busy, but none of the recent deals promise to replenish the diminished supplies of primary reporting, local broadcasting, and original programming that were casualties of the past decade's mega-mergers and acquisitions.

"Fear not," say new media enthusiasts: Concentrated ownership no longer obstructs the free flow of news, culture, and information. There is an infinite supply of content on the Internet, they argue, and with a high-speed connection anyone can get news and entertainment from virtually any place in the world in real time. With a low-cost camera or recording device, anyone with basic media-production skills can create and distribute original content—whether it's citizen journalism, garage rock, bedroom movies, or a video blog—and vie for attention alongside the world's largest conglomerates. In any case, they say, the "old media" of broadcast radio, network television, and printed newspapers are losing their core audience and failing to attract young consumers—another reason not to be concerned about deregulation in that area.

There are countless reasons to be excited about the current communications revolution, including its potential to improve the quality of news and enrich civic life. But we should be wary of corporate lobbyists who glibly argue that new communications systems make the nation's media-ownership restrictions unnecessary. (Some broadcasters, for instance, present the mere existence of online radio as reason enough for Congress and the FCC to further relax or even eliminate local-ownership caps for radio companies.) Their arguments are doubly flawed. First, the existence of new technologies by no means makes older technologies obsolete. Television, radio, and newspapers continue to be enormously influential, and therefore regulation of these media is still quite relevant. Second, new media itself requires regulatory protection, lest corporations rewrite the rules so that they reap the greatest benefits of new communications systems while citizens, communities, and creative cultural producers find their choices diminished.

The fallacy of looking to technology as a cure-all is neither novel nor surprising. "New media," from the telegraph to the television, have routinely generated predictions that an informational utopia is soon to follow. Alas, technology has rarely been used in the way its proponents expect. As the historian of science Steven Shapin writes, "No one is very good at predicting technological futures; new and old technologies coexist; and technological significance and technological novelty are rarely the same—indeed, a given technology's grip on our awareness is often in inverse relationship to its significance in our lives. . . . Technological palimpsests are everywhere; it's the normal state of things."[3] The implication for communications is straightforward: Despite the popularity of the Internet and the iPod, old media will be around for a long time.

Today, for instance, the average household has more television sets than people, and television viewing levels continue climbing to historic highs. According to Nielsen Media Research, during the 2005–06 season average household TV consumption topped eight hours per day, with the typical individual watching TV for a record-setting four hours and thirty-five minutes. What's more, during the 2006–07 season broadcast television companies were responsible for all of the two hundred top-rated programs—not a single show on cable made the list. Newspapers are also surprisingly resilient. Yes, revenues are falling, and paid circulation of printed daily papers has been declining for decades. But nearly all of that drop comes from the disappearance of evening editions, whose circulation plunged from about 36 million in 1965 to about 7 million in 2006. At the same time, circulation of morning editions has nearly doubled in the past forty years, rising from 24 million in 1965 to over 45 million in 2006—a figure that is only slightly lower than 2003's historic high of nearly 47 million.[4]

WHILE THE "OLD MEDIA" ARE FARING BETTER THAN MOST ANALYSTS recognize, the freedoms touted by most advocates of new media are under threat. Consider Internet radio. With endless commercials and predictable programming having driven millions of consumers away from conventional commercial radio, Web sites offering streaming audio (such as Pandora and Live365) are now attracting an estimated 34 million American listeners. But the future of Internet radio was threatened on March 2, 2007, when the Copyright Royalty Board (CRB) announced that it would raise royalty rates for all Internet music radio sites at least threefold. Smaller operators, who would no longer be allowed to calculate royalty payments on the basis of their revenue, would see their rates increase as much as twelvefold. The new rate structure, which would be imposed retroactively to 2006, would likely force the great majority of online music radio companies out of business and push small terrestrial broadcast stations, including college radio outlets, to shut down their Web sites altogether.

Like the Radio Act of 1912 and the Communications Act of 1934, both of which squeezed amateur broadcasters and small businesses off the public spectrum while allowing a few commercial broadcasters to flourish, the CRB's decision would effectively prevent all but a few large corporations from participating in the new medium's most exciting application. The Internet can offer an open space for creative, independent programming, but this openness is not an inevitable or immutable feature of the technology; it requires political protection lest it be shut down. In this case, the party most invested in rewriting rules for the Internet is SoundExchange, a performance rights organization that distributes royalty payments to artists and is associated with the powerful Recording Industry Association of America as well as with companies such as Sony BMG Music Entertainment and Warner Music Group. The CRB, critics allege, lifted the new royalty rate structure directly from SoundExchange's wish list and overlooked the fact that Internet providers already paid more than twice the royalty rate of satellite radio companies.

The recording industry's demands incensed Internet radio operators and listeners, as well as countless recording artists who recognize that the Internet could break out songs that terrestrial stations would never play. Even big broadcast companies opposed the new rate structure, fearing that short-term losses from the onerous fees would slow the pace of new product development online. Within days of the CRB announcement, these parties formed the SaveNetRadio coalition, which organized a march in Washington, D.C., and circulated a petition to challenge the ruling. In April, U.S. Representatives Jay Inslee (D-WA) and Donald Manzullo (R-IL) introduced a bill that would nullify the CRB decision and set new rates designed to keep independent radio operators online. In May, U.S. Senators Ron Wyden (D-OR) and Sam Brownback (R-KS) introduced a companion bill in the Senate. As the summer progressed and the bills worked their way through committee, SoundExhange began negotiating with the National Association of Broadcasters and National Public Radio. Progress has been slow. "This is obviously not the time for people to be launching new ventures," said Jonathan Potter, executive director of the Digital Media Association.[5] For the moment, the cauldron of creative programming on Internet radio has been chilled.

So, too, has some of the free speech that the Internet and wireless communications systems are so well suited to deliver. In 2007, major telecommunications corporations gave citizens reason to fear that, lest Congress create special protections, selective filtering of political speech will soon be part of our "new media" system. In September, Verizon refused to allow NARAL Pro-Choice America to send text messages about its activities to customers who signed up for the updates, even though it allowed other organizations to send such messages. After enormous public outcry, Verizon reversed its position on NARAL, but the company insists that it is legally permitted to select which text messages it carries. In August, AT&T was involved in a similar incident. During a Web-cast performance by Pearl Jam, AT&T silenced the audio as vocalist Eddie Vedder sang the lyrics: "George Bush, leave this world alone . . . George Bush, find yourself another home," to the tune of Pink Floyd's "The Wall." Legally, AT&T owned the content from the performance, so its actions—which a spokesman called "editing" and dismissed as a "mistake"—did not technically amount to censorship. But the company's move to block politically charged speech highlighted the vulnerability of open expression online. As Pearl Jam put it in a formal statement: "AT&T's actions strike at the heart of the public's concerns over the power that corporations have when it comes to determining what the public sees and hears through communications media. . . . This, of course, troubles us as artists but also as citizens concerned with the issue of censorship and the increasingly consolidated control of the media."[6]

The Pearl Jam incident struck a chord with citizens throughout the nation, amplifying interest in the related issue of Net Neutrality. Traditionally, all data traffic on the Internet is treated equally, regardless of its ownership, source, or destination. Internet carriers such as AT&T, Verizon, and Time Warner, however, want to be free to purposely slow down consumer access to some Web sites or applications while speeding up access to others—a scheme that would let them charge fees to any content providers who did not want to have their users forced into the "slow lane." While the carriers have been dismissing concerns about Net Neutrality as largely theoretical, testing by the Associated Press in October 2007 confirmed that Comcast, the second-largest supplier of Internet access in the United States, has been surreptitiously throttling its users' traffic on the BitTorrent file-sharing network. Additional testing showed that other programs, including IBM's business application Lotus Notes, are being throttled as well.[7]

Leading legal scholars Timothy Wu and Lawrence Lessig, along with emerging Internet companies and a grassroots campaign known as the SavetheInternet.com Coalition, have been forcefully arguing that fair competition will be impossible if corporations that control the wires are allowed to discriminate at will against online content of their choosing. In January 2007, U.S. Senators Byron Dorgan (D-ND) and

Olympia Snowe (R-ME) heeded these concerns and introduced the Internet Freedom Preservation Act of 2007, which would prohibit Internet service providers from establishing such tiers of online service. The Bush administration signaled its opposition to the bill in September, when the Department of Justice sided with the telecommunications giants in a filing to the FCC. In comments prepared during the last days of Alberto Gonzales's tenure as attorney general and released soon after his resignation, the Department of Justice told the FCC to "be highly skeptical of calls to substitute special economic regulation of the Internet for free and open competition enforced by the antitrust laws." (In the mirror-world of the DOJ, "free and open competition" means the freedom of Internet carriers to charge content providers for non-degraded service, while "special economic regulation" refers to the legislation that would keep all online traffic safe from such discrimination.) The agency's implicit argument was "Just trust us." Its abysmal record as the guardian of the nation's most cherished political principles, however, undermined the DOJ's position. The Internet Freedom legislation is pending, and the issue is unlikely to be decided until after the 2008 elections. But for now, at least, there is little question that the Net Neutrality advocates have the momentum.

THE EARLY BATTLES OVER INTERNET RADIO, NET NEUTRALITY, AND content filtering suggest that the emerging digital media system will not be open unless it is aggressively defended against those who would place the pursuit of greater profits ahead of the public good. The history of American media gives ample reason to doubt that such a defense can succeed: During previous policy debates, corporations have proven far more influential than citizens, and the financial stakes of the current contests dwarf those from earlier eras. But the rising movement for media democracy has upset the traditional balance of power, and media policy may well become genuinely public policy. For the first time in decades, FCC commissioners face intense scrutiny of their deliberations and their decisions. Elected officials in Congress have heard so much and so often from media activists that they have begun, on occasion, to fight for the public interest.

This is hardly to say that media policy is now fully open to the democratic process. Under its current leadership, the FCC continues to operate without transparency and to share privileged information with media companies but not public interest groups. In September 2007, the Government Accountability Office (GAO) issued a blistering report on corporate favoritism in the FCC's rule-making process. By law, the FCC is prohibited from disclosing information about its voting schedule, yet in a series of four case studies the GAO discovered that "multiple stakeholders"—but not citizen groups—"generally knew when the commission scheduled votes on proposed rules well before FCC notified the public. . . . As a result, stakeholders with advance information about which rules are scheduled for a vote would know when it is most effective to lobby FCC, while stakeholders without this information would not."[8] The report inspired a chorus of demands for the FCC to develop "sunshine laws," which would allow the public to learn how the agency responsible for promoting open communications actually operates.

Such provisions would surely be useful to anyone interested in understanding another crucial yet mysterious part of the FCC's policy-making process: the outsourcing of contracts for official research studies. In 2006, during the latest round of deliberation on media ownership rules, Chairman Kevin Martin waited until the night before Thanksgiving to announce that he had commissioned ten new studies, which were to be conducted by an assortment of consulting firms, ratings agencies, and economists. Michael Copps and Jonathan Adelstein, the two Democratic commissioners, immediately objected. "Today's announcement of the Commission's new media ownership studies, unfortunately, raises more questions in the public's mind than it answers," Copps complained. "How were the contractors selected for the outside projects? How much money is being spent on each project—and on the projects collectively? What kind of peer review process is envisioned?" Martin did not answer.

Few were surprised when, the following July, Martin's handpicked researchers reported findings that would support his preferred policy changes, such as allowing newspaper companies to "cross-own" broadcast television stations in the same market. But Copps and Adelstein were most frustrated by the FCC's demand that all comments and criticisms of the studies be formally submitted within sixty days of their release. Although Martin had made public the data behind the studies, the tight deadline for responses made it practically impossible for anyone to conduct a thorough review. "Just when we hoped an open media ownership process was developing here at the FCC, along comes this bucket of ice water," Copps and Adelstein said in a joint statement. "This is unfair, unnecessary, and ultimately unwise—inviting public, Congressional, and judicial outrage reminiscent of what happened when the FCC tried to loosen media ownership rules four years ago. . . . The Commission's action today does not inspire confidence that this time around we are serious about getting it right."[9]

AS 2007 CAME TO A CLOSE, IT APPEARED LIKELY THAT MARTIN AND HIS Republican colleagues would soon relax media ownership restrictions, despite strong objections from the Democratic commissioners and general opposition from the voting public. In October, the chairman told a Senate committee that he would schedule a vote on new ownership proposals before year's end. The *New York Times* reported that Martin's plan—which the Democratic commissioners had not seen at the time of the Senate committee meeting—involved repealing the thirty-two-year-old cross-ownership ban. Others speculated that radio and television ownership limits would also be loosened. The consequence of such changes would be dramatic. Without the cross-ownership prohibition, a media mogul such as Rupert Murdoch would be able to march into any American city and acquire every newspaper, two or three of its broadcast television stations, and up to eight of its broadcast radio stations. Market competition, which the FCC is charged with protecting, would diminish considerably, as would the diversity of perspectives available from the most popular sources of news and information. And while it's hard to precisely gauge the power and influence that corporations could gain by controlling so many local media outlets, it is easy to see why allowing them to consolidate further is dangerous for democracy.

Chairman Martin's bold attempt to gut media ownership laws—to complete the deregulatory process that his predecessor Michael Powell failed to achieve—surprised many observers of the FCC. To be sure, several influential corporations, including the Tribune Company and Media General, were lobbying for the rule change, and Martin had already declared his sympathy for their position, but allowing media conglomerates to grow even larger would no doubt stir up bipartisan anxiety. The sudden hurry to push through the changes seemed designed to prevent the political fallout from contaminating the Republican candidates in the 2008 electoral campaigns. Moreover, the quick vote would ensure that ownership rules changed before a new president appointed fresh FCC leadership.

Martin's rush to relax media ownership restrictions infuriated Commissioners Copps and Adelstein. Copps, who was in London when he learned of Martin's time frame for the vote, told the *New York Times* that "It is déjà vu all over again. . . . We shouldn't be doing anything without having a credible process and nothing should be done to get in the way of Congressional oversight and more importantly, public oversight. . . . We've got to have that public scrutiny."[10] Adelstein contrasted Martin's rush to serve the interests of Big Media companies with his slow pace for addressing concerns over the declining diversity in media ownership and the diminished public-interest programming produced by broadcasters. Formal proceedings on both of these issues had languished for years, said Adelstein, and Martin's neglect to act on them suggested that the FCC was once again placing private interests ahead of the public good.

Copps and Adelstein were all the more perturbed since, just weeks before, Martin had publicly asserted that the loss of female and minority media owners had become an urgent matter, and promised to take on a personal leadership role in dealing with the issue. In late September, the FCC had held a public hearing in Chicago to focus on minority ownership. It was a fitting location: Chicago, which is roughly 37 percent African American and 26 percent Latino, has the lowest proportion of minority radio station owners in the top twenty-two markets—a mere 5 percent—and only one station owned by a woman of any ethnicity. This is precisely the kind of situation that the U.S. Third Circuit Court of Appeals cited unfavorably in *Prometheus v. FCC*, the case that blocked Michael Powell's attempt to further gut media ownership restrictions in 2003. The court had directed the FCC to address this disparity directly in its future ownership policies, but there were no signs that Martin's plan would do so.

Inevitably, the hundreds of citizens who turned out for the hearing linked the problems of media diversity to the loss of local owners. Only three of Chicago's thirteen full-power broadcast television stations are locally controlled, and Copps suggested that this helped explain why their programming routinely failed to cover many of the city's key issues. The commissioner acknowledged that a handful of media companies are both willing to invest in local journalism and committed to including a diverse set of voices in their offerings. "But I'm worried," he explained, "that in this era of huge consolidated media—with a few broadcasting giants owning so many properties— it's harder for these folks to be captains of their own fates. More and more they are captives to the unforgiving expectations of Wall Street and Madison Avenue. In the process local coverage has diminished, the news has been dumbed down, and diverse local and regional cultures have been subsumed to homogenized, nationalized programming fare."[11]

Local ownership has never guaranteed high-quality local content. Yet—as residents of Los Angeles, and journalists such as Nancy Cleeland, have learned from experience—ownership matters, and the civic indifference of chains and conglomerates has inspired widespread calls for local control. The future of our media system remains uncertain, but today there is no question that Americans of all political persuasions believe media consolidation was a failed experiment. It's time for change.

INTRODUCTION: THE EMPTY STUDIO

1. The account that follows comes from transcripts from the Ward County 911 dispatcher, the Minot Rural Fire Department, and the Minot Police Department, and from the National Transportation Safety Board. *Survival Factors Group Chairman's Factual Report,* June 12, 2002.

2. See the National Transportation Safety Board, *Hazardous Material Factual Report,* June 26, 2002, available at http://www.in-forum.com/specials/minot/NTSBreport/233006.pdf. Dimensions of the toxic cloud were reported by Marion Blakey, chairman, National Transportation Safety Board, during a U.S. Senate Commerce Committee hearing, July 10, 2002.

3. See the EAS fact sheet at http://www.fcc.gov/eb/easfact.html.

4. On Clear Channel's acquisition of all six commercial stations in Minot, see Jennifer 8 Lee, "On Minot, N.D., Radio, A Single Corporate Voice," *New York Times,* March 29, 2003.

5. The accounts of what happened to Kenny Moe and the Grabingers were reported in Steven Wagner, "Lost in the Cloud: Ammonia Spill Leaves Minot in Blind Panic," *Forum,* August 18, 2002.

6. *Law Enforcement News* also reported that Minot officials first tried using the EAS system and then attempted to use EBS when it failed. See Jennifer Nislow, "The Wrong Time to Find out that Emergency Alert System Doesn't Work," *Law Enforcement News,* March 2003.

7. The comments from Steve Davis are available in a Clear Channel news release: http://www.clearchannel.com/Corporate/PressRelease.aspx?PressRelease ID=1558.

8. According to the USINFO, a Web site produced and maintained by the U.S. Department of State's Bureau of International Information Programs, "The average American . . . spends about eight hours a day with the print and electronic media—at home, at work, and traveling by car. This total includes four hours watching television, three hours listening to radio, a half hour listening to recorded music, and another half hour reading the newspaper." http://usinfo. state.gov/usa/infousa/facts/factover/ch12.htm.

9. Rachel Carson, *Silent Spring: 40th Anniversary Edition* (Boston and New York: Mariner Books, 2002), pp. 12–13.

1: IN THE PUBLIC INTEREST

1. Susan Douglas, *Inventing American Broadcasting, 1899–1922* (Baltimore: Johns Hopkins University Press, 1987), p. 227. The account of early radio regulation that follows draws on chapter 7, "The *Titanic* Disaster and the First Radio Regulation."

2. Ibid., pp. 228–29.

3. House Reports, 62nd Congress, 2nd session, December 4, 1911–August 26, 1912, vol. 3, report 582, quoted in ibid., p. 233.

4. Paul Starr suggests that Franklin Delano Roosevelt, who signed the bill that created the FCC, was one of the first national leaders to recognize both the political benefits of appeasing Big Media operators and the hazards of challenging them. "In the 1932 election," Starr writes, "six out of ten newspapers had opposed him, and Roosevelt believed that he was the victim of a deep hatred among newspaper publishers who slanted press coverage against his programs. The radio networks, in contrast, gave the president their full cooperation, opening the airwaves to him whenever he wanted, and Roosevelt used radio to reach the public directly and explain his policies." Such fear and respect for the power of media corporations would become a theme of American politics, from the presidential to the local level, and as Big Media companies grew in size and scale so would their influence on federal and state policies. See Paul Starr, *The Creation of the Media: Political Origins of Modern Communications* (New York: Basic Books, 2004), p. 360.

5. See Robert McChesney, *Telecommunications, Mass Media, and Democracy: The Battle for the Control of U.S. Broadcasting, 1928–1935* (New York: Oxford University Press, 1993).

6. See Alexis de Tocqueville, *Democracy in America*, vol. 1 (New York: Vintage, 1990); Robert Park, "The Natural History of the Newspaper," in Robert Park and Ernest Burgess, *The City: Suggestions for Investigation of Human Behavior in the Urban Environment* (Chicago: University of Chicago Press, 1984), pp. 80–98; Richard Hofstadter, *The Age of Reform* (New York: Vintage, 1960), p. 188; Gunther Barth, *City People: The Rise of Modern City Culture in Nineteenth-Century America* (New York: Oxford University Press, 1980), p. 58.

7. On the increasingly local content of city newspapers during the nineteenth century, see Starr, *The Creation of the Media*, pp. 131–39. For the history of professional city reporting, see Michael Schudson, *Discovering the News* (New York: Basic Books, 1978).

8. The emphasis on primary reporting gave life to another American journalistic tradition: muckraking investigative projects into the uses and abuses of power in local government and business. During the Progressive Era, journalists including Lincoln Steffens, Upton Sinclair, and Ida Tarbell helped to establish a model for truth-seeking, critical, and reform-seeking reporters across the country. In fact, as Michael Schudson argues in ibid., American newspapers have never sponsored muckraking investigations into local power structures as much as their professional mythology would suggest.

9. Lippmann's statement is from a speech in Des Moines, Iowa, quoted in Geneva Overholser, "In the Age of Public Ownership, the Importance of Being Local," *Columbia Journalism Review*, November–December 1999.

10. Phyllis Kaniss, *Making Local News* (Chicago: University of Chicago Press, 1991), p. 8.

11. See the *Bee*'s Pineros series online at http://www.sacbee.com/content/news/projects/pineros/.

12. Harvey Molotch, "The City as a Growth Machine," *American Journal of Sociology* 82 (1976): 309–32.

13. Using the language of economics, Baker claimed that engaged local journalistic organizations produce "positive externalities," public benefits reaped by citizens, whereas the absence of such organizations creates "negative externalities" for the community, because it emboldens powerful, self-serving, and corrupt interests to act with that much less scrutiny. Baker's testimony is available at http://commerce.senate.gov/hearings/testimony.cfm?id=1321&wit_id=3847; he elaborates the argument in his book *Media, Markets, and Democracy* (Cambridge: Cambridge University Press, 2002).

14. Upton Sinclair, *The Brass Check: A Study of American Journalism* (Urbana and Chicago: University of Illinois Press, 2003), pp. 238–39.

15. Jeffrey Mays, "City Council Will Pay for Good News in Newark," *New Jersey Star-Ledger,* October 24, 2005.

16. On Wal-Mart, see Charles Fishman, *The Wal-Mart Effect* (New York: Penguin, 2006). On Costco, see Steven Greenhouse, "How Costco Became the Anti-Wal-Mart," *New York Times,* July 17, 2005. On McDonald's and In-N-Out Burger, see Eric Schlosser, *Fast Food Nation: The Dark Side of the All-American Meal* (Boston and New York: Houghton Mifflin, 2001). Consolidation in the retail industry, best symbolized by the rise of big-box stores such as Wal-Mart and Home Depot and the demise of small local businesses, further defangs local media by reducing the number of potential newspaper advertisers and making media companies more dependent on the national players that remain. A new Wal-Mart might force independent businesses to close and push down prevailing wages, but a national media chain that features reports about the problems Wal-Mart generates risks losing its patronage—not just in one town but in its entire fleet of papers and broadcast stations. Of course, chain media companies are not likely to make a fuss about chain retail companies anyway. Yet media conglomerates are not getting any favors for their support: the largest national retailers are now substituting direct mailings for paid advertisements in print publications, and local media outlets everywhere are watching their marketing revenues sink as a result. "Wal-Mart has a fairly standard policy of doing little to no local newspaper advertising," complains Mike Buffington, president of the National Newspaper Association. "Community newspapers across the nation are all but invisible to Wal-Mart—unless the company is looking for some free PR in our pages." Public letter from Mike Buffington to Wal-Mart, January 14, 2005.

17. For an insider account of how the pressure to produce such high margins has affected media organizations, see Leonard Downie Jr. and Robert Kaiser, *The News about the News: American Journalism in Peril* (New York: Alfred Knopf, 2001).

18. See this statement on the Citadel Web site: http://www.citadelbroadcasting.com/about/markets.cfm.

19. John Dunbar and Aron Pilhofer, "Big Radio Rules in Small Markets," Center for Public Integrity, October 1, 2003, available online at http://www.publicintegrity.org/telecom/report.aspx?aid=63.

20. The account of buying and selling radio stations comes from the Curb Center for Art, Enterprise, and Public Policy at Vanderbilt, *Radio Deregulation and Consolidation: What is Public Interest?* July 12, 2004. Neil Hickey, "So Big: The Telecommunications Act at Year One," *Columbia Journalism Review,* January–February 1997.

21. Anthony DeBarros, "Consolidation Changes Face of Radio," *USA Today,* July 17, 1998.

22. The U.S. Department of Justice ordered Capstar to sell eleven of SFX's stations to comply with antitrust regulations. See the DOJ statement at http://www.usdoj.gov/opa/pr/1998/March/153.htm.html.

23. See the Hickses' bio on the Capstar Web site: http://www.capstarpartners.com/ourteam/bios/s_hicks.php. See also Paul Krugman, "Steps to Wealth," *New York Times,* July 16, 2002; Andrew Wheat, "Legalized Bribery," *Multinational Monitor 3,* March 2001; and Robert Bryce, "The Governor's Sweetheart Deal," *Texas Observer,* January 30, 1998.

24. Quoted in Anna Wilde Matthews, "Clear Channel Uses High-Tech Gear to Perfect the Art of Sounding Local," *Wall Street Journal,* February 25, 2002.

25. The quotes from Alan are reported in ibid.

26. See the Center for Public Integrity's report *On the Road Again,* at http://www.openairwaves.org/telecom/report.aspx?aid=15.

27. The data on political contributions by sector come from the Center for Responsive Politics, a nonpartisan research group that tracks money in politics and assesses its effects on elections and public policy. See http://www .opensecrets.org.

28. The term *reluctant regulators* comes from Barry Cole's book about the FCC, *Reluctant Regulators: The FCC and the Broadcast Audience* (Boston: Addison-Wesley, 1978).

29. Mel Karmazin, testimony before U.S. Senate Committee on Commerce, Science, and Transportation, July 17, 2001.

30. Jack Fuller, testimony before U.S. Senate Committee on Commerce, Science, and Transportation, July 17, 2001.

31. See Dennis FitzSimons's statement at http://www.tribune.com/investors/ transcripts/midyear_05.html. Emphasis added.

32. See Steven Kull, *Misperceptions, the Media, and the Iraq War,* the Program on International Policy Attitudes, University of Maryland, October 2, 2003.

2: REMOTE CONTROL

1. Susan Douglas offers a succinct technical explanation of why AM signals can travel from 100 to 1,500 miles from their transmitters at night: "The lower layers of the ionosphere (called the D and E layers by radio technicians), which are approximately 45 to 75 miles above the earth's surface, act like a huge sponge during the day, absorbing the signals that pass through them. But after the sun sets these layers disappear, and the ones above them—anywhere from 90 to 250 miles above the earth—combine to form a dense layer that acts like a mirror to sky waves." Susan Douglas, *Listening In: Radio and the American Imagination* (New York: Crown, 1999), p. 38.

2. The FCC encouraged this kind of expansion, effectively giving FM licenses to AM stations to help generate activity on what was then the less-crowded side of the dial.

3. See Douglas, *Listening In,* chapter 10, for a rich account of the FM radio revolution.

4. For an account of the early days of KFRE-FM, see Jim Ladd, *Radio Waves: Life and Revolution on the FM Dial* (New York: St. Martin's, 1991), pp. 5–6.

5. See ibid.

6. Historians credit the invention of the Top 40 format during the 1950s to Todd Storz, the director of programming at KOWH AM in Omaha, Nebraska, and its proliferation to Gordon McLendon, the owner of KLIF in Dallas. Bill Drake is the namesake of the "Drake format," a tight playlist in which a small number of popular songs recur regularly and DJ chatter is held to a minimum. See Ben Fong-Torres, *The Hits Just Keep on Coming: The History of Top 40 Radio* (San Francisco: Backbeat Books, 1998). The quotes on FM radio are from Richard Neer, *FM: The Rise and Fall of Rock Radio* (New York: Villard. 2001), p. 2; Ladd, *Radio Waves,* pp. 5–6; and the transcript from "The Rise of Rock FM," Museum of Radio and Television, New York City. T: 32807. See also Douglas, *Listening In,* pp. 269, 273.

7. For a fascinating discussion of the way African American DJs helped achieve cultural desegregation, see chapter 9, "The Kids Take Over," in Douglas, *Listening In.* Jeff Chang discusses the role of local DJs in breaking new hip-hop styles in his book *Can't Stop Won't Stop: A History of the Hip-Hop Generation* (New York: St. Martin's Press, 2005).

8. Asch's statement is from "WNEW: Free Form Format," a panel discussion a the Museum of Radio and Television, New York City, T: 50942.

9. See WLIR's self-reported history on its Web site: http://www.wlir.fm. Bingenheimer is the subject of the documentary *Mayor of the Sunset Strip.* He is

quoted in Kate Sullivan, "A Man Out of Time," *Los Angeles Weekly,* July 13–19, 2003. To read about Maxanne Sartori, see http://www.geocities.com/uridfm/s/maxanne.htm.

10. Douglas, *Listening In,* p. 280.

11. See http://www.prophetsys.com/lines/broadcast/voicetrac.asp. Emphasis added.

12. This and the following quotes from the Fayetteville case are from Tricia Nellessen and Robert Brady, "May I Speak with the DJ? Industry Consolidation, Computer Technologies, and their Impact on Radio in the Late 1990s: A Case Study," *American Communications Journal,* May 2000, available online at http://www.acjournal.org/holdings/vol3/Iss3/articles/nell.html.

13. Lawrence K. Grossman, "The Death of Radio Reporting," *Columbia Journalism Review,* September–October 1998.

14. The NPR audience figures come from the Arbitron ratings service and are cited in Jacques Steinberg, "Money Changes Everything," *New York Times,* March 19, 2006.

15. Deadwood, as its name suggests, has a long history of burning. The town was built by the thousands of miners, cowboys, and gamblers who flocked to the area in the 1870s, during the last great western gold rush. After tiring of their temporary camps, those who decided to settle in the hills constructed new houses from trees downed in previous fires. This was a convenient but unstable arrangement. According to local legend, two major fires, the first of which destroyed over three hundred structures, hit Deadwood during the town's first decade. With gold came new resources, and soon the wealthy prospectors quarried native stone and used it to assemble fire-resistant structures, many of which survive today. Others continued building with wood, however, and despite ample experience dealing with fire hazards, periodically Deadwood ignites. The 1950s, known locally as the "fiery fifties," were especially brutal, with a series of major conflagrations culminating in 1959 with an inferno that consumed 4,500 acres and forced local residents to evacuate. Many of the town's current residents remember the experience today.

3: CLEAR CHANNEL COMES TO TOWN

1. Robert Short, Jr., testimony before the U.S. Senate Committee on Commerce, Science, and Transportation, January 30, 2003, available online at http://commerce.senate.gov/press/03/short013003.pdf. See also Paul Davidson, "Singers Take on Big Radio," *USA Today,* January 30, 2001.

2. For an account of the AMFM merger, see Joseph Weber and Louis Lavelle, "Family, Inc," *BusinessWeek,* November 10, 2003. For the FCC's official approval of the merger, see http://www.fcc.gov/Bureaus/Mass_Media/News_Releases/2000/nrmm0034.html.

3. In December 1996, Jacor spent more than $1 billion for stations owned by Citicasters, Regent Communications, and Mutual Insurance, giving it nearly one hundred outlets. In March 1997, Jacor purchased E.F.M. Media Management for $50 million, which gave it control of the nation's most popular radio program, *The Rush Limbaugh Show.* In June, Jacor bought Premiere Radio, a leading radio syndicator, for $190 million. The *Cincinnati Business Courier* and the *Cincinnati Enquirer* closely tracked Jacor's acquisitions through the period. For a timeline of Jacor and Clear Channel's growth, see "How Clear Channel Became the Biggest," *Cincinnati Enquirer,* March 19, 2000, and Richard Curtis, "Sam Zell May Be Shopping Jacor," *Dayton Business Journal,* October 17, 1997. Jacor CEO and future Clear Channel radio head Randy Michaels had once gained attention by being carried into industry meetings on a throne and wearing disco outfits to embarrass his stodgier colleagues. As *Salon*'s Eric Boehlert reported, "Behind the

mike he made a name for himself back in the '70s and '80s farting on the air, cracking jokes about gays and tantalizing listeners with descriptions of "incredibly horny, wet and ready" naked in-studio guests. Along with getting hit with a sexual harassment suit [which was eventually settled], Michaels pulled in big ratings wherever he went." Eric Boehlert, "Radio's Big Bully: Clear Channel," *Salon,* April 30, 2001.

4. The data on radio industry revenues are from BIA Financial Networks and are included in a report by the Future of Music Coalition, *Radio Deregulation: Has it Served Citizens and Musicians?* Available online at http://www.futureofmusic .org/images/FMCradiostudy.pdf.

5. See Clear Channel's press release on the merger, which valued AMFM at $23.5 billion, including the assumption of $6.1 billion in debt, at http://www .clearchannel.com/Corporate/PressReleases/2001/100199AFMCCU.pdf. See the FCC's approval at http://www.fcc.gov/Bureaus/Mass_Media/News_Releases/2000/ nrmm0034.html. See also the Project for Excellence in Journalism's *State of the News Media* report for 2004, in particular the section on radio ownership, at http://www.stateofthenewsmedia.org/narrative_radio_ownership.asp?cat=5&media=8. Infinity and ABC have a strong presence in the leading and most lucrative markets. Citing BIA Financial Network statistics for 2004, the Center for Public Integrity reported that Clear Channel's 1,195 stations generated revenues of $3.57 billion, while Infinity's 179 stations produced revenues of $2.22 billion. For a list of the largest broadcast radio and television companies, in revenue and stations, see http://www.publicintegrity.org/telecom/industry.aspx?act=broadcast.

6. "Clear Channel Communications, Inc. Fact Sheet," http://www.clearchannel .com/PressRoom/FactSheets/Corporate.pdf. It was alleged in a complaint filed with the FCC that Clear Channel may control an even larger number of stations, since advertisers and competitors have accused the conglomerate of setting up front companies that house "shell stations," which they covertly operate, to get around the remaining local ownership caps. In November 2001, David Ringer, an advertiser in Chillicothe, Ohio, petitioned the FCC to complain that "in situations where Clear Channel cannot operate a station in a particular market, it substitutes Concord Media or some other entity as its alter ego." *Salon* reported that Ringer, who worried that advertising prices would skyrocket if one company dominated local radio, discovered that employees at the Chillicothe station WKKJ were being paid by Clear Channel rather than by its legal owner, Concord Media, that Clear Channel employees worked at Concord's other stations, in Florida and New York, and that the Web site for Concord's outlets in Jacksonville identified them as the "Clear Channel Jacksonville Media Family." See Dan Monk, "Advertiser Fights Radio Titan," *Cincinnati Business Courier,* November 30, 2001; and Eric Boehlert, "Is Clear Channel Playing a 'Shell Game'?" *Salon,* November 20, 2001.

7. See Chris Nolter, "Radio: Static from Clear Channel," *Columbia Journalism Review,* January–February 2002; and see http://www.clearchannel.com/ Radio/rad_ktf.aspx. Before acquiring *Inside Radio,* Clear Channel set up a mock Web site, http://www.insideinsideradio.com, which featured an image of a man with his head in his ass and the caption, "Jerry checks with an inside source."

8. Mays is quoted in Christine Chen, "Clear Channel: Not the Bad Boys of Radio," *Fortune,* March 3, 2003, available online at http://www.fortune.com/ fortune/print/0,15935,423802,00.html.

9. Duncan's American Radio, *Radio Market Guide 2002.*

10. See Clear Channel's self-report at http://documents.clearchannelint.com/ upload62949PM_1.pdf, and "Clear Channel Credit Rating Revised," *Dayton Business Journal,* May 7, 2003.

11. See the testimony of Jon Mandel before the U.S. Senate hearing on media ownership, July 8, 2003.

12. Maria Figueroa, Damone Richardson, and Pam Whitefield, *The Clear Picture on Clear Channel Communications, Inc.* (Ithaca: Cornell University, 2004), p. 29.

13. For reports on Clear Channel's use of voice tracking to cut labor costs, see also Anna Wilde Mathews, "Clear Channel Uses High Tech Gear to Perfect the Art of Sounding Local," *Wall Street Journal*, February 25, 2002; Todd Spencer, "Radio Killed the Radio Star," *Salon*, October 1, 2002; Boehlert, "Radio's Big Bully"; and Figueroa, Richardson, and Whitefield, *The Clear Picture on Clear Channel Communications*, p. 38.

14. Mathews, "Clear Channel Uses High Tech Gear to Perfect the Art of Sounding Local"; and Boehlert, "Radio's Big Bully." Mathews reports that in Florida, Clear Channel agreed to make an eighty-thousand-dollar "contribution" to the Consumer Frauds Trust Fund after the state attorney general began investigating complaints that it deceived listeners with voice-tracked call-in contests.

15. Chris Baker, "Voice Tracking Lets Disc Jockeys Create Radio Shows for Different Cities," *Knight Ridder/Tribune Business News*, Washington, D.C., May 25, 2002.

16. Lowry Mays, testimony before the U.S. Senate Committee on Commerce, Science and Transportation, January 30, 2003.

17. David Rubin, "When Power Went Off, WSYR Failed Listeners," *Syracuse Post-Standard*, August 23, 2003.

18. Bill Carey, "SU Dean Failed to See How WSYR Met Local Needs," *Syracuse Post-Standard*, August 31, 2003.

19. David Rubin, "Radio's Response to Crisis Too Important to Tune Out," *Syracuse Post-Standard*, August 31, 2003.

20. See the testimony of Lewis Dickey Jr. before the Senate Committee hearing on media ownership, July 8, 2003.

21. See the report on the Future of Music Coalition Web site: http://www.futureofmusic.org.

22. Jenny Toomey, "Radio Deregulation: Has It Served Citizens and Musicians?" testimony of the Future of Music Coalition on media ownership, submitted to the U.S. Senate Committee on Commerce, Science, and Transportation, January 30, 2003.

23. Gabriel Rossman, "Concentration of Ownership and Concentration of Content in Rock Radio," unpublished manuscript.

24. The classic account of payola is Fredric Dannen, *Hit Men: Power Brokers and Fast Money Inside the Music Business* (New York: Vintage, 1991). In *Listening In* (1999), Susan Douglas claims that the Payola crackdown contributed to the loss of DJs' control over programming.

25. Eric Boehlert, "Record Companies: Save Us From Ourselves!" *Salon*, March 13, 2002; Eric Boehlert, "Pay for Play?" *Salon*, March 14, 2001; and Eric Boehlert, "Fighting Pay-for-Play," *Salon*, April 3, 2001.

26. See Charles Duhigg and Walter Hamilton, "Paying a Price," *Los Angeles Times*, July 26, 2005.

27. Chuck Taylor, "Hundreds of Radio Stations in Payola Probe," *Mediaweek*, February 13, 2006.

28. Don Henley, testimony before the the U.S. Senate Committee on Commerce, Science, and Transportation, January 30, 2003. The members of the Recording Artists' Coalition include Christina Aguilera, Beck, Mary Chapin Carpenter, Eric Clapton, Dave Matthews Band, Billy Joel, Elton John, Linkin Park, Joni Mitchell, Pearl Jam, Kenny Rogers, Bruce Springsteen, Sting, Stone Temple Pilots, and Tom Waits.

29. Transcribed from "The Rise of Rock FM," Museum of Television and Radio, New York City, T: 32807.

30. See the Web site for the PBS *Frontline* special "The Way the Music Died": http://www.pbs.org/wgbh/pages/frontline/shows/music/perfect/radio.html.

31. See Simon Renshaw, testimony before the U.S. Senate Committee on Commerce, Science, and Transportation, July 8, 2003. Rintels is quoted in Brett Pulley, "Gee, Thanks Dad," *Fortune*, October 18, 2004.

32. See the CPI report on Clear Channel at http://www.publicintegrity.com/telecom/analysis/CompanyProfile.aspx?HOID=183#Financials.

33. A transcript of the interview is available at http://www.reclaimthemedia.org/stories.php?story=02/08/31/6144861.

34. Jeff Chang, "Urban Radio Rage," *San Francisco Bay Guardian*, January 22, 2003.

35. Walker is quoted in Andy Paras, "Morning Radio Co-Host Sues Station that Fired Her," *Greenville News*, July 7, 2003. For Goyette's account of his conflict with Clear Channel, see Charles Goyette, "How to Lose Your Job in Talk Radio: Clear Channel Gags an Antiwar Conservative," *American Conservative*, February 2, 2004.

36. Media Matters provides excerpts of Beck's attack on Berg at http://mediamatters.org/items/200405170002. Clear Channel's Premiere Radio Networks offers photos, news coverage, and audio clips from the rallies on one of its sponsored Web sites: http://www.glennbeck.com/home/rally.shtml.

37. Quoted in Eric Boehlert, "The Passion of Howard Stern," *Salon*, March 4, 2004.

38. See Shakowsky's Web site: http://www.house.gov/schakowsky/article_04_15_03massmedianotes.html.

39. Michelle Garcia, "Antiwar Billboard Nixed in N.Y.," *Washington Post*, July 13, 2004.

40. Scott McKenzie, "Fox News to Partner with Clear Channel," *Billboard Radio Monitor*, December 5, 2004.

41. See http://www.clearchannel.com/Radio/home.aspx.

42. Sarah McBride, "From Conservative Talk Format to All Katrina," *Wall Street Journal*, September 6, 2006.

43. Ellen Barry, "A Lifeline Sent by Airwave," *Los Angeles Times*, September 10, 2005.

44. See the list of press releases at http://www.clearchannel.com/PressRoom/Display.aspx?DivisionID=6.

45. Clear Channel's lobbying expenditures were reported to the U.S Senate Office of Public Records, and posted by the Center for Public Integrity: http://www.publicintegrity.org/telecom/analysis/CompanyProfile.aspx? HOID=183.

46. See "Hertz, Clear Channel Among $88 Billion Falling into Junk Market," *Bloomberg*, October 4, 2005.

47. Quoted in "Clear Channel Renews Bid to Ease Ownership Restrictions," *Reuters*, October 3, 2005.

48. See Katy Bachman, "Clear Channel Divides into Three," *Mediaweek*, May 2, 2005.

49. http://www.xmradio.com/newsroom/screen/press_release_1999_06_08.html.

50. Quoted in Sarah McBride, "Hit by iPod and Satellite, Radio Tries New Tune: Play More Songs," *Wall Street Journal*, March 18, 2005.

51. However, XM Satellite Radio provides weather and traffic reports for twenty-one cities.

52. See Walter Kirn, "Stuck in the Orbit of Satellite Radio," *Time*, May 23, 2005.

4: NEWS FROM NOWHERE

1. In late 2004 Sinclair began selling some of its stations, and it was down to fifty-eight in April 2006.

2. See the transcript for CNN's *American Morning*, October 12, 2004: http://edition.cnn.com/TRANSCRIPTS/0410/12/ltm.06.html.

3. For more on Hyman, see http://www.sinclairwatch.org/sinclair_report.pdf.

4. See "Sinclair and the Public Airwaves: A History of Abuse," *Free Press*, October 11, 2004, http://www.sinclairwatch.org/sinclair_report.pdf. See also http://officialmedia.blogspot.com/; http://web.archive.org/web/20030401200453/www.newscentral.tv/thepoint/thepoint.shtml; http://mediamatters.org/items/200412140002; and http://www.alternet.org/story/15718. In addition to Hyman's editorial, these segments included one called "Truth, Lies and Red Tape," which offered examples of government waste and inefficiency, and news reports broadcast by Sinclair's Washington, D.C., bureau that were so consistently skewed to the right that reporters and producers complained they were having trouble getting moderate or Democratic sources to talk to them.

5. For information about the Norman Lear Center's local news and elections project, see http://www.learcenter.org/html/projects/?cm=news.

6. See Bob Papper, *Local Television News Study of News Directors and the General Public*, Radio and Television News Directors Foundation, 2003, pp. 23–24; and Tom Rosenstiel, Carl Gottlieb, and Lee Ann Brady, "Local TV News: What Works, What Flops, and Why," *Columbia Journalism Review*, January–February 1999.

7. Martin Kaplan, Ken Goldstein, and Matthew Hale, *Local News Coverage of the 2004 Campaigns: An Analysis of Nightly Broadcasts in 11 Markets*, The Lear Center Local News Archive, February 15, 2004. (Emphasis added.)

8. See the state of Washington's report at http://vote.wa.gov/general/recount.aspx.

9. Kaplan, Goldstein, and Hale, "Local News Coverage of the 2004 Campaigns," p. 15.

10. There is a vast literature on the link between television coverage and racial discrimination. See Martin Gilens, *Why Americans Hate Welfare* (Chicago: University of Chicago Press, 1999); Robert Entman and Andrew Rojecki, *The Black Image in the White Mind* (Chicago: University of Chicago Press, 2001); and Jerry Kang, "The Trojan Horses of Race," *Harvard Law Review* 118 (2005); 1491–1593. Neil Postman and Steve Powers condemn the use of actor-anchors: "The fact that the audience is being deluded into thinking that an actor-anchor is a journalist contributes a note of fakery to the enterprise. It encourages producers and news directors to think about what they are doing as artifice, as a show in which trust-telling is less important than the appearance of truth-telling." They are similarly critical of TV consultants: "Consultants are hired by stations to find ways to increase the ratings of news shows, and to do so quickly. The usual way to proceed is by emphasizing 'hair-spray' ethics at the expense of solid journalism." Neil Postman and Steve Powers, *How to Watch TV News* (New York: Penguin, 1992), pp. 32, 77. Also see chapter 6 of Leonard Downie Jr. and Robert Kaiser, *The News about the News: American Journalism in Peril* (New York: Knopf, 2001).

11. Jon Fine, "Local TV's Brave New World," *BusinessWeek*, September 12, 2005.

12. Before 1992, when Congress passed the "Fin-Syn" rule (financial interest and syndication), networks were legally prohibited from producing and syndicating their own shows.

13. See the Project for Excellence in Journalism's annual *State of the News Media* report: http://www.stateofthenewsmedia.org/narrative_localtv_ownership .asp?cat=5&media=6 and http://www.stateofthenewsmedia.org/narrative_localtv_ownership.asp?cat=5&media=6.

14. Ibid.

15. See the Scripps annual report: http://www.scripps.com/2002annualreport/10k/10.html.

16. Alan Frank, statement to U.S. Senate Committee on Commerce, Science, and Transportation, July 17, 2001, http://commerce.senate.gov/hearings/071701 Frank.pdf.

17. Alan Frank, "Keep Cap on Number of TV Stations for One Owner," *USA Today*, February 24, 2002.

18. Dan Ackman, "The Infomercial Triumphant," *Forbes*, November 11, 2002. According to a 2003 study of forty-five local television stations conducted by the Alliance for Better Campaigns, during a typical one-week period paid infomercials filled up about 14.4 percent of programming time, including popular daytime hours, whereas local public-affairs shows comprised under 1 percent of the schedule. The title of this study is *All Politics Is Local: But You Wouldn't Know It from Watching TV.*

19. See Doreen Carvajal, "Is it News, Ad, or Infomercial?" http://www.journalism.indiana.edu/gallery/Ethics/isnews.html.

20. Quoted in Jeff Chester and Gary O. Larson, "Whose First Amendment?" *American Prospect*, December 17, 2001.

21. See http://www.publicintegrity.org/telecom/analysis/CompanyProfile.aspx?HOID=22261.

22. See http://www.stljr.org/. In 2006 the WB and UPN networks merged to form the CW network.

23. "Sinclair's Shame," *Broadcasting and Cable*, May 3, 2004, http://www.broadcastingcable.com/article/CA414506.html?display=Editorials.

24. http://mccain.senate.gov/index.cfm?fuseaction=NewsCenter.ViewPress Release&Content_id=1276.

25. http://www.msnbc.msn.com/id/6293163/site/newsweek/.

26. Moody's: http://www.rbr.com/tvepaper/pages/october04/04-210_news1.html.

27. The Smiths take in handsome salaries for their leadership at Sinclair. But they also keep busy with other enterprises, some of which take advantage of unconventional synergies with their television empire. David has large investments in car dealerships that are among the largest advertisers in Baltimore, and he benefits nicely when they buy commercials on his station. Frederick has a real estate company, Todd Village, which Baltimore Neighborhoods sued in 2004, alleging discrimination against African Americans by refusing to show them residential properties that they willingly showed to whites. See http://www.thewbalchannel.com/news/3805874/detail.html.

28. Critics immediately pointed out that the sale price, $7 million, was suspiciously low given that Sinclair had just paid $55 million for WPGH, while WPTT, which was not sold through a public auction, was transferred to Edwards after he put down $10 for a $7-million loan. On the Edwards loan, see Teresa Lindeman, Rob Owen, and Barbara Vancheri, "Cashing It In: Eddie Edwards Sells WCWB," *Pittsburgh Post-Gazette*, November 18, 1999. Edwards converted WPTT to WCWB in 1998. Sinclair acquired WCWB in 2000, after the FCC relaxed its duopoly restrictions, and changed the call letters to WPMY in 2006.

29. http://www.fcc.gov/Speeches/Copps/Statements/2001/stmjc133.html.

30. http://www.usatoday.com/news/washington/2005-01-06-williams-whitehouse_x.htm.

31. According to the FCC's rules on payola: "When a broadcast licensee has received or been promised payment for the airing of program material, then, at the time of the airing, the station must disclose that fact and identify who paid for or promised to pay for the material. All sponsored material must be explicitly identified at the time of broadcast as paid for and by whom, except when it is clear

that the mention of a product or service constitutes sponsorship identification. Any broadcast station employee who has accepted or agreed to accept payment for the airing of program material, or the person making or promising to make the payment, must disclose this information to the station prior to the airing of the program. Any person involved in the production or preparation of a program who receives or agrees to receive payment for the airing of program material must disclose this information. Broadcast licensees must make reasonable efforts to obtain from their employees and others they deal with for program material the information necessary to make the required sponsorship identification announcements. The information must be provided up the chain of production and distribution before the time of broadcast, so the station can air the required disclosure. These rules apply to all kinds of programs aired over radio and television stations. Some may also apply to cablecasts." See http://www.fcc.gov/cgb/consumerfacts/ PayolaRules.html.

32. Government Accountability Office, *Department of Education—Contract to Obtain Armstrong Williams Services*, September 30, 2005, B-305368.

33. See Howard Kurtz, "Writer Backing Bush Plan Had Gotten Federal Contract," *Washington Post*, January 26, 2005; and Jim Drinkard and Mike Memmott, "HHS Said It Paid Columnist for Help," *USA Today*, January 27, 2005.

34. Anne Kornblut, "Bush Prohibits Paying of Commentators," *New York Times*, January 27, 2005.

35. See the KEF Web site: http://www.kefmedia.com/. Audience research confirms that viewers find VNRs more credible than commercials. Anne Owen and James Karrh, "Video News Releases: Effects on Viewer Recall and Attitudes," *Public Relations Review* 22 (1996): 369–78. See also Anne Owen, "Breaking through the Clutter: The Use of Video News Releases in Integrated Marketing Communications," Ph.D. dissertation, University of Florida, 1996. There are only a small number of academic research articles on how TV stations use VNRs. See Glen Cameron and David Blount, "VNRs and Air Checks: A Content Analysis of the Use of Video News Releases in Television Newscasts," *Journalism and Mass Communications Quarterly* 73, no. 4 (1996): 890–904, and Mark Harmo and Candace White, "How Television News Programs Use Video News Releases," *Public Relations Review* 27 (2001): 213–22.

36. See the transcript of National Public Radio, "Public Relations and the Media," *Talk of the Nation*, March 15, 2005. John Stauber and Sheldon Rampton, *Toxic Sludge Is Good for You! Lies, Damn Lies, and the Public Relations Industry* (Monroe, ME: Common Courage Press, 1995), p. 184.

37. Quoted in David Barstow and Robin Stein, "Under Bush, a New Age of Prepackaged TV News," *New York Times*, March 13, 2005.

38. Marion Just and Tom Rosenstiel, "All the News that's Fed," *New York Times*, March 26, 2005.

39. See Michael Stoll, "News from Nowhere," *Grade the News*, September 4, 2003.

40. Stauber and Rampton, *Toxic Sludge*; and Barstow and Stein, "Under Bush, a New Age of Prepackaged TV News."

41. Government Accountability Office, "To Heads of Departments, Agencies, and Others Concerned: Prepackaged News Stories," memo, February 17, 2005.

42. Quoted in Accuracy In Media Report: *Senator Clinton and the Fake News Scandal—April B*, April 14, 2005, http://www.aim.org/aim_report/2866_0_4_0_C/.

43. See the GAO decision from May 19, 2004, at http://www.gao.gov/ decisions/appro/302710.pdf.

44. Quoted in Robert Pear, "U.S. Videos, for TV News, Come Under Scrutiny," *New York Times*, March 15, 2004.

45. Quoted in Ron Suskind, "Without a Doubt," *New York Times Magazine*, October 17, 2004.

46. Ketchum, the firm that hired Armstrong Williams for the Department of Education, was the largest recipient of government contracts, with $97 million during Bush's first term. See Jim Drinkard, "Report: PR Spending Doubled Under Bush," *USA Today,* January 27, 2005.

47. Barstow and Stein. "Under Bush, a New Age of Prepackaged TV News."

48. See http://democrats.house.gov/news/librarydetail.cfm?library_content_id=632.

5: OWNING IT ALL

1. This quote from Caylor and the quotes from Bingham and Oppegard that follow are from Katharine Seelye, "The Day the News Left Town," *New York Times,* January 30, 2006.

2. On the Bingham family, see Susan Tifft and Alex Jones, *The Patriarch: The Rise and Fall of the Bingham Dynasty* (New York: Summit, 1991). Gannett is formally incorporated in Delaware, where there is no income tax for companies that do not transact business in the state.

3. See Oliver Wendell Holmes, "Bread and the Newspaper," reprinted in *The Oxford Book of American Essays* and available online at http://www.bartleby.com/109/.

4. James Surowiecki, "Printing Money," *New Yorker,* April 3, 2006.

5. The combined print and Web circulation figures from the Newspaper Audience Database are reported in http://www.naa.org/nadbase/2005_NADbase_Report.pdf. The Audit Bureau of Circulations figures are for the six-month period ending on September 30, 2005.

6. The Project for Excellence in Journalism report on newspaper economics is available at http://www.stateofthenewsmedia.org/narrative_newspapers_economics.asp?cat=4&media=2; the Morton Research study was reported in "Something to Discover," *Columbia Journalism Review,* November–December 2005, http://www.cjr.org/issues/2005/6/editorial.asp; Katharine Q. Seelye, "At Newspapers, Some Clipping," *New York Times,* October 10, 2005.

7. The quotes from FitzSimons and Mullen (see next paragraph) are available in the transcript from Tribune Company's Mid-Year Media Review, June 24, 2003, http://www.tribune.com/investors/transcripts/midyear_03.html.

8. Frank Blethen, "Who's Controlling Your Information?" speech at the University of Washington, October 26, 2004.

9. Jack Fuller, testimony before the U.S. Senate Committee on Commerce, Science, and Transportation, July 17, 2001, http://commerce.senate.gov/hearings/071701Fuller.pdf.

10. See the U.S. Bureau of Labor Statistics data at http://www.naa.org/info/facts04/employment.html.

11. Phyllis Kaniss, *Making Local News* (Chicago: University of Chicago Press, 1991), p. 35.

12. A. J. Liebling, *The Press* (New York: Pantheon, 1981).

13. George Ryan, "An Address on the Death Penalty," the University of Chicago Divinity School, June 3, 2002. See http://pewforum.org/events/index.php? EventID=28.

14. Quoted in Gary Washburn, "Daley: Tribune Makes Chicago a Cubs Town," *Chicago Tribune,* October 7, 2005.

15. See the CHA Web site: http://www.thecha.org/relocation/overview.html.

16. Ernest Hollings, statement at the Senate media concentration hearings, July 17, 2001, http://commerce.senate.gov/hearings/071701EFH.pdf.

17. See, for example, the Federal Communications Commission, Media Ownership Working Group, *Study 8: Consumer Survey on Media Usage,* prepared by Nielsen Media Research, September 2002 (see especially questions 1 and 8); the

Consumer Federation of America report *New Survey Finds Americans Rely on Newspapers Much More than Other Media for Local News and Information,* January 2004; and the Newspaper Association of America NADbase report for 2005, at http://www.naa.org/nadbase/.

18. For cautionary stories about cross-ownership in Milwaukee, Tampa, Dallas, Columbus, and Atlanta, see the Consumers Union, "Loss of Diversity, Local and Independent Voices Harms the Public Interest: Some Recent Examples," March 11, 2003, http://www.consumersunion.org/telecom/media-d-report.htm. For an account of the Wisconsin State Senate's stadium-financing debate, see Steve Fainaru, "Selig Plays Hardball on Stadium Deals," *Washington Post,* June 27, 2004.

19. Federal Communications Commission, "FCC Issues Broadcast Ownership Biennial Review Report," press release, May 30, 2000. In an article published by the American Bar Association, Harold Feld and Cheryl Leanza, from the Media Access Project, wrote: "At best, these multimedia conglomerates will homogenize news and entertainment into a single 'infotainment' package leveraged across multimedia platforms and targeted primarily at advertiser-coveted demographics. At worst, the few media gatekeepers may suppress news or perspectives that run counter to their economic or ideological interests, or to curry favor with the government." Cheryl Leanza and Harold Feld, "More than a Toaster with Pictures: Defending Media Ownership Limits," *Communications Lawyer* 21, no. 3 (2003): 12, 18–22.

20. According to U.S. Senate records, Tribune's lobbying expenses were $72,000 in 2000, $121,000 in 2001, $147,000 in 2002, and $153,000 in 2003, the year of the FCC's decision. See http://www.openairwaves.org/telecom/analysis/CompanyProfile.aspx?HOID=8033#Lobby.

21. Quoted in James Squires, *Read All About It! The Corporate Takeover of America's Newspapers* (New York: Crown, 1993), p. 82; and Ken Auletta, "Synergy City," *American Journalism Review,* May 1998.

22. Some reporters and editors at Media General and Tribune were given anonymity or pseudonyms as a condition of my observational research.

23. John Pavlik, the executive director of Columbia University's Center for New Media, reports that "newspapers that have not set up a separate new media staff have put incredible demands on their reporters, who must now report for both the newspapers and online. People are putting in sixteen- to twenty-hour days and getting burned out." *Journalism and New Media* (New York: Columbia University Press, 2001), p. 101.

24. Although computers and digital production programs allow for more efficient internal circulation of articles once they are written, writers and editors have not found that the high-tech editorial systems have given them more time to work. Summarizing the research on new editing technologies in 1991, the communications scholars David Weaver and Cleveland Wilhoit reported that with video display terminals and computers, "editing speed is reduced, because of the need for more proofreading, more keystrokes to make changes, and greater manual dexterity." David Weaver and Cleveland Wilhoit, *The American Journalist: A Portrait of U.S. News People and Their Work,* 2nd. ed. (Bloomington: Indiana University Press, 1991), p. 149.

25. The same anxieties are the basis of television criticism from Neil Postman, the late media scholar who authored *Amusing Ourselves to Death* (New York: Viking, 1985), and Pierre Bourdieu, the late sociologist whose book, *On Television* (New York: New Press, 1999) sparked a national debate about how television degraded both journalistic and public discourse in France.

26. http://www.journalism.org/resources/research/reports/ownership/default.asp.

27. James Squires, *Read All About It! The Corporate Takeover of America's Newspapers* (New York: Crown, 1993), pp. 220, 210; Leonard Downie Jr. and

Robert Kaiser, *The News about the News: American Journalism in Peril* (New York: Alfred Knopf, 2001), pp. 10–11, 92.

28. Davis Merritt, *Knightfall: Knight Ridder and How the Erosion of Newspaper Journalism Is Putting Democracy at Risk* (New York: Amacom, 2005), p. 4; Richard McCord, *The Chain Gang: One Newspaper versus the Gannett Empire* (Columbia: University of Missouri Press, 1996).

29. The account of Gannett's plans to establish a monopoly presence in Salem comes from McCord, *The Chain Gang,* chapters 2 to 5.

30. Ibid., p. 91.

31. Aurora Wallace, *Newspapers and the Making of Modern America: A History* (Westport, CT: Greenwood Press, 2005), p. 4. On Gannett's relationship to the Newseum complex, see Thomas Frank, *One Market under God: Extreme Capitalism, Market Populism, and the End of Economic Democracy* (New York: Doubleday, 2000).

32. Geneva Overholser, "In the Age of Public Ownership, the Importance of Being Local," *Columbia Journalism Review,* November–December 1999.

33. For an extensive profile of Black, including an account of his relationship with Radler, see Dominic Rushe, "Black Narcissi," *Sunday Times,* March 28, 2004, http://business.timesonline.co.uk/article/0,,9071-1044025,00.html.

34. The series is available online at http://www.suntimes.com/special_sections/clout/ and http://www.suntimes.com/special_sections/clout/followup/hired_020905.html.

35. The report by the Hollinger International special committee is available online at http://sec.gov/Archives/edgar/data/868512/000095012304010413/y01437exv99w2.htm. Hollinger International's own journalists provided some of the best reports on Black's and Radler's "corporate kleptocracy." See, for example, Eric Herman, "The Looting of the Sun-Times," *Chicago Sun-Times,* September 1, 2004.

36. See Richard Siklos, "Hollinger Board Rides Out Criticism," *New York Times,* September 26, 2005; Elena Cherney, "Radler Plea Deal Vows Cooperation in Hollinger Probe," *Wall Street Journal,* September 20, 2005; and Elena Cherney, "Hollinger's Black Is Likely to Face Broad Indictment," *Wall Street Journal,* October 13, 2005.

37. For an excellent account of the business media's failure to cover Enron, see Scott Sherman, "Enron: Uncovering the Uncovered Story," *Columbia Journalism Review,* March–April 2002. The *Houston Chronicle* has archived its ongoing coverage of Enron, which is online at http://www.chron.com/content/chronicle/special/01/enron/oct01/nudex.html.

38. See Charles Layton and Mary Walton, "Missing the Story at the Statehouse," *American Journalism Review,* July–August 1998; and Neil Gordon, "State Lobbyists Near the $1 Billion Mark: For Every Lawmaker, There Are About Five Lobbyists," *Public Interest,* Center for Public Integrity, August 10, 2005.

39. Wallace, *Newspapers and the Making of Modern America,* p. 145.

40. For an account of Carroll's frustrations with Tribune, see Ken Auletta, "Fault Line," *New Yorker,* October 10, 2005. On the Tribune's $1-billion tax burden, see Kate Berry, "The Billion-Dollar Bite: Everything Went Wrong with Times' Tax Gamble," *Los Angeles Business Journal,* October 3, 2005.

41. On the loss of local journalism at the *Times,* see Auletta, "Fault Line." See also Steve Wasserman, "Chicago Agonistes: The Plight of the L.A. Times," Truthdig.com, November 28, 2005; and Joseph Hallinan, "Los Angeles Paper Bets on Softer News, Shorter Stories," *Wall Street Journal,* October 3, 2005.

42. Quoted in Gadi Dechter, "London Falling," *Baltimore City Paper,* October 12, 2005.

43. Associated Press, "Recent Newspaper Cuts," November 18, 2005. By summer 2006 the Chandler family, which had sold Times Mirror to Tribune and become the company's second-largest shareholder, announced that they too were fed up with Tribune's business strategy. That June the Chandlers wrote an open letter calling for Tribune to break up and sell off the corporation.

44. The September 12 letter from Los Angeles civic leaders to Tribune is addressed to Mr. FitzSimons and Members of the Board of Directors. It was published in the Opinion section of the *Los Angeles Times* on September 19, 2006.

6: CHAINING THE ALTERNATIVES

1. See Jarrett Murphy, "Paper Route: Buying and Selling the Voice," *Village Voice*, November 1, 2005, p. 31, for a brief account of the paper's owners; and Alexander Cockburn, "Guess Who's Paying for Dinner? Rupert Murdoch Buys the Voice," *Village Voice*, January 10, 1977 (reprinted in November 1, 2005, p. 60), for the response to Murdoch's takeover.

2. On the early history of the *Voice*, see Kevin McAuliffe, *The Great American Newspaper: The Rise and Fall of the Village Voice* (New York: Charles Scribner's Sons, 1978).

3. Wolf is quoted in ibid., p. 92, and McAuliffe's line is from ibid., p. 96. McAuliffe has an excellent account of the *Voice*'s role in the fight to save Washington Square Park, pp. 91–99.

4. Calvin Trillin, "U.S. Journal: Seattle, Wash.: Alternatives," *New Yorker*, April 10, 1978.

5. See the Project for Excellence in Journalism report on alt weeklies at http://www.stateofthenewsmedia.org/chartland.asp?id=332&ct=line&dir=&sort=&col1_box=1.

6. See the AAN's overview of the report at http://aan.org/gyrobase/Aan/ViewPage?oid=145320, or the executive summary at http://aan.org/files/inf.pdf.

7. Sandra Yin, "The Weekly Reader," *American Demographics*, May 1, 2002.

8. Lacey is quoted in Eric Bates, "Chaining the Alternatives," *Nation*, June 29, 1998.

9. Mark Jurkowitz, "No Alternative," *Boston Phoenix*, August 31, 2005.

10. Lacey is quoted in Bates, "Chaining the Alternatives."

11. See the transcript from "The Future of Alternative Newspapers," NPR, *Talk of the Nation*, October 27, 2005.

12. Mike Lacey, "Brugmann's Brain Vomit," *San Francisco Weekly*, September 7, 2005.

13. Mark Jacobson, "The Voice from Beyond the Grave," *New York*, November 14, 2005.

14. Harold Meyerson, "Hold the Politics," *Los Angeles Weekly*, January 24–30, 2003.

15. Marc Cooper, "Return of New Times," *Los Angeles Weekly*, November 4–10, 2005.

16. Rodney Benson, "Commercialism and Critique: California's Alternative Weeklies," in Nick Couldry and James Curran, eds., *Contesting Media Power: Alternative Media in a Networked World* (Lanham: Rowman and Littlefield, 2003), pp. 117, 119.

17. Their comments explain Benson's discovery that, compared to other alt weekly publishers, "New Times papers are the most consistently anti-protest. Activists appearing in their pages always play comic roles. For instance, the *SF Weekly* delights in exposing what it calls the 'only in San Francisco' protests . . . [and] typical *LA Weekly* headlines include 'Review this Book or Else: The Latest Gripes from the "Gun-Toting Lesbians"' and 'Three Guys and a Megaphone: The

JDL's Shrinking Role in Jewish Extremism.'" See Benson, "Commercialism and Critique," p. 118.

18. John Mecklin, "Mecklin," *San Francisco Weekly,* June 9, 1999.

19. See *San Francisco Bay Guardian*'s chronology, "The First 30 Years," *San Francisco Bay Guardian,* thirty-year anniversary issue, 1996.

20. Ibid.

21. Tim Redmond, "The Predatory Chain," *San Francisco Bay Guardian,* March 6, 2002.

22. John Mecklin, "It's the Journalism, Bruce," *San Francisco Weekly,* March 13, 2002.

23. Amy Jenniges reports that "according to a memo obtained by the *Bay Guardian,* Schneiderman told New Times execs earlier this year that VVM's San Francisco and Cleveland papers were 'locked in a brutal struggle . . . with no sign of success.' He wrote: 'In the 2004 Calendar year, *SF Weekly, East Bay Express,* and the *Cleveland Scene* racked up losses of $4 million.'" Amy Jenniges, "Chain Gang," *Seattle Stranger,* October 27–November 2, 2005.

24. Quoted in Tim Redmond, "Bay Guardian Sues New Times Chain for Predatory Pricing," *San Francisco Bay Guardian,* October 20–26, 2005.

25. See Tim Redmond, "Chain Gang," *San Francisco Bay Guardian,* May 25–31, 2005; and "SOS: No Secret New Times-Village Voice Media Deal," *San Francisco Bay Guardian,* August 24, 2005.

26. Tim Redmond, "Merger on the March," *San Francisco Bay Guardian,* August 31–September 6, 2005.

27. The press release is available at http://www.villagevoice.com/aboutus/index.php?page=merger.

28. The press release is available at ibid.

29. "Mike Lacey to Village Voice: Drop Dead!" *San Francisco Bay Guardian,* November 9–16, 2005.

30. "The Final Merger Battle," *San Francisco Bay Guardian,* November 30–December 6, 2005.

31. http://www.cantstopwontstop.com/blog/2005/10/eulogy-for-alt-weekly.cfm.

7: THE NET AND THE NEWS

1. At Marketwatch.com, Jon Friedman wrote that "although New Orleans is certainly a prominent (and beloved) American city, many of the national network reporters seemed to have little real feeling for or understanding of the city's psyche. The onrushing media practically acted as if they had been dropped into Zimbabwe." See Jon Friedman, "TV Employs a Familiar Hurricane Script," August 31, 2005.

2. See Joab Jackson, "Telephone Infrastructure Was No Match for Katrina," *Washington Technology,* November 7, 2005.

3. For an account of how the *New Orleans Times-Picayune* managed to continue publishing, see the three-part series by Paul McCleary, "The Times-Picayune: How They Did it," *CJR Daily,* September 12, 2005; "Embedded with the Times-Picayune in New Orleans," *CJR Daily,* September 13, 2005; and "In New Orleans, Everyone's a Critic," *CJR Daily,* September 14, 2005.

4. I wrote this rough transcript while watching the webcast on August 31, 2005.

5. Transcript of "Showdown at the FCC," *NewsHour with Jim Lehrer* (PBS), May 15, 2003.

6. James Gattuso, "The Myth of Media Concentration: Why the FCC's Ownership Rules are Unnecessary," the Heritage Foundation Web Memo no. 284 (May 2003).

7. See Powell's interview with the University of Southern California Annenberg School's *Online Journalism Review* at http://www.ojr.org/ojr/law/powell.php.

8. For a useful summary of the differentiated-use aspect of the digital-divide problem, see Paul DiMaggio, Eszter Hargittai, Coral Celeste, and Steven Shafer, "From Unequal Access to Differentiated Use: A Literature Review and Agenda for Research on Digital Inequality," in Katherine Neckerman, ed., *Social Inequality* (New York: Russell Sage, 2004), pp. 355–400; and Leslie Harris and Associates, *Bringing a Nation Online*, http://www.civilrights.org/publications/reports/nation_online/bringing_a_nation.pdf. The statistics on Internet usage are from the Center for the Digital Future at the University of Southern California's Annenberg School, *2005 Digital Future Report*. The highlights are available online: http://www.digitalcenter.org/pdf/Center-for-the-Digital-Future-2005-Highlights.pdf.

9. See the PEJ 2006 report at http://www.stateofthemedia.org/2006.

10. Transcript of "Showdown at the FCC.

11. Johnnie Roberts and Barry Diller, "Is Big Media Bad?" *Newsweek,* http://www.msnbc.msn.com/id/3606172/.

12. http://www.stateofthemedia.org/2005/narrative_online_intro.asp?cat=1&media=3.

13. The high-profile cases involving major U.S. media companies that failed to accurately report on issues of local, national, and international significance have compromised public confidence in the major media. Even after earning broad acclaim and a heightened national audience for its coverage of Hurricane Katrina, the "mass media" enjoyed the trust of only half of the population, compared to the more than 70 percent trust levels it enjoyed in the 1970s. According to the annual Gallup governance survey, 68 percent of Americans trusted the mass media in 1972, rising to a highpoint of 72 percent who expressed a good deal or fair amount of trust in the media in 1976. Public confidence in mass media had declined to 53 percent by 1997, when Internet news sites began to proliferate, and it remained there until 2003, when it dropped to a record low of 44 percent amid high-profile journalistic scandals, some of which involved credulous coverage of the U.S. government's case for war in Iraq. Gallup conducted another survey in late September 2005, immediately after the media had aggressively covered Hurricane Katrina, and 50 percent of respondents reported having a "great deal" (13 percent) or "a fair amount" (37 percent) of trust in mass media. See Joseph Carroll, "Trust in Media Rebounds Somewhat this Year," *Newswatch*, September 27, 2005.

14. Dan Gillmor, *We the Media: Grassroots Journalism by the People, For the People* (Sebastopol, CA: O'Reilly, 2004), p. 74. The story of Wal-Mart's use of bloggers for public relations is reported in Michael Barbaro, "Wal-Mart Enlists Bloggers in Its Public Relations Campaign," *New York Times,* March 7, 2006. *BusinessWeek Online,* reported that during Katrina, Wal-Mart achieved a "PR coup" by enlisting bloggers to spread its self-promotional story line: "Government doesn't work, Wal-Mart does." See Stephen Baker, "Edelman Shows Wal-Mart the Power of Blogs," *BusinessWeek Online,* October 26, 2005.

15. "For the Record," *Los Angeles Times,* December 28, 2005.

16. The transcript was published in the *New York Times* and is available at http://select.nytimes.com/gst/abstract.html?res=F30615F83B580C7A8CDDA90994D8404482. See the Urban Legends Web site for an account of the Federal Bill 602P hoax, http://www.snopes.com/business/taxes/bill602p.asp.

17. See the site at http://www.dhmo.org.

18. Gillmor, *We the Media,* p. 188.

19. The statement of purpose is available at http://www.gothamgazette.com.

20. See Mark Glaser, "Holy Policy Wonks, Batman! Gotham Gazette Aces Civic Duty," *Online Journalism Review,* November 20, 2003, http://www.ojr.org/ojr/glaser/1069368190.php.

21. Archives of the *Gazette*'s 2001 election coverage are available online at http://www.gothamgazette.com/searchlight2001/index.shtml.

22. Jonathan Mandell, "Behind the Scenes: Gotham Gazette's Rebuilding NYC," *Cyberjournalist,* http://www.cyberjournalist.net/features/behindthescenes/gothamgazette.html. In 2006 the staff writer Joshua Brustein reported on the death of James Zadroga, a thirty-four-year-old detective who spent 470 hours cleaning up Ground Zero and five years later died of lung disease and mercury poisoning—"a condition that hasn't been a widespread occupational hazard for over a century when hatters were sickened as they dyed beaver pelts." The *Gazette,* providing links to scattered news reports and the 9/11 Health Registry, speculated that the deaths of some twenty workers may be related to toxic poisoning at "the pile," and that about five thousand of the forty thousand people who participated in the cleanup are not getting necessary health care. See Joshua Brustein, "The Heroes of 9/11 Are Getting Sick," January 2006, http://www.gothamgazette.com/article/health/20060130/9/1742.

23. See two studies released by the Pew Internet and American Life Project: Elena Larsen and Lee Rainie, *Digital Town Hall: How Local Officials Use the Internet and the Civic Benefits They Cite from Dealing with Constituents Online* (Washington, DC: Pew Internet and American Life Project, 2002); and John Horrigan, *How Americans Get in Touch with Government* (Washington, DC: Pew Internet and American Life Project, 2004).

24. Patrick Healy, "Weld Aides Find a Way to Deal with Negative Press: Re-edit It," *New York Times,* February 4, 2006. There is an emerging academic literature on e-government, most of which concludes that it is too early to make conclusive claims about the effects of government Web sites. In one of the few empirical studies, the public-policy scholars Donald F. Morris and M. Jae Moon found that "few local governments reported impacts from e-government, and not all the reported impacts have been positive (such as increased work for staff) and some anticipated positive impacts have not occurred (such as revenue production, staff reductions, and lowered administrative costs)." Donald F. Morris and M. Jae Moon, "Advancing E-Government at the Grassroots: Tortoise or Hare?" *Public Administration Review* 65, no. 1 (2005): 64–75. Darrell West, a policy scholar at Brown University, publishes an annual *Urban E-Government Report* on his Web site, http://www.insidepolitics.org, and is the author of *Digital Government: Technology and Public Sector Performance* (Princeton: Princeton University Press, 2005).

25. See Daniel Drezner and Henry Ferrell, "The Power and Politics of Blogs," http://www.utsc.utoronto.ca/~farrell/blogpaperfinal.pdf.

26. A rave review from the influential music Web site Pitchfork was even more important in launching the band, generating thousands of sales on http://www.insound.com, which is a popular way that independent bands without major labels distribute their albums.

27. http://www.gothamist.com/archives/2005/11/20/opinionist_corp.php.

28. See the BBC news coverage at http://news.bbc.co.uk/2/hi/americas/4567236.stm; the *Wired* coverage at http://www.wired.com/news/culture/0,69741-0.html?tw=wn_tophead_13; and the *Washington Post* coverage at http://www.washingtonpost.com/wp-dyn/content/article/2005/12/25/AR2005122500589.html.

29. The story is told in Bernard Lefkowitz, *Our Guys: The Glen Ridge Rape and the Secret Life of the Perfect Suburb* (New York: Vintage, 1997).

30. The post is online at http://www.baristanet.com/barista/2005/12/our_ hiphop_guys.html.

31. http://www.baristanet.com/barista/2006/05/what_do_mothers.html.

32. Michael Getler, "The News in Black and White," *Washington Post*, September 25, 2005.

33. The most exhaustive and compelling version of this argument comes from the historical sociologist Paul Starr, *The Creation of the Media: Political Origins of Modern Communications* (New York: Basic Books, 2004).

8: FIGHTING FOR AIR

1. Thomas Bleha, "Down to the Wire," *Foreign Affairs*, May–June 2005. For an account of how the U.S. public sector developed the Internet, see Janet Abbate, *Inventing the Internet* (Cambridge: MIT Press, 1999).

2. See Michael Calabrese and Matt Barranca, "Reclaiming the Public Airwaves," in Robert McChesney, Russel Newman, and Ben Scott, eds., *The Future of Media* (New York: Seven Stories Press, 2004), pp. 207–18. A group of economists at MIT and Carnegie Mellon recently found initial evidence that "broadband positively affects economic activity in ways that are consistent with qualitative stories told by broadband advocates. Even after controlling for economic-level factors known to influence broadband availability and economic activity, we find that between 1998 and 2002, communities in which mass-market broadband was available by December 1999 experience more rapid growth in (1) employment, (2) the number of businesses overall, and (3) businesses in IT-intensive sectors." See William Lehr, Carlos Osorio, Sharon Gillett, and Marvin Sirbu, *Measuring Broadband's Economic Impact*, report prepared for the U.S. Department of Commerce, Economic Development Administration. February 2006. Small cities are beginning to see high-speed Internet access as a key tool for development, and if private companies do not make it available they build it themselves. According to Robert McChesney and John Podesta, "When three major employers in Scottsburg, Ind. (pop. 6,040), threatened to leave town because they didn't have the communications infrastructure needed to deal with their customers and suppliers, the town's mayor, Bill Graham, went to the major cable and telephone companies for help. They told him that extending high-speed broadband services to Scottsburg wasn't profitable enough. So the city decided to build a municipal wireless "cloud" using transmitters placed on water and electric towers that reach more than 90 percent of the surrounding county's 23,000 residents . . . Scottsburg's investment worked—the employers stayed." See Robert McChesney and John Podesta, "Let There Be Wi-Fi," *Washington Monthly*, January–February 2006.

3. The quotes from Rabe and Street are from a *NewsHour with Jim Lehrer* broadcast, "Philadelphia Plans Citywide Wireless Internet," http://www.pbs.org/ newshour/bb/cyberspace/july-dec05/philadelphia_11-22.html.

4. On the telecom industry's lobbying campaign to ban municipal wireless, see Mark Levy, "Lobbyists Try to Kill Philly Wireless Plan," Associated Press, November 23, 2004, and other articles about the legislative process on the Free Press webpage dedicated to Pennsylvania's wireless legislation, http://www .freepress.net/communityinternet/=PA. On Cohen's political influence, see "Ex-Rendell Staff Chief Tops the List of Powerful," *Philadelphia Business Journal*, May 23, 2003. On the telecom industry's lobbying in Pennsylvania, see the Center for Public Integrity report, *Well-Connected.*

5. Matt Richtel, "Pennsylvania Limits Cities in Offering Net Access," *New York Times*, December 2, 2004.

6. Chester is quoted in Jesse Drucker, "Verizon, Philadelphia Discuss Deal on City's Wi-Fi Proposal," *Wall Street Journal*, November 30, 2004.

7. David Baumgarten, *More Cities Offering Wireless Internet Access,* the Center for Public Integrity, September 29, 2005.

8. Although in *Nixon v. Missouri Municipal League et al.,* the U.S. Supreme Court ruled that states are entitled to regulate how municipalities offer telecommunications services. Free Press has made an interactive map with information about community wireless projects across the United States. See http://www .freepress.net/communityinternet/networks.php.

9. Robert McChesney, *The Problem of the Media* (New York: Monthly Review, 2004), p. 283. See Wayne LaPierre, "Speak Out vs. FCC While You Can," *New York Daily News,* July 18, 2003. Boxer is quoted in Jube Shiver Jr., Richard Simon, and Edmund Sanders, "FCC Ruling Puts Rivals on the Same Wavelength," *Los Angeles Times,* June 9, 2003. McChesney also reports that in December 2003 *Lou Dobbs Tonight* polled its viewers on the question "Do you agree big media companies should be broken up?" More than 96 percent of the five-thousand-plus respondents said yes.

10. Robert McChesney and John Nichols, *Tragedy and Farce: How the American Media Sell Wars, Spin Elections, and Destroy Democracy* (New York: New Press, 2005), p. 178.

11. Adelstein is quoted in the transcript of his interview with Rick Karr for the PBS show *NOW,* April 4, 2003, available at http://www.pbs.org/now/ transcript/transcript_adelstein.html.

12. Jackson is quoted in Robert McChesney and John Nichols, "The Making of a Movement," *Nation,* January 7, 2002.

13. The best historical account of the organized opposition to the private-sector and initial government plans for regulating broadcast media is Robert McChesney, *Telecommunications, Mass Media, and Democracy: The Battle for the Control of U.S. Broadcasting, 1928–1935* (New York: Oxford University Press, 1993). See also Paul Starr, *The Creation of the Media: Political Origins of Modern Communications* (New York: Basic Books, 2004). On the campaign led by the Office of Communications of the United Church of Christ, see Kay Mills, *Changing Channels: The Civil Rights Case that Transformed Television* (Oxford: University of Mississippi Press, 2004).

14. The quoted passages here are from Robert Horwitz, "Broadcast Reform Revisited: Reverend Everett C. Parker and the 'Standing' Case," *Communication Review* 2, no. 3 (1997): 311–48. My account of the case between the UCC and FCC draws heavily on Horwitz's article.

15. Horwitz, "Broadcast Reform Revisited."

16. Ibid. The source for WLBT's employment and audience statistics is from Kay Mills, "Changing Channels," *U.S. National Archives and Records Administration* 36, no. 3 (Fall 2004).

17. *Office of Communication of United Church of Christ v. FCC,* 1966, p. 1003.

18. Horwitz, "Broadcast Reform Revisited."

19. Bozell's comments are from his testimony before the U.S. Senate hearing on indecency, sponsored by the Committee on Commerce, Science, and Transportation, November 29, 2005. The ACLU letter is available online at http://www.aclu.org//freespeech/commercial/10964leg20040210.html.

20. McCain's remarks are available at http://commerce.senate.gov/hearings/ testimony.cfm?id=1127&wit_id=2532.

21. See the FCC press release: "FCC Media Bureau Finds Substantial Consumer Benefits in A La Carte Model of Delivering Video Programming," February 9, 2006.

22. McCain is quoted in U.S. PIRG, *The Failure of Cable Deregulation,* August 2003.

23. U.S. General Accounting Office, *Wire-Based Competition Benefited Consumers in Selected Markets*, GAO-04-241, February 2004, pp. 60–61.

24. See Kimmelman's testimony before the U.S. Senate Committee on Commerce, Science, and Transportation, in a hearing on escalating cable rates, March 25, 2004. The figures on cable ownership come from U.S. PIRG, *The Failure of Cable Deregulation*.

25. The testimony of James Robbins at the hearing on escalating cable rates is available at http://commerce.senate.gov/hearings/testimony.cfm?id=1127&wit_id=2835. The Cox Communications annual report for 2003 is available at http://media.corporate-ir.net/media_files/IROL/76/76341/reports/AR_2003/letter.html.

26. Roberts is quoted in a Comcast press release, http://www.cmcsk.com/phoenix.zhtml?c=118591&p=irol-newsArticle&ID=670027. The Comcast annual reports are available at http://www.cmcsk.com/phoenix.zhtml?c=118591&p=irol-reportsAnnual#.

27. A Center for Digital Democracy report on how cable companies campaigned against à la carte pricing is at http://www.democraticmedia.org/news/marketwatch/cablelies.html.

28. L. Brent Bozell's testimony is from the U.S. Senate Committee on Commerce, Science, and Transportation, indecency hearing, January 19, 2005.

29. See the original article, Mark Rahner, "FCC Indecency Fight Chilling Free Speech?" *Seattle Times*, April 24, 2004.

30. Michael Copps, testimony before the U.S. House Subcommittee on Telecommunications and the Internet, February 11, 2004. A recent study by Jonathan Rintels, executive director of the Center for Creative Voices in Media, and Phil Napoli, a professor of communications and media management at Fordham University, supports Copps's claim for the radio industry. In "Ownership Concentration and Indecency in Broadcasting: Is there a Link?" the authors show that "ninety-six percent of the FCC indecency fines from 2000 to 2003 were levied against four of the nation's largest radio station ownership groups: Clear Channel, Viacom, Entercom and Emmis. The percentage of overall indecency fines incurred by these four companies was nearly double their 48.6 percent share of the national audience. In contrast, the 11,750 other U.S. radio stations not owned by these companies—88 percent of the country's stations—received just four FCC indecency violations. Eighty-two percent of the radio programs that generated FCC indecency fines were owned by large, vertically integrated radio station ownership groups." The report is available online at http://www.creativevoices.us/cgi-upload/news/news_article/FINALReport 090605.pdf.

31. On the value of ESPN for Disney, and the consumer survey of cable viewers, see Leslie Cauley, "How We Pay for Cable May Be About to Change," *USA Today*, March 1, 2006.

32. L. Brent Bozell and Gene Kimmelman, "Enough with the 'All or Nothing' Bit," *Dallas-Fort Worth Star-Telegram*, February 5, 2006.

33. Parents Television Council, "PTC Calls Time Warner's 'Family Tier' a 'Very Bad Joke,'" December 15, 2005.

34. See the FCC press release "FCC Media Bureau Finds Substantial Consumer Benefits in A La Carte Model of Delivering Video Programming," February 9, 2006.

35. Ken Belson, "FCC Sees Cable Savings in a la Carte," *New York Times*, February 10, 2006; Kimmelman and Bozell are quoted in Leslie Cauley, "Study: A la Carte Cable Would be Cheaper," *USA Today*, February 10, 2006.

36. *Speaking for Ourselves* is available at http://www.youthmediacouncil.org/pdfs/speaking.pdf.

37. *Is KMEL the People's Station?* is available at http://www.youthmediacouncil.org/pdfs/BuildAPeoplesStation.pdf.

9: THE MEDIA AND DEMOCRACY

1. For reports on the lobbying expenditures of media companies, see http://www.opensecrets.org.

2. Patricia Aufderheide, *Communications Policy and the Public Interest: The Telecommunications Act of 1996* (New York: Guilford Press, 1999). p. 1.

3. Hundt's comment about his fortunate seat assignment appears in Ken Auletta, "Selling the Air," *New Yorker,* February 13, 1995. The remarks about the 1996 Telecom Act from Clinton, Gore, and Hundt are available at http://usinfo.state.gov/usa/infousa/laws/majorlaw/telecomc.htm.

4. See the Common Cause Education Fund, *The Fallout from the Telecommunications Act of 1996: Unintended Consequences and Lessons Learned,* 2005.

5. William Safire, "The Five Sisters," *New York Times,* February 16, 2004.

6. See Frank Rose, "Big Media or Bust," *Wired,* March 2002; Eric Boehlert, "The Media Borg's Man in Washington," *Salon,* August 6, 2001; and Paul Davidson, "'Team Player' Powell Takes Over as FCC Chairman," *USA Today,* January 23, 2001.

7. Hundt is quoted in Frank Rose, "Big Media or Bust," *Wired,* March 2002.

8. A transcript of the House hearing is available at http://www.energy commerce.house.gov/107/action/107-21.pdf. Hollings is quoted in Boehlert, "The Media Borg's Man in Washington." The FCC news release on the waiver is available at http://www.fcc.gov/Bureaus/Mass_Media/News_Releases/2001/nrmm0108 .html, and Commissioner Tristani's dissent is at http://www.fcc.gov/Speeches/ Tristani/Statements/2001/stgt149.html.

9. Michael Powell, "The Public Interest Standard: A New Regulator's Search for Enlightenment," April 5, 1998. For a transcript, see http://www.fcc.gov/ Speeches/Powell/spmkp806.html.

10. William Safire, "The Urge to Converge," *New York Times,* March 7, 2002.

11. William Safire, "Merger Mania Can Hurt Media," *New York Times,* January 20, 2003.

12. William Safire, "Regulate the F.C.C.," *New York Times,* June 16, 2003.

13. William Safire, "The Great Media Gulp," *New York Times,* May 22, 2003.

14. See the full text of Trent Lott's statement at http://lott.senate.gov/news/ 2000/0606.fcc.html.

15. Richard Burr and Jesse Helms, "Keep Control of Local TV," *Charlotte Observer,* October 19, 2003.

16. Wayne LaPierre, "Speak Out vs. FCC," *New York Daily News,* July 18, 2003; and National Rifle Association, "Urgent NRA Bulletin: Media Monopoly Alert," May 14, 2003.

17. The two CPI reports are online: *On the Road Again—and Again* is available at http://www.openairwaves.org/telecom/report.aspx?aid=15, and *Behind Closed Doors* is at http://publicintegrity.org/telecom/report.aspx?aid=83.

18. This remark and the Copps statements quoted below are available on his FCC Web site, http://www.fcc.gov/commissioners/copps/welcome.html.

19. Quoted in Catherine Yang, "The FCC's Loner Is no Longer so Lonely," *BusinessWeek,* March 24, 2003.

20. See Robert McChesney, *The Problem of the Media,* chapter 7, "The Uprising of 2003" (New York: Monthly Review Press, 2004). Quotes from the hearing are reported in Bob Rayner and McGregor McCance, "Media Issue Gets Full Venting," *Richmond Times-Dispatch,* February 28, 2003.

21. Copps's speech at the University of Southern California is available at http://hraunfoss.fcc.gov/edocs_public/attachmatch/DOC-233924A1.pdf.

22. According to an *American Journalism Review* study, commercial television and the cable networks had forced a "News Blackout" on the FCC's ownership policy debate, providing "virtually no coverage" on the matter during the first five

months of 2003. See Charles Layton, "News Blackout," *American Journalism Review,* December–January 2004.

23. The texts of Copps's call for hearings are available at http://hraunfoss.fcc.gov/edocs_public/attachmatch/DOC-229233A1.pdf and http://hraunfoss.fcc.gov/edocs_public/attachmatch/DOC-230981A1.pdf. The quote by Adelstein is from his interview with Rick Karr on the PBS show *NOW,* April 4, 2003. The transcript is available at http://www.pbs.org/now/transcript/transcript_adelstein.html.

24. Adelstein is quoted in McChesney, *The Problem of the Media,* p. 275.

25. The quotes from Adelstein and Powell come from PBS's *NewsHour with Jim Lehrer,* June 2, 2003. The transcript is available at http://www.pbs.org/newshour/bb/media/jan-june03/powell_6-2.html.

26. MoveOn.org Civic Action is a 501(c)(4) organization, which is legally permitted to lobby for legislation but not to intervene in political campaigns. MoveOn.org Political Action is a federal PAC, and it is allowed to raise hard money for political candidates.

27. Powell claimed to be a surrogate for the people on the PBS show *NOW,* April 4, 2003. See http://www.pbs.org/now/transcript/transcript_powell.html.

28. McChesney, *The Problem of the Media,* p. 285.

29. Safire, "The Great Media Gulp." Michael Copps, "Statement at USC Media Consolidation Forum," April 28, 2003.

30. See the June 2 *NewsHour with Jim Lehrer* at http://www.pbs.org/newshour/bb/media/jan-june03/powell_6-2.html.

31. The *NewsHour with Jim Lehrer* Web site has the dissenting statements from both Copps and Adelstein. See http://www.pbs.org/newshour/media/conglomeration/.

32. Hollings and Wyden are quoted in Dominic Timms, "U.S. Media Bill Faces Further Revolt," *Guardian,* July 16, 2003.

33. The Media Access Project's petition is available at http://www.mediaaccess.org/programs/diversity/PrometheusPetReview.pdf.

34. Quoted in Leon Lazaroff, "Radio Activists Take on FCC, Media," *Chicago Tribune,* October 16, 2003.

10: LOW POWER TO THE PEOPLE

1. Greg Ruggiero, *Microradio and Democracy: (Low) Power to the People* (New York: Seven Stories Press, 1999), p. 17.

2. There is an accessible account of the Class D licensing history at http://www.diymedia.net/feature/fhistlpfm.htm.

3. See Matt Spangler, "FCC Tries to Sink Pirate Operation," *Radio and Records,* November 7, 1997; and visit the Web site for Beat Radio, at http://www.beatworld.com/.

4. Korn is quoted in a press release released by Prometheus, available online at http://www.prometheusradio.org/releaseaug99.shtml.

5. The FCC statement, docket 99-25, is available at http://hraunfoss.fcc.gov/edocs_public/attachmatch/FCC-00-19A1.pdf.

6. Dunifer's e-mail is quoted in Ron Sakolsky, "The LPFM Fiasco," *LiP Magazine,* January 17, 2001.

7. See the FCC's document "Low Power FM Radio Service: Allegations and Facts," available at http://www.fcc.gov/Bureaus/Mass_Media/Factsheets/lpfmfact032900.html.

8. For a sample of the NAB's statements on LPFM, including the audio file of signal interference, see http://www.nab.org/newsroom/issues/lpfm/default.asp. The FCC's response to the NAB's claims about cross-talk interference is available at http://www.fcc.gov/Bureaus/Mass_Media/Factsheets/lpfmfact032900.html.

9. See the NPR statement at http://www.npr.org/about/press/000406
.lpfmlegislation.html.

10. See Pete Tridish and Kate Coyer, "A Radio Station in Your Hands Is Worth
500 Channels of Mush!" in Elliot Cohen, ed., *News Incorporated: Corporate
Media Ownership and Its Threat to Democracy* (Amherst, NY: Prometheus
Books, 2005), p. 300.

11. Quoted in Alex Markels, "Radio Active," *Wired,* June 2000, http://
wiredvig.wired.com/wired/archive/8.06/radio.html?pg=5&topic=&topic_set=.

12. Quoted in Tridish and Coyer, "A Radio Station in Your Hands," p. 300.
The full document is available at http://www.fcc.gov/Bureaus/Engineering_
Technology/News_Releases/2000/nret0005.html.

13. The FCC document is available at http://www.fcc.gov/mb/audio/lpfm/
index.html#RETURN.

14. Tridish and Coyer, "A Radio Station in Your Hands," p. 300.

15. See Mary Louise Wrabley, "Two Little Radio Stations that Could,"
Chesapeake BayWeekly.com, March 10–16, 2005.

16. See the *Washington Post*'s report on the barn raising at http://www
.prometheusradio.org/barnartpost.shtml.

17. For statements on the boycott and resolution, see http://www.ciw-online.org/
contact.html.

18. Jim Ridley, "Low Power to the People," *Nashville Scene,* April 14–20,
2005.

19. See ibid.

CONCLUSION: THE DIGITAL FRONTIER

1. All the quotes from the hearing are in the transcript of the U.S. Court of
Appeals for the Third Circuit, *Prometheus Radio Project v. Federal Communications
Commission,* February 11, 2004.

2. Quotes from the Third Circuit Court's decision are from the Media
Access Project, "Prometheus v. FCC: Summary of the Third Circuit Opinion,"
June 24, 2004.

3. See Andrew Ross Sorkin, "Former FCC Chief to Join Providence Equity,"
New York Times, August 11, 2005; Olga Kharif, "Why Did Providence Hire
Michael Powell?," *BusinessWeek Online,* August 14, 2005; and James Granelli,
Sallie Hofmeister, and Jon Healey, "FCC Finds Itself Up to Its Neck in Hot
Issues," *Los Angeles Times,* January 24, 2005.

4. Merritt is quoted in Paul Nowell, "FCC Holds Hearing on 'Localism' in
Charlotte Media," Associated Press, October 22, 2003. Klenz is quoted in Mark
Washburn, "Hearing Gauges Media's Service," *Charlotte Observer,* October 23,
2003.

5. L. A. Lorek and Travis E. Poling, "Complaints and Praise Heard in S.A.,"
San Antonio Express-News, January 29, 2004.

6. See Dirk Lammers, "FCC Opens Airwaves at Hearings," *Aberdeen News,*
May 26, 2004.

7. "Adelstein Hosts Town Meeting in Iowa on Deregulation," *Friday Morning
Quarterback,* October 7, 2005.

8. Keith Brown and Peter Alexander, "Do Local Owners Deliver More Localism? Some Evidence from Local Broadcast News," Federal Communications Commission Media Bureau, June 17, 2004.

9. John Dunbar, "Lawyer Says FCC Ordered Study Destroyed," Associated
Press, September 14, 2006.

10. Quoted in Peter Kiefer, "John Kerry," *Hollywood Reporter,* January 27, 2004.

11. U.S. representative Henry Waxman, a Democrat from California, asked
NBC to turn over videotapes of the studio on election night that were rumored to

show whether or not Welch pushed the news reporters to call the election. NBC refused his request.

12. For XM Satellite's statement explaining why Clear Channel has the right to broadcast its programs and advertisements, see http://www.xmradio.com/lineup/letter.jsp.

13. Radley Balko, "Broadcast Lobby Fighting Satellite Radio," FoxNews.com, July 4, 2004.

14. For Knight Ridder's 2005 financial summary, see http://knightridderinfo.com/releases/index.php?id=810407. See Joseph Menn and James Rainey, "As Knight Ridder Goes, So May News Industry," *Los Angeles Times,* November 8, 2005.

15. In summer 2006, for example, members of the Chandler family, which had sold Times Mirror to Tribune Company and become the corporation's second-largest shareholder group, publicy demanded that Tribune break up its divisions and consider selling off the parts.

16. See Davis Merritt, *Knightfall: Knight Ridder and How the Erosion of Newspaper Journalism Is Putting Democracy at Risk* (New York: Amacom, 2005).

17. See Katharine Seelye and Andrew Ross Sorkin, "Newspaper Chain Agrees to a Sale for $4.5 Billion," *New York Times,* March 12, 2006.

18. Pruitt's interview aired on CNBC, March 14, 2006.

19. Simmons is quoted in Steve Levingston and Terence O'Hara, "McClatchy's Paper Chase," *Washington Post,* March 14, 2006.

20. See Joseph Menn, "Burkle May Bid High for Newspapers," *Los Angeles Times,* April 6, 2006.

21. Holcomb is quoted in Joseph DiStefano and Thomas Ginsberg, "It's Back to Bidding for City's Papers," *Philadelphia Inquirer,* March 14, 2006.

22. The quotes from Foley and the Newspaper Guild are in Jennifer Saba, "Newspaper Guild Calls for Emergency Meeting over MediaNews Deal," *Editor and Publisher,* April 27, 2006.

23. See Mike Cassidy, "A Sense of Relief, for Now, over Boss," *San Jose Mercury News,* April 27, 2006; Joseph Menn and James Rainey, "Deal Set for Three Bay Area Papers," *Los Angeles Times,* April 27, 2006; and Carolyn Said, "MediaNews to Acquire More Bay Area Papers," *San Francisco Chronicle,* April 27, 2006.

24. The quote from Durbin and the report about fired staff members are cited in Gabriel Sherman, "Can Voice Make it Without Its Lefty Zest? *New York Observer,* April 24, 2006. Michael Lacey did not reply to my request to interview him about the *Voice.*

25. See the transcript from *Democracy Now!* April 13, 2006, available at www.democracynow.org/article.pl?sid=06/04/13/145245.

26. Randall Stross, "Hey, Baby Bells: Information Still Wants to Be Free," *New York Times,* January 15, 2006.

27. Chester's quote is from the Pacifica talk show *Democracy Now!* April 13, 2006. The U.S. Supreme Court could have helped to establish network neutrality protections in 2005, when it considered *FCC v. Brand X,* a case involving the question of whether cable companies were required to share their infrastructure with Internet service providers, including the small California company Brand X. Brand X argued that the Internet is a "telecommunications service," and that—just as telephone companies are obligated to share their lines with competitors—cable companies should be treated as "common carriers" ("a company that provides the transmission of communications services to the general public"), obligated to give competitors access to the network for a reasonable fee. The FCC, however, claimed that the Internet is an "information service," and that cable companies who offer it have no common-carrier responsibilities. In a six-to-three decision, the Court ruled in favor of the FCC, paving the way for discriminatory

pricing of Internet services. For a useful overview of the Brand X case, see Marguerite Reardon, "FAQ: What Is Brand X Really About," available online at http://news.com.

28. See the SavetheInternet.com press release at http://www.savetheinternet .com/=press2.

29. See http://www.twu-canada.ca/cgi-bin/news/fullnews.cgi?newsid 1122447600,4516.

30. Martin is quoted in Mark Fitzgerald, "FCC Chairman Martin: Repeal of Cross-Ownership Ban Overdue," *Editor and Publisher,* April 4, 2006.

31. Eddie Fritts, opening speech to the National Association of Broadcasters, Las Vegas, April 18, 2005.

32. Jonathan Segal, "Commissioners Get an Earful from the Public," *Monterey Herald,* July 22, 2004.

33. Remarks of Commissioner Michael Copps at the FCC hearing on localism and license renewal, Monterey, California, July 21, 2004.

AFTERWORD

1. Macpherson was quoted in the May 11 edition of *Newsweek* online: http://www.msnbc.msn.com/id/18619929/.

2. Nancy Cleeland, "Why I'm Leaving the *LA Times,*" *Huffington Post,* May 28, 2007, available at http://www.huffingtonpost.com/nancy-cleeland-/ why-im-leaving-the-l_b_49697.html.

3. Steven Shapin, "What Else Is New?" *The New Yorker,* May 14, 2007.

4. The newspaper circulation figures are available from the Newspaper Association of America at http://web.naa.org/thesource/14.asp#circulation.

5. Quoted in Seth Sutel, "Deals Could Be Close on Internet Radio," Associated Press, September 10, 2007.

6. The full statement is available at http://www.pearljam.com.

7. Peter Svensson, "Comcast Blocks Some Internet Traffic," Associated Press, October 19, 2007. SavetheInternet.com Coalition, "Discrimination Isn't Comcastic," http://www.savetheinternet.com/blog/2007/10/23/discrimination-isnt-comcastic/.

8. See GAO-07-1046: "Telecommunications: FCC Should Take Steps to Ensure Equal Access to Rulemaking Information," available at http://www.gao .gov/new.items/d071046.pdf.

9. The statement is available at http://fjallfoss.fcc.gov/edocs_public/ attachmatch/DOC-275674A1.pdf.

10. Copps is quoted in Stephen Labaton, "Plan Would Ease Limits on Media Owners," *New York Times,* October 18, 2007.

11. Michael Copps, Statement at Chicago Ownership Hearing, September 20, 2007.

ACKNOWLEDGMENTS

Fighting for Air is a work of public sociology, written narratively to provide an accessible account of how and why the U.S. media has changed so dramatically during the past decade, and to identify the emergence of an improbable social movement for media reform. The book is based on five years of fieldwork and extensive travel across the media field: in the radio, television, newspapers, alternative weekly, and Internet industries, and from the newsrooms where journalists perform their craft to the marketing departments and executive suites; in the political agencies responsible for regulating media markets and setting communications policy; in the town halls and convention centers where citizens congregate to discuss the state of their media; in the neighborhoods where residents consume (and increasingly produce their own) news, information, and entertainment; and in the places where civic groups, old and new, are uniting to demand the media that they need.

After decades of scientific specialization and technical debates that shut out nonprofessional readers, public sociology—long associated with scholars such as Daniel Bell, W. E. B. DuBois, Kai Erikson, Arlie Hochschild, C. Wright Mills, David Riesman, and Richard Sennett—is now experiencing a renaissance, and without it this book would not be possible. Michael Burawoy, former president of the American Sociological Association, and Craig Calhoun, president of the Social Science Research Council, have led the revival of American public sociology, and I thank them for doing so.

During my research a number of journalists and broadcast personalities confided that they had long wanted to produce stories about how media consolidation has devasted their profession, but could not because their editors or producers refused to cover the state of their own industry, or because they feared the career repercussions. As I have learned, today people in the industry are all too aware that a dwindling number of companies employ a dwindling number of reporters, editors, DJs, music programmers, and anchors, and the resulting job insecurity means that most media workers—from top national television news anchors to interns in small-town newspapers—are reluctant to speak out or write about how chains and conglomerates are quietly compromising the quality of American democratic and cultural life. The chilling effect of media concentration on free and open speech about the media, in the media, is just one of consolidation's many hidden costs. It also makes the public sociology of culture and communications especially necessary today.

The pressure not to report on the social and political consequences of media consolidation makes it especially important to acknowledge the journalists who do so anyway. Eric Boehlert, Amy Goodman, Jim Lehrer, Bill Moyers, John Nichols, and William Safire deserve special mention for their relentless efforts to cover the rise of Big Media and the fall of the federal government's public interest commitments, as do the journalists Ken Auletta, Katherine Seelye, and Sara Mathews, whose thorough beat reporting on the media business proved invaluable during my research. I owe an incalculable debt to Eric Bates, at *Rolling Stone*, and Serge Halimi, at *Le Monde Diplomatique*, who not only commissioned some of the stories told in this book but also ensured that they were well told.

Scholarship from media studies and sociology provided the foundations for this book. In particular, I drew on the work of Manuel Castells, Susan Douglas, Herbert Gans, Todd Gitlin, Robert Horwitz, Robert McChesney, Michael Schudson, Paul Starr, and Barbie Zelizer. I'm also fortunate to have friends and colleagues—at New York University and beyond—whose suggestions for research and editorial comments improved the manuscript. Thanks to Rodney Benson, Sarah Deming, Peter DiCola, Jerry Frug, Jodi Kantor, Danielle Klinenberg, John Lavine, Ronald Lieber, Jeff Manza, Harvey Molotch, Jay Rosen, Siva Vaidhyanathan, Aurora Wallace, and Matt Wray.

Undergraduate and graduate student research assistants also provided tremendous help. Aaron Platt transcribed interviews and conducted thorough reporting on the media business, while Claudio Benzecry, Ellen Berrey, Katy Gilpatric, Jennifer Jones, Robin Kello, Monika Krause, and Allison McKim dug up crucial evidence. Their work, and much of my own, was supported by the Charles A. Ryskamp Research Fellowship from the American Council of Learned Societies, the Stephen Vladeck Faculty Fellowship from New York University, the Social Science Research Council, the Overbrook Foundation, and the NYU Faculty of Arts and Sciences.

Tina Bennett helped in so many ways that no single title—*über*-agent, advocate, key source—adequately describes her contributions to this project. Svetlana Katz was always there when I needed help. Not many authors get an editorial team like the one that worked on *Fighting for Air*. Vanessa Mobley, my initial editor, treated the manuscript with her signature intelligence and care. Patrick Clark, Grigory Tovbis, and Megan Quirk kept things steady and organized, while Riva Hocherman gave the beginning sections a close read. Sara Bershtel, my editor at Metropolitan Books, intuitively understood both the big picture and every little frame inside it, and she masterfully shepherded the book into print.

My parents, Rona Talcott and Edward Klinenberg, kept our family in the heart of Chicago when so many others around us abandoned the city, instilling a commitment to ideals of urban civic life that anchors this book. My wife, Caitlin Zaloom, makes city living a distinctive pleasure, since she has an eye for little treasures that I would never have discovered on my own. She also brought us Cyrus, the greatest treasure of all, and both were considerate enough to let me finish writing just days before letting their own labor begin. I'm lucky that Caitlin happens to be a brilliant scholar and wonderful writer. She put so much of herself into this project that dedicating the book to her, as I do, might falsely imply that it is not already ours.

INDEX

ERIC KLINENBERG is an associate professor of sociology at New York University. His first book, *Heat Wave: A Social Autopsy of Disaster in Chicago,* was praised as "a dense and subtle portrait" (Malcolm Gladwell, *The New Yorker*); "a remarkable, riveting account" (*American Prospect*); "intellectually exciting" (Amartya Sen); and a "trenchant, persuasive tale of slow murder by public policy" (*Salon*). The recipient of numerous academic awards and fellowships, Klinenberg has written for *Rolling Stone, The Nation, The Washington Post,* and *Slate.*

CPSIA information can be obtained at www.ICGtesting.com
Printed in the USA
LVOW11s1240300716

498413LV00001B/2/P